D1498194

# From Wodehouse to Wittgenstein

# ANTHONY QUINTON

✳ ℐ ⬥ ⬥ § ❀ ❦ ⤳

# FROM WODEHOUSE TO WITTGENSTEIN

*Essays*

St. Martin's Press
New York

*To Hedy with love and thanks*

FROM WODEHOUSE TO WITTGENSTEIN

The author thanks the editors and publishers of the essays they originally published for permission to reprint them here.

St Martin's Press, Scholarly and Reference Division, 175 Fifth Avenue, New York, N.Y. 10010

First published in the United States of America in 1998

Printed in Great Britain

ISBN: 0-312-21161-9

Library of Congress Cataloging-in-Publication Data
Quinton, Anthony.
       From Wodehouse to Wittgenstein/by Anthony Quinton.
          p. cm.
       Includes bibliographical references and index.
       ISBN 0-312-21161-9 (cloth)
       1. Philosophy. 2. Science—Philosophy. 3. Religion—Philosophy.
    4. Wittgenstein, Ludwig. 1889–1951. I. Title.
    B29 0557 1997
    100—dc21                                          97-40491
                                                          CIP

# Contents

I

# Religion and Science in Three Great Civilisations

The most important event in the history of mankind since the neolithic revolution which turned human beings into farmers is industrialisation. It began in a small way in Britain in the middle of the eighteenth century, transformed Europe and North America in the nineteenth century and continues to develop explosively in technological sophistication and geographical range today. Eight or nine thousand years ago our species began to give up the hunting and food-gathering on which, like other animals, it had relied for subsistence since its inception perhaps a hundred thousand years before.

In broad terms the industrial revolution reproduces many of the novel features of its predecessor. First of all, each has made possible a vast increase in human numbers by enlarging the supply of food. Secondly, each has drawn people closer together: once in villages and market towns; now in great urban centres. The original agricultural surplus allowed for a division of labour which separated specialists in learning, religion and warfare from the general productive mass. Industrialisation has gone some way in the opposite direction with universal education and the mass, conscript army. But at each stage mankind has become less exclusively bound to satisfying the requirements of subsistence.

Industrial technology is a Western invention. I mean by Western here 'of European origin' and intend it to cover Russia as well as the West as it is defined in current political discourse. It remained a complete Western monopoly until comparatively recent times. Aspects of it were imposed marginally on India, particularly in the form of a railway system, by the British colonial rulers and it is still only weakly installed there now that they have left. In China, much less thoroughly colonised, it was even more superficial until resolutely imposed at the command of rulers professing an imported Western ideology. Japan adopted it with enthusiastic vigour a hundred years ago, without a major break in the continuity of its culture, and has become today the world's economically most successful power. But the West is still dominant as a source of new technological ideas.

Industrial technology is clearly associated with the uniquely advanced natural science of the West. But it would be wrong to suppose that the connection between the two is altogether straightforward: in particular, to suppose that Western technology is a direct and immediate causal consequence of the scientific revolution. Science and technology are now inextricably bound up with each other. But there was a time lag of about a century and a half between their respective beginnings and again between their respective maturities. Furthermore, the first and the most crucial inventors were not scientists but craftsmen. I shall come back to this at the end. For the time being I shall simply assume that the two are aspects of a single, complex phenomenon and hope to justify the assumption in due course.

In *Science and the Modern World* Whitehead wrote: 'Having regard to the span of time and the population involved, China forms the largest volume of civilisation which the world has seen. There is no reason to doubt the intrinsic capacity of individual Chinamen for the pursuit of science. And yet Chinese science is practically negligible. There is no reason to believe that China if left to itself would ever have produced any progress in science. The same,' he goes on, 'may be said of India.'

These words were written sixty years ago and the parochialism of which the word 'Chinamen' is a symptom has been considerably dispelled. We now have at our disposal the numerous volumes of Joseph Needham's *Science and Civilisation in China*. In considering the matter we must not let ourselves become entangled in the variety of meanings of the word 'science'. It is, of course, true that China and India acquired and conveyed substantial bodies of organised knowledge about the workings of nature. They also had and used technology, if by that is meant a broad range of practical skills, some of them industrial at least in scale, such as building and irrigation.

What they did not have is the kind of theoretical natural science that came so brilliantly into existence during the course of the seventeenth century, one which combines in a systematic way mathematically formulated laws of the workings and the fine structure of nature, empirically controlled by observation, typically aided by instruments, exact measurement and experimentation. Likewise, they never made the crucial technological advance to mechanical power and thus to repetitive, standardised factory production and to the easy transport of great weights of goods over land. Both China and India are still largely societies of peasant agriculturalists.

The main thesis I want to put forward is that the unique Western achievement of theoretical science, and – to the extent that it depends on that science – industrial technology, reflects and has been significantly influenced by the Christian religion that was proprietary to the West, and that the absence of any such science and of the capacity to use it in China and India is similarly related to the Confucianism and Hinduism on which those two civilisations are respectively founded.

I shall begin by describing the difference between Eastern and Western sciences and technologies in more detail. I shall go on to identify the relevantly influential elements in the three great religious systems. I shall look briefly at an alternative style of explanation of the scientific revolution of the seventeenth century. I shall consider the problem posed by the fact that something much more like the science of Galileo and Newton than anything in China or India was produced in classical Greece and something much more like Western technology than anything in the East was developed in Hellenistic Alexandria, both in the half-millennium before Christ. I shall come back finally to the question of the nature of the connection between Western theoretical science and industrial technology.

China has always been more isolated from the rest of the world than India. Its great distance from other centres of power and population encouraged both a practice and a principle of self-sufficiency. Conquerors from the surrounding steppes brought little with them but marauding energy and were soon absorbed into the stable continuity of Chinese culture: bureaucratic, hedonistic, learned, peaceful.

The fact that iron came to China comparatively late, in the sixth century BC, six to nine hundred years after it was first exploited in Babylon, is of no great significance. Chinese inventiveness was evident during the Han dynasty, between the second century BC and the second century AD. In that period paper was invented, the properties of the magnet were recognised, iron was cast and the water-wheel used as a source of power. By 800 AD printing had been invented. At approximately two hundred year intervals between the eleventh and the fifteenth centuries movable type in clay, wood and metal successively was employed, all in advance of Gutenberg in mid-fifteenth century Europe. Gunpowder appeared around 800 AD – the third, along with printing and, in the eleventh century, the compass, of the three revolutionary inventions picked out as crucial by Francis Bacon. Marco Polo saw firearms in China in the late thirteenth century and about a hundred years after that, cannon were being made, at much the same time as that of their first appearance in

Europe. It is not true, as is often said, that the Chinese, having invented gunpowder, used it for nothing but fireworks.

But there is an underlying truth in the firework myth. Chinese weapon technology remained stuck in its first, unreliable, short-range stage. The compass was used for a short period for some large and heroic voyages of exploration in the early fifteenth century. But in 1424 the emperor forbade sea-going vessels, and China backed away from the possibilities of an empire overseas, leaving the coast of China open to the pirates of neighbouring, more barbarous nations. The printing press was used only to supply a small educated class with editions of traditional classics. The brilliant early inventiveness of the Chinese was thus minimally exploited. And it neither encouraged nor was stimulated by anything much in the way of scientific research.

The real weakness of Chinese science lay in its deficient mathematics. Certainly a great deal of mathematical lore was accumulated. But it was at once complicated and unsystematic. Although China had place-value numerals and zero by the mid-thirteenth century, these two vital inventions, of the same kind of importance as the development of a phonetic alphabet, whose absence was a persistent obstacle to Chinese intellectual progress, were available to the Indians from the fifth and seventh centuries respectively, to be conveyed in due time to Europe by the Arabs from whom our number system is misnamed. Chinese mathematics was essentially a reckoning device, an aid to the practical work of surveying and accountancy. It never properly took off on it own as it did in India, Greece and, as the inheritor of both, the European West.

It is noteworthy that the field of Chinese natural knowledge that has most admirers in the modern Western world is its almost purely empirical medicine. Admirable therapeutic rules of thumb were devised without the benefit of any theoretical backing. The rules connect manipulation to beneficial result without passing through any explanatory substructure, whether largely fanciful like the old theory of humours, or more serious and anatomical, in the style of the great dissectors, from Galen in second-century Pergamum to Vesalius in sixteenth-century Padua.

Where Chinese science is almost exclusively practical in purpose and empirical in style, Indian science is at the opposite, abstract extreme. Its achievements in pure mathematics reach a sophisticated level long before the post-classical West. Fruitful intellectual contacts were the outcome of relative geographical proximity to other centres of civilisation and of the exposure to military intrusion which that entailed. Babylonian influence is shown in the concentration of Indian mathematicians on algebra, rather than as with the Greeks, on geometry. Some Greek astronomy, not the best, made its way to India. But it was handled in a different, algebraic way. Although averse to observation, Indian astronomers took the earth to be spherical and in the sixth century the hypothesis that the earth rotates on its axis was put forward.

In pure mathematics Indians studied the summation of series, attempted to solve quadratic equations and introduced the trigonometric concept of the sine of an angle. Important work continued to be done until the twelfth century. But after that the flow of invention seems to have petered out, smothered, perhaps, by the tropical luxuriance of Hindu religiosity.

Indian medicine was for the most part superstitious and fantastic, and was wholly unsupported by anatomical study, although there is a competent fourth-century manual of surgery. The chemical properties of matter attracted the usual alchemical attention from those anxious to develop an elixir of life or a method of transmuting base metal into gold, but this did not develop into chemistry proper.

The revival and vulgarisation of Hinduism that began in the seventh century had a discouraging effect on India's first scientific development. Tantric magic and superstition came to be incorporated into religion and, indeed, every part of the life of the mind. India's rulers worked to seal their culture off from alien, potentially civilising influences, particularly Muslim ones. Religious dominance allowed only one rational discipline to flourish: the linguistic study of Sanskrit, the sacred language of the Vedas, and even that became ossified.

Since their enterprising beginnings in the first millennium AD, both Chinese and Indian civilisation have stagnated. The successful stability of the Chinese social system and its seclusion from outside interference allowed China to retreat within itself, looking resolutely backward and cultivating its traditional practices. India's exposure to the rest of the world led to military conquest and exploitation rather than intellectual stimulus. Without Chinese social equilibrium and without the high level of Chinese artistic culture, it fell back on other-worldliness to endure the this-worldly misfortunes so heavily imposed upon it.

The scientific revolution which created the modern Western world is rightly described as taking place in the seventeenth century. Certainly the first signal achievement, the publication of Copernicus's heliocentric theory, occurred in 1548. But the main work was done in the following century. Copernicus's theory of the heavens was comparatively speculative, even if it benefited from improvements in observational astronomy which had come about in response to the needs of navigation. But the work of Kepler, Galileo and, culminatingly, Newton, was based on an altogether more exalted variety of empirical evidence about the movements of heavenly bodies.

Galileo's main contribution was in mechanics, the mathematically formulated theory of the movement of matter, starting out from the study of projectiles and falling bodies. It lent support to the heliocentrism of Copernicus. So did Galileo's use of his improved telescope to discover imperfections on the sun and moon which undermined the old theory that the heavens are made of different material from the earth and are subject to different laws. Newton's *Principia* brought the movements of matter in the heavens and on the earth under a single scheme of laws which seemed to have attained an unimprovable completeness. The implication of seventeenth-century physics that the physical universe as a whole is a vast machine was extended to cover the human body. The first step here was Harvey's discovery of the circulation of the blood, which was actually observed by Leeuwenhoek, who also used the microscope to observe micro-organisms.

The central feature of these advances is that they involve the explanation of straightforwardly observable things by what is not straightforwardly observable. In some cases the unobserved explanatory factors turn out to be discoverable by instrumentally assisted observation – hitherto unknown planets by the telescope, spermatozoa by the microscope. In other cases the hidden factor is an intuitively unobvious order which makes systematic sense of what appears at first to be a confused variety, as in celestial mechanics. The lesson of these developments is that the world is not what it appears to be. The earth is not at rest but is in axial and orbital rotation. And there is more to the world than there appears to be: the corpuscles that prefigure the developed atomism of nineteenth-century physics and chemistry and the micro-organisms that prefigure the cells of nineteenth-century biology.

This, more or less ontological aspect of the scientific revolution is bound up with its most important methodological characteristic: the application of mathematics to natural fact embodied in the practice of exact numerical measurement. There were new mathematical developments which directly served the investigation of nature. Some of these were notational: Stevin's decimals and Napier's logarithms.

Others were substantive new disciplines: Descartes' analytic geometry, Pascal's probability theory and, above all, the calculus of Newton and Liebniz.

The general upshot was the idea that the essential determinants of natural happenings are the measurable properties of things, many of them beyond the range of unassisted observation, acting in accordance with mathematically formulated laws whose values are to be established by or inferred from observation and experiment.

The immediate technological fruit was not so much productive as instrumental. The theory of projectiles was of use to artillerymen; the theory of chances to gamblers. But the primary technological application of the new scientific knowledge was in the production of instruments for the acquisition of further knowledge and not for the Baconian purpose of the relief of man's estate: accurate pendulum clocks, reliable compasses, telescopes, microscopes, barometers, thermometers.

It was only in the eighteenth century that the absolutely transforming event of the introduction of steam power took place. The first steam engines were used to pump water out of mines and so enable immense new deposits of coal to be mined. Then came the use of steam to convey railway wagons and to drive textile machinery, which thus become independent of human muscles and a convenient supply of falling water.

The development of mechanical power enormously accelerated in the nineteenth century. Oil supplemented coal as a source of steam. The petrol-burning internal combustion engine increased human mobility on land and in the air. Electricity was recruited to supply light, heat and, eventually, power. A scientific revolution in chemistry took place in the nineteenth century in close association with the development of the chemical industry, a process, beginning with synthetic dyes, that was soon to supply mankind with a host of new, artificial materials.

Electromagnetic theory led to the discovery of radio waves with the result of enormously increased long-distance communication and, in due course, a major change in the human use of leisure.

The governing idea behind this complex of Western scientific and technological advances is that the natural world and everything in it is mechanical in character, that every natural process, from the movements of the planets to the circulation of the blood, operates in accordance with mathematically formulated laws, which we must rely on observational or experimental measurement to establish. What differentiates it most radically from the more rudimentary sciences of China and India is that it brings the empiricism of the Chinese, unsystematised and commonsensically qualitative, into an explosively fruitful conjunction with the abstract formalism of the Indians.

The hitherto orthodox form of European science which the scientific revolution displaced had to some extent the empiricist superficiality of Chinese science. Aristotle's physics was qualitative and unsystematic. It registered the evident distinguishing features of different natural kinds and classified them on the basis of their evident similarities. It could explain what happened sufficiently to appease a curiosity that was not too penetrating by saying that things act as they do because it is their nature to do so. But if it was cognitively comforting it was practically useless since it was unable to predict. All action is directed towards the future. As agents we want to know what will happen if we do this or do not do that. Explanation that is not tied to prediction gratifies a merely contemplative appetite.

In the Renaissance the authority of Plato had been invoked to combat that of Aristotle. For the most part the effect of this revival of Plato was confined to the humanities. Dog-Latin, syllogistic logic and metaphysical theology were discarded for Ciceronian Latin, rhetoric and scholarly cultivation. It is an historical mistake, which many have absorbed from the Renaissance humanists, to suppose that the authority of Aristotle in the Christian West stretches right back to the beginning of the Middle Ages. Although a fragment of his logic was available from the first, the main body of his writings did not come into the possession of the European West until it was retrieved from the Arabs from the mid-twelfth century onwards and that was after the deaths of the first generation of truly medieval philosophers: Anselm, Abelard, and Peter Lombard, compiler of the *Sentences* which became the formal basis of the bulk of later medieval thought. Before the recovery of Aristotle, medieval thought had been Platonic and, in particular, neo-Platonic. The Platonic dialogue most influential in the early Middle Ages was the *Timaeus*, Plato's Pythagorean cosmological speculation, which puts forward a mathematical conception of the world as fashioned by a Demiurge out of geometrical figures.

The Platonic notion of the physical world, prominent in the Augustinian phase of medieval thought, has a measure of affinity with the Indian concept of nature. For Plato, as for most Indian thought, the physical world is not wholly real. All that is real, all that can be truly known, is timeless. For both, the physical world, to the extent that it can be known, must be understood by pure mathematical speculation. The astronomical teaching Plato recommends in the *Republic* has just the same unempirical character as Indian astronomy.

The conscious opposition of the scientific revolution of the seventeenth century to Aristotle's doctrine of the physical world received some impulsion from the fifteenth and sixteenth century revival of Plato. But the Pythagorean mysticism which holds that all that exists is made of numbers was brought down to earth by the idea that the numbers which matter are the measured characteristics of empirically observable things. It was a crucial moment in the process of deliverance from Platonism when Kepler was forced by his devotion to truth to admit that the planets move, not in perfect circles, but in elliptical orbits.

The main thesis that I wish to propose is that the differences between the sciences of China, India and the West can be attributed to their respective religions, in particular to the cosmological element, the general theory of the nature of the world, which in each case the corresponding religion embodies. It is sometimes maintained that Confucianism, just because its cosmological aspect is so negative or marginal, is not really a religion at all. At any rate, such as it is, it is firmly this-worldly or commonsensically naturalistic. It is a religion of immanence. Confucius was a critic of spiritualistic superstition. The heaven to which reference is made in the traditional doctrine of Chinese imperial authority is not theistic, but at most a deistic principle of cosmic harmony and order. There are no Chinese scriptures bringing a revelation from beyond, only the recorded wisdom of sages. Confucius, the chief prophet, is entirely human. Like Socrates he did not consider the natural world to be a serious or worthy object of consideration. But he did not deny that it exists. For him, indeed, it is all that there is.

The Confucian cosmology is perfectly congruous with the nature and achievements of Chinese science. That science did not look for theoretical explanations or seek to penetrate the hidden fine structure of things. It was content to register practically useful relationships between one straightforwardly observable state of affairs and another. Its mathematics was for counting coins and measuring acres, not for weighing atoms or determining the distance of stars.

Indian religion is at the other extreme from Confucianism. Hinduism is unremittingly transcendentalist, exclusively otherworldly. It takes the natural world present to the senses to be illusion or *maya*. The right management of life is a business of freeing the soul from its painful entanglement with the illusions of the sensible world through meditative disciplines of detachment. For the enlightened the illusory natural world falls away and with it the corresponding illusion of individual selfhood, as the soul is absorbed into the impersonal, all-inclusive soul-stuff or *atman*, which is ultimately identical with *Brahman*, the featureless, undifferentiated Unity, which is all that truly exists.

The Indian repudiation of the perceptible, empirical world in space and time is entirely congruous with Indian science, such as it is, that is to say, an abstract mathematics in which the emphasis is algebraic, and thus as far as possible from the actual world, and not geometrical, and so involved with space, the stage on which the processes of nature are played out.

Christianity, finally, occupies a position in a sense in between the other two, or at any rate incorporates elements of both. On the one hand it accepts the reality of the sensible world: on the other it affirms a supernatural order in which the omnipotent creator of the natural world is located, together with other spiritual beings, intervening in nature once he has created it by means of miracles and other revelations of his existence and purposes, and, most dramatically, by his personal incarnation in it in human form. In the reverse direction, so to speak, the immortality of the soul is linked in Christianity with the doctrine of the resurrection of the body. One of the first heresies proscribed by Christianity is Gnosticism with its conception of the natural world as evil, and although during the neo-Platonic phase of Christian theology the secondary, derivative, more or less minimal reality of the natural world is affirmed, it was never declared to be an illusion in the manner of Hinduism.

Two aspects of the orthodox Christian cosmology serve as foundation stones for the great Western scientific constructions of the seventeenth century. First there is the idea of God as a rational intelligence setting his creation to work in accordance with a unitary scheme of intelligible laws. Secondly, there is the idea of God as something behind the perceptible surface of the world but constantly involved with it. Under these assumptions the sensible world is neither a chaos nor autonomous. It works in accordance with unobvious laws and the ultimate cause of what happens is also unobvious, hidden behind its perceptible surface. The scientific revolution naturalises these two notions: the underlying causes of what is perceived are not absolutely or metaphysically transcendental, but simply beyond the reach of straightforward observation and the fundamental laws in accordance with which the perceptible world works are not perceptible regularities, but laws of the behaviour of hidden explanatory factors. Newton's first law of motion illustrates the second point: nothing that we perceive is in direct conformity with it, nothing that we perceive continues permanently in the same state of motion, since everything we perceive is subject to impressed forces of some kind or other.

The three cosmologies – Confucian immanence, Hindu transcendence and Christian dualism – correspond to three distinct attitudes to the life of mankind on earth. For the Confucian, the right mode of life is one of peaceful coexistence with nature, taking such convenient advantage of it as one can, but for the most part accommodating oneself harmoniously to it. For the Hindu, nature is a kind of bad dream to which one should take up an attitude of passive submission, principally concerning oneself while it lasts with the search for liberation from it, like a prisoner who does not seek to make himself comfortable in jail, but is always preoccupied with thoughts of escape. Indian magical beliefs are a marginal mitigation of this cast of mind, like the unpredictable benevolence of a guard, a chink in the system that leads nowhere beyond itself. For the Western, nature is a field of opportunity, for adventure and enterprise, a gift to be made use of. The technological implications of these attitudes hardly need to be set out in detail.

There is a final parallel which I shall mention briefly. In the history of philosophical reflection on scientific knowledge three main competing theories have been developed. The first of these, which takes a formal deductive system as the ideal model of a science, rests such knowledge on the rational intuition of axiomatic first principles. The second, instrumentalism, takes the theoretical elements of science to be a kind of conceptual shorthand for propositions about what can be directly perceived. The third, realistic doctrine, takes scientific theory to be inferred but literal truth about the hidden, fine structure of the physical world. Intuitionism, the doctrine of Plato and Descartes, has an affinity with Indian assumptions about nature and our knowledge of it. Instrumentalism, the theory of scientific knowledge of the pragmatists, and before them of Berkeley and Ernst Mach, is Chinese in spirit. (So also is the practice of Aristotle, even if in theory he shows his dependence on Plato by endorsing an axiomatic theory of the nature of scientific knowledge.) Realism is broadly the position of Locke in all its none too coherent good sense. I must confess that I share the belief attributed to my distinguished Oxford predecessor, H.A. Prichard: 'In the end, when the truth is known, I think it will turn out to be not very far from the philosophy of Locke.' Locke regards the hidden reality of the material world as altogether too inaccessible and takes too subjective a view of the direct objects of perception. But no major structural modifications are needed.

It could be objected to what I have been arguing that all I have done is to show some rough general parallel between the cosmologies of Confucianism, Hinduism and Christianity on the one hand and, respectively, the sciences of China, India and the West on the other. But I have surely wanted to claim more than that, specifically that the religious cosmologies are causally related to the corresponding bodies of scientific knowledge and belief. I do indeed want to make that claim. The principal justification for doing so must be that which must support any such claim: in each case the alleged cause is precedent in time and contiguous in space to the alleged effect. Together with the fact – and I have tried to make out that it is a fact – of the near-identity of content between the cosmological teaching of the religions and the operating assumptions of the corresponding sciences, that ought to be enough.

But to prevent some possibilities of misinterpretation, some qualifications must be made. In particular, I am not claiming that the cosmologies are the sole and entire cause of the forms of science to which they are connected, nor am I claiming that they are the indispensably necessary conditions of the sciences that correspond to them. My claim, in other words, is limited by acknowledging the two factors called by Mill the complexity and the plurality of causes.

The cosmological assumptions I have picked out as causes are, as is usual in such cases of explanation, each only one of the factors which, in the circumstances of each case, had to be present for the effect to ensue. There are plenty of societies with traditional religious cosmologies which have not produced any science at all, nothing even to be compared with the comparatively limited or partial scientific achievement of the Chinese and Indian civilisations. Clearly social factors must also be taken into account: stability, a degree of prosperity to provide the requisite leisure for scientific work, some urbanisation to provide for the development of a critical community of investigators, a fairly substantial amount of literacy.

Some historians of thought, attracted to more or less Marxist styles of historical explanation, have attributed the rise of modern Western science to the existence of a confident and secure merchant class, not preoccupied with politics and war, nor constrained by the disciplines imposed by priestly status, their minds broadened by the trader's awareness of a world wider than his own. It is certainly true that the mercantile class of early modern European history answers much more closely to this description than the merchants of China, who were traditionally looked down upon, or than the merchants of India, who were hampered and kept on the run by social turmoil and arbitrary government. But that factor would seem to be more a standing than a precipitating cause of the thing to be explained, a relatively higher fertility of the soil in which Western science grew than the seed from which it actually developed.

As to the other qualification, the Christian cosmology or even a theistic cosmology of the Christian type, which sees the perceptible world as determined in all its details by the workings of a single rational intelligence behind the sciences, does not seem to be an indispensable condition of the kind of scientific and technological development which has enabled the West to dominate the world, first politically and then culturally. In classical Greece there was a great deal of mathematically formulated natural science. In the Athenian, pre-Alexandrian period this took the form of pure mathematics on the one hand and largely speculative physics and astronomy on the mechanics of Archimedes on the other. Aristarchus, the first great Alexandrian astronomer, maintained that the sun and stars did not move. Thirty or forty years later, Eratosthenes made a remarkably accurate calculation of the diameter of the earth from pole to pole. This anticipation of Copernicus did not take hold. Hipparchus returned to the idea that the earth is the unmoving centre of the heavens but his astronomical measurements achieved a high level of accuracy. Alexandrian medical scientists practised dissection and got all that could be got from it with the naked eye, correcting, among other things, the erroneous belief of Aristotle that the heart, and not the brain, is the seat of the intellect.

Hellenistic science finally succumbed to the unmathematical practicality of the Romans, symbolised by the casual death of Archimedes. Alexander himself, like Napoleon, travelled with engineers and surveyors and the museum founded by Ptolemy, his successor as ruler of Egypt, was, in effect, an institute for scientific research, although subsequent rulers of his line were increasingly unsympathetic to scientific inquiry. Hero devised a steam engine, but it was used for amusement only. Archimedes constructed a planetarium and invented a water-pumping device as well as developing the theory of buoyancy for which he is particularly celebrated.

What lay behind this first, aborted flowering of a movement of thought, closer than any other in form and sophistication to the science of the seventeenth century, was not a religious cosmology but the purely naturalistic physical speculations of the Ionian philosophers of nature. Thales, the first of them, is the traditional inaugurator of the history of philosophy. This scheme of ideas reached its culmination in the work of Democritus, who was an approximate contemporary of Socrates. We know of him largely through the writings of Epicurus, half a century later, and the *De Rerum Natura* of Lucretius, living two centuries later still. By that time the redirection of Greek philosophy from the study of nature to the study of man and society, encouraged as profitable by the Sophists and as desirable by Socrates, had been completed, even though the science it inspired had two centuries of Alexandrian life left in it.

In the hands of Epicurus and Lucretius, the atomistic materialism of Democritus was used in a negative way, to curb the pretensions of religion. It no longer served as a stimulus to scientific inquiry. The important point for the purpose in hand is that this was a limitation, not a perversion. The atomistic philosophy of nature had from the beginning been irreligious, although it had been a great deal else as well. Thus, something broadly comparable to Western science and technology did arise in the later stages of Greek civilisation, before it was mentally trivialised by the dominance of Rome, and it came about without a religious cosmology of the Christian type to initiate it.

I suggest that in the intellectual circumstances of post-medieval Europe the only form in which the general dualist assumption about the determination of the palpable surface of nature by forces hidden behind it could be effective was a religious one. Medieval Europe had emerged from totally unintellectual barbarism through the agency of the Christian church, which maintained its intellectual monopoly. The institutional foundation of that monopoly lay in the fact that, with meagre exceptions, only clerics were literate, an arrangement incorporated in the phrase 'benefit of clergy'. The church controlled education in curriculum and practice; it controlled higher learning. The only aspect of culture which had some secular footing was the non-edifying imaginative literature and art of the epoch. What, I suggest, is necessary for theoretical science is the dualism, which in the form of the Christian cosmology, lay behind the scientific revolution of the seventeenth century. The specifically religious clothing in which it was arrayed was simply what it had to put on in order to be effective at the time.

So far I have been speaking in general terms about the Christian cosmology which I have been putting forward as the precipitating intellectual cause of the scientific revolution. In a reference to the orthodox proscription of Gnosticism as a heresy, I claimed that there is a firm commitment in Christian theology to the reality of the natural world. Nevertheless that commitment has wavered at times. In what I have called the Augustinian period, before the recovery from the Arabs of the main body of the writings of Aristotle, the neo-Platonic philosophy which was relied upon to articulate revealed Christian dogma ascribed to matter an exceedingly marginal role in the total scheme of things, as the least and lowest emanation from the One and thus, in its remoteness from the source of all being, as endowed with the weakest hold on reality.

By the fourteenth century this kind of spiritualistic conception of the universe was no longer sustained except in the writings of more or less isolated mystics. But even if the reality of nature was not in doubt there was still a strong tradition of moral hostility to it, according to which it was not a worthy or even proper object of study. The formula which bids us abjure it along with the flesh and the devil casts no doubt on the existence of any of them, but it calls upon us to have as little to do with them as possible.

In the early, Augustinian phase of medieval thought, the material world was, then, neo-Platonically downgraded in respect of its existence and ascetically depreciated in respect of its value. The Thomist synthesis of Christian doctrine and the whole corpus of Aristotle's writings attributed unqualified reality to the natural world but was in two ways obstructive to the investigation of nature. First, in holding that reason could independently establish much of revealed doctrinal truth and that it needed to be applied to develop the implications of that truth, it took theology to be the primary, if not quite exclusive, field of reason's proper employment. Secondly, its attitude toward Aristotle's philosophy of nature was that it should be piously received and digested, not used as a springboard for new advances in the knowledge of nature.

Aquinas's harmonising conception of the mutually corroborative relations of faith and reason was negatively criticised by Duns Scotus, who minimised the capacity of human reason to arrive at religious truth. Ockham combined this fideism in theology with a positive enthusiasm for the use of reason to acquire the knowledge of nature, which, in his view, it was specifically fitted to acquire. In his own time there was a productive school of pure mathematicians at work in Oxford. Of more significance, both for the purpose in hand and in itself, is the group of Ockham's followers in Paris, starting with his pupil Jean Buridan. From the middle of the fourteenth century Buridan developed a mathematical physics in opposition to Aristotle which, if still only vestigially empirical and making no effective use of experiment, anticipated much that was to be put on a solider basis two or three centuries later.

The chief achievement of the Parisians was their theory of impetus, which replaced Aristotle's doctrine that moving bodies not in direct contact with other bodies that are exerting force on them are pushed forward by the air turbulence set up behind them by their forward motion. Buridan held that motion could go on indefinitely so long as there is no air resistance. Oresme invented the graphical representation of functional relationships, argued that the earth rotates daily on its axis and that the velocity of a freely falling object is directly proportional to the time of its fall, and has nothing to do with its weight. The possibility of a vacuum was also accepted, although not until the seventeenth century was Pascal able to demonstrate it empirically, against the fallacious proof of the opposite by Descartes, by the economical device of sending his brother-in-law up the Puy-de-Dome with a rudimentary barometer.

The literary humanism of the Renaissance diverted attention from the study of nature to its aesthetic enjoyment. The variegated occultisms prevailing in the period sought to control nature by magical practices, derived from fantastic speculations about correspondences and analogies. The Biblical fideism of the Protestant Reformation left no room for the scientific study of nature since it took every reference to the natural order in the Bible to be divinely inspired and so beyond the reach of legitimate questioning. The only place in Europe where the scientific spirit of Ockham's followers survived was Padua, university city of the independently and unreliably Catholic republic of Venice, steadily resistant to the thought control of the counter-reformation. It was in Padua, of course, that Galileo in the eighteen years before he moved to Florence in 1610, carried out his investigations in mechanics.

It was at this time that Francis Bacon clearly identified the three main obstacles to the progress of natural knowledge and outlined what he believed was the one correct method for the development of sciences that would contribute to the relief of man's estate. The enemies were the disputatious learning of Aristotelian scholasticism, the delicate learning of the literary humanists and the fantastical learning of the enthusiasts for the occult. The method of eliminative induction that he proposed was really more suitable for the biological than for the physical sciences. The conventional and correct view of its limitations is that, first, it aspired, like most seventeenth century theories of method, to an unattainable level of certainty; secondly, that it ignored the role of imagination in framing the set of alternative possible hypotheses to which the process of inductive selection was to be applied; and, finally, that his conception of the 'forms', which were to be the ultimately explanatory factors in the new sciences, misconceived them in a qualitative, non-mathematical fashion.

For all that, he was extremely influential, not as a scientist but as the prophet of science. The Royal Society was set up in conscious compliance with his recommendations, as a somewhat gentlemanly version of the research institute, Salomon's House, that he described in his *New Atlantis*. In Hooke's statutes it is laid down that 'the business and design of the Royal Society is to improve the knowledge of all natural things and all useful arts, manufactures, mechanic practices, engines and inventions by experiment'. The declared emphasis on experiment and technological application was adhered to in actual fact.

Bacon had been brought up in the atmosphere of his mother's strict Calvinist Protestantism. It is clear that in his maturity he was wholly devoid of religious enthusiasm and possibly devoid of religious faith. He was as determined as Ockham to keep apart the supernatural domain of faith and the natural world open to reason. The way in which he insists on their separation betrays much more concern to free science from entanglement with religious controversy than to accord equal rights to both realms of human interest. It was characteristic of the Calvinism of Bacon's age to insist on work in the world; however uncomfortably that activism consorted with the doctrine of predestination. The idea of active vocation may be seen as a religious prefiguring of Bacon's valuation of science for its practical utility in much the same way as, according to my thesis, Christian cosmology prefigures the conception of nature and of our knowledge of it present in the scientific revolution.

Bacon's valuation of science for the practical contribution it could make to the satisfaction of the material needs of mankind was, as I suggested earlier, somewhat premature. James Watt's steam engine, which was the storming of the Bastille of the industrial revolution, came into existence a century and a half after Bacon's death and nearly a hundred years after Newton's *Principia*, which, in its apparent perfection and completeness, brought the development of science to a kind of consolidating halt for a time. It is this gap between the maturity of the scientific revolution and the onset of the industrial revolution that puts in question the view that Western science and Western technology are two aspects of a single phenomenon, or two phases of a single process.

What is clear is that the type of productive technology Bacon had in mind as the source of science's value for mankind took some time to emerge. The technology which advanced hand in hand with seventeenth-century science was instrumental. Precise instruments of measurement – clocks, thermometers and barometers – were indispensable if the intellectual machinery of mathematics was to get a grip on the empirical world. Precise instruments of observation – the telescope and the microscope – were indispensable if things hidden from ordinary observation by their remoteness or minute size were to be discovered. It was the scientists themselves who carried out much of the work of instrumental improvement. Galileo's work on the telescope is only the most notable instance. Even so apparently cerebral a person as Pascal designed a calculating machine and a kind of barometer.

James Watt was a practical craftsman or engineer, not a scientist strictly speaking. But he was employed as an instrument-maker at the University of Glasgow and he discussed technical problems with Joseph Black, professor of chemistry there, who was, after Lavoisier, the greatest chemist of the eighteenth century. His chief problem was the relatively low efficiency, due to waste of heat, of small engines. Making use of Black's findings about latent heat, he constructed an engine greatly superior in efficiency to that of his predecessor, Newcomen. Newcomen, a Devonshire blacksmith, may seem at a casual glance to be an even more scientifically isolated and unprofessional figure than Watt. But in fact his work was inspired and guided, in its early stages, by Robert Hooke, associate of Newton and curator of the Royal Society, who had formed the view that mechanical energy could be conveyed over a distance by the condensation of steam.

Despite first appearances, then, there was a continuous interaction between the new science and the productive, practically useful kind of technology. I have said a little about the early history of the steam engine. A similar conclusion could be drawn from the history of the development of the pump, which was the first applicance to benefit significantly from steam power. In the early seventeenth century there were metaphysical disputes about the possibility of a vacuum. By the middle of the century experimental work on vacuum pumps was preparing the way for mining at hitherto unreachable depths. The advance provided the coal that was both to supply power to railway engines and to constitute much of the freight they were to pull, being delivered to factories where new textile machinery had enormously multiplied output.

For all its dependence on advances in scientific theory, the development of steam power preceded the full working out of the fundamental theory of its own operation. The thermodynamics of the conversion of heat into mechanical energy was first seriously taken up by Carnot in the 1820s. But from the mid-nineteenth century onwards, science and technology became indissolubly connected with the emergence of the German chemical industry under the intellectual guidance of Liebig. Thus, when the apparent gap between the scientific and industrial revolutions is looked at a little more closely it turns out to be occupied by continuous lines of connection, in very much the same way as the apparent intellectual abyss between the Aristotelian scholasticism of the late Middle Ages and seventeenth-century science is found to contain the mathematical physics of Ockham's followers in Paris.

It should not be necessary to say that in ascribing the relative backwardness of Chinese and Indian science and technology to the cosmologies embodied in the religious systems that constituted the intellectual nucleus of the two civilisations there is no suggestion of any innate incapacity for scientific thinking as it is understood in the modern Western world. That notion is sufficiently refuted by the number of Chinese, Japanese and Indian scientists who have won Nobel prizes, a perhaps superficial but still presumably reliable indicator of scientific work of fundamental importance and originality. This appropriation of Western styles of thought, furthermore, has not been as the expense of traditional Eastern intellectual skills. The Indian tradition in pure mathematics revealed its continuing vitality with particular vividness in the case of G.H. Hardy's brilliant pupil, S. Ramanujan, of whom it could be said, as Newton said, with sublime modesty, about his pupil, Cotes, 'if he had lived we might have learned something'. In Japan, historically a cultural dependency of China, recent developments in electronics are continuous with the Chinese tradition of consummate practical skill.

One other final comment should be made. The vast increase in the quantity and quality of the knowledge of the world we live in that has flowed from the scientific revolution does not stand in the kind of logical relation to the Christian cosmology which I contend, inspired it, that lends any evidential support to that cosmology. The latter is a metaphysical anticipation in imaginative almost pictorial, form of the scientific world-picture. It is not a more general theory from which that world-picture is deducible. It is an allegory in need of interpretation, rather than a system of first principles whose consequences need to be deduced. It stands to the scientific world-picture in much the same relation as the philosophy of Schopenhauer does to the Freudian account of human personality. Even if Freud were right about human nature, it would not at all follow that the world as a whole was, in reality, blind, unconscious will.

The substantial truth of the doctrine that behind the straightforwardly perceptible surface of the natural world there is a mathematically measurable and also entirely natural fine structure which explains it does nothing to confirm the idea that behind the natural world in space and in time there is a supernatural system or a supernatural intelligence. As the example of Ionian cosmology and Greek and Alexandrian science and technology shows, it is possible for something that is reasonably approximate to Western science and technology to come into existence under the influence of a purely naturalistic cosmology, one that is wholly devoid of religious embodiment. Nevertheless I remain sure that the unprecedentedly lavish and powerful science and technology of the West are the result not of some underground, esoteric fidelity to Democritus, but of the suggestively Democritean shape of the theory of the universe incorporated in Christian doctrine, disguised as it often was by that doctrine's successive submissions to the authority of Plato and Aristotle.

*Delivered as a Humanities Council Distinguished Lecture at New York University on 17 April 1985.*

# Philosophy as an Institution

I propose to explore a subject which I have never seen discussed in anything but an occasional aside in writings pointed in an entirely different direction: the history of philosophy as an organised institution. For the most part philosophy is treated as an accumulation of arguments and conclusions, ordinarily in conflict with each other and only loosely anchored in persons, times and places. There are many accounts of the nature or essence of philosophy. That is understandable enough in the light of an old-fashioned view of it as a reflective inquiry into the nature or essence of an array of important things and ideas of high generality: existence, knowledge, truth, the good, science, history and art, for example. Philosophy itself is one of those large and interesting generalities which are fit for philosophical examination.

Philosophers often make rather heavy weather of the business of defining philosophy. But historians of philosophy, at any rate, must have some principle at the back of their minds to guide them in choosing what to include and what to leave out of their books. Very conventional ones, however, will get by with confining themselves to just those bodies of thought that were considered by their predecessors.

Most histories of philosophy are thoroughly impersonal. They set out, in more or less chronological order, a sequence of theses and of arguments for and against them. For the most part these are presented as the work of disembodied intellects, influenced by and influencing the work of other pure intelligences of the same passionless and immaterial sort. The personal names attached to the bodies of thought described are convenient devices for keeping complex assemblages of reasoning together for the reader's assistance. There are usually, it should be admitted, some marginal concessions to the human weakness of the readers. The account of a particular thinker will start off with some perfunctory biographical details: place and date of birth and death, jobs, whether professorial and relevant to philosophy or not, teachers and other influences, associates the subject was in touch with, a list of writings, possibly religious and political affiliations. Aspects of a philosopher's personality or circumstances are mentioned only if they have an evident bearing on his philosophy. So everyone soon learns that Berkeley was a bishop. Some find out that Hume was oppressed in early life by his mother's rigid Calvinism. A more sophisticated version of that sort of thing is Popper's explanation of Plato's view that only timeless abstract ideas are truly real and that the world of change is penetrated by illusion. He refers this to the fact that Plato was an aristocrat, two of whose uncles were put to death after the democratic revolution that followed Athens's final defeat in the Peloponnesian war. Passionately hostile to change in society, Plato expelled it from the real constitution of the world. Anything more than this austere provision is regarded, it seems, as mere gossip, a sugar coating of human interest to help get the harsh philosophical medicine down. In my own case it was only after being closely involved with philosophy for about fifty years that I found out that Aristotle was well known as a natty dresser and was sometimes mocked for his thin legs. (I got that from the *Encyclopaedia Britannica* in the course of checking a date. I do hope it is correct.)

There are some exceptions, but they are distinctly exceptional. In the late nineteenth century the *Biographical History of Philosophy* by George Henry Lewes, George Eliot's long-term companion, sold well. There have been some systematic works about the personality traits of philosophers: one by Alexander Herzberg, another by Ben-Ami Scharfstein. These are concerned with such things as the degree of introversion of philosophers, the high incidence of celibacy among them, even when they are not Catholic priests, their drinking habits, their private pleasures.

That sort of thing may satisfy an understandable, if undignified, kind of curiosity. Much more interesting are the relations between philosophy and its social and intellectual environment. Since philosophy is the mother from which all other intellectual disciplines have emerged – natural science, dogmatic theology, economics, psychology, sociology and linguistics to name only the most prominent cases – it would be interesting to examine the interaction between the parent and her children after they have left home and set up on their own. An impressive attempt at this was made by Wilhelm Windelband in the late nineteenth century in what is still, I would contend, the best one-volume history of philosophy. Windelband describes philosophy as part of general intellectual culture. Bertrand Russell cast his net wider, subtitling his *History of Western Philosophy* 'its connection with political and social circumstances from the earliest times to the present day'. It is generally agreed that, for all its considerable entertainment value, the net did not draw up much of any importance for the understanding of philosophy. The circumstances he attended to were on too large a scale, things like the fall of the Roman Empire, the rise of Christianity, the Crusades, the eclipse of the papacy and so on. What is more, after about 1500, the social and political circumstances recede into the background.

My topic is a much smaller and, in a way, intimate one. It is to consider philosophy as a social activity itself, and not in relation to its social environment. For, like the procreation and rearing of children, it is an essentially social undertaking. The pure intelligences of standard histories of philosophy, related abstractly by influence, exert and respond to influences in a number of concrete ways. They constitute schools, some with actual buildings, more without. They communicate most effectively and fruitfully by face-to-face encounter or by the approximation to it of personal correspondence. It is only exceptionally *taught* by post, to interested inhabitants of remote islands. Dialogue is its bloodstream, as shown by the fondness of philosophers for dialogue as a literary form: Plato on everything, Berkeley on human knowledge, Hume on natural religion. The argumentative conversational encounters of philosophers are not isolated occurrences. They take on a stable form such as Plato's Academy, which was a lecture hall and gymnasium in a public park, and lasted for more than 900 years; Aristotle's Lyceum, with its covered walkway in which to do philosophy peripatetically; Epicurus's garden; the monasteries, cathedral schools and universities of the Middle Ages; the Florentine Academy of the Renaissance; the Abbé Mersenne's amazing circle; Edinburgh dining clubs; the salons of eighteenth-century Paris; Jeremy Bentham's utilitarian group; French existentialist cafés; the departments and associations of our own epoch.

It is the combatively co-operative sociability of philosophers that distinguishes them from sages. The ideal type of sage is isolated; he is a hermit, who carries on a one-way traffic in wisdom with those seeking to acquire it on a short visit. (He may have some disciples, but it is not their role to answer back.) He does not enter into critical discussion with his visitors and disciples; he tells them. He is usually, and always represented as, old and venerable. His aphoristic pronouncements, after all, are normally the fruit of long and varied experience, followed by withdrawal from the world for protracted meditation. Philosophers proper, by contrast, are usually at their best when young, if not quite to the same extent as mathematicians. Duns Scotus died around the age of forty, Berkeley published his main thoughts at the age of twenty-five, Hume published his when he was twenty-eight. Schopenhauer and Bertrand Russell produced their best books at around thirty. The sage distils his wisdom in small droplets. Philosophers erect complex intellectual structures of argument, without which their conclusions are of little interest, and because they are so complex they are intrinsically rickety and in constant need of critical reinforcement, or, painfully often, dismantling.

The kind of inquiry I am proposing could be seen, not just as social, but as economic. Philosophy is a form of intellectual production. By reason of its social character it is not a one-man craft or cottage industry, to be undertaken on one's own. Questions arise from this. Why is it supplied? What is the demand for it, since it is publicly offered and not just a matter of the private satisfaction of the producer? What makes it flourish or stagnate?

I have suggested that it is primarily conducted by word of mouth, by conversation, hearsay, oral teaching, conferences. But it also operates by way of the circulation of written matter: by books from the earliest times, by letters (some of Plato's have survived, those of Descartes, Locke and Leibniz are philosophically important) and, with increasing intensity in the last hundred years, by periodicals.

Why is it produced? Partly, like many other things, for the internal reason of being valued for its own sake, to serve what Aristotle called wonder and could be more dismissively described as curiosity. It is, or purports to be, the pursuit of interesting and important truths. The pursuit is, in a way, everybody's business. We all have some capacity to discriminate between sound and unsound reasoning, between those beliefs that are thrust on us which deserve our acceptance and those that do not. Philosophy, among other things that it does, aims to make explicit the principles involved.

From outside there is the demand for it from powerful institutions, church and state above all, for educational or instructive purposes of varying degrees of purity. In classical antiquity the subject was pursued simply from love of the thing in Greece and as a polite, civilised acquisition in Rome. Various Greek philosophers were put on trial for impiety, such as Anaxagoras and Socrates. Philosophers were banished from Rome by Domitian in AD 90 and the philosophical schools of Athens were closed down by Justinian in 529. But an alternative is to fight the philosophy you do not like with a comparably cogent philosophy that you favour. Part of the organisation of Christianity as a cosmopolitan religion out of its modest beginnings as a radical Jewish sect was the work of equipping it with a philosophically articulate body of doctrine to fight off opponents who, for one reason or another, could not be dealt with by brute force. This was the task of the Fathers of the Church, most notably St Augustine, the greater part of whose writings are polemics against various kinds of heretic and infidel.

In the West, and even more in the Byzantine empire, philosophy remained the *ancilla theologiae,* the handmaid of theology, to the exclusion of any other role until the Renaissance, and continued to do so within the sphere of influence of the Catholic church. Like other handmaids in real life it was not perfectly docile and obedient and frequently showed that it had a mind of its own. Many philosophers of the high Middle Ages got into trouble with the Pope and the ecclesiastical authorities, Ockham and Wyclif being conspicuous examples. Both of them were taken up by secular rulers because of their agreeably anti-papal beliefs.

In our own time the vast quasi-religious system of Marxism has been at once encouraged and controlled by the Russian state in a manner for which there is no Western precedent, but which closely resembles the position of philosophy under the emperors of Byzantium, for whom it was a servile ingredient of the state-run church.

Two instances of much milder ideological pressure are worth a brief consideration. In the United States in the nineteenth century the philosophical orthodoxy taught in the still rather unenlightened universities was an imported article, the Scottish philosophy of common sense. This, which began as a reasonable and intellectually respectable answer to Hume, was attractive to institutions much involved with the training of future clergymen because of its moderation. It navigated comfortably between hell-fire Calvinism on the one hand and more or less sceptical or materialistic doctrines, generally hostile to religion, on the other. It was introduced by John Witherspoon, a signer of the Declaration of Independence and an early president of Princeton, and flourished until well after the arrival from Scotland of James McCosh, a latter-day member of the school, in 1868 to hold the same post for twenty years.

A second example is the form of anglicised Hegelianism which rapidly came to dominate the philosophical scene in the last quarter of the nineteenth century in Britain. Its philosophical dilution of religion served to protect the latter, at a cost, from various forms of aggressive naturalism that were prevalent in that post-Darwinian age and it argued for social responsibility against the devil-take-the-hindmost individualism of Herbert Spencer. Holding out in Scotland for a long time, it had succumbed in England by 1920 to the analytical philosophy of Russell and Moore.

The external pressures considered so far have been defensive, like the reluctant acquisition of nuclear submarines by an established nation that feels obliged to protect the possessions it would prefer to enjoy in peace. There is a more positive, more genuinely educational variety of external pressure which is favourable to philosophy. The earliest version of this is the training in the arts of effective argument – in which logic and rhetoric both play a part – of aspirant lawyers by the Greek sophists, of whom Socrates was a very idiosyncratic instance. The logical instruction which came to predominate in the curriculum of the major medieval universities was a training for the literate clerical administrators needed by the only fitfully literate rulers of the epoch. In late nineteenth-century Oxford Plato's *Republic,* in a mildly Hegelianised form, was installed by Benjamin Jowett as a manual for the instruction, and self-definition as a ruling élite, of imperial administrators.

A final source of demand for philosophy, in virtue of its historical prestige, is as a part of high culture. That seems to have been fairly marginal in Greece, although the devotion of the very chic Alcibiades to Socrates may be an example of it. It came to predominate in Rome, where it was understood that every truly cultivated man had to spend some time at the philosophical schools of Athens, which lasted until well after the fall of the western Roman empire. I think it is fair to say that the Roman republic and empire produced no philosopher above the third rank, with the possible exception of Lucretius. If his arguments and conclusions are almost entirely derived from Epicurus and his school, he has the merit of writing not only the one philosophical poem that has solid argumentation in it but one that is also a literary masterpiece. Nearly all the other recognised Roman philosophers were important public figures: Seneca, Cicero and the emperor Marcus Aurelius. They, like the freed slave Epictetus, were all satisfied with the literary embellishment of Stoicism, to which they brought nothing significantly new.

The Romans are not the only publicly important philosophers. From Anselm onwards a number of the philosophers of medieval England rose to be archbishops of Canterbury and, as such, to the summit of political life. Francis Bacon, after holding other leading posts, became Lord Chancellor. At the end of the last century and the beginning of this, two leading British politicians, Balfour, who became prime minister, and R.B. Haldane, were thoroughly competent philosophers as was the South African General Smuts, up to a point. I know of no literal examples, besides Marcus Aurelius, of philosopher-kings, laid down as the ideal rulers of the ideal state by Plato. The closest realisations are Heraclitus, who turned down the kingship of Ephesus to which he was entitled by heredity, and Thomas Masaryk, the first president of Czechoslovakia.

The cultural attraction of philosophy is not primarily due to its intellectual content. It has often been of the highest literary excellence. Well-informed people, whose knowledge of Greek is much better than mine, speak of the writings of Plato as among the finest examples of classical Greek prose. Lucretius is one of the greatest Roman poets. The philosophers of the Middle Ages neither aimed at nor achieved formal literary distinction. The only virtue of their dog-Latin is that it is much easier for us to understand than the comparatively convoluted Latin of Cicero. With the Renaissance, style came back, first with the revival of Ciceronian Latin and then, more significantly, with the writing of philosophy in vernacular languages, appropriate for an age of printing and secular literacy.

In Britain and France, which were both philosophically productive from the beginning of the seventeenth century until well on into the eighteenth, many of the most admirable literary productions were philosophical. Francis Bacon, the first important British philosopher to write in the vernacular, is one of the glories of English prose. So, in a somewhat more rough and ready way, is Thomas Hobbes, who was for a time Bacon's amanuensis. Descartes, along with Pascal, transformed French prose, replacing the confused, rambling multitudinousness of Rabelais with what has come to be called la clarté française and which has served ever since, despite some recent Heideggerian pollution, as a marvellously lucid instrument of exposition. Voltaire and Rousseau are its supreme exponents. After Bacon and Hobbes, although Locke was not a major prose writer, with Berkeley, above all, and, not far behind him, Hume, English philosophical prose reaches its highest point. Dugald Stewart, leader, after Thomas Reid, of the Scottish school, displayed a certain distinguished sonority and John Stuart Mill wrote with marvellous clarity even if a degree of flatness. (Someone said of him that he wrote clearly enough to be found out.) The first great modern German philosopher, Leibniz, wrote in Latin and French. Kant wrote abominably, as did his successors, Fichte, Schelling and Hegel. Schopenhauer, Hegel's infuriated opponent, wrote superbly as did Nietzsche, the philosopher he inspired, an influence acknowledged in Nietzsche's Schopenhauer as educator. It should be remembered that Walter Pater, the most deliberate and refined of late Victorian prose stylists, was a teacher of philosophy. It may be that his teaching was not of the sort to secure his pupils good examination results, but, in *Plato and Platonism,* he wrote a genuinely philosophical book. The greatest English prose writer of the Victorian age, J.H. Newman, was also a philosopher, along with much else, even if the brilliance of his prose is less evident in his strictly philosophical *Grammar of Assent,* than his *Apologia,* his *Idea of a University,* and in his often superbly entertaining polemical works, such as *The Present Position of Catholics in England.*

This apparent digression into the subject of philosophy as prose literature serves to introduce a topic more obviously relevant to my general subject. This is that there is an alternation in the history of philosophy between predominantly academic or scholarly phases and predominantly literary ones.

In its beginnings on the Ionian coast of Asia Minor in the city of Miletus, it seems, for all we can tell, to have been a matter of free speculation by far-seeing individuals. The fact that they all lived in the same place, however, suggests some measure of organisation. Perhaps there were regular discussions in a favoured tavern or public building in which any interested passer-by could take part. With Pythagoras and his circle we encounter an early aberration. For the Pythagoreans constituted a religious order, with firm discipline and ritual. A crucial dogma was the transmigration of souls; a central practice abstention from eating beans. Bertrand Russell describes Pythagoras as a combination of Einstein (on account of his important mathematical achievements) and Mrs Mary Baker Eddy.

In the Ionians and the Pythagoreans we find exemplified two persisting misconceptions of the way in which philosophy is carried on. The Ionian model, for lack of information, is taken to be that of free, unassociated individuals, working things out for themselves, with no tradition to start from and no competent critics to confront. The Pythagoreans convey the impression of philosophers as initiates of an esoteric mystery, an anomaly which was to come to the surface again in an epoch of magical thinking in the sixteenth century, whose principal exponent was Paracelsus. This was the intellectual world of the hermetic writings and the Kabbala, of the alchemical transmutation of base metals into gold, of mystic correspondences and analogies between macrocosm and microcosm. In our own century its main results have been the Rosicrucian inspiration of much of the poetry of W.B. Yeats and, on the negative side, the more or less comically disgraceful practices of Aleister Crowley. It made no lasting contribution to philosophy.

With the Sophists of the fifth century BC, philosophy takes on the form which it has intermittently had ever since, but above all in the high Middle Ages and for the last century. It became a training in clear and effective thought and speech for young men intending to follow careers in public life, particularly as lawyers. That was the background of the work of Socrates, who accused the Sophists, corrupted by the money they received for their teaching, of indifference to truth and preoccupation with argumentative success. I do not think any fair-minded person of ordinary logical capacity could absolve Socrates of the charge of being himself much given to sophistical refutations of his critics, if Plato's accounts of how he argued are to be believed. Nevertheless his very devoted pupil Plato and Plato's somewhat less devoted pupil Aristotle greatly enlarged the scope of philosophy and greatly elaborated and purified the reasonings of which it was composed. They have remained the paradigms of true philosophy ever since. Roughly speaking, Plato supplied the bright ideas, including most of those on which Aristotle drew for the purpose of criticising him; Aristotle set them out in the comparatively precise and logically orderly way.

Each of them founded a school and Plato's Academy, as I have mentioned, persisted in some form or other for about nine hundred years, until AD 529. These were broadly speaking universities, continuing centres of research and teaching. They undoubtedly showed signs of ossification as time passed. After Alexander the Great extinguished the independence of Athens and other Greek city-states, the intellectual interests of the better-off turned from public to private concerns. Stoics, Epicureans and Sceptics largely, but by no means exclusively, concentrated on ethical issues, specifically that of how life should be lived, how *ataraxia* or peace of mind could be secured. But the Stoics made important advances on the formal logic of Aristotle, which were reinvented in the middle of the nineteenth century, the Stoic contribution being unknown until that reinvention, although they had been lurking in the works of Sextus Empiricus, which had been available to Western European philosophers since perhaps as early as 1441. The Sceptics' theory of knowledge, or of the obstacles to it, were, however, immediately influential after their rediscovery, most conspicuously in Descartes. The sceptical arguments he aimed to refute were familiar from Montaigne's *Apology of Raymond Sebond*, which was provoked by reading Sextus Empiricus, and the more philosophically professional attack of Gassendi on Aristotelianism. Chrysippus, the major contributor to Stoic logic, lived in the third century BC, a hundred and fifty years after Plato. Sextus Empiricus produced his great compilation of sceptical reasonings some four hundred years later, summing up a philosophical tradition of almost six centuries in length. But although Cicero and Augustine, respectively about half way through, and after the end of, that tradition, both wrote books about scepticism, Roman interest in Greek philosophy, after Lucretius at any rate, was almost entirely ethical and literary. It began in the circle of admirers of Greek culture that was centred on Scipio Africanus, the conqueror of Carthage, who was taught by a pupil of Chrysippus, and petered out with Marcus Aurelius around AD 200.

The great creative age of ancient philosophy lasted for some two hundred and fifty years. A serious intellectual tradition persisted in Greece for a while. But with Rome in political control of the eastern Mediterranean from the mid-second century BC and with cultivated members of the Roman élite being the chief consumers of Greek philosophical learning, its more austere, theoretical elements sank into comparative oblivion. Plotinus, in the third century AD, who studied in Alexandria and settled in Rome, was a truly theoretical philosopher and a portent for the future, most of all because of his influence on Augustine. As the Roman world was falling to pieces his version of Platonism became, in Augustine's hands, the intellectual bone-structure of Christian theology, a position it maintained until the greater part of the works of Aristotle were recovered for the West, by way of Moslem intermediaries, in the twelfth century, nine hundred years after Plotinus and seven hundred years after Augustine.

In terms of my picture of the history of philosophy as an alternation of academic and literary phases, the philosophy of the ancient world, after an inevitably exceptional and idiosyncratic start with the Ionians and Pythagoreans, has a great creative period of at most two and a half centuries which fairly soon settled into an academic form. Schools established themselves and endured, if in an increasingly imitative and derivative manner. A large political change, the submission of Greece to Rome, introduced a new cultivated clientele for philosophy, whose taste was less for abstract theory than for what may be called human philosophy, wisdom about the conduct of life, but still based on reasoning, unlike the dogmatic pronouncements of sages.

The theoretical needs of the church, developing in conditions of political and social breakdown, then revived theoretical philosophy sufficiently for Christian doctrine to be given a seriously philosophical form. But after Augustine and the fall of the Western empire in the fifth century, the circumstances of barbarian invasion and economic collapse in effect ruled out the effective pursuit of the subject. It became, at best, an ancient treasure to be preserved.

The only philosophers of note between Augustine in the fifth century and Anselm in the late eleventh are Boethius, important more as communicating the seed of the problem of universals to thinkers who revived philosophy with it half a millennium later, and John Scotus Erigena. Erigena, the most remarkable figure in the dark age Irish culture that was obliterated almost without trace by the Vikings, was called to the court of Charles the Bald, to assist with the false start of the Carolingian renaissance. With Anselm, two hundred years later, theoretical philosophy revived with a degree of vigour that propelled it forward for two hundred and fifty years until it sank into repetitive torpor after Ockham, the Black Death of which he died, the subordination of the papacy to the French crown and the final indignity of the Great Schism and the existence for some years of three different claimants to the papal title. These were difficult times for free thought. Wyclif in late fourteenth century England died in his bed, but his disciple John Huss, like him an anticipator of the Protestant reformers of the sixteenth century, was put to death, as were many of Wyclif's followers.

In the great years of medieval philosophy, between Anselm and Ockham, it was thoroughly academic. Its typical expression was in highly formalised disputations. It had no literary pretensions and was of no interest to those such as Petrarch who first exhibited the literary concerns of the Renaissance. It was practised in monasteries and in the schools associated both with them and with cathedrals. In due course it came to be centred in universities, beginning with Paris and Oxford in the late twelfth century. Although subject to a good deal of orthodox doctrinal interference, condemnations for heresy and proscriptions of theses, it lived a life of its own. It, and the universities in which it was pursued and taught, were protected by secular rulers, who relied on those universities to turn out clear-headed and mentally disciplined administrators.

Scholasticism declined from the mid-fourteenth century, but has remained alive to this day. In Spain there was nothing to compete with it. In all Christian countries, Protestant ones included, Aristotle remained the primary philosophical authority in universities until the nineteenth century. I sometimes think he still is in Oxford. Bacon, Hobbes and Locke were all propelled into philosophy by disgusted reaction to the dead Aristotelian lore drummed into their heads when they were students.

The characteristic philosophers of the early Renaissance were secular scholars of a literary bent, like Ficino and Pico della Mirandola, working not in church-controlled universities, but in academies, supported by secular rulers. But for all their merits, such as Valla's proof that the Donation of Constantine was a forgery, they made no contribution to philosophy with anything like the substance of their major scholastic predecessors or their great seventeenth-century successors. With the latter, with the philosophical heroes of Whitehead's century of genius: Bacon, Descartes, Hobbes, Locke, Spinoza and Leibniz, it is one of the three great philosophical ages. It spread over into the first half of the eighteenth century, with Berkeley and Hume. None of these thinkers was a professional university philosopher. Most of them had received, and contemptuously rejected, an academic training in Aristotelian philosophy. Locke was employed in Oxford for quite a time, but as a medical man. He did not take up philosophy until he was middle-aged. His great *Essay on Human Understanding* was the by-product of a private discussion group devoted to problems about religion and morality, neither of which gets much attention in it. Hobbes was in the entourage of a noble family; Spinoza, cast out by the Jewish community of Amsterdam, made a living by grinding lenses. Leibniz, after a short time as a professor, went into the service of the ruling family of Hanover at the age of twenty-seven and stayed in it for the rest of his life, most of it as a court librarian.

This was the great epoch of philosophical letter-writing. With the exception of the perhaps excessively self-confident Bacon and the excessively self-sufficient Hobbes, all the great seventeenth-century philosophers carried on much of their work by correspondence, and even Hobbes engaged in angry polemics with those who criticised him: a bishop who assailed his determinism, abler mathematicians who proved to everyone's satisfaction but his that he had failed to square the circle. An interesting innovation in modes of contact between philosophers was Marin Mersenne's recruitment of a number of important contemporaries to comment on, and, indeed to object to, Descartes' *Meditations*, among them Hobbes, Gassendi and Arnauld, and to publish them, along with Descartes' frequently indignant responses. Mersenne was a member of a severe religious order, the Minimi, and in the thirty years of his active life as a philosophical impresario in Paris, lived in a monastic cell. There he received visitors, but one by one presumably. Only in an abstract way did he anticipate the great cultural innovation of the eighteenth century: the salon. It was at the salons of Mme d'Holbach and Mme Helvétius that the *philosophes* gathered and discussed the great array of ideas incorporated in the *Encyclopedie*. Two of them, Diderot and Holbach, were of substantial, if secondary, importance. These gatherings were a revival of the kind of conversational dinner-party described in Plato's *Symposium*. No doubt the food was much better and the drink less liberally circulated. In the world of Cicero and Seneca there may well have been more thoughtful and dignified versions of the feast of Trimalchio described in Petronius's *Satyricon*.

Dining or drinking clubs of an intellectual kind, with a large admixture of philosophy, were a feature of Edinburgh social life in the eighteenth century. Hume was a genial and active presence, even if he had originally worked out his revolutionary doctrines in seclusion in France. Other participants were Adam Smith and Adam Ferguson. But this non-academic form of philosophical collaboration overlapped the Scottish revival of the universities. Scottish Protestantism was enthusiastic to the point of being fanatical. But its lack of central authority allowed the Scottish universities to operate in a secular spirit, even if most of their principals and professors (Ferguson and Thomas Reid, for example) were ministers. Professors were appointed by the town councils of the cities where they were situated. Orthodox religious influence was strong enough to keep Hume out of a chair. But the councils were dominated by lawyers and that kept religious interference more or less at bay.

Absolute ecclesiastical control ensured that the British universities remained philosophically torpid until the reforms of the mid-nineteenth century swept away the requirements of ordination and celibacy for teachers and of subscription to the Thirty-Nine Articles of the church for students. The church-controlled universities of France were more or less obliterated by the Revolution and after it Napoleon introduced new, more utilitarian institutions of higher education such as the Ecole Normale, which remained under firm political control under the various governments of nineteenth-century France until 1870. Until then French philosophy of any significance was non-academic: Maine de Biran was an administrator and politician, Comte a private if loquacious person, Renan and Taine were only very loosely anchored in the university system.

The first secular universities to come to life again were those of Germany, where they were encouraged by states, particularly Prussia, which authoritatively controlled the churches within their domains. At Halle, the first of these universities, was Christian

Wolff, the devoted Leibnizian who was the chief thinker of the German Enlightenment. Dismissed from it by one king of Prussia, he was recalled by another, by Frederick the Great, host to Voltaire and La Mettrie, and an influentially interested amateur of philosophy. Kant, spending his life uninterruptedly in the remote East Prussian fastness of Königsberg, was the finest product of the German professorial tradition. He became something of a model for German philosophers ever since, apart from exasperated exceptions such as Schopenhauer and Nietzsche. A rigorously systematic thinker, he did not much engage in discussion or meetings with other philosophers. Generally, German philosophers have elaborated their thoughts in a dogmatic fashion within the security of an academic institution, in which respect for established authority has overwhelmed the free play of criticism. The sheer number of universities in Germany has encouraged this sage-like development as contrasted with England where for long there have been actually, and for even longer effectively, only two and in France where there has been only one. Remote from each other, and dotted about all over the place, serious German thinkers have ploughed ahead with their systematic constructions, not looking up from their desks. Their students mitigated the effect of this hermetic individualism by moving from one university to another, to escape total absorption in one master's way of thinking – Karl Marx's student wanderings from Bonn to Berlin are an example of this.

In England, while the universities slept peaceably in the bosom of the church, such philosophy as there was was of the salon variety, if that is not too elegant a term to apply to such modest gatherings of those of the circle in which Priestley and Godwin moved, or the somewhat more comfortable arrangements for the utilitarians at Jeremy Bentham's well-appointed country house. The philosophical radicals, of whom he was the passive and eccentric leader, made use of a means of communication which had been available for the learned for some time: the periodical or magazine. The French *Journal des Savants* had been in existence since 1655, the *Acta Eruditorum,* inspired by Leibniz, since 1685, but they contained little philosophy. The great periodicals of nineteenth-century Britain, particularly the *Edinburgh Review,* which published James Mill and his son's target, Sir William Hamilton, and the *Westminster Review,* which the group brought out to express its views more effectively and copiously, were more hospitable.

From the mid-nineteenth century to the present day philosophy has everywhere become increasingly academic and has, perhaps unfortunately, more and more addressed itself to an academic, thoroughly professionalised audience. This is true of Britain from about 1860, of France from 1870 and of the United States since the 1880s, with the beginning of the teaching careers of James and Royce, and with the academically minded, but academically unemployable, Charles Sanders Peirce in the background. In France the solidly academic foundation of philosophy in this century has been obscured by some superficial reversion to the bellelettristic style of the salon or, in our day, café. Bergson lectured to large audiences in which ladies of fashion were conspicuous. But he had a steady job at the Collège de France. Sartre may have held forth at the Café de Flore, but he came up by a hard academic route, though he never held a chair. Merleau-Ponty did, and so did Foucault and Derrida, at the summit of the university system.

In speaking of an alternation between epochs of academic and literary philosophy, of Greeks, scholastics and modern professionals, on the one hand, with socially elevated Romans and the uninstitutionalised philosophical men of letters from the Renaissance to Rousseau, on the other, I have not meant to suggest that it follows a rigid pattern. To start with there have been two large gaps of nothing in particular: between the fall of Rome and the eleventh century, due to general social and political convulsion, and between the mid-fourteenth century and, to all intents and purposes, the beginning of the seventeenth century, due to protracted religious conflict. But academic philosophy tends towards an introversion which is scholastic in the bad sense of the word and from which it can be rescued only by individual initiatives of thought from outside.

Nor have I wanted to convey the idea that the academic professionals are superior to the private men of letters. Considered as institutions, both modes of philosophical activity have a strongly social character. Sages, unlike philosophers proper, do not meet in salons or dining clubs, do not have a large technical correspondence, do not turn up at conferences or contribute to specialised periodicals. That is not to say that many prominent philosophers are not sages under the skin, longing for wholly docile disciples and vehemently resistant to criticism. It is, I think, no accident that the two most intimidating and despotic of philosophers in the twentieth century English-speaking world, Wittgenstein and Popper, were both of German, more exactly Austrian, origin. But that is an aberration, against which the institutional history of the subject unequivocally pronounces.

In a way the most notable institutional fact about philosophy today is the unprecedently large number of its exponents and, since they are almost all university teachers, of their students. But it would be odd if that were not the case. Populations have increased, as have the proportion of them that goes into higher education. Journalists lament the subject's esotericism and unintelligibility. Philosophy has been generally readable at times, in its non-academic periods, but this is not one of them. Is Quine really less accessible than Kant or Duns Scotus? In any case there are numerous and capable popularisers for those who want to consult them. A further ground of complaint is the persisting estrangement of the narrowly cognitive but wholly rational philosophy of the English-speaking world, and a few like- minded outposts, from the humanly interesting but prophetically irrational style of philosophy of continental Europe. Alternatively, the two parties might agree to co-exist peacefully, as do physics and literary criticism, although this would be a makeshift since the two modes of thought intrinsically undermine each other. Anglo-Saxon philosophy, like that of the Sophists and the Scholastics, at least has a clear social purpose: the training of the intellect. A culture that does not provide for that lacks one of the essentials of civilisation.

*Delivered in the Presidential lecture series at Brown University, 1994.*

# Character and Will in Modern Ethics

My subject is obviously an appropriate one for a seminar which is held in honour of the memory of Lionel Trilling. The bent of his mind together with the public circumstances of his last years led him to be entirely explicit about the question. In 1973, in 'Art, Will and Necessity', he wrote:

> The concept of the will no longer figures significantly in the systematic psychology of our day. Those of us who are old enough to have been brought up in the shadow of the nineteenth century can recall how important the will was once thought to be in the conduct of the personal life, how confidently our parents and teachers pointed to the practical as well as the moral advantages of having a will of developed strength and discipline. Nothing could be more alien to the contemporary style of rearing and teaching the young. In the nineteenth century the will was a central and controlling topic in psychological and ethical theory – as how could it not be, given an economic system in which the unshakeable resolve of the industrial entrepreneur was of the essence, and given the temperaments of its great cultural figures? (*The Last Decade*, p. 130)

It is my purpose to reopen the question, to inquire what character and will actually are, mindful of the fact that the word 'ethics' means different things in the two main English-speaking countries – moral practice in America, moral theory in England. Then I shall consider the declining presence of character and will in actual moral life and their distinctly marginal, even furtive, role in organised thinking about morality. What I have to say will, then, fall into four parts. I shall begin, pretty much in character as a philosopher from Oxford, with what may seem to be lexicographical needlework at first, but may well appear on further reflection to be the exercise of a rougher, more legislative conceptual trade. I shall go on to cover some familiar ground in rehearsing the ever more residual place occupied by character and will in the more usual and accepted styles of moral personality in our age, to which I shall add some equally familiar thoughts about the causes of this phenomenon, social and intellectual. Thirdly, I shall turn to the place of character and will, conceived particularly as virtue or the system of virtues, in moral philosophy, where they have had an increasingly thin time since the classical world succumbed to 'barbarism and religion'. The last thing I wish to do is to be edifying, so I shall leave that to the end.

## 1. Character and will: lexicographical preliminaries

I begin my attempt to articulate the form of the idea of character by a comparison of it with other ideas which we use, as we use it, to distinguish what may be called the *performance* of human beings. (The analogy implied by that word is with the assessment of the qualities of motor cars, rather than with theatrical performers, but has no mechanistic bias or intention.)

In the first place, character is different from personality. Personality is the style or form of a person's presentation of himself, typically in more or less short-lived encounters. It is, therefore, something that can be put on and taken off more or less at will, like clothing or make-up, the device which makes it possible to be all things to all men for those who want to be so. The derivation of the word from *persona*, a mask, is not evidence, but is at least symptomatic. Character, by contrast, is something more deeply-rooted, not, as I shall argue, innate or unalterable, but at least a fairly hard-won achievement. Character is the reality, I am inclined to say, of which personality is the appearance. I am treating personality here in the sense which it usually has in colloquial speech. Psychologists engaged in the study of what they call personality apply the word much more widely to cover the whole range of a person's dispositions to conduct, character and personality colloquially understood being among those dispositions but not exhausting them. In support of my account of the colloquial conception of personality is the fact that we commonly assess personalities in terms appropriate to clothing, or at any rate the surfaces of things: as agreeable, pleasant, attractive and, of course, their opposites.

Character is also different from temperament. Temperament is the modern equivalent of the humours of an earlier age. It has been suggested that the four humours – the sanguine, the phlegmatic, the choleric and the melancholy – correspond to four main possibilities of combination of two dimensions along which temperaments may vary, dimensions that are independent of each other. One runs from optimism to pessimism, the other from extraversion to introversion.

Thus the sanguine and phlegmatic are extraverted, the sanguine and choleric are optimistic. Certainly the aptest terms for the description of temperaments fit this scheme: outgoing or withdrawn, cheerful or gloomy. Now temperament, so understood, would seem to be something innate or constitutional. It is the most stable part of the total personality. To the extent that it does alter, we attribute the fact to physiological change or to emotional crisis (positive as well as negative). Character, however, is not given but acquired, by habituation, if Aristotle is right, but at any rate under the influence of teachers or one's own self-modifying resolve.

Thirdly, character is different from appetites or tastes, the primary, given impulses which are the initial and ultimate determinants of conduct. The kind of food or entertainment or place to live a person favours is something important to know about him, but it is not something that he can be admired or despised for or expected to do anything about on the whole. There are, of course, what are considered to be perverted tastes, for human flesh as food, for example, or for young children as sexual objects. There are good reasons why these tastes should not be indulged and the condemnation due to acts that indulge them naturally gets extended to the tastes themselves, as liable to express themselves in such acts. But pity might be a more appropriate response than blame. In so far as tastes are such as to lead to objectionable conduct, it is the role of character to ensure that they do not; it is not just another, competing taste.

Character is sometimes thought of as the system of a person's virtues or moral dispositions. There is something in this, but qualification is needed. There is an ancient idea of the virtues, still bearing the authority that endorsement by Aristotle supplies, which takes a very broad range of good human qualities as virtues, intellectual excellences along with moral ones. This is to understand virtue in much the same way as we do when we speak of the virtues of a furniture wax or a cold reliever. Now intelligence and imagination and fertility of ideas and so forth are undoubtedly good human qualities and worthy of admiration. But they are not, I feel, properly described as qualities of character. They are more like a fourth aspect of human performance from which character needs to be distinguished: abilities and skills. These, like character, are acquired by learning, and, in particular, by habituation, whether imposed by parents and teachers or by oneself. But they are comparatively specific, where character is more general. On the other hand, general intellectual power, which shares the generality of character, is not like character (and particular skills, for that matter) modifiable by teaching or training.

So far I have been approaching the idea of character obliquely, by distinguishing it from neighbouring things which it is not. It is essential or fundamental, and not as is personality, a matter of the surface, even a form of communication. It is modifiable by teaching, and, in a way, by effort, unlike such innate and constitutional things as temperament, tastes and intellectual power. It is comparatively unspecific, unlike abilities and skills. It is time to consider more directly what it positively is. My main claim is that it is in essence resolution, determination, a matter of pursuing purposes of varying kinds of largeness without being distracted by passing impulses. It is something that is measured in terms of its strength. Its strength, indeed, is its existence, for the weaker it is the closer it comes to non-existence. In that respect it is like the will, as we ordinarily conceive it. To have a will is to have a fairly strong one. To have a very weak will is the next best thing to having no will at all.

Is this a peculiar, idiosyncratic notion of character? It comprises, at any rate, three of the four virtues that Plato took to be most important: prudence, courage, moderation. In so far as his fourth virtue, justice, is taken to be impartiality or fairness, that is as the power to resist the promptings of immediate affection or favour, it is also a quality of character. I am not so sure about justice as a form of general benevolence, that is as the self-denying suppression of one's own interests for the sake of people other than oneself. I say a little more about benevolence later.

Human life, being social, involves not just interaction, but collaboration. A strong character is at least a necessary requirement in an effective collaborator. It is not sufficient, since he may apply his strong character in pursuit of purposes of his own, and not the declared purposes of the collaboration. In writing a reference for someone the matters one is meant to give first consideration in describing his character (and not his special skills, general intelligence and personality, for which there are ordinarily special sections) are his firmness of purpose, reliability, honesty and good sense or prudence. Temperance is taken for granted unless its absence is very pronounced.

The qualities of character I have mentioned are all dispositions to resist the immediate solicitations of impulse. Prudence is a settled resistance to whim, courage to fear, temperance to greed, justice to selfishness or particular affections. One could add industriousness as resistance to laziness, reliability as resistance to taking the easiest way. They are, generally speaking, ways of deferring gratification, of protecting the achievement of some valued object in the future from being undermined by the pull of lesser objects near at hand.

When in the Aristotelian way, courage and prudence are described as moral virtues, one's thoughts at once turn to the brave and resolute malefactor. Clarendon, in his *History of the Great Rebellion*, referred to Oliver Cromwell as 'a bold, bad man'. In doing so he was admitting that Cromwell was a man of character, while affirming that he was not a good man. His strength of character was brought to bear in the service of evil purposes, in Clarendon's view: the destruction of the ancient constitution of church and state. He was quite a different kind of person from, on a plausible interpretation, the emperor Caligula, whose brief career of cruelty and grossness was throughout the indulgence of capricious passion.

Just as a man of character may be good or bad, so the qualities that make up his character may be morally admirable but may also not. Stalin, one may suppose, was a steady worker. But his industriousness was used for vile purposes. Yet if not morally admirable, it is still admirable, in contrast to the trivial motivation of the less statistically frightful killings ordered by Caligula. This is a variation on the theme of *corruptio optimi pessima*. The devil, according to the founder of the Salvation Army, had all the best tunes. He also, if *Paradise Lost* is to be trusted, has some fine qualities of character.

In the light of these considerations I propose the theory that the idea of character is procedural rather than substantive. It is not a matter of having a particular set of desires alongside the instinctive, impulsive desires we share with other animals. It is the disposition or habit of controlling one's immediate, impulsive desires so that we do not let them issue in action until we have considered the bearing of that action on the achievement of other, remoter objects of desire. So understood, character is much the same thing as self-control or strength of will. Like them it may be used for bad purposes. But one may suspect that only those of the most delightful innate temperament and preferences can achieve much morally without it, and then only if their circumstances are very safe and easy, that is, where all that is required of a moral agent is kindliness.

The cognitive distinguishing mark of the human species is its reasoning power, the ability that we have, conferred by language, to think about what is outside the immediate zone of perception and, by drawing inferences with the aid of regularities we observe, to work out what to do to produce or prevent future possibilities, contingent on our action, that we find attractive or repellent. Strength of character, by holding in check impulses excited by what is immediately present, allows the cognitive harvest of our reasoning powers to have an effect on what we do. To conceive character in this way is to give an acceptable sense to the idea that reason can and should control the passions. Even Hume, who, correctly, given his understanding of reason, believed it was and ought to be the slave of the passions, admitted that there was a practical rationality about the agent in whom the calm passions, informed by the longer view, were such as to prevail over the violent passions of immediate instinct.

I said at the beginning that what first appeared as lexicography might, on a second look, seem more like legislation. I do not pretend that the account I have given of character, as in effect strength of will, the self-disciplined control of impulse for the sake of long-term aims, is a simple transcription of what we ordinarily mean by the word. I am not thinking so much here of such things as calling someone 'a character' or 'a real character' who, although equipped with a gaudy personality and some insistent tastes, may have no strength of character or readiness for deferred gratification at all. More to the point is the fact that we talk of people as having nice characters who, in my terms, have perhaps an agreeable personality or an amiable temperament. We could as well have said of them that they are simply nice people or, a bit more archaically, that they have nice natures. All I would claim is that the sense I have articulated is one that has long been dominant and still widely prevails. To the extent that the boundaries of the word's application are often less determinate and more inclusive in our present speech, that may reflect the widespread distaste for the quality of human beings that I use the word for and to whose position in current moral practice I now turn.

## 2. Character and will in the moral history of our age

In the English-speaking world we live and move amid the ruins of Victorian morality in which character and will had an important place. Its central theme was one of strenuous self-discipline. It was itself a reaction against the consciously non-strenuous morality of the eighteenth century which preceded it and which was, in its turn, a reversal of the gloomy fanaticism of the seventeenth century and the epoch of the wars of religion. Character and strength of will were not repudiated by the secular good sense of the Augustans. Long-term aims were essential for the rational management of life and for morality, which was seen as an indispensable part of that code of rational living. But the aims now approved were secular and terrestrial, to be pursued by steady and prudent application, not with guilty fanatical enthusiasm. Hume's words for morally desirable qualities of character are representative: they are, he maintained, those that are 'agreeable or useful', the properties, we might feel, more of an ideal weekend guest than of a collaborator in some risky and ambitious undertaking.

The morality of the eighteenth century was a relaxed and elegant version of the ideal of life of the Protestant commercial middle class which had been progressively reconciled to life on this sinful earth by the worldly success that had accrued to its hard work and foresight. It was such sober and prudent people who established the first European settlement in north America, people of such moderate outlook as to be capable of using turkey for purposes of celebration. Acquiescing in their own good fortune, they found an emblem, after a century and a half, in Benjamin Franklin, a believer in only the most judicious and economical repression of instinct. By the middle of the nineteenth century an altogether more severe and ascetic ideal of like had replaced his genial accommodation of long-term goals and short-term needs.

If we go further still into the past, there stretches back to the beginnings of recorded moral history a sequence of aristocratic moralities, idealising many different kinds of aristocrat – the Renaissance virtuoso, the medieval knight, the Stoic citizen of the Roman republic, Aristotle's great-souled man and the dim, militant heroes of epic poetry. Common to them all is an insistence of honour, the maintenance of a public standard of behaviour, whose military appurtenances, the chase and the duel, outlasted the military usefulness of the ideal. There were no serious relics of this to obstruct the triumph of Victorianism in the United States, although the idea of it was there to trouble the literary imagination of the South. In continental Europe feudal morality was propped up by dynastic monarchies who preferred to be served by its exponents. In Britain a large and powerful aristocratic class followed the lead of the queen into complete submission to middle-class moral ideas. Palmerston died in 1865. Lord Steyne, a more complete and much less attractive expression of the previous mode of life, was embalmed in *Vanity Fair* in 1848.

The main ingredients of Victorianism are nearly all aspects of an ideal of self-reliance. At the top is industry, in which effort is accompanied by scrupulous workmanship. Honesty and fidelity to promises, so advantageous in the nineteenth-century business world of small enterprises, are seen as required in all people's activities. Waste is deplored, both so that opportunity should not be let slip and so that provision is made against ill fortune. Sexuality is narrowly confined within the limits of monogamy. Benevolence is confined to the unfortunate; the merely pitiable do not as such deserve it, since they may be simply failures. Decorum must be maintained, serving as a kind of fireproof matting to keep down smouldering impulses to passion and extravagance.

This morality was overcome by two main lines of attack. The first of them is the rationalism of a group of late nineteenth and early twentieth century thinkers who sought to revive the Enlightenment, notably Samuel Butler, Shaw and Bertrand Russell. They attacked Victorian ideas about sex, property, the relations of men to women and of adults to children and, consequentially, the decorum that they saw as preserving the moral errors they attacked at one level and the religion they saw as sanctifying them at another. These late-Victorian and Edwardian moral reformers were themselves people of strong character, richly endowed with will. Shaw and Russell were very hard workers and Shaw was physically ascetic above and beyond the call of Victorianism, undefiled by drink, meat or sexuality.

They believed that people in general worked too hard, that they endured unnecessary economic and sexual deprivation, that their domestic relationships were marred by authoritarian harshness and that decorum and religion deceived them about the conditions of their own happiness. They hoped that a new, more rational morality would free people to perfect themselves. They did not predict the looting employee, the consumer of pornography, the absent or indifferent parent, the hooligan adolescent.

The other line of attack on Victorianism was, as far as England and, no doubt, the English-speaking world in general is concerned, an import from continental Europe, particularly France. What I have in mind is a sequence of hedonisms, by no means closely related to each other or sympathetic to each other. To start with there is the decadence of the 1890s, in its politer form aestheticism, the Paterian life of intense private sensation. After 1918 the sensations pursued become rougher and more primordial, but there is the same desire to shock and to ridicule older pieties. Vulgar Freudianism, the idea that all 'inhibition' is bad, unhealthy, the cause of neurosis, helps to fill the sails of this pleasure-boat. Just as aestheticism had a kind of rural correlate in sandal-wearing communities of admirers of Ruskin, given to free love or the drinking of fruit juice, so the rural arm of the hedonism of the 1920s was the instinctualism of D.H. Lawrence, who recruited Freud for his own special uses as did the heroines of F. Scott Fitzgerald and the early Evelyn Waugh.

In our time everyday morality, emancipated from Victorianism, takes two principal forms, corresponding in their rough and popular way to the two lines of moral reform I have described. The first is the negatively permissive morality whose ideal of life is one of passive consumption, of the more or less inert enjoyment of material and, one might say, recreational satisfactions. An important feature is the unloading on to something called 'society' of the duty of ensuring that the means of satisfaction are available at minimal cost in effort, as also of the responsibility for the failures and crimes of individuals. The quality most admired is kindness, an immediate amiability of response, a sort of uncritical endorsement of the wants and acts of others, free from all trace of censoriousness.

The second is the ecstatic morality that enjoins the unrestricted indulgence of instinct, up to, and even beyond, the limits of ordinary self-preservation. It is less widespread than permissiveness, being largely confined to the young. On this view all frustration or inhibition is bad and unhealthy. Older ideas of the natural goodness of mankind are reanimated, often with the qualification that innocence can survive only in communities sequestered from the corrupting influences of the urban, industrial world. In this system of thought the freaked-out adolescent takes over the role of Wordsworth's baby as 'mighty prophet, seer blest!'

At their worst these styles of morality are exhibited, in the permissive case, by the crowd who do nothing to help the rape victim or the looters who pick around in the wreckage of an air crash, and in the ecstatic case, by the circle of Charles Manson. But Victorianism has its prisons and orphanages to its discredit.

Both moral styles are, even at their best, hostile to character and will. For the permissive, strength of character is tiresome and embarrassing, a source of unnecessary trouble, spoiling things by its imposition of disagreeable restraints, souring the enjoyment of life with irrational guilt. For the ecstatic, strength of character is more like a disease, a neurotic deformation of personality fostered by individualism and to be helped by immersion in a collectivity in which selfhood is dismantled. From a point of view which neither would accept, both are juvenile: permissiveness in its idealisation of the style of life of the pampered child, receiving presents and having fun; ecstaticism in its idealisation of the wholly uncontrolled or runaway child, living wildly with a gang.

The development of these moral styles has its parallels in twentieth-century fiction. The heroes of Kafka and Beckett are respectively blanks and residual puddles or fragments of personality. Technically progressive novelists, reflecting on their art, have consistently repudiated the emphasis on character of the great bourgeois novelists from Balzac and Dickens to Thomas Mann and Proust. In the French *nouveau roman* of comparatively recent memory, characterless narrators record the scene around them without interpretation. Personalities of a sort are to be found in the academically admired subjectivistic phantasmagorias of recent American fiction but the chaoses they inhabit are not a medium in which long-term purposes can be pursued any more than a portrait bust can be made out of minestrone.

There is a great deal of social commentary or description in which the decline of character and will has been recorded, with and without implied attitudes of welcome or distaste. Riesman's other-directed man lacks the will of his inner-directed father or grandfather, and is thought the less of by his identifier on that account. Goffman, on the other hand, seems to delight in the central vacuity of the selves whose theatrical devices of personal presentation he articulates, although perhaps the glee is really a response to the cruel accuracy of the articulation. McLuhan groups his passive collectivity round the television set.

There is also a great deal of explanatory material to hand, ranging from the influence of theories at one extreme to that of new modes of social organisation at the other. Of theories the most relevant are those that affirm the motivation of human conduct by forces that agents are not aware of, above all Freudian psychoanalysis. In particular, the Freudian account of the conscience or superego as the product of aggression turned by the individual against himself through fear of the withdrawal of parental love suggests that obedience to its commands is some sort of self-mutilation. Perhaps Freud did not intend his theory of superego to have the comprehensively undermining effect that it has had. To argue that conscientiousness or a sense of guilt can be pathologically exaggerated need not show conscientiousness in general to be a sickness, let alone that character or strength of will is. Freud himself was the unashamed possessor of a will of great strength. There is an instructive aspect to his account of conscience in what he says about civilisation. Although he sees it as having some of the qualities of a collective neurosis, he takes the renunciation of instinct it requires to be preferable to the alternative of uncontrolled aggressiveness.

Another, rather platitudinously, favourable factor in the emergence of the characterless self is the decline of religion, or, at least,
its transformation into radical agitation in the interests of various
species of underdog. Fear of eternal punishment may have induced
some people to the cultivation of character. It is plain that belief
in immortality, or in anything else of a supernatural sort, is not
required in a person of strong character or will. Roman virtue owed
it proverbial status to its early, republican style. It was corrupted by
oriental habits of luxury at much the same time as the earth-bound
Roman intellect was clouded with oriental fantasies about other
worlds than this.

Other features of our times that might be cited in an explanatory
way are the prospect of total extinction by nuclear war, the relapse
to seventeenth-century levels of brutality in politics, intensified by
improved technology, the general disappointment of enlightened
liberal expectations by way of the increase of crime at home and
despotism abroad, particularly in those parts of the world that have
secured political independence from the West.

More to the point, I believe, is the enlargement of the institutions
in which people work or with which they are otherwise involved. In
the first place, that instils feelings of powerlessness and dependence
and so contracts the sphere of action of character and will. Secondly,
conscientiousness diminishes when the actions to which it prompts
us concern our relations to remote, impersonal organisations rather
than concrete individuals. It seems less bad to steal from or do
shoddy work for a railway or the state than a person with whom one
is actually acquainted.

Whatever the correct explanation may be, there can be no doubt
of the fact that a large moral change has taken place in the Western,
or at any rate English-speaking world in the twentieth century. Many
would see it as primarily a change in the content of morality, in our
conceptions of what actions are right and wrong and of what states
of affairs our actions should be morally applied to produce or
prevent. That change of content would be seen to consist in the
replacement of Victorian sexual asceticism by the view that all sexual
activity engaged in by consenting adults is harmless, so long as
unwanted children do not result from it; the replacement of Victorian
authoritarianism by a condition of things in which hitherto dominant adult males are on the same footing with women and children;
and the subordination of the supposed rights of those who earn and
own to the claims of those who want and need, the agenda of social
justice and 'compassion'.

What I am suggesting is that such an account of what has happened does not go far enough and that these changes of content or substance are less fundamental than changes of form which have accompanied them and have altered the whole conception of the moral agent. The liberal or progressive proposers of the changes of moral content that have taken place hoped they would provide conditions in which the dominated or unfortunate would be free to express their strength of character in achievement previously impossible for them. Instead we have the Playboy enterprises and cocaine-sniffing.

### 3 Character and will in ethical theory

I come now to the third and last main part of what I have to say, a consideration of the position occupied by character and will in moral philosophy to see what light may be thrown on them from that quarter. And I begin with a quotation from G.H. von Wright's *Varieties of Goodness*, one of the most sensible and least dotty books of moral philosophy since a kind of Gadarene silliness overtook a good many of the moral philosophers of the English-speaking world after the publication of G.E. Moore's *Principia Ethica* in 1903. 'The concept of character', von Wright says, 'is one of the obviously most important but at the same time most strangely neglected concepts of moral philosophy.'

It has, it is generally agreed, been very much neglected in modern times, that is to say since philosophical reflection on morality began to be conducted in an independently rational manner, abstracted from, although not necessarily in conflict with, the morality of religion, in the seventeenth century. In the century that followed, Butler, Hume and Kant still all concerned themselves with the topic of virtue, which is closely connected with character, since partly constitutive of it. But their prime interest was in rightness or duty, which is a property of actions, and only secondarily with the dispositions in agents from which right actions flow. Butler's account of conscience is more concerned with its alleged intellectual role, as that to which we refer to find out what we ought to do, than with its executive role in which it gets us to do it. Hume distinguished benevolence, the desire for the happiness of others, as a natural virtue, from the artificial virtues of fidelity, or promise-keeping, and justice – which he curiously defined as respect for property – that are needed to supplement the natural limitation of the scope of benevolence to the happiness of those who are comparatively near and dear to us. In the intricate tangle of Kant's moral philosophy duty and our motive for doing it are, at first glance, inextricably bound up with one another. His ringing formula, 'duty is the necessity of acting out of reverence for the law' seems to mean that an act is one's duty if it is an act to which one is motivated by one's disposition to do one's duty. That is either a triviality, if it means that if one is motivated to do one's duty then if one takes something to be one's duty one will be motivated to do it, or a hopeless circularity, if it means that to find out what one's duty is one should see what one's disposition to do one's duty disposes one to do. It turns out that duty and not our disposition to do it is primary, to the extent that its rightness is a logically intrinsic, formal characteristic of actions, being possessed by those actions whose implied principle can be consistently laid down as applicable universally. Reverence for the law, *the* moral virtue, is the disposition to perform actions because they have this formal property. Other motives, benevolence, for example, may lead us to do such dutiful acts as helping the afflicted, but, from the moral point of view that is, as Kant see it, irrelevant. Benevolence is likeable but without moral worth. Only doing duty for duty's sake is deserving of moral credit.

Since Hume and Kant the topic of virtue has been largely of marginal concern to moral philosophers. Their main concern has been with the question of whether the rightness of acts is intrinsic to them, as Kant and other rationalists such as Samuel Clarke supposed, or is a function of the goodness of the consequences which actions of the kind in question can be reasonably expected to produce. Agreeing in general that virtue is the disposition to right action, they have divided into those who see as virtuous only the Kantian motive, which is more or less guaranteed to lead to right action, and those less rigoristic thinkers who admit as virtuous any disposition of agents which tends as a matter of fact to right action in most cases.

Until I started thinking about the subject again for this occasion, I was satisfied with the Humean view. What I now reject in it is the assimilation it makes of virtues in particular, and, by implication, of qualities of character in general, to desires, conceived either as settled preferences or as qualities of temperament. Virtues and qualities of character are, I am now convinced, not just given elements in an agent's appetitive constitution, but cultivated and disciplined modes of choice, by which passive appetites are held in check and so brought into contention with longer-term purposes. The distinction can be conveniently illuminated by contrasting two ways in which the slightly archaic word 'benevolence' can be taken. On the one hand it can be used to refer to a direct appetite or preference for the happiness of others or, again, to settled amiability of temperament. On the other, it can be taken as something more in the nature of a policy or principle of giving weight in one's decisions to others' happiness or well-being.

The point I am making, which treats virtues, on the authority of Aristotle, as qualities of character in the sense of character which I proposed at the beginning of these remarks – that is a s a disposition to control impulsive desires and not just as further desires themselves – is made in different but, I think, recognisably similar terms by J.L. Mackie. 'The good life', he writes, 'will consist in activities that manifest and realize developed dispositions for choice. To say this is to avoid two contrary errors. These activities will manifest *dispositions*, that is the good life is not just a collection of choices… or of equally separate pleasures and satisfactions… But on the other hand these are dispositions for choice… not just instinct or habits' (*Ethics*, p. 188).

The emphasis was once very different in philosophical reflection on morality. In the classical world the notion of virtue was the primary or fundamental moral notion. The chief question for the moral philosopher, according to Plato and Aristotle, was not so much 'what should I do?', asked at some specific juncture, but 'how should I live?' or, more exactly, 'what sort of person should I be?' Since the early modern period and the resecularisation of philosophy the question has become 'how am I to find out what I should do?' It is not that that question did not arise for the classical moral thinkers. But the Thrasymachus with whom Socrates argues in the early part of Plato's *Republic* is more a man who does not see that he has a motive for acting justly or rightly than one who is sceptical of conventional beliefs about what it is right or just to do.

Modern moral philosophy, congruously with the rest of philosophy, is inveterately epistemological. And from that point of view the picking out of certain human dispositions as virtues or morally good qualities of character is secondary. Both Hume and Kant determine the virtuousness of benevolence and fidelity in the one case and conscientiousness in the other by their relation to the independently established moral qualities of actions, that is, their rightness. Cognitively speaking, then, the moral quality of agents is derivative from the moral quality of actions. For consequentialists the moral quality of actions is derivative in its turn from the value of the states of affairs to which those actions can be reasonably expected to lead.

So for them the moral quality of agents is at a yet further remove of dependence.

This point about the cognitively secondary nature of virtue is sometimes put by saying that value of agents and their dispositions is not intrinsic. The implication that the value of moral excellence is instrumental is, it seems, emotionally disagreeable to some people to the point of unacceptability. The stirring phrase with which Kant begins the main text of his chief ethical work serves as a motto for this distaste. 'Nothing in this world or out of it', he said, 'is good without qualification but a good will.' To take that as saying that nothing is good itself and independently of anything else is defensible neither on its own account nor as an interpretation of what Kant was trying to say. His thesis was that only reverence for the moral law, the sense of duty as he understood it, is in all circumstances morally good. Other qualities, such as courage, when possessed by otherwise bad men, only intensify the wrongness of their actions. As for the idea that a good will, or virtue in general, is intrinsically good, it is fairly plain that their goodness is not an immediately discernible property like the yellowness of a daffodil, but can and needs to be reasoned for on the basis of their contribution to the personal and social economy of human action. Perhaps it may just be sensible to add that virtues are still good if unexercised for lack of opportunity, just as a knife can be a good one although never used to cut anything. A disposition is a *potentiality*, not a track record.

I have argued that the cognitive preoccupations of moral philosophers in recent times have led them to ignore virtue, and character generally. It is as if they had seen their task as that of considering the activities of the moral agent in the thick of choice, of the moral critic hoping for some ratification of his critical authority, of the moral disputant involved in disagreement with someone who rejects his moral convictions. There is another perspective in which virtue and character bulk larger. This is the perspective of the moral educator. You have to have some confident idea about what is morally right before you can set about getting people to do it. But it is little use knowing what should be done unless you can get people to do it.

Moral philosophers with the cognitive preoccupation I have discussed tend to give the impression that the executive task of getting people to act rightly, whether others or oneself, is best carried on by simply telling them what they ought to do and then, if they disagree, arguing with them. But the effectiveness of argument and, *a fortiori*, of simple assertion in morals, is going to depend on the moral disposition of the person being argued with or adjured. Moral dispositions are only to a negligible extent innate. Hume's limited natural sympathy needs to be augmented by artificial virtues, as he called them, which are not natural and instinctive.

In general outline it seems clear enough that two factors operate in the moral development of the normally brought-up child. The first is simple imitation, the second that pursuit of parental approval which Freud painted in such funereal colours. The fact that virtue and character have such humble beginnings does not undermine or invalidate them. Since we start as minute savages it is inevitable that all our higher achievements should start in some more or less deplorable or undignified Yeatsian rag and bone shop. A flower is still a flower, even if wholly explainable in terms of seed and some manure. The genetic fallacy involved in denying that is a curious survival of the pre-Darwinian superstition that the greater cannot come out of the less.

Not all development or improvement of character is externally induced. There is such an activity as self-examination; it was a habit for our pious forebears, but we are more likely to be pushed into it by some conspicuous occasion for disgust with ourselves. Morally mature human beings ordinarily acquire certain moral preferences, for courage over cowardice, for equability over petulance and so on. There is no paradox in saying that one can be led by these preferences into the effort of seeking to improve one's character such as determination still does not generate the paradox of using a trait of character to bring itself into existence. The man who says to himself 'I really must cultivate more resolution' is in a bit of a fix if he has none whatever. You cannot enter the game with nothing at all, or develop the muscle in a missing limb. But that, surely, is an unrealistically extreme case.

In the last few years several moral philosophers have addressed themselves to the topic of virtue after its long neglect. So far as I know no one has got very far with the task of systematising the virtues or sorting them into fundamental kinds. I have been dealing with them only obliquely here, as that element in the range of interests of moral philosophers which overlaps the notion of character and, in its everyday sense, of will. Alasdair MacIntyre, in his extremely exciting but to me far from totally persuasive book *After Virtue*, argues that in our moral plight, if we are not to embark on Nietzschean self-affirmation, we must renovate something like Aristotle's idea of virtue as the central moral idea. That seems to me a much more imperial project than the one I have been supporting by implication. That is that we should reinstate character in life and in education and regard childhood, not as an ideal end-state for human beings, but as a receptive phase in which autonomous individuals can develop.

I promised a spot of edification at the end but now that I have started on it I feel reluctant to continue further into the shallow waters of platitude. Why should we seek to develop character and strength of will in ourselves and in those for whose personal development we become responsible? As far as oneself is concerned, it is, from one side, a matter of self-respect. If that looks like a kind of moral aestheticism, it can be replied at least that self-respect is not the same thing as self-satisfaction, it does not have the relaxed, slippered, even terminal quality of the latter. As bearing on others, that without which one cannot respect oneself is the proper object of admiration or at least a high opinion. Does one want willess or characterless friends, let alone collaborators? Friendship is necessarily a fairly persisting relationship and of a friend we ask more than we do of an occasional social companion.

At this point the claims of character and will are coming to be seen as more than attractive in themselves, as also serviceable for further purposes. The characterless person is disarmed in face of the variability of fortune. He is manipulable and without the resources to accommodate himself to change. I find it hard to restrain myself from applauding character as nothing other than spiritual health. As the Cromwell example shows, character and will are not always virtuous, although I have argued that the traditional virtues are constituents of character and will. But a bold, bad man can sometimes be redirected so that he becomes a bold good one; a weak and passive one just continues to flow in the direction imposed on him by the last outside influence he has felt the force of.

There is a weird piece of argument in the ethics of Kant which I always used to ridicule. He said that if nature had intended men to make happiness their overriding end, they would have been fitted out with instincts that led them automatically to it. But, since we have reason, our proper purpose must be something different. I am not yet ready to swallow this whole, but I do now have some sympathy for it. Our instincts are not enough; evolution has organised and modified them, and provided us with a long infancy in which the formation of character can take place. If for no more dignified reason, we should hang on to character for self-defence, as the porcupine does to his prickles or the lobster to his shell.

*Delivered at the Lionel Trilling Seminar, Columbia University, 1983.*

II

# Alien Intelligences:
# Reflections on the Remoteness of
# the European Mind

The large gap between what is called philosophy in the English-speaking world and what goes by appropriate versions of that name in the western part of continental Europe has for some time been a commonplace. It became fairly obvious with the liberation of Paris in 1944. Closely in the wake of the liberating armies came the cultural journalists. They were soon sending back messages about existentialist philosophy and the highly reportable activities of its chief exponent, Sartre. The novels and plays of existentialist writers were widely read in the Anglo-Saxon world. But Anglo-Saxon philosophers generally gave little serious attention to the more narrowly philosophical work that was going on on the other side of the Channel. There was an occasional bluntly argued dismissal, as in various articles by A.J. Ayer. There were a few well-disposed expositors, William Barrett and Iris Murdoch, for example. But there was no practising existentialist movement in the English-speaking world.

Things have moved on since 1944. Existentialism was supplanted by structuralism in the early 1960s. Saussure's ideas about language were applied with increasing amplitude to anthropology by Levi-Strauss, to criticism by Barthes, to social theory by Althusser, to psychoanalysis by Lacan. By the end of the 1960s, by which time Foucault's main books had been published, post-structuralism had installed itself. Its detachment from its predecessor was established in the work of Derrida, who brought out three large books in 1967. Then in the mid-1970s, as a kind of intellectual reaction to the anarchic turbulence of 1968, there was the short-lived flowering of *la nouvelle philosophie*. But that recall to tradition did not really unseat Foucault and Derrida, although it served to open up the French philosophical market-place to some extent. Given the gap between the two philosophical cultures, that is about as far as we can expect to keep up. Structuralism and its unruly post-structuralist offspring have been noted and reported on in the English-speaking world. The structuralists and Derrida, but not Foucault, have had a very

pronounced influence on literary studies. But, with the single exception of Richard Rorty, no Anglo-Saxon philosopher of note or repute
has come to share their views and very few have given them anything
but the most casual and fleeting attention.

In 1992 the process of European unification is planned to make
a large step forward. So it is an appropriate moment to consider how
the philosophical estrangement between Anglo-Saxon and continental Europe came about and to ask whether it would be beneficial
to either side to come closer to the other. I shall begin by tracing the
past history of the division in order to show that, in its recent and
current thoroughness, it is something new. I shall go on to outline
the main points of difference between the two styles of philosophy,
to examine the distinguishing methods and some of the distinguishing doctrines of modern European philosophy and to ask what,
if anything, there is that we should learn from them.

Before the Renaissance and the Reformation, European intellectual unity was ensured by the existence of a common learned
language and by the influence of the beliefs and institutions of a
single church. Descartes and Bacon inaugurated the modern epoch
in philosophy almost as much by writing in the vernacular and by
their distinct forms of indifference to the detail of Christian belief as
by taking a new topic as central – and by treating it in an argumentative style that was unencumbered by deference to authority.

But these innovations did not lead to the breaking up of the
republic of letters into its national parts. Hobbes and Locke were
both thoroughly familiar with the work of Descartes and Locke was
much influenced by it, as he was also by Gassendi. Locke wrote a
book about Malebranche. Locke was the hero of Voltaire and of the
French enlightenment generally, as Bacon was of the *encylopédistes*.
As everyone knows it was Hume who, in Kant's words, 'woke him
from his dogmatic slumbers'. Kant was known to the leading figures
of the Scottish philosophy of common sense in its later phases: to
Hamilton, who did not know very much, and to Mansel, who knew
quite a lot. The Scottish philosophy, in its turn, was drawn on extensively by Victor Cousin, the principal philosopher of France during
the Orleanist monarchy in the second quarter of the nineteenth
century. The British Utilitarians learnt much from the philosophers
of the French enlightenment, in particular from Helvétius, and for
some time John Stuart Mill was in close intellectual contact with
Comte. The British idealists of the last quarter of the nineteenth
century were thoroughly dependent on Hegel. He, admittedly, had
died nearly fifty years before their movement began. But they were

also interested in Lotze, who died in 1881, and they arranged the translation of his main works into English.

All this is evidence of an effective international community of philosophers, at least in Britain, France and Germany and they, after all, were the only places in which, from the end of the sixteenth century up to that time, original philosophy had been produced. The beginnings of analytic philosophy, in a reasonably inclusive sense of the term, can be dated from 1903: the year of Russell's *Principles of Mathematics* and G.E. Moore's *Principia Ethica*. Russell's immediate inspiration for his attempt to derive mathematics from logic was an Italian mathematician, Peano. He soon found that his project had been anticipated by the then unknown German philosopher-mathematician Frege. Moore's ideas about the workings of the mind, and, perhaps, some of his realism, were much influenced by the Austrian Brentano. Now Husserl, whose phenomenology provided the technical foundation of the *Weltanschauung* of existentialism and who was the teacher of Heidegger, was himself a pupil and follower of Brentano. Furthermore he was converted from a psychologistic theory of the nature of mathematics, broadly like Mill's view of the matter, by a severe review of his book on the philosophy of arithmetic written by Frege, who had been equally scathing about Mill. Russell and Moore in Britain, that is to say, and Husserl in Germany, the ancestors of the two main and deeply divided lines of philosophical development in the English-speaking world and in Europe in this century, both reacted against the psychologism of Mill under the influence of the objectivism of Frege and Brentano. The beginning of twentieth-century philosophy was, therefore, in Henry James's phrase, 'an international episode'.

But from that point on national self-sufficiency came to prevail. British and American philosophers showed hardly any interest in what was going on in continental Europe. The only Europeans to take any interest whatever in Anglo-Saxon philosophy were the completely isolated sect of logical positivists and they, for the most part, followed their wayward prophet Wittgenstein to the English-speaking world between Hitler's rise to power and the outbreak of war in 1939. Nothing reveals this more starkly than the complete failure of Bergson and Croce to make any serious headway in English-speaking philosophy. Both were, of course, noticed and both became the subject of brief fads. Professional philosophers who had mounted one or other of the bandwagons either got off again, as did the adherents of Bergson, or worked hard to conceal the alien source of their ideas, as Collingwood did in the case of Croce. A solitary and surprising exception is to be found in the earliest interests of that most British of modern British philosophers, Gilbert Ryle. He made a close and sympathetic study of Brentano, Husserl and the phenomenological movement and his first substantial publication was a long review of Heidegger's *Being and Time* which he brought out in 1929.

The first significant philosophical writings in German were those of Wolff in the early eighteenth century, expounding the ideas of his master, Leibnitz (who himself wrote in Latin and French). The distinguished scholar of German philosophy, Lewis White Beck, says 'Wolff's deadly style and unmatched prolixity make it difficult to understand his immense popularity. His writing combines the worst features of scholastic pedantry and a specious mathematical form'.[1] He turned out to be a model for all subsequent German philosophers of importance, with the shining exceptions of Schopenhauer and Nietzsche. The thoughts of German philosophers were rendered inaccessible by their villainous ugliness and obscurity to foreign readers prepared to make the linguistic effort involved.

British philosophy has always been well-written, at least in its higher reaches. Bacon, Hobbes, Berkeley, Hume, Mill and Russell are writers of the highest excellence and of superb lucidity. The same was true of France until this century. Descartes, Pascal and Voltaire are among the glories of French literature as, in the nineteenth century, were the two great positivists: Renan and Taine. But something terrible happened in the twentieth century. Bergson was, indeed, a distinguished and elegant stylist, even if far from ideally intelligible. But the French philosophers of the second half of the century, from Sartre to Derrida, seem to have applied themselves to the self-mutilating task of copying the most repellent features of German philosophical prose. At dreadful cost in 1918 and in a humiliatingly dependent way in 1945, France emerged formally victorious from wars with Germany. But French philosophy has surrendered unconditionally to the Germans. When the victorious allies imposed liberal democracy by force on their docile and defeated enemy it is a pity that they did not take steps to bring about stylistic denazification or, perhaps one should say deGermanisation. If anything, present day Germans do not write quite such awful philosophical prose as the French, although that of Germany's leading philosopher, Habermas, is as obscure as that of Foucault and considerably uglier. Foucault at least has a certain wild, poetic vitality.

1. Lewis White Beck 'German philosophy', in *Encyclopedia of Philosophy*, ed. Paul Edwards (1967), 3 : 299.

It may be that the assimilation of French and German philosophical writing is just a facet of the general rapprochement between the two countries arising from the experience, which they shared and the Anglo-Saxon nations did not, of being fought over and occupied. But why should the assimilation have gone in the wrong direction? It is, at any rate, possible to identify with some precision the date at which the process really began. Between 1933 and the outbreak of war, the Russian emigré Alexandre Kojève lectured on Hegel's *Phenomenology of Mind* at the Ecole Pratique des Hautes Etudes in Paris to an audience that included many of the most notable names in French post-war intellectual life, and who have testified to its influence on them. The lectures interpreted Hegel in melodramatic terms as a meditation on the end of history. They installed Hegel at the centre of French philosophical consciousness, where he was to reign, along with Husserl and Heidegger, until the arrival of structuralism. More important, they introduced the rhapsodic style, scintillating with resonant phrases and contemptuous of the decencies of logical explicitness, which has predominated in French, more even than in German, philosophy ever since.

So much for the history of philosophy's international relations. It is time to examine the main differences between the two kinds of philosophy under consideration. Anglo-Saxon philosophy is, above all, *cognitive*. It is concerned with knowledge and seeks to arrive at knowledge about it. The kinds of knowledge it concerns itself with are the most objective and impersonal: our commonsense knowledge of the material world and of ourselves and other people, scientific knowledge of nature and the mathematical knowledge that serves it. These are the kinds of knowledge about which there is least disagreement and which are least involved with our desires and emotions. Much less attention is given to more questionable and disputed fields in which knowledge is claimed: history, the social sciences, art, religion.

Secondly, it is *analytic* in the sense of being logically explicit. The senses of terms are carefully distinguished and demarcated. Forms of argument are set out in detail and referred critically to an agreed canon of logical principles.

Analytic philosophy since Russell and Moore inaugurated it in 1903 is by no means homogeneous. There was an early, realist period during which it was gradually becoming aware of its own interests and procedures. That was followed by the era of logical positivism, running from the late 1920s to 1945, to be followed by the linguistic philosophy of the later Wittgenstein and of Ryle and Austin. Since the early 1960s three has been a move back to something closer to logical positivism, during the epoch of Quine and Popper, in which natural science rather than common sense has been the paradigm of knowledge and formal logic, rather than everyday rationality and our natural sense for the meaning of words, has been the canon of validity.

The philosophy dominant in continental Europe has been either indifferent to natural science or positively hostile to it. Heidegger was inspired by his dislike of technologically based civilisation to call philosophers back to the study of Being itself, an elusive activity of intellectually purifying preliminaries designed to prepare ourselves for passive receptiveness to the intimations Being might give us of itself. In his earlier, less amorphous work in *Being and Time*, which set the agenda for French existentialism, he carried out a phenomenological, and therefore not natural-scientific, investigation of *Dasein* or human existence. The human existence being studied was not the impersonal cognitive subject or pure intelligence, the Cartesian ego, presupposed by analytic philosophy. It was an anxiety-ridden thing, conscious of the need to create itself through the exercise of will in choice and of its finite and temporal nature.

With structuralism indifference or hostility to natural science persists, but the point of view is reversed. The autonomous human individual is no longer the point of departure. He turns out, indeed, to be a myth, as Foucault proclaimed in his slogan 'the death of Man'. Man is made what he is by language, which is a transpersonal, thoroughly integrated system of signs and determines the way man conceives of himself and the world around him, his social institutions, the way in which his unconscious desires express themselves, even such humdrum things as the way in which he clothes himself. In the phase of structuralism proper, this underlying structure was seen as something timeless and universal, or was, at any rate, treated as if it were. Foucault, however, reflecting speculatively about various social practices and bodies of doctrine, identified a historical sequence of 'epistemes', each organising the world, and particularly the self and society, in its own way and each serving the interest in power of some group for whom that way of looking at things and people was advantageous. Finally, with the later Barthes and Derrida, the principle that all our thinking is conducted within an integrated system of signs gave rise to the idea that all thought is a passage from one sign to another which interprets it, so that everything we can think about is really text or discourse, and to the even more subversive notion that there is no limit to the free play of developing interpretations.

Despite their opposition of content, existentialism on the one hand and structuralism and post-structuralism on the other are very close in style and procedure. That agreement reflects their shared rejection of the methodical pursuit of objectivity in natural science. They are, first of all, both literary, or even poetic. The proportion of metaphor is very high compared with that of Anglo-Saxon philosophical prose. There is a lack of orderly sequence, a constant eruption of conceptual surprises. This is in accord with a central doctrine of Derrida's which holds that philosophy is just one form of writing among others and accessible to the sort of critical interpretation that seeks to reveal hidden or underlying meanings. In particular, philosophical texts, according to Derrida, are proper objects of deconstruction, a process which elicits an underlying message which is in some way inconsistent with the text's manifest content.

Secondly, there is a kind of argumentative frivolity about continental European philosophers. Their writings are liberally equipped with terms indicating logical relationships such as 'because', 'therefore', 'it follows that' and so forth, but these are, on the whole, ornamental. Arguments are deployed with a view to sustaining strange propositions, but there is no practice of considering possible objections. The counter-example is a species for which there is no place in their menagerie. I shall shortly be looking at a number of quasi- or pseudo-arguments for strategically crucial conclusions drawn by European philosophers in order to justify this claim.

I mentioned earlier the pursuit by Anglo-Saxon philosophy of knowledge about knowledge. In the same spirit Ryle speaks of talk about talk, Quine of lore about lore. That is to ascribe to philosophy a second order status, as a critical or judicial approach to other bodies of thought on whose claim to be worthy of belief it proposes to decide. Such an attitude, as Rorty observes, is undoubtedly presumptuous. But it does not follow that it is therefore mistaken. Certainly if the philosopher claims the authority of a special kind of insight into the beliefs of common sense, science, history or theology he does not deserve attention. But analytic philosophers appeal to sources of validation that are universally available and familiar. They are three in number: our common capacity to understand, and to some extent to define, the meaning or meanings of words; our common capacity to judge the validity of trains of reasoning and to acquire an understanding of the implicit principles involved as set out in logic; and our common agreement as to the obvious truth of some matters of fact. None of these need be taken to be fixed or final. Our grasp of meaning is always improvable. Our intuitive judgements of logical consequence and consistency are corrigible and our logical systems often caricature or oversimplify the implicit rules of our thinking. What we all agree to be obviously true may be vulnerable to criticism. But by setting out our arguments as clearly as possible and with as much logical explicitness as possible, and by exposing them to the criticism of others and acknowledging an obligation to respond to those criticisms by something other than an indeterminate claim to have been misunderstood, we may hope to take part fruitfully in what Samuel Johnson called 'the common pursuit of true judgement'.

To the analytic philosopher his continental European counterpart seems at once self-indulgent and oracular. That, it might be held, is a partisan reaction. But the party involved is a large and historically distinguished one. So far as its methods are concerned analytic philosophy is the legitimate successor of the central philosophical tradition from Plato and Aristotle, by way of Augustine, Aquinas and Ockham, through to Descartes and Locke, Hume and Kant.

That is not a conclusive consideration, of course. Galileo and Newton did not just have different beliefs about the nature of the physical world from those of Aristotle and Aquinas; they arrived at them in a radically new way. A more direct appeal on behalf of what analytic philosophers regard as rational method is to the sincerity of those who disparage it. In their dealings with real life – with tax men, landlords, business competitors, in planning their own activities, in looking after their families and making provision for them – do they not rely on common distinctions of meaning, on a common logic, on a shared background of obvious truths? Would post-structuralists not feel apprehensive if it were suggested that their wills or the contracts they have entered into should be deconstructed? Poetry can have truth embedded in it, but the sentences of which it is composed do not typically aim at literal truth. Those of analytic philosophy do and those of existentialism and structuralism undoubtedly appear to. But they do not set about the task in a way that is calculated to succeed. Their contentions are often suggestive, sometimes excitingly so. Occasionally they strike one as possibly true or at least worthy of belief. But despite the argumentative ornamentation with which they are presented they do little to establish that they are true or worth believing. To resort to an image: the difference between the two kinds of philosophising is the difference between the two settings in which they would be most at home. Anglo-Saxon philosophy is the philosophy of the law court; a ritualised undertaking in which, by way of adversarial exchanges and with all words being carefully measured, a final outcome is pursued. The philosophy of continental Europe is the philosophy of the café; nobody speaks under oath or expects to be held responsible for what he says; everyone, to secure attention, speaks at the top of his voice and exaggerates; the whole undertaking has no determinate purpose beyond itself, the activity is justified by its intrinsic delightfulness.

It is time to support what I have said about the nature of philosophical argument in Europe with some examples. I shall offer several and I have tried to take strategically central instances, not just casual scintillations.

I begin with Heidegger, the early Heidegger of *Being and Time* who established the agenda for existentialism with his account of human existence or *Dasein*. He begins by saying that man is *thrown* into the world. That seems to be just a dramatic way of saying that human life is finite or has a beginning. At one moment I did not exist, at another I did. To describe one's arrival on the scene of existence as being thrown suggests that it is passive and possibly painful, both of which are correct, and that it is sudden, which is not. Throwing presupposes a thrower in ordinary circumstances, but Heidegger does not mean this. What he does mean is that human beings are forlorn, alienated things who come to a consciousness of themselves in a world they did not make and which was not made for them. In fact, many human beings pass their lives in emotionally and socially protective and comfortable surroundings. All the same, everyone, even they, must have times when they have feelings of general desolation. But it is not clear why these feelings should be more metaphysically reliable than the mystic's sense of oneness with all being or the practical man's conviction that the world is his oyster. The pathos of Heigdegger's account of the human situation is not self-authenticating.

It may be thought to look forward for support to the general account of man that follows. Heidegger says that man is a self-transcending being, with no fixed nature, a being that has to choose what it will be. Existentialists inflate the extent to which human nature is unfixed. Humans, like animals and plants, change a good deal in time. But there is the difference that human beings alone change in some accordance with their ideas of what they think they ought to be – morally or prudentially or aesthetically. However, from the fact that men alone can, and sometimes do, choose what they are going to be it does not follow that they are entirely self-made. That is an example of a form of argument to which European philosophers are particularly liable and of which I shall produce more examples. One

might call it *hypernegation*. It infers from the falsity of some generalisation – all aspects of human nature are fixed, say – that its
contrary is true – no aspects of human nature are fixed. Even if one
is convinced that inheritance and environment do not account for
everything about people, it is simply absurd to maintain that they
account for nothing.

Heidegger goes on to insist, quite correctly, that men are temporal
beings. That is not the same as to say that their occupancy of time
begins and ends, although that is also true. Man, he says, is conscious
of non-being within himself and of the inevitability of his total non-
being, his death, in the future. One's present non-being is a little hard
to pin down. Is it everything that might be true of one but in fact is
not? Or is it everything that might be but is not true of one which
one could, or believes one could, bring about? Heidegger maintains
that our consciousness of the non-being within oneself is expressed
in *Angst*. Certainly some choices are risky. So when we have staked
a lot on them, the likelihood of failure is worrying. But if the stake
is trivial there is no cause for anxiety. I can throw a piece of paper
into the waste basket, with little expectation of success, without the
smallest emotional disturbance.

The major negation of death is, indeed, an intelligible ground for
anxiety. That comes out in the constant and varied efforts we make
to put if off: watching when we cross the road, avoiding cholesterol,
not walking alone in certain areas late at night. But, if we reflect, it
is rather the event of dying or becoming dead that we should worry
about, rather than the fact of *being dead*. Most ways of becoming
dead are fairly horrible. But being dead, as Heidegger says, is being
in no state whatever. Nevertheless we can reasonably fear it in
advance. We may be concerned about the well-being of people who
depend on us or, more self-regardingly, about the annihilation of
projects in which we suppose ourselves to be indispensably involved.

Heidegger goes on to contend that authentic living requires us not
to hide from the fact of our own death, not to push it to the margins
of our consciousness. We must, he says, confront it resolutely. Does
this mean admitting death's inevitability when the topic arises? Or
does it mean persistently dwelling on the subject? Perhaps thinking
about it a good deal is necessary to vivify belief in it, so that when
it does come close it does not do so with too great a shock. That
seems sensible, but no more heroic than the opposite view of Spinoza
that the free man thinks of nothing as little as he does of death. So,
to sum up, the capacity of annihilation to induce anxiety does not
show that the partial elements of nothingness Heidegger identifies in

us when we are alive should worry us, although, of course, some of them may. Nor does the fact of approaching annihilation dictate what sort of attitude we should adopt to it. Should we live as if we were going to live for ever or live every day as if it were going to be our last, or, as I imagine most people do, oscillate from one to the other, depending on whether our mood is active or contemplative?

This conception of man's situation in the world was taken over more or less *en bloc* by Sartre but redecorated in an urban style. Where Heidegger sought to open himself to Being by walking in the woods with a volume of Hölderlin, Sartre is preoccupied with the inescapable bad faith of waiters, all acting away at pretending to be waiters. He is even more insistent than Heidegger on the absolute freedom of man and he produces an interesting argument for it. Suppose a man attempts to climb a mountain in a day and, when night is falling, finally collapses exhausted, half way up. He can never be sure that he could not have gone at least a little further. We can never be sure that, in athletic language, our personal best is our possible best.

There is the scent here of a sorites paradox. A man with no hair on his head is bald. You do not make a bald man non-bald by adding one hair. Therefore all men are bald. But I would not ascribe to Sartre the theory that anyone can do anything. What he does do is infer, from the fact that we, in the light of familiar defects of resolution, can never be sure when we have given something up as impossible that we could not in fact have done more, that we can always do more than we did. It is a form of what I have labelled hypernegation to go from *I am not sure that I cannot* to *I am sure that I can*. The most we could reasonably believe is that we could have tried harder and that is, perhaps, more in the nature of a resolution to do better next time than a report on how things were with us at the moment of exhausted collapse.

Let me turn now to Foucault on the other side of the structuralist revolution. In content existentialism and structuralism are utterly opposed. The existentialists proclaim the autonomy of man. The structuralists see him as made what he is by external factors. These are not the natural forces impinging on the body that were taken to be decisive by nineteenth-century materialism. They are structures of a generally linguistic character, above all language itself. But the rhapsodic style of exposition is common to both groups. Foucault's starting point is various institutions and associated habits of mind which identify some people as abnormal and, therefore, as properly subject to various forms of compulsion. He began with madness, went on to ordinary illness, then to crime and, finally, in a more free-wheeling way, to sexuality and its alleged perversions. From these studies he drew two main conclusions. The first and more structuralist one is that in the course of post-medieval history, thinking about his chosen topics and others as well has taken place within a framework of attitudes and assumptions, constituting what he calls an *episteme*. These epistemes succeed one another abruptly. There are four of them: a Renaissance age of symbolism, a classical age of representation, the nineteenth-century age of self-reference and finally a new age, that of the 'death of man', which is in the course of replacing it. In each of these epochs there are underlying parallels between all levels of culture and between the bodies of doctrine prevailing in them and they are sharply separated from one another.

The second conclusion is more Nietzschean. It is that the supposed knowledge used in different ages to pick out some people from the rest as deviant in some way and to subject them to treatment is in fact an instrument of power. It enables the part of the community not subject to exclusion to dominate those who are subject to it. Both of these conclusions have a sceptical, relativist or, as the favoured adjective puts it, unmasking character. To call a doctrine an instrument of power is implicitly to describe it as a put-up job, an illusion, fastened on victims by exploiters. To reveal a sequence of abruptly changing styles of thought is to suggest that there is no progressive improvement but something more like a switch of fashion. No episteme can claim to be more rational than others. Each defines rationality in its own terms.

Like the existentialism of Sartre and the early Heidegger this is at least intelligible in broad terms, however puzzling the small print may be. It also raises an issue that the scientism of analytic philosophy has generally ignored. Psychiatry, medicine and criminology are regarded as real sciences, with the same prestige of objectivity as physics. But, in fact, the criteria for the identification of their subject-matters – the mad, the ill, the criminal – are controversial or contestable. The distinctions they draw are not like those between circles and squares or between trees and flowers. They involve an evaluation. Hypernegation comes in with the inference that since they are evaluative and contestable they are therefore arbitrary and, in aspiring to objective status, a cover for the pursuit of desired, interested ends which it would be inconvenient to acknowledge.

It is a modest, but not unimportant, truth that political dissidents have been incarcerated as insane, healthy people treated as sick (e.g. the left handed) and people punished as criminals under absurd laws (e.g. witches). But there is a large core in each category of not seriously disputable cases. Most people, except those whom most agree are mad, agree about who is mad, while the mad, so identified, disagree with each other as well as with the agreeing majority. The very great majority of those who are said to be ill by the medical profession agree that they are ill and are keen to be treated. Many criminals enthusiastically endorse the laws that impinge on them by indignantly invoking them when the fruit of their thefts is stolen from them. Others endorse the idea of law in general by the claim that their acts are in pursuit of a justice that is not catered for by existing law. The main point is that there can be room for reasonable dispute about where precisely a line should be drawn without any reflection on the propriety of drawing it somewhere.

There is much more to be said about Foucault: about his whimsical use of historical evidence, the wildness of many of his episteme-defining analogies and his idea that if a belief serves a desire for power it is not really knowledge. But I want to give some attention to Derrida, the most ecstatic, even delirious, of these prophets of irrationality. A brief example of his way of proceeding will serve as introduction.

'The signifying value of (the pronoun) "I" does not depend on the life of the speaking subject... My death is structurally necessary to the uttering of "I".'[2] The perfectly correct premise here is that I can understand the use, in a written text, of the word 'I' by someone who is now dead. It follows that it will be possible for someone to understand my use of the word 'I' if he comes across it, after I am dead, in something I have written. However, my death is not necessary, structurally or in any other way, to my use of the word. All that follows is that my death does not make my use of the word thereafter unintelligible. What is necessary, however, is that I should not be dead when I utter it. Dead men tell no tales, whether deconstructible or not.

Derrida accuses all previous philosophy of commitment to a mistaken 'metaphysics of presence'. This is the belief in and search for some self-evident and incorrigible foundation for knowledge. His choice of the term 'presence' rather than 'foundation' or 'absolute certainty' reflects his initial involvement with Husserl and his project of basing philosophy on intuitions of essence. And, as a Frenchman, he has in the back of his mind the clear and distinct perception chosen

2. Jacques Derrida, *Speech and Phenomena*, trans. D.B. Allison, (1973, original, 1967), p. 108.

by Descartes as his foundation, exemplified by *cogito ergo sum*.

There is a sound point being made here. It is that philosophy does not have to base knowledge on foundations with absolute certainty. It is as well that it does not, since the only plausible claimants to absolute certainty are insufficient for the task in hand. Derrida sketches a good argument for this position, at least in a common Anglo-Saxon form. The certainties of immediate experience are momentary and fading. The sense-datum of half a minute ago is now only an unreliable memory.

But that is not really what interests Derrida. In the first place he wants to stamp out 'presence' altogether. Presence, he rightly says, is a notion defined by its difference from, its exclusion of, other notions. But in thus implying 'absence', he weirdly concludes, it is infested with 'absence' and so there is really no such thing. That pattern of argument would prove that there are no consistent concepts whatever, including, of course, those with whose aid it is formulated.

Many Anglo-Saxon philosophers are nowadays fallibilists, convinced that knowledge cannot have absolutely certain foundations, incorrigibly reporting matters of fact. That does not show, however, that nothing can be justified, that all is the free play of interpretation, that all thought is about itself, that there is nothing but text about other texts. Here once more hypernegation is at work. That there is not absolute certainty does not imply that there is no certainty whatever, or even that there is no cumulative certainty, as one might put it, that is certainty achieved by the consilience of a multitude of evidences, none of them on its own beyond doubt.

Derrida's contention that all texts are openly, infinitely interpretable and that interpretation never comes to rest in a reality external to texts seems to be based on the consideration that the most direct way of explaining what something means is by way of paraphrase, of translation into other words that are superficially or deeply equivalent in meaning. He says: 'reading... cannot legitimately transcend the text toward something other than it, toward the referent... or toward a signifier outside the text whose content could take place, could have taken place, outside of language... There is nothing outside of the text.'[3]

The most obvious protest that this invites is that unless at some point the interpreting words are connected by the hearer to a reality he has experienced he can make nothing of what is said. We all have to learn the meaning of the words we use and claim to understand

3. Jacques Derrida, *Grammatology*, trans. G. Spivak (1976; original 1974), p. 158.

when spoken or written by others, however much the underlying grammar of language may be innate. That process of learning must begin by hearing words uttered in the presence of what they signify. At that point no other, already understood words are available for the purpose of a purely verbal interpretation. The operation of linking words to their extra-linguistic signifiers goes on long after the first stages of learning. Even Derrida will say 'show me' when his interior decorator suggests that he cover his sofa in material in an unfamiliar, decorator's colour like chartreuse or taupe.

Derrida's call for unlimited freedom of interpretation, carried through fully, is really a kind of logical nihilism, the project of a complete liquefaction of intellectual activity, of meaningful thought and reasonable inference. These two things are a humdrum basis as necessary to poetry as it is to mathematical physics. Metaphorical flights have to take off from a platform of literal, everyday meaning. His position is a philosophical version of what Freud called infantile fantasies of omnipotence, in which the pleasure-principle completely obliterates the reality-principle. If thoroughly followed through it would result in literal dehumanisation, a return to the merely instinctive mode of life of the most primitive animals in whom there is a flicker of consciousness.

Derrida's attack on the 'metaphysics of presence' is seen by Rorty as a fatal assault on the pretensions of philosophy to sit in judgement on the validity of other forms of thought and discourse. 'Who are these people to decide about the credentials of what we are doing?' is the question he puts into the mouths of the exponents of the disciplines judged. This expression of intellectual egalitarianism has an obvious appeal. In particular cases it can also have a good deal of force. Philosophers often make mistaken assumptions about the actual procedures of those they criticise and propose irrelevant and unrealistic alternatives. Carnap's philosophy of science and Hempel's philosophy of history are notable instances.

But the general thesis embodies an incorrect analogy. Critical philosophers are not legislators or even judges but rather policemen. They apply rules of words, but they do not endow those words with meaning. They make logical principles explicit and use them to criticise instances of reasoning but they do not invent those principles; they find them embedded in ordinary thinking in its most widely agreed and reflective form. The epistemological profession is open to all comers, it is not a closed esoteric caste, bringing secret mysteries to an unenlightened populace. Again, like the police, it could be dispensed with. Public order could be preserved in principle by the activity of public-spirited citizens. In the same way intellectual order could be preserved by the self-critical thoughtfulness of anyone with a sensitivity to the meaning of words and to the cogency of argument.

This analogy of critical philosophers with policemen is itself pretty defective. Its main virtue is that it ascribes no intrinsic intellectual authority to such philosophers. But it must be acknowledged that this intellectual police force seems to spend most of its time investigating the offences of other policemen. That failure in public usefulness is to some extent compensated for by the weakness of the sanctions at its disposal. True policemen can arrest; epistemologists can only scold and can safely be ignored.

All the same they, and epistemologically-minded thinkers of any kind, do perform a public service. To introduce another analogy, they help to keep our intellectual instruments clean and sharp. Unless the meanings of words are fixed and generally agreed upon communication is obstructed, up to the point of complete breakdown. Unless discourse is consistent it either amounts to nothing or requires its hearers to repair it in some more or less speculative and contestable way. This is a negative service but so is that of doctors. And just as doctors are more reliable and therefore respected than callisthenists and body-builders, so epistemologists are more reliable, and should be more highly regarded, than speculative metaphysicians.

Derrida attaches to his critique of the 'metaphysics of presence' the intellectually egalitarian proposition that philosophy is just one kind of writing along with others. Like fiction or poetry it has its own rhetoric, is subject as much as they to interpretation, is accessible, as they are, to the process of deconstruction which finds hidden, undermining messages beneath the obvious surface of texts. That is true, and it reflects a certain literary-cum-methodological impurity in critical philosophy. It would not be true if philosophy were typically written, as it in practice occasionally is, in the manner of treatises on mathematics and physics. Such treatises can be judged as better and worse written than each other but it is merely a sophisticated joke to seek for underlying meanings in them, let alone to deconstruct them. The rhetorical aspect of philosophical writings is really secondary, contingent and ignorable, even if not wholly without interest. One can treat the doctrines of the British idealists of the late nineteenth and early twentieth century as a single system despite the enormous differences of style and quality between the writing of Green, Bradley, McTaggart and Collingwood.

The philosophers of continental Europe, even at their most anti-rational extreme as with Derrida, do at least supply material for serious consideration, although it can be a heavy labour to extract it. Derrida's attack on the metaphysics of presence and the connected view that philosophy is just one kind of writing among others, however muddled and evasive the argumentation on which they are based, do lead to an examination of assumptions about the nature of their activities which analytic or critical philosophers ordinarily take for granted. I believe that those assumptions are not only defensible but correct, but it is better to have reflected on the matter than not. That is pretty faint praise, rather like applauding a massive conflagration in some valuable buildings for providing an admirably strong test for some new fire-fighting equipment. For all his perversities, Derrida is plainly an ingenious, learned and, in a corrupted way, intelligent man. He could have served his useful intellectual purposes without the paraphernalia of his substantial monographs by means of a collection of Neitzschean aphorisms. Selected from the chaotic verbal tissue in which they are presented his lively, or at any rate provocative, thoughts would have been less trouble to identify and would have appeared more rather than less worthy of examination.

By contrast Foucault is an almost pedestrian figure. His three main ideas are all reasonably familiar. The first and most valuable of them, that the kinds of deviance which are taken to justify institutional confinement rest on contestable criteria, is both true and, because of its practical implications, important. Its truth has been concealed from view by a certain naivety about the genuinely scientific credentials of the human or social sciences, both among philosophers and the interested or involved part of the general public. Philosophical questioning of the social sciences has tended to fasten on the more collective disciplines – politics, economics, sociology – rather than on the more individual ones – pathology, medical psychiatry, criminology, the psychiatry of sex.

His second idea that social thinking in post-medieval Europe takes the form of a sequence of abruptly successive *epistemes* or systems of assumptions has a broad similarity to the doctrine of Spengler and a closer one to Kuhn's theory of the history of natural science as a sequence of revolutions. In his wayward use of historical evidence, however, he is closer to Spengler. As it stands the thesis is not very plausible. Assumptions come and go, but not all at once and not overnight. Even if they did a sceptical inference from the fact would not be inescapable. Nor is such an inference necessary from Foucault's third main idea, that knowledge is an instrument of men's pursuit of power.

His three leading ideas do hang together. The history of changing attitudes to deviance supplies evidence for the theory of epistemes and, more circuitously for the thesis that knowledge, or what passes for knowledge, is in the service of power. But this extracted essence is at a very large distance from his mannered, allusive text. He and Derrida deserve the comment of their philosophically renegade compatriot, Jacques Bouverese, who writes:

> We are witnessing... the proliferation of a type of work which attempts, with a very relative degree of success, to compensate for the absence of properly philosophical argumentation by means of literary effects and for the absence of properly literary qualities by means of philosophical pretensions. In general, contemporary French philosophers are past masters in the art of making themselves quite impossible to grasp, that is to say they are never to be found at the precise point where criticism might possibly reach them. Structuralism which constituted in principle a return in strength of 'scientific' objectivism and which had made the disappearance of the 'subject' and of the 'author' one of its favourite themes, has given rise to the most detestable forms of narcissistic self-celebration, of unconditional submission to the master, of the cult of the personality and of the star system, along with an almost total inhibition of the most elementary of critical reflexes.[4]

Such forceful language is no doubt best left to members of the immediate family. The style of philosophical behaviour to which it refers is not unknown in the English-speaking world, most conspicuously in the Wittgenstein cult. The prevalence of such a style, however, although it is hostile to the rational examination of doctrines, need not rule it out altogether. Where, as I hope it is here, a critically rational spirit is well-established the best thing we can do is to try to spread it. And the way to do that is to seek out discussable theses in works of alien philosophy, to supply or reconstruct arguments in favour of them and to see if they are strong enough to withstand criticism. Confidence in our methods should not lead us to suppose that we have a monopoly of insights.

I turn finally to the merits of existentialism. A primary source of

---

4. Jacques Bourveresse, 'Why I am so very unFrench', in *Philosophy in France Today*, ed. A. Montefiore (1983), p. 31.

its appeal to the English-speaking intellectual community generally was its concern with interesting, humanly compelling topics, with death, love, authenticity, choice, bad faith and sincerity. Anglo-Saxon philosophy, with its generally rigid concentration on the cognitive, treats human beings in a strangely attenuated way. For the most part it sees them as knowers or, at any rate, inquirers. As agents it considers them either as, more or less inexplicably, following principles of morality, in a narrow sense of the term, or as motivated by a largely undifferentiated swirl in which impulse, self-interest and prudence are indiscrimately mixed. Philosophical interest in human beings is largely confined to the forensic matter of personal identity through time, to the justification of anyone's belief that other people have a mental life at all and to the relations between such primordial mental events as perception and decision and their physical correlates of sensory stimulation and bodily movement. The detailed architecture of personality – the topic of seventeenth- and eighteenth-century accounts of the 'passions of the soul' – is, with a few honourable exceptions, ignored.

Since the death of ideology was prematurely announced by Daniel Bell in 1960 there has been a marked revival of social and political philosophy, in the work, most notably, of Rawls, Nozick, Dworkin and Barry. What one might call human philosophy is still rather sparse, although it too has its landmarks: Nagel's *Mortal Questions*, Singer's *Applied Ethics*, Scruton's *Sexual Desire*. Clarification of fundamentals need not exclude clarification of humanly interesting detail.

What I have called the narrowly cognitive interests of analytic philosophers may be psychologically connected to the practice of analytic philosophy itself. The unemotional dissection of ideas and beliefs may come most easily to those without much in the way of emotions to obstruct them. Since I believe that analytic philosophers use the only reliable method for arriving at justified conclusions, I hope that is not an insurmountable obstacle to the enlargement of their philosophical agenda. If it is, we should still do better to rely on aphorists and poets, who offer their thoughts without pretence of argument, than on the Bacchanalian revels of unreason with which the most admired of recent European philosophers mockingly parody the real thing.

*The Charles Carter Lecture, delivered at the University of Lancaster on 14 November 1989.*

# On the Ethics of Belief

## I

In recent discussions of the subject, such as that of Chisholm in his
*Perceiving*,[1] the idea of the ethics of belief is used to draw attention
to the normative character of the theory of knowledge. C.I. Lewis,
in a general consideration of the nature of the right, argues for an
analogy between the rightness, epistemic or cognitive, of belief and
of inference (or, as he calls it, 'concluding').[2] Ayer, in a familiar definition of knowledge, singles out as one of its constituents the right
to be sure.[3] To call something an item of knowledge, to say that a
belief is reasonable or evident or certain, is to evaluate it critically,
to recommend its adoption to some extent or other.

That point of view was adopted with a measure of explicitness
and self-consciousness by Locke, even if it seems none too consistent
with his claim to follow a historical, plain method in his enquiry into
the human understanding. A few lines further on in the introduction,
where that method is referred to, he says of his undertaking, 'it is
therefore worth while to search out the bounds between opinion and
knowledge; and examine by what measures, in things, whereof we
have no certain knowledge, we ought to regulate our assent and
moderate our persuasions'.[4] In Book IV he concludes that we do not
have certain knowledge of most of what we need or should like to
know for the practical purposes of life. We must, therefore, make do
with what we can best judge to be probably the case. He goes on to
lay down the general principle that we should not entertain 'any
proposition with a greater assurance than the proofs it is built upon
will warrant'.[5] In the form in which it has been articulated by H.H.
Price that principle has been put forward as a definition of rationality, 'the degree of our assent to a proposition ought to be
proportioned to the strength of the evidence for that proposition'.[6]

1. R. M. Chisholm, *Perceiving* (Ithaca, 1957).
2. C.I. Lewis, *The Ground and Nature of the Right* (New York, 1955).
3. A.J. Ayer, *The Problem of Knowledge* (London, 1956), p. 34.
4. J. Locke, *Essay Concerning Human Understanding*, ed. P.H. Nidditch (Oxford,
   1975), p. 44.
5. Ibid., p. 687.
6. H.H. Price, *Belief* (London, 1969), p. 131.

The alternative conception of the theory of knowledge is the naturalistic one proclaimed, but none too securely followed, by Hume and described by him as the introduction of 'the experimental method of reasoning into moral subjects',[7] the study of the human mind by observation and experiment. In our own time the idea has been reaffirmed as a matter of explicit principle by Quine, who maintains that a properly naturalised epistemology must be understood as a part of psychology.[8]

That thesis, which appears to be both epistemological and prescriptive, has an air of self-refutation about it. But it is nevertheless true that theorists of knowledge can get quite a long way without making any explicit epistemic valuations of their own. They can adopt a position like that of the investigator of a legal system who observes that there is a range of activities among the people subject to that system, which, although not complying altogether with the set of laws which they invoke, is strongly influenced by it in regard to their decisions about their own conduct and their critical observations on the conduct of others. In human cognitive activity there is a reasonably coherent set of principles of epistemic appraisal in constant use. Theorists of knowledge do not pronounce on the cognitive activities of mankind from a position wholly external to them. They have to build on the intimations of rationally critical order that they find in them. To paraphrase Locke: God did not make men barely two-legged and leave it to Locke to make them reasonable. The epistemologist, like the legal theorist, aims to develop into an explicit system a complex of practices of regulation that already exists. Just as legal theorists cannot intelligibly explain how decisions are arrived at in court when they define the law as what the courts decide, so naturalistic epistemologists cannot account for the critical reflections of ordinary rational persons about the degree of assent they should give to what it occurs to them, or is offered to them, to believe.

In its original coinage by W.K. Clifford the phrase 'ethics of belief' was in no way metaphorical or figurative and it introduced a highly moralistic, and indeed indignant, discussion of the right ordering of our beliefs.[9] Taking the word 'ethics' literally, as concerned with an agent's relations to others, Clifford distinguished two ways in which

7. D. Hume, *A Treatise of Human Nature*, ed. L.A. Selby-Bigge (Oxford, 1975), p. vii (title page on original edition).
8. W.V. Quine, *Ontological Relativity and Other Essays* (New York, 1969), pp. 69–90.
9. W.K. Clifford, *Lectures and Essays* (London, 1979), 2 : 177–211.

belief is publicly influential. In the first place, beliefs are publicly expressed. To have a belief is to be ready, in a wide range of circumstances, to express it. Some beliefs go unexpressed because of their triviality; others because their expression would be in some way disadvantageous, dangerous or embarrassing to the believer. But the usual case is that any belief that is at all important and not plainly imprudent to avow will somehow be put forward as a contribution to the stock of what passes for common knowledge.

Secondly, to have a belief, at least where this is of a more or less concrete or practical character, is to be disposed to act in some ways rather than others. Some beliefs, strictly evaluative ones, are directly tied to action, in that failure to act in the appropriate way undermines the claim to hold the belief, unless it can be shown that it is overridden by some competing valuation. In that case, however, it will still reveal itself in a secondary fashion, by way of reluctance to act against it and of regret afterwards for having done so. Other beliefs imply action of a particular sort when accompanied by preferences and desires. There are few beliefs that do not figure somewhere in complicated chains of practical reasoning which lead to action that goes beyond mere verbal expression of the belief, in answer to a question, perhaps, or as part of an examination performance, or simply to fill a gap in conversation, unless they are too trivial and transitory to find an opportunity to influence conduct or are about topics too remote to engage at all with the practical management of life.

Our beliefs tend to get expressed, then. In the very numerous cases where those to whom they are expressed do not have any firm conflicting belief about the topic to which they relate, they tend, furthermore, to get accepted, unless the hearer has some special reason to distrust the speaker, or at any rate an attitude, reasoned or not, of distrust towards him or her. Most of the beliefs we arrive at entirely on our own, and without reliance on the testimony of others, are of a trivial, passing, commonsensically atomic variety. Correspondingly most of the important beliefs that we have are derived, partly or wholly, from the spoken or written expression of the beliefs of others or from what, in cases of insincerity or misunderstanding, we take to be their beliefs.

Clifford points out that there are two ways in which our ostensible expressions of belief may be deficient. The belief-expression may be insincere. It may, on the other hand, be cognitively rather than morally defective, be, as he puts it, a failure in knowledge and judgement rather than in veracity. If we are dishonest we act so as to inspire beliefs that we suppose to be false or unreasonable. If we are mistaken or unreasonable we inspire beliefs that actually are false or unjustified.

To deplore the communication of false beliefs is to assume that it is disadvantageous to believe what is not true. That is a reasonable assumption on the whole, although it is not, of course, universally correct. It is an advantage not to know, as most of us most of the time do not, the precise date on which we are going to die. It is probably best that we do not have precise and detailed true beliefs about what everybody we encounter thinks of us. We may be helped to survive dangerous situations by inadequate information as to just how dangerous they are. All these are cases where true belief is emotionally unmanageable and disabling to us. In all of them some measure of rational belief about the matter in hand, that falls short of disabling us, is of positive value. I can order my affairs more sensibly in such humdrum things as date of retirement and insurance planning if I have some rough idea of my expectation of life. It is of very great importance to be aware of the hypothetical truth that if I do not change my way of life I shall be dead very soon. In the same way it is valuable to have some rough notion of what the people one most associates with think of one, or that a situation that one is in is dangerous and calls for caution.

The general principle that true belief is advantageous rests to a large extent on the fact that most of what we do is not done for its own sake but as a means to some further desired or chosen end. Everything that we do directly or immediately, all our basic actions that are not done by doing something else, are bodily movements and, unless we are dancers or need to stretch a cramped limb, our bodily movements are in themselves of little interest to us. To achieve what we want or value, therefore, we have to rely on beliefs about the outcome, at any degree of remoteness we can manage, of the bodily movements that are all that we can directly bring about. If these beliefs are false it will be an unusual fluke to achieve the end we had in view, in spite of them. It is the exceptional character of this kind of happy ending which makes it comic. Another, perhaps slightly less exceptional, possibility is that we bring about a resultant state of affairs that is in fact preferable to the one we were aiming at. In that case two mistakes have cancelled each other out: one about the best thing to aim for, the other about how to achieve it. But the usual case when we act on a false belief is that we fail to get what we want and commonly get in its place, not just something that, as an alternative to what we are aiming at, we are indifferent to, but something we should much rather not have, something that we do not want.

The actions I am led to by false or unreasonable beliefs of my own are not quite so directly harmful to others as is the communication of false or unreasonable belief to them. It will be so to the extent that my action is directed to their well-being, whether animated by a benevolent or protective impulse or, as is perhaps more common, by my having undertaken to perform some service for them. Actions of mine which have been inspired by false or unreasonable beliefs will be advantageous to others principally in the circumstance – which I hope it is not too Panglossian to suppose to be comparatively unusual – that I am intent on doing them harm. Most of us, I imagine, do more harm to others because we are indifferent to the effect on them of our actions in pursuit of our own interests than because of positive hostility or malice. In this case my acting on false or unreasonable beliefs does not seem to make a difference one way or the other, unless I have defective beliefs about what the collateral effects on others of my actions will be. More to the point here is absence of belief, rather than its falsity or unreasonableness. I may simply not be aware of, perhaps because I have not thought about, the effect of my actions on others.

In arguing for the general correctness of the assumption that my defective beliefs are harmful to others, either as communicated to them or as leading to conduct that affects them, I have taken arguments for the disadvantageous implications of false beliefs to support conclusions about the undesirability of communicating or acting upon unreasonable beliefs as well. Unreasonable beliefs can, of course, be true. But, one is inclined to reply, unreasonable beliefs are unlikely to be true. That claim seems to say more about the cognitive helpfulness of the world – namely, that most reasonable beliefs are in fact true – than the modestly tautological contention that we have more reason to suppose reasonable beliefs to be true than to be false. But that very watery truism is, in fact, sufficient for the purpose in hand. For if the general assumption that false beliefs are disadvantageous is correct, then we have more reason to accept the parallel assumption about unreasonable beliefs than to reject it. And that is enough to be going on with.

## II

In what follows I shall confine myself to the ethics of communicating beliefs rather than of acting on them and, in particular, to the educational communication of beliefs. There are several distinguishing features of the educational relationship between teacher and taught which intensify the moral significance of right belief. In the first place, teachers occupy a position of power and authority; there is a measure of compulsion on the pupils to attend to what they say and to accept it, at least to the possibly habit-forming extent of reproducing it in examinations. Secondly, teachers have, or at any rate express, beliefs about matters which by and large their pupils have ordinarily no opinion one way or the other, because of their comparative youth and inexperience. This combination of institutionalised power with a lack of resources for intellectual resistance to their influence imposes a particular responsibility on teachers for the right ordering of the beliefs they express in their professional capacity. In social life and ordinary conversation beliefs are expressed on equal terms and in circumstances where there is no pressure on any of the participants to accept what anyone else affirms. I do not have to listen at the dinner party; I can close the book or paper; I can turn off the television. But the educational audience is the most abject of all in its captivity. In its innocence, furthermore, it is the most suggestible and responsive.

The ethics of the communication of belief, then, takes on its starkest and most demanding form in the responsibilities of teachers. But everyone who thinks about education nowadays must be on their guard against the conception of it as, in essence, the imparting of information from someone who possesses it to someone who does not. When the idea that education should be an activity of learning, not a passive reception of influence, is combined with the philosophical idea of the primacy of 'knowing how' to 'knowing that', the role in it of the propositional furnishing of empty minds is redefined in an acceptably modest way. The supplying of information is not in fact what education has ever wholly or even mainly consisted in, however much its practitioners thought it was and may have tried to make it so. Nor ought information-supplying to be more than a part of the whole. To be merely well-informed is, in a way, to be knowing; it is not to be well-educated.

Nevertheless, a good deal of the content of normal school education is propositional. Geography and history are initially taught in order to acquaint pupils with the main features of tracts of space and time that fall outside their own experience. There is a descriptively geographical element also in what we learn at school about the heavens, about species of animals and plants, about the varieties and constitution of matter. But knowledge about these comparatively unobvious things is of limited significance in itself. The facts of natural history, in the broadest sense, are not just for ownership and possible display. They have to be possessed before the more important business of gaining an understanding of them can be embarked upon. To understand them is to become aware of their systematic interconnection, of the laws in the light of which some are explanatory conditions of others. In a less sophisticated way the same is true of history and, least of all until very recent times, of geography, that reservoir of obstinately brute facts, the seemingly random contingencies of rivers and mountain ranges and coastlines.

Other familiar, customarily demarcated chunks of school education are, however, barely propositional at all. Mathematics and linguistic studies in composition and translation are skills, in which much of what is first presented as brute fact becomes rediscoverable by pupils on their own account, if all goes well, when they have mastered the appropriate operations. In both cases a vocabulary of some kind has to be learnt and retained. But the point of learning it is the subsequent ability to construct proofs or sentences out of it, to interpret such constructions when they are presented by others and, where appropriate, to correct them.

To understand the propositions that we are educationally encouraged to accept, in the sense in which I have described it, is to go some way towards learning what reasons there are for accepting them, what evidence there is for supposing them to be true. That is something that leads directly into the ability to find out for oneself whether they are true or reasonable to believe. Sometimes, no doubt, it does not lead very far. School historians can get to know quite a lot of history without having more than the vaguest idea about the technique of making use of the primary sources. But even if they have not mastered the technique of securing the primary evidence for historical conclusions, they will know at least what sort of evidence those conclusions rest on and how it serves to support them.

To the extent that learners grasp the evidence on which what they are invited to believe is grounded and, if only sketchily, how to set about checking the evidence for themselves, they are in a position to test the reliability of the authorities on which they must depend for most of what they claim to believe. Teachers will not ordinarily present what they teach as if it were all their own work. They will rather act as a channel through which the content of textbooks and treatises is conveyed and they will, ideally, be a channel with a critical filter in it. If the authorities they invoke in teaching do not agree among themselves, their activity will be frustrated unless they can make a rational discrimination between the conflicting parties.

Non-dogmatic teaching, which goes beyond the dictated recital of propositions to be memorised for later regurgitation, should provide those to whom it is given with something that will protect them against its inadequacies, at least its inadequacies of detail. Rational, critical teachers will instil into those they teach the capacity to be rationally critical of them. For this reason it does not very much matter if the basic raw material of the teaching is out of date and full of what, from the point of view of current scholarly chic, is infected with error. It does not matter that the general inventory of what there is and has been in the world which they supply contains a lot of mistakes, so long as there goes with it a training in the ability to put them right. Any special obligation on teachers arising from their doubly powerful position in relation to the beliefs of those they teach is at least indirectly met if, by teaching non-dogmatically, they in effect attach a critical question-mark to the primary propositions they affirm and equip their pupils with the capacity to answer the critical questions thus posed for themselves.

## III

But that is really too perfectionist or Utopian as a comprehensive specification of the responsibilities of teachers. We cannot get very far with the mastery of the processes of discovery and justification in the whole range of subjects that we study. Many people, no doubt, never acquire any such skill in any subject. Nevertheless they should know the difference between evidence that does support a conclusion and evidence that does not, even if they are not able to find the evidence for themselves. We can also acquire what might be called intellectual taste, a sense of the comparative soundness of the claims made on us to accept beliefs of different kinds. Like other forms of taste, this is a matter of controversy.

At one extreme is straightforward scientism, the idea that observation, experiment, induction and deduction constitute a single scientific method which is readily distinguishable from other modes of arriving at conclusions and which marks off the enquiries approved by the Royal Society from the activities of theologians, mystics, cranks, charlatans, astrologers, alchemists, spiritualists, fortune-tellers, Freudians, Marxists and so forth. At the furthest opposite extreme to this is the cognitive anarchism of Paul Feyerabend, for whom anything goes, all affirmations of belief are on a level.

In a way this is an unreal dispute. Normal science, to use Kuhn's phrase, is at odds with two different kinds of cognitive undertaking, which may be called 'pseudo-science' and 'non-science'. There are many bodies of doctrine in which findings are presented in a rational manner, the obligation of providing supporting evidence is acknowledged and adhered to. Other bodies of doctrine are put forward merely assertively, in an inspired or prophetic fashion. In either case the fact that their claims are inconsistent with what is accepted by the prevailing consensus as well-founded creates a presumption against them. But it creates only a presumption. In the case of what I have called, presumptuously, pseudo-science, as if the question has already been decided to its disadvantage, the evidence offered has to be considered on its merits. It is an implication of the claim of rationality made on behalf of normal science that the theories it propounds are never certain, never guaranteed against the possibility of reasonable doubt. The mere fact of inconsistency with it, therefore, does not entail falsehood. So the steady work of rational unmaskers of pseudo-science like Martin Gardner[10] cannot be dispensed with or regarded as superfluous.

Non-science is a different matter. It is not necessary to go the whole way with Popper's conception of science to agree that hypotheses, at least those that go beyond the straightforwardly observable regularities of natural history, are the fruit of imagination or intuition, a creative activity that cannot be mechanised or reduced to rule. (Even natural history has its non-mechanical aspects, as is made clear by the history of the reclassification of natural kinds, in the light of greater knowledge of structure and development.) But interesting or challenging hypotheses are not contributions to knowledge or rational belief. We have good empirical grounds, although they are un-Popperianly inductive, for supposing that most of them are false, namely the fact that most of them that have been put forward hitherto have turned out to be. Until someone attracted by them, most naturally their original framers, supplies them with supporting evidence, which looks as if it could turn out to be as strong as that which supports the established beliefs they conflict with, there is no call to take them seriously.

10.  cf. *Fads and Fallacies* (New York, 1957)

What I have called pseudo-science is really that part of minority science that has been falsified or otherwise shown to be rationally deficient, for example, to be based on tainted, over-selective or insufficient evidence. But all majority science at any given time was once minority science. The situation is analogous to that in politics which is described in the familiar stanza: Treason doth never prosper, here's the reason: if treason prosper, none dare call it treason. No irony is involved in the scientific case. Minority science keeps science alive, since it is where new and better science comes from, even though most of it is cast aside. It keeps science cognitively healthy to the extent that it implies that although majority science may at any given time claim to be, on the whole, superior in rationality to anything else that anyone believes, that is no certain guarantee either of its truth or against its eventual replacement.

## IV

I have been arguing that it is the moral responsibility of teachers, and so, to some extent, of every communicator of belief, not just to tell what they believe to be the truth, but to tell only what they have good reason to believe is the truth. Clifford applies that principle to belief itself when he says 'it is wrong everywhere and for anyone, to believe anything on insufficient evidence'.[11] In a way that is a truism, since it can be taken to mean that one is not justified in believing anything one is not justified in believing. What it fails to take into account is that evidence and justification, on the one hand, and belief, on the other, can vary in strength. Like many others, notably Chisholm, Clifford adopts an exceedingly constricted view of possible belief-attitudes – namely, that one can believe or disbelieve or suspend judgement altogether, that is neither believe nor disbelieve. That attenuated repertoire is, I think, demonstrably inadequate to our actual needs and circumstances.

The proof is very simple. All the practical beliefs that we require for rational conduct relate, in so far as they are to guide conduct, to the future. No belief about the future is certain. Therefore no belief we can act on is certain. The first premise is itself certainly true. The only actions that can be guided by belief are actions that have not yet taken place. The role of belief in the guidance of action is to select from a range of possible but as yet unperformed actions the one

11. W.K. Clifford, op. cit., p. 186.

which will lead most satisfactorily to some end we have chosen.

The second premise is rather more questionable. That one day I shall die, that the sun will rise tomorrow (visibly or not) are surely propositions that only an epistemologist, in a state of occupational imbalance brought on by over-indulgence in hyperbolic scepticism, could regard as matters for reasonable doubt. Nevertheless, as rationally grounded beliefs about future events, they rest on inductive generalisations which are not susceptible of complete verification. It could be argued, however, as it has been by Strawson,[12] that complete verification is not the same thing as conclusive support. That is to say, the evidence we have for the general propositions that all people are mortal and that each part of the earth's surface faces the sun every twenty-four hours is so massive and systematic that there is no rational need for any more to be acquired. It is no argument against this that both propositions can be denied without self-contradiction, nor that many people, namely Jehovah's Witnesses, believe, as they put it, that 'thousands now living will never die'. It is, perhaps, rather more to the point that we have good reason to think the present orbital relationship of the earth to the sun will not persist for ever, even if it is not clear whether it will end in the sun's explosion into a nova or, later, when the sun ceases to radiate light as a black dwarf. In this case it could be said that the generalisation at least conclusively establishes predictions about the near future, which is all we are concerned with in the great bulk of our actions. (To avoid a sorites paradox we should have to claim that the day of judgement or a solar explosion would have to announce themselves in advance in some way or other.)

It is not essential to settle this question for the purpose in hand. The reason is that even if there are some empirical generalisations that are conclusively supported or established beyond reasonable doubt, they do not include the generalisations on which our actions are for very much the most part based. A man takes out life insurance, not because all men are mortal, but because he thinks it is probable that he will die before his wife does or before his children are securely launched in the world. Butler's thesis can be strengthened: probability *has* to be the guide of life.

In other words we almost always have to act under uncertainty. All but the most basic of our actions are connected to the purposes for which we choose them by beliefs that are only more or less probable. To take this to amount to the position that our practical beliefs

12. P.F. Strawson, *Introduction to Logical Theory* (London, 1952, pp. 237–8.

are ones to which we are justified in giving only a qualified degree of assent is to say that a statement of probability is an expression of qualified assent. It could be objected that it expresses not qualified assent about a matter of categorical fact, but an unqualified assent to the assignment of a probability.

That is, I think, doubly mistaken. In the first place, rather confusingly, some of our assignments of probability are, or are taken by us to be, less than fully justified. If I have evidence from only a dozen potatoes from a lorry-load that nine of them are free from defect, I shall rightly have limited confidence in the statement that three-quarters of the potatoes in the load are sound and, correspondingly, in the statement that there are three chances out of four that the next potato I take out will be so. As the sample available to me gets larger, my confidence in the correctness of the probability-assignment will rightly increase. It may not unplausibly be urged that the first assignment of probability is in fact a categorical assertion about the proportion of sound potatoes in the whole load. But the assignment of a probability to that cannot be a disguised categorical assertion about the proportion of samples of that size that turn out to be representative without regressively raising the question of the probability of the generalisation about the accuracy of samples.

The second point has a less pettifoggingly elaborate character. Suppose I am rightly confident that three-quarters of the load is sound, in the light of the stability of the proportion as a sample I have investigated gets larger. I shall then indeed be quite confident that the probability of the next potato's soundness is three-quarters. But what my action in selecting potatoes is directed to is the separation of those suitable for the kitchen from those to be served to a less exigent clientele in the chicken-run. What matters is the soundness of the next potato I pick out. and that is something I can have only a limited degree of belief in, given the circumstances described.

There is a further line of argument for the view that the ethics of belief concerns continuously variable degrees of belief and not just the decision between believing a proposition, believing its contradictory and suspending judgement. This is that the more constricted idea either leaves us cognitively unprepared for practical life by forbidding us to believe everything we need for purposes of action or is absurdly permissive, indeed dangerously so. Chisholm says there are evident beliefs that we ought to believe and beliefs that we ought to reject, those whose contradictories are evident.[13] In his view

---

13. R.M. Chisholm, op. cit., ch. 1.

all the rest are acceptable, in the sense that it is all right to believe them, we are not obliged to accept their contradictories; and also rejectable, in the sense that it is all right to disbelieve them, we are not obliged to believe them. So as far as all, or at any rate most, of the beliefs we need in practice are concerned, we are allowed freely to choose whether to believe, disbelieve or, presumably, suspend judgement. That guidance is practically useless and epistemically antinomian. The stricter alternative, which would require to us to believe only the evident and otherwise suspend judgement, is equally unhelpful for practice.

The binary obsession of theorists of belief which I have been criticising corresponds to an ethical deficiency in the management of beliefs which is exceedingly widespread and to which we are all, no doubt, liable. This is the vice of intellectual intemperance, of asserting beliefs without qualification when some measure of qualification is rationally in order, when we have some reason, but not conclusive reason for taking them to be true.

## V

Intellectual temperance is a crucial ingredient in rationality. The corresponding vice is not the same thing as credulousness, which is an over-readiness to adopt from others with unqualified assent beliefs that are inadequately supported or even have no rational support at all, but it includes it, along with an over-readiness to assent without qualification to beliefs that one has arrived at on one's own, rather than been supplied with by others. Intellectual intemperance in general, as well as credulousness in particular – creditive lustfulness and seducibility – arise from the uncomfortable character of doubt. As Peirce says in *The Fixation of Belief*, 'doubt is an uneasy and dissatisfied state from which we struggle to free ourselves and pass into the state of belief; while the latter is a calm and satisfactory state which we do not wish to avoid, or to change to a belief in anything else. On the contrary, we cling tenaciously, not merely to believing, but to believing just what we do believe.'[14]

The reason for the comparative unpleasantness of doubt or incomplete assent is that it leaves things unsettled, in the cognitive pending tray. The next potato is going to be sound or it is going to be unsound. So long as I am not sure which, the matter is open for

14. C.S. Peirce, *The Philosophy of Peirce*, ed. J. Buchler (London, 1940), p. 10.

further investigation, and indeed calls for it. But once I have decided which, once my mind is made up, there is no need to go on thinking about the subject. It ceases to hang over me.

To some extent intellectual intemperance is little more than a conversational idiom, a habit of fanciful exaggeration. People say, 'He can't bear the sight of her', where what is present is a mild distaste. In the same spirit we tend to say, 'He'll never get there in time', when we should properly say that there is an appreciable chance of his missing the appointment because of the familiar contingencies of travel. Ordinarily these categorical outbursts are neither intended nor taken seriously. Faced with the reply, 'Well in that case we had better go on without waiting for him', the utterer of, 'He'll never get here in time' will back off with some such oblique disclaimer as, 'Let's just wait till the time we agreed, anyway, in case he does make it.'

But there are more dangerous indulgences in this intellectual vice. The most conspicuous is the placing of unqualified confidence in very large general systems of doctrine which entail, or are thought to entail, important practical consequences, above all religions and political ideologies. In religion a Pascalian emphasis on the infinite value of the matters at stake combines with dogmatic acceptance of articles of faith, understood as propositions it is sinful to doubt, to produce fearful results of persecution and oppressive harassment. It never seems to be thought that since God has made us imperfect in so many other respects, He might also have limited our capacity to find out precisely what He wants us to do.

Huge numbers of people have been tortured or killed for failing to believe things so fatuous or trivial that it is hard to credit the sanity, let alone the rationality, of those who were absolutely convinced of the necessity of believing them rather than not doing so. In the case of crusading Marxism, certainty about the direction of history takes the place occupied in crusading, persecuting Christianity by certainty about the wishes of God. If it had been guaranteed that Stalin's cruelties were the sole but infallible means for the inauguration of Utopia there would have been an argument for them, although not necessarily a compelling one. In fact, the cruelties were certain, the Utopian effect at the faintest lower limit of probability.

Between the extremes of conversational exaggeration and the all-inclusive claims of a dogmatic faith there is a continuous series of styles and patterns of belief that are intemperately expressed and invite intemperate assent. Among representative examples are theories in psychiatry and economics, medical and dietary regimes, conceptions of national character. In the crowded world of beliefs there is plenty to be intemperate about.

Temperance, it must be admitted, is a fairly grey, dispiriting virtue. In its intellectual form, as applied to belief, it seems to imply a kind of timid, elderly, valetudinarian cautiousness of the kind expressed in E.M. Forster's version of Landor:

> I strove with none, for none was worth my strife.
> Reason I loved and, next to Reason, Doubt.
> I warmed both hands before the fire of life
> And put it out.

It is, however, perfectly consistent and combinable with another intellectual virtue of a more positive and colourful kind, that of intellectual courage. That does not consist in bravely risking the danger of acting on beliefs which there is not much reason to suppose are true. Rather, it is a matter of incurring the risk of lost time and effort that is involved in trying to find out if reasonable grounds exist for new and adventurous thoughts and, in particular, in the serious and effortful business of questioning the credentials of things it is customary to believe.

Here, as in the literal case, courage does not have to rest on intemperance. It is more real, less Dutch, if it does not. An unusual, original, even ridiculous-looking hypothesis can be put forward for consideration without the pretence or illusion that it is some kind of indubitable revelation, the product of incorrigible insight, rather than of imaginative speculation. Without the taking of intellectual risks, human knowledge, as we politely call the corpus of general beliefs that are widely acknowledged to be well-founded, will stagnate. Since the conditions of human life keep changing, unless our knowledge keeps pace with them, there are likely to be unpleasant consequences. The major changes we are at present anxious about – in population, the supply of natural resources, the weapons of war, the nature of work – are themselves the outcome of advancing knowledge. But the knowledge that gave rise to them does not include any provision for controlling or mitigating their unpleasant effects. We have to keep moving to maintain such measure of equilibrium as we have managed to achieve.

There are two other, more private, intellectual virtues which fill out the notion of a non-metaphorical ethics of belief a little further. The first of them is a kind of intellectual justice or fairness, which consists in open-minded readiness to consider beliefs that are inconsistent with or count against one's own. The point of this is not respect for the holders of the conflicting beliefs or concern for their *amour propre*, worthy as these considerations may be in their own right. The immediate purpose is the acquisition of better, more reasonable beliefs for oneself. This is, I have argued, a literally moral purpose because of the tendency our beliefs have to be communicated to others and also because of the influence they have on our conduct and thus on the welfare of others.

The second of these more private intellectual virtues is a different kind of thing altogether. It might be called intellectual charity. In its more straightforward form it is a matter of couching one's expressions of belief in such a way as to minimise the pain they cause to those to whom they are expressed. It recognises a human need that is brushed aside by those who prepare one for home truths with the formula, 'I know you would like me to be perfectly frank', an assumption, of course, which is usually false. Charity of utterance can run all the way from euphemism to plain lying, and some considerable time before it reaches the disreputable limit a conflict of duties is set up. But this really has nothing to do with the management, in particular with the right formation, of one's beliefs; it is simply a matter of discrimination in their expression.

The general idea of addressing oneself to one's beliefs in a charitable frame of mind can, however, take another more serious form. The unappetising phrase that comes to mind to embrace its whole scope is 'positive thinking'. Friends adjure us to think of them in a kindly way; moral mentors encourage us to think the best of people. Tolstoy, in very much that spirit, said that it is better to be deceived than to be suspicious. Look on the bright side, says folk wisdom, hope for the best. Hope has a traditional association with charity and, more disconcertingly for anyone concerned with the rationality of belief, with faith.

Unless there is reason to think that one has a constitutional tendency to think the worst of people or to take the gloomiest view of things in general this prescription cannot be endorsed. If some people are melancholic by nature, others are sanguine and should be addressed in quite the contrary spirit. We all have our emotional biases and it is rational to try to find out what they are and to correct for them. This, like a lot of other things about one's personality, is something that other people, in flat defiance of Descartes, know more about than one does oneself. These are Bacon's idols of the cave, individual propensities to error of a particular kind for which there can be no general prescription.

It is an analytic truth that we ought to believe what it is epistemically right to believe, in other words, what there is good reason to believe. And from that it follows that we ought morally to believe only what there is good reason to believe (and we ought prudentially to believe only that as well). But the implication is not rigidly deductive. It is morally desirable for my beliefs to be reasonable to the extent that if I have them I will have a tendency to express them, whose indulgence is on the whole more calculated to influence other people to accept those beliefs than, perhaps because of obstinate counter-suggestibility, to reject them. Since beliefs may remain unexpressed and may be resisted when they are expressed there is a twofold weakening of the connection between the epistemic improvement of one person's beliefs and the advantage to others which we can rationally expect to accrue from the possibly consequential improvement of their beliefs. But so long as it has some tendency that way and none to speak of in the other – which it is also reasonable to suppose – it is clearly morally desirable. And that is particularly the case in the educational relationship where the two loose connections are considerably tightened up.

## VI

So far I have referred freely to what is rational or to what we have reason to believe in a general way without going into detail about what it is that makes a belief rational. Perhaps something not altogether vapid can be said on the subject fairly briefly. The paradigm of a rational belief is one for which there is favourable evidence, that is to say, one that can be inferentially arrived at from other, justified, beliefs by a reliable method of inference. Some of that support must owe its acceptability to something other than further acceptable beliefs. The ordinarily acknowledged sources of primary or direct evidence are perception – whether of the physical world or of one's own state of mind – and memory, in the first instance of past perceptions. Further beliefs are derived from this initial stock by inference. Since deductive inference only extracts and makes explicit the content of its premises, it is through non-deductive inference that substantially new knowledge or rational belief must come. But a very great deal of what we believe is acquired on the testimony of others and we need to have principles for the acceptance of testimony. (The actual content of the testimony we get by perception, by hearing what others say or reading what they have written.)

Theorists of knowledge have tried to find some kind of primary evidence which is incorrigibly certain. But none of our perceptual beliefs about the physical world or, I should argue, any matter of empirical fact, is incorrigibly certain. Indeed I think that no perceptual belief is in itself, so to speak, beyond reasonable doubt. What the senses prompt us to believe becomes something that is beyond reasonable doubt only when it is supported by a whole lot of other reasonable but individually dubitable beliefs. Certainty is achieved, not given. As Ryle said, it is something we ascertain or make certain of.[15] Knowledge can be arrived at, then, from the rational organisation of beliefs none of which is certain or known to be true taken on its own. We do not require knowledge, properly so called, anyway to manage our lives. Rational belief is enough.

The main argument for the thesis that there is reason, even if not conclusive reason, to believe in the ordinary deliverances of perception is simple, if indirect. It is that we can have no reason to question those deliverances unless they conflict with others of the same kind, a conflict that cannot break out unless laws are brought in which the majority of our perceptions serve to confirm. We have reason to doubt only what conflicts with the greater and most readily systematisable part of what perception induces us to believe. And that, inevitably, must be the exceptional case. No one can be in the minority unless there is a majority.

No present perception is, on its own, inconsistent with any other of my present perceptions. Only if laws, resting on past, and for some time remembered, perceptions are invoked can such conflicts arise. But that entails a reliance, non-dogmatic but fairly general, both on the reliability of memory and of the inductive procedure by which the observed pattern, revealed in the remembered past, is extrapolated to apply to the world as a whole.

There is equally no reason to doubt the promptings of memory unless we are justified in accepting our recollections of cases in which it has failed us in the past and in inductively inferring, from the liability to failure we have reason to ascribe to it in the past, to its present and future imperfection. The general acceptability of perception, memory and induction, although not the infallibility of any of them, or of any part of them, is presupposed by the supposition in any particular case that we have reason to doubt any of them.

The argument for the general reliability of testimony, at least

15. G. Ryle, *The Concept of Mind* (London, 1949), p. 238.

about primary matters of fact, is that unless we take most of what people say about what is currently observable to be true we shall be unable to attach any meaning to what they say, in particular the meaning that we, imitating them, ordinarily attach to the words they utter. In the same way, the logical truths they accept are revealed in their inferential practices and are determined by their attaching the meaning they do to the logical words. For the rest we have to rely on the checks we can make for ourselves on their general reliability.

As I come to the end of these remarks I wonder if I have not offended against my own moralising injunction against intellectual intemperance. In a properly edifying spirit let me conclude by saying that, without putting the claims I have made forward as undiscussable certainties, I hope I have given some reasons for their acceptance.

*Delivered as a Richard Peters Lecture at the University of London Institute of Education in 1985.*

# Education and Damage Control

## The nature of teaching

From one point of view, teaching can be seen as a way of causing beliefs – or at any rate of trying to cause them. That places it alongside some parallel human activities and invites one to inquire what it is that differentiates it from them. Other deliberate belief-causing agencies are advertising, journalism, political oratory, the pleadings of lawyers. Unlike the followers of most of these practices, the teacher is characteristically free from direct interest in the effects of his work. He does not want or expect it to enhance the sale of some product, increase the number of those voting for a political party or lead a jury to bring in a particular verdict. The benefit of the recipient is the teacher's avowed, and, of course, usual aim, whatever side-benefits in the way of professional pride, promotion or gratitude may be achieved as well.

As far as ordinary teaching of the young is concerned there are distinctive peculiarities in the relations of teacher to taught, peculiarities not to be found in a driving-school or a foreign-language course. The pupils are under some measure of compulsion in regard to attendance, attentiveness and, in a way, performance. They are also intellectually, as well as institutionally, defenceless, or at any rate at a disadvantage, as compared with their teachers. They are generally not well enough equipped to criticise the teaching they receive in any but the most superficial or cosmetic way. They can condemn it as boring or confusing, that is to say in terms of the perceived quality of their immediate reaction to it. But they are not ordinarily in a position to assess the intrinsic quality of the beliefs that are communicated to them. Intruded into an empty space, these beliefs do not have their passage obstructed by any serious critical filter. Conventionally considered, that puts a responsibility on the teacher for ensuring that the beliefs he teaches deserve to be taught.

It may be objected that to define teaching as a way of causing belief is to persist in an antiquated and distressingly one-sided idea of it. Teaching is not just the imparting of granules of information or even of systematically organised bodies of information. The most important element in education of all varieties is teaching how, a further respect in which it differs from advertising and journalism. It includes teaching how to think, to calculate and to apply calculation to concrete states of affairs; how to observe and how to weigh evidence and judge probabilities; how to set about finding things out, by observation and experiment or by looking them up; how to judge the reliability of the beliefs that are presented to or merely occur to one. These teachings-how are intellectual or epistemic skills. Other teachings-how are of a practical nature: how to exercise certain techniques and, more informally, how to behave, how to manage one's life sensibly, how to act rightly.

The account of teaching as belief-causation can be defended from the charge of limiting it to the transfer of bits of information by the consideration that all these teachings-how have a belief aspect. They do not consist simply in bringing about the acquisition of skills or habits or knacks by way of mere of imitative contagion. The pupil in being taught a skill is conscious of what he is learning, he believes that what he is doing is the right thing to do, in a sense of 'right' that extends far beyond the usual application of the word, although it includes it. That is not to say that every exercise of a learnt skill or good habit is accompanied by the conscious thought 'now at this point the right thing to do is so-and-so'. But such a thought is implicit in the action in a way that is not in the various hand-movements someone has got into the habit of making under mild stress or, it seems reasonable to suppose, in the actions of a cat manifesting a learnt capacity to stalk birds. A learnt practice takes the form of a practical belief to the extent that its exponent can be articulately conscious of what he is doing. And in the other direction it is a condition of genuinely holding a practical belief that the believer is committed to following the course of action it prescribes as the right thing to do unless there is some suitable countervailing consideration, such as that it was physically impossible in the circumstances or that he was too upset or frightened to do it.

For something to be part of the content of education it must be capable of being taught (in the way that violin-playing can be taught only to those who can hear) and is, in some way or other, worth learning. From the intellectual or epistemic point of view this means at least that the beliefs involved should be true or, what we often have to be satisfied with, reasonable to believe. That is not enough, they must also be interesting or useful, but it is nevertheless indispensable. On the practical side, the belief that this is the right or a good way of doing something means at least that the way in question is an effective one and that it is better than any other known and available one. Here too the end to which the action involved is a means must be something that is worth doing, but the effectiveness and relative efficiency of the action designed to produce it are also indispensable.

## The demoralisation of teachers

Teachers, as we all know, are in a depressed state of mind at present, even demoralised. Much of that is due to external or social factors. Recent governments have been critical of, even hostile to, the teaching profession and in being so would seem to reflect attitudes towards education that are widespread in society as a whole. The right things, by which is commonly meant the vocationally useful things, are not taught. What is taught is often not taught well. Some of what is taught ought not to be taught at all, that is to say radical ideology, embodying the attitudes of the underclass, ethnic minorities and sexual deviants.

Secondly, and more impersonally, there is the demographic fact of falling rolls, of a generally smaller school-age population, particularly in large urban areas. These two factors put together lead to a relative decline in income for teachers, to a decline in the status of the teaching profession and a decline in the quality of new recruits to it. The teaching profession, indeed, appears to be going the way of the clergy, which it once extensively overlapped. In the mid-nineteenth century, something like half the graduates of the two ancient universities were ordained. Now the proportion cannot be more than about one in fifty. The proportion of graduates going into teaching is steadily going down too.

The pragmatic or vocational emphasis in thinking about the content of education undermines the traditional curriculum which was formerly sustained by the autonomous authority of the teaching profession and acquiesced in, with varying degrees of satisfaction, by everyone else. A more ideologically intrusive style of local government – operating in a quite different, but still anti-traditional direction – also erodes the autonomy of teaching.

On top of all this the general intellectual tendencies of our age are calculated to destroy the confidence of teachers in the more elemental or indispensable value of what they teach, not its interest or utility, but its validity, its claim to be believed. That influence is most obviously present in the field of morals and politics, but easily extends itself to any region of thought where explicit value-judgements are involved. It is now bearing down on the theoretical domain which has hitherto seemed secure. Sceptical and subjectivist doctrines about morality have been joined by similar attitudes to science and, in continental Europe at any rate, to knowledge, or what conventionally passes for knowledge, as a whole, which is conceived in Nietzschean terms as primarily an instrument in the struggle for power.

When many teachers were clergymen, or worked under the supervision of clergymen, schools conveyed the value-system of institutional religion, whose authority was only furtively or marginally contested. Even where the educational system and organised religion were opposed, as in France, for example, teachers had a substitute religion to fall back on to authorise the values they sought to instil, the secular, republican ideology of the Enlightenment, which was hardly more sceptical and subjectivistic than its Christian opponent.

It is this intellectual, and corrosive, scepticism about value, and, as it has developed, about science and what conventionally passes for knowledge in general, that I propose to examine, to see how far it is justified, and to the extent that it is, what its implications are for the activity of teaching.

## Scepticism about values

Scepticism about virtue is ordinarily supposed to have originated with the Sophists, but it was rather an accidental by-product of their setting themselves up as professional teachers of virtue than a considered and explicit doctrine. Just as those who reject the claims of metaphysics often turn out to have a metaphysics of their own they are anxious to peddle, so the Sophists, in criticising conventional morality for its inconsistencies and lack of clear foundations, were in fact the exponents of a new, less heroic and more down to earth morality of their own.

Hobbes is sometimes held to be a thoroughgoing ethical subjectivist. He did, after all, maintain that 'whatsoever is the object of any man's appetite or desire that is it which he for his part calleth good.' But although he goes on to say 'these words of good, evil and contemptible are ever used with relation to the person that useth them: there being nothing simply or absolutely so; nor nay common rule of good and evil to be taken from the objects themselves', he does in fact assume that the preservation of life is a supreme and overriding good and it supplies the foundation for a system of universally applicable rules of conduct, so long as they are embodied in law and enforced by the coercive power of the state.

There is a sense of subjectivism – but I shall not use the word in that sense – in which it does not have irresistibly sceptical consequences and it is in that sense that Hobbes and may other moral philosophers are subjectivists. This is the view that morality is not an aspect of the world independent of human beings, part of the extra-human nature of things. It is thus in conflict with the ethical rationalism that takes moral truths to be eternally and necessarily true in the same way as the truths of mathematics. It is also at odds with the idea that the principles of morality are divine commands.

To believe that morality essentially involves human beings and, more specificially, as this doctrine usually contends, that it is based on the emotional reactions of human beings, on 'the passions' as they once were called, does not necessarily subjectivise morality, either fully, by making moral convictions matters of private, individual decision, or, in the manner of ethical relativism, by basing them on the shared and socially shaped attitudes of a given community.

An anthropocentric conception of morality, if it is to avoid subjectivism, would seem to presuppose a certain stability and a basic community of human nature. But even if human liabilities to suffering and sources of well-being were very much more various than they are, there would still be a place for the universal rules 'do not act so as to cause suffering in others' and 'act so as to diminish the suffering of others'.

Subjectivism is often inspired by the realisation that societies other than one's own appear to subscribe to quite different moral principles from those one's own does. The conclusion is expressed in the proposition: what is right in one place is often not right in another. But that, of course, does not mean that what is right is whatever anyone happens to think is right. The circumstances of people in different societies differ so that means to ends that all could agree are good could differ without there being any fundamental disagreement. Secondly, what people believe about the consequences of particular kinds of action (compelling the naturally left-handed to use their right hands, for example) may differ and disagreement about what is the right thing to do would disappear with the correction of the erroneous belief about consequences. Finally, human nature is not an immutable fixity. It is to some extent responsive to its social setting so that human reactions, on which all else depends, will vary from one society to another.

## The death of God

It is necessary to distinguish ethical anthropocentrism and relativism (which are not inevitably subjectivist) from subjectivism proper, since the most favoured explanation of the currency of ethical subjectivism does not very directly imply it. The death of God which Nietzsche proclaimed undoubtedly *encourages* ethical scepticism. In the words of Dostoevsky, 'If God does not exist everything is permitted.' But it does not by any means logically entail it. Dostoevsky's proposition is not an incontrovertible truth. A secular or naturalist account of morality as objective can be sustained independently of God.

For Kant, indeed, the boot was on the other foot. The nearest he thought himself entitled to come to a proof of God's existence was to say that it was a presupposition of the categorical or absolutely binding character which he ascribed to moral principles.

Generally philosophers, however devout, have been critical of what they see as the naïvety of the doctrine that moral principles are divine commands. It represents an infinite, and so only marginally intelligible, being in an excessively anthropomorphic way. There is something quaintly primitive about supposing the creator and ruler of the universe to be minutely concerned with the bureaucratic small-print of human conduct. It might be argued, instead, that unless God is conceived in an unplausibly anthropomorphic fashion his existence is compatible with the truth of ethical scepticism.

The traditional ground of a non-theological kind for ethical scepticism is the fact of moral disagreement. But disagreement may be due to the fact that one party is right and the other wrong. To carry any sceptical weight, disagreement has to be somehow insoluble. In the moral domain, it seems reasonable to say, it persists unresolved more obdurately than anywhere else than perhaps aesthetics. But we do not find the differing opinions of others about aesthetic values anything like as worrying as opposed moral values. The moral convictions of others will determine how they treat one while their aesthetic preferences determine only what poetry they will admire and what pictures they will choose to look at. In consequence much more effort is put into the elimination of moral than of aesthetic disagreement. That, at least, strengthens the inductive support given by the persistence of unresolved disagreement to the conclusion that it is, ultimately, at least in some cases, insoluble.

But philosophers, although many of them recommend induction to others, tend to dismiss its adequacy in their own operations. At best, they feel, it can result in suggestions that can inspire the search for a proof. In the case in hand, such a proof has seemed to emerge in pursuing the intimations of Moore's inductive conclusion, from a rather meagre sample of instances, that all definitions of 'good' and other evaluative words in terms of words for what he called 'rational' properties were incorrect.

The proof consists in an explanation of the alleged logical autonomy of morals, that is to say, its irreducibility to any other, less problematic area of belief, such as facts about the role of human action in the causation and prevention of suffering. Morality could be autonomous and still be objective. It might all depend eventually for its rational justification on a basic moral principle or a handful of such principles which was or were self-evidently necessary, something or some things it would be self-contradictory to deny.

What has been claimed is that the autonomy of morals is the demonstrable consequence of the essentially practical or action-guiding nature of moral convictions. Moral affirmations, it is held, in most cases, consist of a directly practical or action-guiding element, an imperative addressed to everyone, together with an implicit allusion to some unproblematically factual feature of what is morally judged which constitutes a reason for morally enjoining or forbidding it. To specify the relevant feature is to connect it, directly or indirectly, to something that is ultimately valued or disvalued for its own sake, in other words to subsume it under an ultimate moral principle. Such a principle, just because it is ultimate, falls under no higher principle; it is a purely imperative injunction or prohibition of whatever it is that is ultimately valued. As the indispensable terminus of argument it cannot be argued for; it is a matter of personal choice or decision or, as it is sometimes put, a proposal. It can be persuasively presented by tracing out its detailed implications for conduct so that the full scope of the choice is made clear for comparison with the implications of alternative and conflicting ultimate principles but that does not establish its truth, it ensures only that the choice is made, or declined, with a full understanding of what is involved. In a way, therefore, these ultimate moral decisions of principle are arbitrary, an arbitrariness that is not much attenuated by being made in an informed and reflective manner. Conflicts between ultimate choices do not show that at least one party to the disagreement must be mistaken.

## Non-moral value

One objection to this attempt to prove that there can easily be moral disagreements that are wholly irresoluble by rational means is that practicality, the feature on which it turns, is not peculiar to moral judgements. It must be present just as much in any explicit judgement of value, any assertion in which such pure evaluative words as 'good', and 'right' and their opposites occur or an assertion which is equivalent to one in which they are to be found, such as 'he is a thief' which means the same as 'he takes things wrongly'.

Included in the very long list of evaluations of this explicit kind that are not moral are aesthetic judgements (*'Bleak House* is Dickens' *best* book'), prudential ones ('you *ought* to take out more insurance'), medical ones ('fibre in the diet is *good* for you'), technical ones ('that is not the *right* way to lift a heavy weight'). Aesthetic disagreements seem quite as irresoluble as moral disagreements but it is disconcerting to have to admit that judgements about prudence, technical efficiency and health rest on arbitrary personal decisions.

One reaction to this difficulty makes use of the distinction Kant saw between the supposedly categorical imperatives of morality ('you ought to keep your promise') and the hypothetical imperatives of the other fields of evaluation. If, but only if, you want to maximise your prospects of advantage in the long run, take out more insurance; if, but only if, you want to keep heating costs down, insulate the roof; if, but only if, you want to stay healthy, eat a good deal of fibre. The element of personal decision is extruded from these judgements, which are in themselves straightforwardly factual, and becomes the independent issue of whether or not their antecedent clauses are actualised or not.

That manoeuvre underestimates the contestable or controversial value of the supposed ends in one way and overestimates it in another. Everyone wants as much advantage as possible, but they differ about what state of affairs is most advantageous. Similarly, everyone wants to be healthy but they may not agree with the doctor as to what being healthy in fact consists in, for them at any rate. Assessments of the comparative cost of alternative techniques can be objectivised if cost is measured by the relative market-price of materials, labour and so forth, but to do that is to identify efficiency with cheapness and applies only where each of the alternative produces results which it is impossible to discriminate between. How, to take a modest specific instance, can it be decided whether it is better to shave with an electric razor or an old-fashioned safety razor? How do we weigh the need for an electrical supply plus general lack of mess minus failure to get rid of some long whiskers on the neck against the economy of getting one's face more or less washed in one operation with shaving minus a chance of drawing blood from surface irregularities on the skin? In other words, either the purpose proposed as the antecedent of the hypothetical imperative is not definite enough for the hypothetical to be true or it is specific enough but is then itself a topic for contestable evaluation.

For my purpose here it is not necessary to pursue this point further with regard to explicit non-moral value-judgements in general. It is enough to have raised the question of their practicality and of the ensuing possibility of there being ultimately irresoluble disagreement about them. I want, rather, to consider a further kind of non-moral evaluation.

## Logical and methodological valuation

This is the field of logical and epistemic or methodological evaluation. Logic is often said to be a normative science, even by people in whom this description might be expected to induce a measure of anxiety. It is plainly not a natural science of thought-processes but a systematisation of principles about how one *ought* to think. The same is true of methodology which is concerned with reasons that are less than deductively compelling. Although, like logic proper, it relies to some extent on information about how people do reason as a matter of fact, it has to reject some actual reasonings as invalid so as to arrive at a unified and self-consistent system which is exemplified by the rest.

Let me concentrate for a moment on the logical relation of entailment. To say that A entails B is to say that B follows from or is a logical consequence of A. It is equivalent in meaning to the assertion that anyone who believes or states that A ought not to believe or state that B is not the case, and that he ought to believe or be ready to assert that B.

Given that, an argument can be constructed which appears to serve as some sort of *reductio ad absurdum* of the doctrine that since judgements of value are practical they cannot be established except by premises, one of which is both practical and ultimate and therefore a matter of arbitrary personal decision. That doctrine in attenuated form states that premises of an objectively true or false kind (premises, that is to say, none of which is a matter of personal decision) never entail a judgement of value. But that doctrine, in saying that premises of a certain kind never entail a certain other kind of conclusion is itself a judgement of value and, on that account, not a statement proper, true or false, but an imperative, that is to say a decision or the consequence of one.

I said only that it was 'some sort of *reductio ad absurdum*' because the argument does not show that the doctrine being considered implied its own *falsity*. What it does do is imply its own arbitrariness, or to put it another way, undermines its own implicit claim to truth.

This argument has been sketched in various places but has not been much discussed. C.I. Lewis put forward a version of it in a chapter whose title – right believing and right concluding – drew attention to the analogy between logical and epistemic valuation on the one hand and moral valuation on the other. The view that the principles of reasoning are in the same boat or arbitrariness as moral principles was advanced by the late David Pole in a book called *Conditions of Rational Inquiry* and his treatment is of interest since it called forth a rather peevish and dismissive response in a subsequent anonymous (but, I think, stylistically penetrable) review in the *Times Literary Supplement*.

Pole's critic asks: what is evaluative about the principles of scientific reasoning? Is it that they imply that they are good principles to follow? It is conceivable that they do in an indirect way, but what is really to the point is that they explicitly lay down what sort of conclusions one *ought* to derive from given bodies of evidence. The writer states that Pole may have shown that evaluation of the ultimate aims of reasoning are arbitrary but oddly goes on to claim that that does not show that principles validated by those aims (presumably by serviceability to them) are arbitrary too. That conclusion could be avoided in the circumstances only if there was also some other, non-arbitrary way of validating them but nothing of the sort is alluded to, let alone sketched, by Pole's critic.

Pole takes his argument to undermine the doctrine of the ultimate arbitrariness of valuation because that doctrine implies something that he finds, and assumes that everyone else, on reflection, would find, to be utterly unacceptable, the thesis that the principles of reasoning are arbitrary, matters of decision that are neither sustainable by reasoning or in some way self-sustaining.

In fact those who have reflected on the subject have not all found wholly unacceptable the idea that the principles of reasoning are ultimately arbitrary. Confining attention for the moment to methodological principles, and postponing consideration of logic strictly so-called, the account of scientific method given in Popper's *Logik der Forschung* is not only put forward as a set of recommendations for good scientific practice, but the ungroundedness of the recommendations is emphatically recognised. Popper contrasts his own conception of methodological rules as conventional, as being proposed for acceptance in comparison with alternatives, with what he calls the naturalistic view, which takes them to be mere empirical descriptions of the practice of scientists. The latter ignores the fact that a conventional decision is involved in the bestowal of the honorific label of 'scientist' on someone. He emphasises the point by describing methodological rules as 'the rules of the game called science'.

Such ideas about method, about the rational justification of beliefs have been carried further by Kuhn and Feyerabend. Kuhn presents a picture of the development of science that contrasts sharply with the optimistic nineteenth-century view of it as a steadily progressive accumulation of well-founded laws and theories. He discerns, rather, a sequence of periods in which a particular paradigm or style of theorisation prevails more or less unchallenged, interrupted by revolutionary episodes in which, for no very obviously justifying reasons, a new paradigm is introduced and the old orthodoxy or normal science is cast aside.

Feyerabend goes even further and seeks to reinstate the most conventionally disreputable ways of thinking about nature, seeing astrology and alchemy as resting their claim to attention on no weaker, if also no stronger, foundations than astronomy and chemistry. That perhaps has the virtue of disturbing the complacency of the practitioners of orthodox science. But even if they reject unorthodox theorists as cranks or charlatans, that does not mean that there is no examination by the partisans of orthodoxy of the assertions of the dissenters. The work of exposure is a relatively humble one. Martin Gardner (see *Science: Fads and Fallacies*) and the late Christopher Evans (see *Cults of Unreason*) are not the recipients of Nobel Prizes or fellowships of the Royal Society, but, like loyal guard dogs in the grounds of a ducal mansion, they provide a vital protective service.

The notion that authoritative claims to knowledge rest on arbitrary foundations is carried even further by such flamboyant post-structuralists as Foucault and Derrida. They follow Nietzsche in taking knowledge-claims as disguised instruments for the exercise of power, a disguise that can hide this fact about the nature of the instruments they use from those who wield them. Bacon, of course, held that knowledge is power, but did not conclude that therefore it was not really knowledge. The sort of power he had in mind was that of using the natural world so as to enlarge the ability of human beings to get what they want. It could not be acquired unless the causal beliefs on which it was founded were true or, at any rate, implied further particular beliefs that turned out to be true for the most part.

### Is scientific rationality arbitrary?

In these proposals of the doctrine that what passes for rational scientific method rests on arbitrary foundations, we find a reversal of the intentions of those who originally contended that method is as much an evaluative matter as morality. The original purpose of stressing the analogy between morality and method was to show that since, as it was assumed, method is obviously not arbitrary, but is nevertheless evaluative, it does not follow from the evaluativeness of morality that it too is arbitrary. It is as if a weak-looking structure were tied to a strong-looking one to strengthen it and then the weak one brought the strong one crashing down with it.

The most straightforward argument against this second, destructive use of the analogy of morality and method is a rather concisely practical one. Great scientists are, no doubt, inspired to their work by a cognitive impulse, a desire to understand the nature and workings of the world. But their much more numerous clients are interested in the technological applications of their findings. And body-scanners, based on orthodox science, give more reliable results than do black-box inspections of blood samples, which are not so based. Astronomical predictions of eclipses are very exact; astrological predictions fail to conceal their untrustworthiness even by the extreme vagueness with which they are expressed.

In short orthodox science works, unorthodox science does not. An objection to that is that it would be more correct to say that orthodox science *has* worked hitherto, but that to regard that as establishing its general superiority is to take for granted the inductive principle which has traditionally been held to be the first rule of scientific procedure.

It might be possible to circumvent this objection by inquiring if the opponents of the claim of orthodox science to be objectively superior to the alternatives are really sincere. Does Feyerabend want to fly in a plane based on some mystical doctrine; to be medically tested with magical potions? Does Derrida want his lawyer to deconstruct his will or the finance office of the Collège de France to deconstruct the text setting out his pension arrangements? It might be replied that all their conventional reactions in these matters would show is that they have not fully shaken off the practical implications of a theory they have come to reject, like some champion of free love who remains obstinately virginal.

## The case of logic

Earlier I postponed the case of logic, strictly so called, formal deductive logic, for later consideration. It may prove constructive at this stage of the argument to turn attention to it. Systems of logic are commonly set out as bodies of logical truths, connected in various ways. But to every logical truth corresponds some rule of inference, most evidently when the logical truth is in a conditional form. To say that 'if p and q then p' is a logical truth is to say you can infer 'p' from 'p and q', or, more to the purpose here, you ought not to accept both 'p and q' and 'not p'.

Why ought one not to assert both of these things? Because it would be inconsistent. What is so wonderful about consistency? Do not poets often inveigh against it? The answer is very straightforward. Unless a fair degree of consistency is maintained in straightforwardly purposeful discourse, communication breaks down, people do not find each other's utterances intelligible, at any rate above the most elemental level of signalling or emotional contagion. The preservation of a mutually intelligible means of communication is a justifying aim which it is hard to conceive being abandoned. Even the most misanthropic of hermits uses the social gift of language in order, as it were, to communicate with himself, to register his thoughts and reflect on his experiences. In other words, the imperatives of formal logic are justified by so unexceptionable an aim that they can be taken to be categorical; no attention need be paid to the implied condition 'if you want to maintain language in being then...'

There are, of course, many different systems of logic, but to a very large extent they concur in finding a place within themselves for an unquestioned set of logical truths. There are, indeed, genuinely alternative logics, not just different ways of systematically arranging a more or less fixed body of material, but systems that understand the basic logical notions in different ways. Reasons have been adduced for the proposal that we might think in terms of a logic without a law of excluded middle for certain purposes (in quantum physics, for example). But it seems clear that we do not, in fact, do so.

The final conclusion to which this leads is that every field of imperatives or evaluations is dependent for the justification of its constituents on the indispensability of what is recommended to the pursuit of some justifying aim: mutually intelligible means of communication in the case of logic, reliable predictions in the case of scientific method and the type of everyday thinking that underlies it and on which the ordinary management of life depends, efficiency in the case of technology, long-run personal advantage in the case of prudence and so on.

Is there any such aim to be found in the case of morality? Or are those Kantian spirits right who suppose right conduct to be its own purpose and neither to require nor even to be susceptible of any ulterior justification in terms of good consequences?

I do not propose to argue for this in any but the most cursory fashion. It is very natural to turn to the consequences of types of action about whose moral correctness there is disagreement in the attempt to resolve it. Changes either in the actual consequences of types of action for human suffering or well-being, and in beliefs about the consequences of action, can be invoked to explain many of the observed variations in what is commonly held to be morally right. If the relevance of consequences of action to moral rightness is denied, such disagreement becomes an irresoluble clash of intuitions.

## The implications of consequentialism

Consequentialism has the merit that it at once allows intelligibly for a good deal of disagreement, at levels short of the ultimate at least, and points the way towards the rational resolution of disagreement. That is bought at what many will feel to be a high price, the conclusion that not much certainty is rationally attainable in moral matters. It will seldom, if ever, be true that the consequences of a given type of action are *always* good or *always* bad. The actions it is primarily important to judge, we must remember, are those that have not yet been done and all prediction of possible future consequences is infected with uncertainty.

Consequentialism implies, then, that principles and judgements about morally right or wrong action are generally fallible and open to correction. It is not reasonable to hold them in an unqualified and unrevisable form. That conclusion is only reinforced if the justifying aim of morality is itself not very precise and also if it is not a single monolithic aim but a multiplicity between whose elements there may be competition. But this rational support for the abandonment of moral dogmatism does not endorse a free-for-all in the way that the doctrine of the ultimate arbitrariness of evaluation seems to. What it does endorse is a readiness to discuss, to reconsider one's own moral beliefs in the light of the criticisms of others and, since this implies that one may be mistaken and others more correct, a tolerance of moral attitudes that are not consistent with one's own.

It is often the case that those who are ostensibly committed to the doctrine that evaluation is ultimately arbitrary are often as dogmatic in their moral attitudes as those who adopt an ethical theory that rationalises their rigidity in moral attitudes; Russell is a familiar example of this combination. What should someone who accepts the arbitrariness theory really do; how should he manage his moral attitudes? Since no one can rationally correct his convictions, provided they are intellectually consistent and he really does hold them, there is no rational ground for his paying attention to what anyone else says in criticism of them, unless they claim to detect inconsistency in him.

An alternative idea is that since each person's moral system is rationally neither superior nor inferior to anyone else's, they should all be treated alike, at any rate to the extent that any one person has no reason to expect any one else to share his convictions or to be indignant if they do not.

I think it is not worth exploring either of these tentative and radically opposed inferences further. For, as in the analogous case of scientific anarchism, it is hard to accept that those who have been driven by philosophical argument into accepting the arbitrariness doctrine really endorse it as an operative, practical belief. To contend that ultimate moral beliefs are arbitrary is to express readiness for a degree of wildness in the variety of beliefs which does not exist and, if it did, would be found exceedingly disturbing. Someone who supposed the supreme and overriding justifying purpose of the rules of human conduct to be the multiplication and protection of flowering plants, in the light of which all else should be judged and, in case of conflict, to which all else would be sacrificed, would be regarded as a lunatic not a lonely moral dissenter. The field of alternatives is not really anything like as broad as the nothing-to-choose theory implies.

## The complexity of morals

Very broadly speaking, the conflicts of moral belief are not over-whelmingly large in comparison with the range of moral consensus that prevails, not only in one's own time and community, but also as between one age and another, one society and another. What differs much more than the *content* of morality is what may be called its field of application, the constituency recognised as the 'others' whose interests and welfare are to be taken into account. In different times and places the line between genuine fellow-creatures and game in open season is differently drawn. The moral history of mankind viewed through fairly rosy spectacles, may seem to show a steady extension of the field of fellow-creatures with a correlative diminution of the domain of the unlimitedly exploitable.

Twentieth-century totalitarianism, especially in its genocidal form in Nazism, seems, against the background of an optimistic view of human moral development, to be a dreadful reversion to primitive habits of thought and conduct. Many technically primitive societies have practices for the hospitable treatment of strangers that are far more helpful and generous than what is enjoined by the morality of the modern liberal West. Foreign groups have always inspired fear and aggression more than foreign individuals no doubt. Perhaps there is a faint residue of this division of response in the way we are happy to put ourselves out for a single foreigner, while regarding the disembarkation of a noisy and over-colourfully dressed mob of them from a coach with altogether less amiable feelings.

What should be recognised is that morality is not unitary. There is a central core of rules concerning the effect of an individual's actions on others which has a certain primacy and compulsiveness and is to be found in the moral systems of all times and places. It requires that we should not act so as to harm others, above all by physically assaulting them so as to cause injury or death. Alongside this are the rules of truth-telling and promise-keeping, whose general observance is needed to maintain effective communication and co-operation between people.

This is distinguishable from two other regions of morality which concern the choice of a style of life and the political management of the community. We are inclined to deplore styles of life which do not attract us on the grounds that they set a bad example (obviously a secondary or parasitic defect), that they involve the waste or misdi-rection of human powers, and, least defensibly, that they are unpleasant to contemplate. Uniformity in clothing, recreations, modes of speech, attitudes to work and leisure is not really required for social peace and the minimisation of mutual harmfulness. The intensity with which it has often been enforced seems to suggest, as a measure of enlightenment or moral progress, the disposition to be shocked by the right things.

As for political morality, its chief defect of rationality is a kind of utopianism which, seizing on some more or less definable public end, is ready to forego all other ends in pursuit of it (the classless society, racial purity, national greatness). But the ends in question are usually seriously confused – class, race and greatness are radically imprecise and, so to speak, Protean notions. Furthermore the means chosen to pursue these elusive ends tend to produce something very different from the vague ideal to which they were directed.

We can afford to bicker about politics and styles of life. It is not advantageous to treat them as on a level with the essential core of personal morality.

## Damage control

Sceptical and subjectivist doctrines about knowledge and morality undermine the intellectual authority of the teacher, not vis-à-vis his pupils, at least if they are fairly young, but in his own eyes and in those of parents and others who have an interest in what he does. There is damage and, as far as the teacher's authority in the moral field is concerned, there is a historical or institutional reason for thinking it to be irreversible.

I have argued that the most solid reason for ethical subjectivism, namely the practical or evaluative character of moral beliefs, is also a reason for subjectivism about science, since the principles of scientific reasoning or method, indeed of rational thinking in general, are also evaluative. The argument seems inconclusive at first since it can be taken either as a *reductio ad absurdum* of the thesis that ultimate morality is arbitrary or as showing that science and all of what passes for knowledge is arbitrary too.

One support for the former conclusion is the fact that the proponents of scientific subjectivism can hardly be sincere. Also, although there are conflicting moral outlooks of comparable intellectual weight, there is really no very serious competition to ordinary scientific method, only conflicting scientific *doctrines* which seem largely to have been arrived at by uncontrolled intuition and to have been maintained by careful neglect of evidence, rather than its maximal exploitation.

An important difference between morality and science is that the latter is institutionalised in a way that morality is not. There is an apparatus of professional associations and societies, of honours and prizes, of respected periodicals whose critical reviews carry authority, of university departments and congresses and government support. There is a conscious, self-defining and self-authenticating minority of scientists. The rest of the public, dependent on them at various removes, as engineers or doctors, rail travellers or outpatients, accepts their authority more or less on trust.

In the past the clergy stood in something of the same relation to the public at large in the field of moral belief. But in our age morality has been democratised. It is a measure of the extent which its democratisation has reached that people have been so easy to convince that morality is inescapably a matter of free individual decision.

Authoritative moral certainty has been damaged, then, but the damage can be contained and moral education kept afloat. If it is clear that it is not rational to take principles of right conduct to be self-evident and incontrovertible, to be affirmed without acknowledgement of any possibility of criticism and correction, it is still possible to see them as well-founded to various degrees, particularly those which concern individual treatment of other people.

The strong institutional front presented by science leaves much of its authority intact, but styles of theorisation do conflict. The most influential of modern theorists of method goes so far as to say that in science 'we do not know, we can only guess'. Here too fallibilism is appropriate. It is important above all for those who might be able to improve our inherited accumulation of scientific beliefs to be trained in criticism of the intellectual status quo. But there is nothing very obvious to be gained by inculcating an unquestioning passivity in those who will be no more than the clients and beneficiaries of science. What is to be lost is the critical attitude that might dispel irrationally dogmatic adhesion to pseudo science and antiscience.

*Not previously published.*

# Reflections on the Graduate School

I am going to begin my consideration of the future of graduate education with a short and selective survey of its past. In its first medieval beginnings the university was a place of graduate education. The earliest universities were wholly graduate schools. Salerno was a school of medicine, Bologna a school of law. With Paris and Oxford in the twelfth century something more stable, and more recognisable as a university, came into being. In both there is a clearly marked distinction between the basic, preliminary studies in arts and the higher studies in theology, medicine, and canon and civil law for which alone doctorates were granted. The basic arts course of study was the liberal aspect of the whole undertaking. Its components, after all, are the original liberal arts: logic, grammar, rhetoric, mathematics, and astronomy. The higher studies for which a master's degree in arts was a required condition were all vocational. They trained men for the professions of lawyer, medical man, and ecclesiastic. Most students who matriculated in the medieval university failed to graduate in arts and only a minority of those who did went on to work for a higher degree.

The graduate aspect of the university was one of the casualties of the decline of universities in the early modern period. Doctorates were still awarded, but in an honorary or virtually honorary fashion. That process of decline is most clearly observed in England, the most progressive country of the epoch. The extraordinary intellectual vitality of Oxford in the thirteenth and fourteenth centuries was severely reduced by the Black Death. But it was not finally extinguished until early in the fifteenth century with official suppression of the Wycliffite heresy. The advancement of knowledge then ceased at the university, to be carried on for the next four or five hundred years almost exclusively by private individuals working outside any learned institution. What the great English thinkers of the seventeenth century acquired from their universities was a settled hostility to the Aristotelian system they had been subjected to there. Bacon, Hobbes, and Locke were all in self-conscious revolt against the type of learning with which the university seemed to them to be indissolubly identified. Bacon supported his mature studies by his successes as lawyer, politician, and judge. Hobbes and Locke had earls as patrons. Where the new learning had an institutional connection it was comparatively informal and unrelated to the university. The Royal Society may have been conceived in Wadham College, Oxford, during the Cromwellian interregnum. It came to fruition only in Restoration London as a club for intellectual gentlemen.

The universities conveyed to their students the old mixture of inert medieval lore, lightened here and there with a little Renaissance polish put on by way of the reading and imitation of classical authors. The undergraduate body consisted in part of well-born young men with no practical reason to bother themselves with degree getting and, in larger but less conspicuous part, of future clergy, now more usually the younger sons of gentry, than the socially humbler scholars of the middle ages. The end result of the process was the Oxford of Edward Gibbon, a kind of academic Sodom in which it would have been hard to find half a dozen intellectually active and distinguished men among the permanent residents. Attention should be given to the time scale of university history. Oxford had two and a half centuries of vigour between its mid-twelfth century beginnings and the onset of stagnation in the early fifteenth century. Four hundred years of torpor then ensued, until at the beginning of the nineteenth century various signs of life began to emerge.

The reformers of the mid-nineteenth century were more interested in ensuring that the university earned its endowment income by the effective teaching of properly selected students by properly qualified teachers than in its revival as a place for the advancement of knowledge. Jowett's conception of the university as the finishing school for the ruling class of the chief imperial nation of the age prevailed. Another reforming point of view was that of Mark Pattison, who wanted the university to concentrate on pure scholarship, the accumulation of knowledge, and the fostering of truly learned men. That policy, which had none of the public appeal of Jowett's scheme of a training camp for philosopher-kings, was, of course, inspired by the nineteenth-century triumph of the German universities.

The universities of Germany had also had their period of decadence. Their historian, Friedrich Paulsen, points out that by the late eighteenth century they were ignored by such intellectually distinguished figures as Leibniz and Lessing. But they revived much sooner than the universities of England. In the late eighteenth century, with Halle, the first Prussian university, and Göttingen leading the way, they had developed the distinctive qualities that made the German universities of the nineteenth century so productive and so much admired. The principles of *Lehrfreiheit* and *Lernfreibeit* encouraged scholarly specialisation by both teachers and pupils. Emphasised in the university of Berlin, founded by Humboldt in 1810, they soon came to permeate the entire German-speaking university system. The double freedom in question meant that the studies of the university were not subordinated to any externally determined principles of social usefulness, whether liberal and general or vocational and particular. The freedom was not abused. Germany in the nineteenth century had the benefit of universal recognition of the fact that its universities were the best in the world. Much more original and substantial work came from them than from the universities of Britain and America. Their graduates were altogether more learned than graduates anywhere else.

It was the conception of the university exemplified in nineteenth-century Germany that inspired the development of a university system really deserving the name in the United States. Before the 1870s and the Johns Hopkins of Gilman, the American college had been a kind of demure and conventional high school. In much the same way as the revived but not yet truly reformed universities of early nineteenth-century England, American colleges were staffed by young men of no great expertise who taught all the subjects offered and were ruled by clergymen more concerned with orthodoxy and decorum than with learning. Gilman's conception of the university as a graduate school on German lines linked up with the element of *Lernfreiheit* embodied in the elective system, the development of serious professional schools and a generally widespread secularisation to establish the vast American university of the present age, with its undergraduate college, its academic and professional graduate schools, its research institutes, and the various kinds of socially purposive educational institutions that are attached to it.

English universities have increasingly come to follow the American pattern, within limits set by poverty and insular complacency. That is particularly true of the urban universities founded in the late nineteenth century, the 'Redbricks', whose theorist, 'Bruce Truscot', claimed were more genuine universities than Oxford and Cambridge on the ground that a university is possible without undergraduates but not without research, which, in his view, the urban universities emphasised. Now all English universities have more or less plausible arrangements for graduate study. In the last few years the possession of advanced degrees, which has for a long time characterised all recruits to the academic profession from the natural sciences, has, for the first time, come to be true of most recruits from the humanities.

The reform of the older English universities in the middle and late nineteenth century does seem to show that organised graduate study is not an indispensable condition of academic respectability. If the private Carlyle and Macaulay, Mill and Spencer gave way to the professorial Stubbs and Maitland, Bradley and Sidgwick, the latter did not have doctorates until encumbered with them *honoris causa* at an advanced age. By English-speaking standards the German universities have for the last two centuries been almost wholly graduate schools. It was by the addition of the graduate school, particularly the academic graduate school of arts and sciences, to the old undergraduate college that the modern American university was brought into being out of comparatively unpromising raw material. Even if the old English universities revived without any perceptible emphasis on graduate studies, they have in the course of this century come to accord almost as important a place to them as they are given in all but the most insistently graduate-oriented American universities.

So far I have done nothing to define graduate education explicitly, but have assumed that the phrase will be uniformly interpreted. An obvious criterion might be the directing of a course of study toward a doctorate. Unfortunately there are many bachelor's and master's degrees that are earned only by what is clearly graduate work such as bachelor's degrees in law, medicine, and divinity, and master's of arts degrees where that is not, as in Scotland, the first degree or, as in Oxford and Cambridge, an automatic sequel to the Bachelor of Arts. A more serious difficulty is that being directed toward a doctorate, even if proposed only as a sufficient condition of the graduate character of a course of study, is defectively superficial in relying on a convention of naming. It is reasonable to award a doctorate for the successful completion of a course only if that course is in its nature of the graduate kind. It is worth noting in this connection that the main degree of the German university is the doctorate. Matthew Arnold and Abraham Flexner were not simply bewitched by a word when they took the completion of the course at the traditional German gymnasium to be equivalent to a first degree in the English-speaking world. The nature of the German university student's work from the outset was such as to make the doctorate an appropriate reward for bringing it to completion.

The idea of independent study has some attractions as a criterion, but the relativeness of the concept of independence makes the idea vague. In comparison to the drilled note-takers whose main academic work is attending lectures and memorising the contents of text-books, the essay-writing undergraduate of the Oxford tutorial system, sent off with a topic and a reading list to come back with an essay a week later, is studying independently. Yet this kind of tutorial procedure is to be found in the sixth forms where the pupils in the better British secondary schools spend their last two or three years before going to the university at all. On the other hand, most graduate programmes involve course work of a more or less authoritatively instructional kind, at least in their earlier phases, and in graduate professional schools such course work bulks very large indeed.

To move back toward a more formal and conventional indication of graduate character, there is the matter of a central part being played by the thesis or dissertation. The distinguishing power of this feature is weakened by such things as the American undergraduate's term paper or the long essays British undergraduates are now often allowed to offer in place of a timed and invigilated examination script in their final examinations, although such papers and essays will ordinarily be a good deal shorter than anything acceptable for a master's or, even more, a doctor's degree.

A further suggestion comes from etymology and history. One who has successfully completed a course of graduate study is a doctor or, at least, a master, and both of these terms imply being qualified to teach others. The master is one who has mastered a craft or art, who knows how to exercise a skill and is thus fit to be imitated by apprentices. The doctor is one who has mastered a science, is the possessor of knowledge that certain things are the case, and is qualified to convey that knowledge to others, a capacity that involves understanding the grounds on which the knowledge rests. This notion of graduate study as directed toward a qualification to teach applies more neatly to academic than to professional graduate work. The latter is concerned to produce qualified practitioners rather than theory builders.

Etymology is, of course, a questionable witness in this kind of case. But its suggestions may survive the tests they have to be given. I think what is suggested here has one very solid virtue. In the universities of the English-speaking world, academic graduate schools, graduate schools of arts and sciences, are now professional schools, for intending entrants to the academic profession. Almost all students of academic graduate schools intended, when they started, to become professional academics. That is no doubt more true of the humanities than of the natural and social sciences. Natural scientists may enter graduate school intending to follow the careers in scientific research for government or industry that they actually go into. Intending diplomats or journalists may well seek doctorates in political science or international relations, intending investment analysts in economics. There are no non-educational professional openings of that degree of closeness to graduate work in philosophy, history or literature.

In what follows I shall assume that our main concern is with the academic graduate school. There are reasonably clearly demarcated bodies of knowledge and levels of competence in applying them which can be used to define professional qualifications in medicine, law, engineering, accountancy, architecture, even social work and school teaching. And the professions in question serve definite, persisting, and fairly uncontroversial needs. These factors make the graduate school for professionals comparatively unproblematic. Neither applies in the case of the academic graduate school. Every profession ought to take stock of itself from time to time. What has made this particularly urgent for the academic profession is the increasing disparity between the numbers of those who seek such a career and of the occupational places open to them. The practical problem that lies behind our presence here is the way in which various factors, most substantially demographic ones, have reduced the demand for academic professionals.

There are two main ways in which the training of professionals generally is and has been carried on. The first is, in effect, on-the-job training, made necessary by the incapacity of the higher faculties of the universities to serve the purpose for which they were apparently designed. Lawyers in England have for centuries received their training in the Inns of Court in the form of apprenticeship to a practising master. Doctors have been trained in hospitals and where these are near enough to universities to be associated institutionally with them the association is often of a very formal nature. The degree of connection between professional training generally and the universities varies between these two limiting cases, both of them pretty remote, at least in every profession except the academic. But for the academic, of course, to be trained at the university is to be trained on the job to the extent that the academic's job is that of being a university teacher.

The alternative, American, method is to have professional schools as genuinely included parts of universities. The actual difference between the two modes of proceeding should not be exaggerated.

What makes it a little less profound than might at first appear is that in British undergraduate courses a good deal of the curriculum of an American law school or medical school is to be found. The difference is, nevertheless, a real one.

The point of drawing attention to the difference is that non-academic professional training, which is now such a very large statistical part of the American graduate school as a whole, stands in no very close or necessary relation to the university. There could well be, as there largely are in Britain, wholly separate schools for the training of entrants into the non-academic professions. It is not even necessary that such schools should require their students to have obtained a first degree at a university. In England there is no such requirement and many people entering the legal and medical professions there even today have not come to them from undergraduate university study.

If there are academic graduate schools attached to universities, it is natural that other non-academic professional schools should cluster around them. Both types of institution give further instruction to the products of undergraduate colleges, even in England, both are concerned with the maintenance of standards. There are also considerations of convenience. Where the interests of academic and strictly professional schools overlap, there can be a sharing of such expensive things as libraries, visiting experts and ancillary courses. A liberal arts college can afford a Bach choir or a rock-climbing society, but for a consort of ancient musical instruments or a stilt-walking group you probably need something on the scale of the modern multiversity.

Let us turn, then, to the academic graduate school proper, the graduate school of arts and sciences. These are, of course, usually associated with undergraduate colleges in universities. As I said earlier, if we assume that the purpose of academic graduate schools is to train university teachers, then that association makes such schools instances of on-the-job training of the English type. Indeed, given the extent to which the teaching of undergraduates is put in the hands of graduate students, that is not just a matter of institutional form. The student as apprentice engages fully in the firsthand work of the profession. But, continuing with the assumption, the comparatively sequestered, more American option is a possible one. Academic graduate schools could be, as a very few of them actually are, altogether independent of undergraduate colleges. If that arrangement became general it might compel the recognition of a possible infinite regress of academic professionalism. There would then be two rather clearly distinct kinds of academic teacher: the teacher of undergraduates, employed by a college, and the teacher of future college teachers, employed by a graduate school. Where, it might now be asked, should the latter be equipped for their special function of professor-training and by whom? In fact the regress could be stopped quite painlessly by allowing the academic graduate school to replenish its own staff. In any educational system of finite complexity there must be a highest kind of teacher whose final training is received from teachers of his own kind and not a higher one.

There can be no doubt that, in actual practice, the main work of most of those who successfully complete their courses at academic graduate schools is university teaching of undergraduates and often of graduates as well. It is equally evident that the courses followed in academic graduate schools contain no formal instruction in the technique of university teaching. What is supplied in abundance is practical experience of the humbler varieties of such teaching. It is often so amply provided that, by absorbing so much of the energy that should be applied to the more central aspects of the course, it causes its completion to be seriously delayed. So, even if university teaching is what those who emerge successfully from graduate schools actually do, it is not what they are directly and explicitly prepared for. We should then examine the assumption that what academic graduate schools are intended to produce is university teachers.

As we all know, academic graduate schools devote themselves to producing scholars, learned men, or, to be quite precise about the present state of things, researchers, advancers of knowledge. That final, Baconian aim is enshrined in the formula defining the appropriate duality of the doctoral dissertation that is the crucial element of the graduate's pursuit of his doctorate, that it should make an original contribution to knowledge.

I argued a little while ago against the assumption that the training of university teachers is the intended or acknowledged purpose of the academic graduate school, that such schools give no instruction in the technique of university teaching. To see some force in that argument is not to suppose that an instruction in those techniques alone would be sufficient to qualify someone for teaching in a university. The technique of communicating knowledge and understanding is empty without some content to communicate. The trained university teacher must be a scholar, in the sense of being an appropriately informed or learned person, as well as an instructor. But does that mean that he has to be a researcher, to be equipped with the capacity to add to knowledge? I do not think it does.

I touched earlier on a point about the nature of knowledge from which it follows that one who possesses knowledge or reasonable belief, in the self-conscious or self-critical way it must be possessed if it is to be authoritatively communicated, cannot be just a repository of truths and of well-grounded beliefs. He must understand that what he is communicating is knowledge or reasonable belief and why it is so. It could be held that the main point of the propositions and theories he puts across is the service they give as examples, through attention to which the power of critically assessing beliefs can be developed.

The scholar or learned person, I maintain, must have not just knowledge but, rather, a critical understanding of the extent to which what he believes in his particular field of study is knowledge. A scholar on this view is not simply a person who knows a great deal. But to insist that he is more than that is not to hold that he must be a researcher in the full, Baconian understanding of the term. He needs to have a critical mastery of the current state of discussion and should not see it as a steady accumulation of uncontroversial truths. He must be familiar, not just with the results of past discussion, but with the way in which those results were supported and the way in which they succeeded in displacing alternative views. The crucial point is that although playing a game may be a good way of acquiring a critical understanding of it, it is by no means the only or the usual way. Every interesting game has many more skilled and critical spectators than it has really gifted players.

The issue I am concerned with is often presented as a problem about the proper relation between teaching and research in the academic career. On the whole it is success in research that is esteemed and rewarded, so it is not surprising that it is research rather than teaching that academics want, or think or say that they want, to do. But the community at large is more ready to pay them for teaching. The received doctrine on this topic is that the two activities are necessary to each other, so that the community cannot have teaching of the quality it wants unless it allows and encourages its university teachers to engage in research. More particularly, it is maintained that teaching without research is flat, lifeless, and uninspired, while research without teaching, which is less painful for the academic mind to contemplate, may become precious, overspecialised, out of touch with life.

I do not think that anyone takes the argument against research without teaching very seriously. Governments and industry, as well as intellectual philanthropy, often set up research institutes and employ highly intelligent people in full-time research but they are not criticised on these sort of grounds. What is commonly objected to about research institutes is the morally or socially deficient character of their objects, such as chemical weapons or cheaper and nastier foodstuffs. Even where the objects of research are criticised for excessive inwardness, refinement, or hyperacademic triviality, it is not suggested that the best way to divert attention to more valuable objects of study is the introduction of some teaching work into the researcher's programme. But resistance to research without teaching is really only there for the sake of symmetry. It is the alleged necessity of research to teaching that is the important case.

Is teaching without research inevitably defective? It seems to me that this constantly affirmed principle is bluff. It is, of course, exciting and generally splendid when a really original contributor to the advancement of knowledge in some field is a gifted and willing teacher of it as well. There are such people. Who were our own most effective teachers, and, of those whom we encountered in our undergraduate years, who were the most creative advancers of knowledge? Were they generally the same? In my own case there was rather little overlap and for an intelligible reason Those active in research tended to use their teaching as ancillary to what they saw as their main business. They generally managed to ensure that the instruction they gave was confined to the area of their current preoccupation. That is at any rate to be preferred to a not uncommon alternative: the perfunctory and more or less exasperated discharge by a researcher of his teaching duties.

The claim that teaching, on the scale required for present-day undergraduate populations, is best carried on without requirement or expectation of research from those who give it is hard to support with familiar examples of great, non-researching teachers. Teaching prowess on its own tends to secure only a local fame. It would not be all that relevant to produce such instances if they were available, since the material consideration is good teaching, not great teaching. But some indirect support is surely given by the large and superfluous mass of low-grade academic publication that is generated by the requirement, ordinarily crucial for tenure and promotion, that the university teacher should be a researcher.

To deny the necessity of the research requirement is not to deny something with which, I suspect, it is quite often confused by those who take it to be a precondition of lively and stimulating teaching. That is the entirely different requirement that the teacher should be 'abreast' of his subject , that he should have a good idea of what is going on in the areas of growth within it. I suspect that this condition is not important for its own sake but more as a symptom of a live interest in his subject on the part of the teacher. Research, it must be said, is often hostile to it. The most creatively productive academics are often ill-informed about what is going on in the rest of their discipline.

Research, I am arguing, is not necessary to preserve the life and freshness of a university teacher's teaching work. But, even if that is correct, there may well be other good reasons for combining the two functions in one profession. There are indeed reasons for the different principle of combining teachers and researchers in the same institution. The chief of these, perhaps, is that the two groups provide, respectively, critical and constructive environments for each other that are valuable. That is simply an institutional version of the arguments I have questioned which affirm the necessity to each other of teaching and research in each academic individual. But it is, I think, more plausible than they are. However, what I am concerned with at the moment is the individual version of the principle.

There are two somewhat pedestrian considerations of a practical kind which may be brought forward in support of it. The first is that the kind of intellectual creativeness that is needed in research work is in various ways fitful and unpredictable. Early signs of originality may turn out to have been deceptive. Bouts of inspiration may be separated from one another by relatively stagnant periods. Something that is irresistibly obvious in mathematics may be more widely diffused in a less unmistakable way through all the fields of higher study: the tendency of creativeness to die away with age. The combination of the two academic functions smooths out the ups and downs of intellectual creativeness by extorting the appearances of research in various forms from the more or less uncreative while providing steady teaching jobs for the creative to fall back on as and when their creative powers dry up. This strategy, at the very least, avoids embarrassment, getting around the problem of the academic counterpart of the superannuated sports star.

A second practical reason for the combination is that it is a convenient device for getting fundamental research paid for. Governments and business firms are anxious to support research for what seem straightforwardly advantageous purposes. But the institutional consumers of knowledge who are in a position to pay for it do not take the same view of the questions which research should be directed to answering as the intellectually creative producers of knowledge do themselves. That is not to say that official and commercial funding of research is always or, even predominantly, philistine. It is remarkable how much unpractical-looking academic inquiry government and business do endorse in one way or another. But as institutions they are accountable, formally to the electorate or the shareholders, more realistically to politicians and finance directors, and that sets limits to the possibilities of intellectual philanthropy open to them.

How else is comparatively unpractical, comparatively academic research to be supported? The founders of the colleges of Oxford and Cambridge handed over large chunks of often questionably accumulated wealth to the colleges, for, among other things, the pursuit of learning for its own sake. It must be acknowledged that in this respect they did not get value for their money. The misuse of endowments during the four to five centuries of torpor entirely justified the principle of ultimate control by public legislation that underlay the highly fruitful reforms of the nineteenth century.

This is really more of a problem for the humanities than for the natural and social sciences. For the latter there are numerous research institutes in every advanced country which, while certainly carrying on some research of a practical and directly usable kind, are not confined to it. Staff of the highest quality is attracted to such places by the opportunity they give for the pursuit of research interests with the best equipment and without the hindrance of teaching duties. It is not fanciful to imagine that all research in the natural and social sciences should be carried on in such establishments. Future researchers, furthermore, could be trained as apprentices in them, coming directly on from undergraduate courses. But that does not seem a plausible solution for the problem of supporting research in the humanities.

An old device that I alluded to when I mentioned the great non-academic thinkers of seventeenth-century England is patronage. That is insecure, as shown by the relations between Bertrand Russell and Dr Albert C. Barnes, and increasingly thin on the ground in an epoch of confiscatory taxation. There is also the marketplace, which by way of his bestselling history of philosophy, supported Russell for the rest of his life, relying while he wrote it on money Dr Barnes had to pay him for unjust dismissal. The trouble here is that the crucial things do not get supported. The great works of mathematical philosophy Russell wrote in the first decade of this century may not yet have covered the cost of their production.

What in fact happens is that research is subsidised, particularly in the humanities, out of the general income of the universities in which academics, conceived, unless they are administrators, as both teachers and researchers, are employed. It must, therefore, depend to some extent on the income derived from student fees. If the endowment income were not spent on sabbaticals, study leave, travel grants, research assistants, and other expensive instrumentalities of the non-teaching roles of academics, it could be used to reduce student fees in general or to supply more scholarships. In a way, then, the student helps to subsidise the research that is supposed, in my view questionably, to improve the quality of the teaching that he receives.

Before jumping to that conclusion, let me reconsider a proposal I dismissed as implausible a little while ago: that of research institutes in the humanities. Things going by that name exist and serve respectable purposes, such as the institute of historical research attached to the University of London. But the phrase is misleading. What are called research institutes in the humanities are not comparable in size or autonomy to research institutes in the natural and social sciences. In general, research in the humanities does not offer the same kind of return to co-operation as it does in the sciences, nor does it rely on physical equipment, apart from books and documents, to any marked extent.

A much more fundamental point, however, is that what is called research in the humanities is a very different thing from what is done under that name in the sciences. Of course original thinking has its place in the development of the humane disciplines, but the maintenance of the tradition of the discipline has an importance to which nothing corresponds in the sciences. A civilised physicist or economist will know something about the history of his discipline. But he does not need to be a civilised physicist or economist to be a good one. The humanities are to a great extent textual disciplines, in which a traditional set of major articulations of human experience is kept alive. It is more appropriate to call them fields of learning than of research. Dr Johnson's engaging definition of scholarship as preserving the remains of ancient literature applies to them, if allowance is made for a certain archaism of phrase. This is true of philosophy considered in a historical manner, of the more familiar and less scientistic kinds of history and, obviously, of literature. It would be possible to study philosophy without ever meeting the names or reading the words of the major philosophers of the past, but it would be an absurd *tour de force*, since in any adequate presentation of the subject they would be present but hidden. The ideas, arguments and points of view that the student of philosophy studies are all rooted in some text. I should argue that history ought to have a historiographical component, not just as in classical history for lack of other evidence than what is to be found in the pages of Thucydides and Herodotus, Livy and Tacitus, but because to understand an age one must find out what its historical consciousness of itself was. The raw, unreflective, practical documents are too raw to yield enlightenment on their own.

This kind of scholarly, textual apprehension of a tradition of thought and expression, at a fairly simple level, makes up the background of general knowledge, or, in an older idiom, of polite learning, that many feel has so nearly evaporated in our own age through the abandonment of widespread study of the Bible and classical literature and then of the literature of our own language, or other current languages, before the present century. An undergraduate course in the humanities does not ordinarily allow for sufficient specialised attention to the acquisition of scholarly competence of this kind to qualify a person for teaching it to other undergraduates. But it is something that is obviously needed by university teachers of the humanities in a way that a research potential, which in this area is both hard to define and hard to discern, is not. It is something that a graduate school, consciously devoted to the training of university teachers as its main task, should continue to perform. The curriculum for it, while more specialised than that of an elective undergraduate course, need not lay the kind of stress that is now usual on the dissertation.

Of course the study of the humanities is not exclusively textual in the way I have described, although I believe that most of it should be, certainly more than usually is now. To some extent the subject matter of the humanities is absorbed into other, more scientifically methodical disciplines. Beyond its elements logic is a part of mathematics, social history (for example, family studies) is a kind of retrospective sociology, some part of the study of literature is contained in linguistics. Of more interest and importance, however, is the kind of really substantial innovation to be found in the work of philosophers like Russell and Wittgenstein, historians like Namier, critics like Leavis. Of these four only Leavis was a full-time academic for most of his adult life and even then it was in a marginal and rather angrily detached way. The others had only fitful and more or less idiosyncratic university connections.

That suggests something that is independently altogether credible: true innovation in the humanities, as distinguished from the preservation of a tradition of scholarly understanding, is rare, unpredictable and not an object that can be institutionally planned for or cultivated. But our present conception of the academic profession, and so of the way in which new entrants ought to be prepared for it, rests on a different assumption, which is that the ideal academic is a creative virtuoso in his field. From that the requirement follows that in order to qualify, a candidate must, in his graduate work, make an original contribution to knowledge in his field. A further result is the rather large number of academics who do not really compensate for a certain barbarousness of specialisation in the their fields by the capacity to make a real addition to them. We should shift the emphasis from pioneering to cultivation.

I am inclined to suspect, furthermore, that what is true of the humanities is at least partially applicable to the natural and social sciences. Direct involvement, in the manner of an apprentice, in research work in natural or social science is essential for those who are going to be researchers proper in those fields. But a fairly advanced understanding of science is needed by many whose careers will not consist in directly enlarging its scope. The management of science-based industries and such jobs as journalism, banking and public administration come to mind in this connection. If the work of conveying understanding of the sciences appropriate to these purposes is carried on under the same institutional umbrella as the fostering of original research in them, the two activities should be recognised to be as different as they are.

Reality is perhaps closer to what I have said ought to be the case than might at first appear. Plenty of respected academics after a ritual obeisance to the virtuoso principle with their Ph.D.'s publish nothing much more afterward. But the principle does take its toll, particularly on candidates for entrance to the academic profession. The painfully long interval between B.A. and Ph.D. in most cases provides a pool of inexpensive teaching labour for universities at the cost of a good deal of distress to those who supply it. For the graduate student in the humanities who is aiming at an academic career, or in the sciences, aiming either at an academic career or at a science-related one, the style of dissertation ordinarily exacted, which is what drags out the length of the course, is really irrelevant.

Invited to talk about the philosophy of graduate education I have allowed myself the indulgence of unpracticality. I have argued that the main role of the academic graduate school is and ought to be the training of university teachers, and that there is no compelling reason why the non-academic professional school should be associated with it in the university. I have argued that it is indeed the university teacher and not the advancer of knowledge through research, with whom the academic graduate school should concern itself. Research proper could well be carried on, as it increasingly is, in separate institutes, which would train their new entrants as apprentices. The aim of the academic graduate school should not be the production of virtuosos, since all that is achieved if that goal is pursued is for the most part anxious and hollow imitations of the rare and gifted ideal. What can be trained is the person equipped with a lively understanding of the current state of discussion in an intellectual domain and where, as particularly in the humanities, it is appropriate, of the way in which it arrived at the position it now occupies. Starting from a rather narrowly vocational conception of the immediate aims of the academic graduate school, I hope I have arrived at a liberal conclusion about the manner in which it should pursue it.

*Published in* The Philosophy and Future of Graduate Education, *edited by William K. Frankena (Ann Arbor: University of Michigan Press, 1980).*

# The Idea of A University:
# Newman's and Others'

## 1. Newman's achievement

Perhaps the most remarkable of the many noteworthy features of Newman's *The Idea of a University* is its originality. The institution itself was at least seven and a half centuries old when he wrote, if we trace it back no further than its first full realisation in Paris around 1100. A hundred years more and there is legally specialised Bologna; a hundred years before that, medically specialised Salerno. One could even go further, to Plato's Academy and Aristotle's Lyceum. In the early 1850s, when he wrote and delivered the original discourses, there was still no general study of the essential nature of universities.

There had been some colourful, but not very critical, histories, particularly the seventeenth-century chronicles of Paris by du Boulay and of Oxford by Anthony à Wood. Newman refers to them in his *Rise and Progress of Universities* as he does also to Huber, whose book on English universities had been translated by Newman's younger brother Francis in 1843. Rashdall is uncomplimentary about Huber. He wrote, it 'is one of the most worthless university histories it has been my lot to peruse: it may be described as a history written without materials'.

More to Newman's purpose, there was available to him a good deal of polemical writing about universities. In the seventeenth century Bacon, Hobbes and Locke all condemned the universities as intellectual museums, trading in an ossified and corrupted Aristotelianism. Bacon, in *The Advancement of Learning*, had gone on to make a number of concrete recommendations, for the most part still to the point: calling for an enlarged role for fundamental research, better stipends for lecturers, for laboratory equipment, for visitation and assessment, for more contact between the universities of different countries and for the inclusion of neglected subjects in the field of recognised studies. Hobbes had a special hostility to universities as strongholds from which the churches, whether

Catholic or Puritan, could seek to undermine the secular state.

Nearer to hand for Newman were two large-scale assaults on the English university system (and Oxford in particular) launched by the *Edinburgh Review*. The first of these was in the years 1808 and 1809, Sydney Smith being one of the authors contributing to the series. This onslaught was replied to with affronted dignity by Provost Copleston of Oriel in 1810, head of the college when Newman arrived there in 1823. His views will be examined in detail later, as will Newman's considerable, and clearly acknowledged, indebtedness to him.

In 1830 another set of criticisms of Oxford by the learned Scottish metaphysician, Sir William Hamilton, came out in the *Edinburgh Review*. These were much more substantial than the rather crude debating-points of Sydney Smith and his colleagues. But Newman made no reference to them or to Hamilton's interesting historical theory of the decline of Oxford from its medieval glory. Hamilton's thesis was that Oxford had been perverted from being a university proper, dominated by professors, into a federation of colleges, dominated by tutors. Real education of the intellectually deserving had been supplanted by the practice of applying a superficial polish to young gentlemen, the advancement of learning by self-indulgent exploitation of endowments. Hamilton's essays had been reprinted in 1852, the year before Newman's lectures in Dublin, in his *discussions of Philosophy and Literature*. Newman not only makes no mention of them but does not address the point of view they advance. With his readiness to remit research to academies, he would clearly not have been in sympathy with them.

Essentially Newman was correct, then, when he wrote in his ninth discourse: 'I have been in want neither of authoritative principles or distinct precedent, but of treatises *in extenso* on the subject on which I have written – the finished work of writers who, by their acknowledged judgement and erudition, might furnish me for my private guidance with a running instruction on each point which successively came under review' (*IU*, p. xx).

It is worth noticing that there has been nothing very much since *The Idea of a University*, which first came out in 1853 and achieved its final and complete form twenty years later, to compare with it in largeness of design. Ortega y Gasset's *Mission of the University*, Walter Moberly's *The University and the Modern World* and Clark Kerr's *Uses of the University* are the nearest approaches. There was a cascade of books inspired by the student disturbances of the late 1960s. But these were *livres d'occasion* and none of them seems to have survived its historical moment.

As for the matter of predecessors: it is significant that 'Bruce Truscot', the ardent champion of British Redbrick universities, refers to no one who wrote earlier than Abraham Flexner in 1930, except for Newman.

## 2. The lectures and their publication

Only five of the nine discourses which make up the first and principal part of The Idea of University were actually delivered as lectures in 1852. All nine were published in 1853 as Discourses on University Education. Lectures and Essays on University Subjects, a miscellaneous collection of pieces written or delivered in the intervening years, came out in 1858. Both were brought together under the name of The Idea of a University in 1873, the discourses having been lightly revised. An earlier plan to bring them out with all references to the project of a Catholic university in Dublin removed from them was abandoned. There had also been an abridged version of the discourses in 1859 under the title Scope and Nature of University Education.

It was to the finished work, under its familiar title, that Pater referred in his essay on Style in 1888, describing it as 'the perfect handling of a theory' and associating it with Lycidas as a perfect poem and Esmond as a perfect fiction.

The original lectures were very successful. Newman described them as a 'hit', a pleasingly early date – and unexpectedly cultivated user – for that sense of the term. But the immediate enthusiasm did not persist. Newman was disappointed by the lack of general interest excited by their publication in book form. But, as Pater's remark shows, they eventually won general recognition and admiration. They may have been thought at first to have been of only local Irish and sectarian Catholic interest.

The circumstances of their composition make their achievement of classic status, when only minimally revised, very remarkable. The Catholic university of Dublin was a project that had been endorsed by the Pope. Newman had been appointed its rector in 1851. His immediate purpose, that of persuading Irish Catholics to support the new university, was nevertheless confronted with a number of serious obstacles.

There were two sets of people he needed to convince: the clergy who would be called upon to authorise the undertaking, and the middle-class Irish Catholic laity, who would have to pay for it. Among Newman's problems were inescapable things about him calculated to arouse suspicion in these two constituencies. In the first place he was an Englishman and so naturally to be suspected of limited understanding of Irish conditions and limited sympathy for Irish needs. Secondly, he was a recent convert to the faith. Only seven years had passed since he had been received into the Church. His Englishness and his long period as an ardent, and often combative, Anglican added up to a kind of double Oxonian burden to be carried by one who was intending to create and lead an idealised version of Oxford for the Catholics of Ireland.

From the point of view of the Irish clergy he was not reliably Catholic enough. He was imperfectly saturated with the type of uncritical piety favoured by Irish Catholicism. What they wanted was a seminary, in which theology was dominant and everything was under the strictest clerical control. There was little place for intellectual culture in this conception. But there was not much more in the university as it was conceived by the laity. Their aim was an institution in which the monopoly of the Protestant establishment over entry to the professions was brought to an end, an instrument for the social and economic advance of capable members of the variously oppressed majority of the Irish population. For them Newman was too unworldly, above all in his worship of intellectual culture and comparative indifference to useful knowledge.

There is a measure of irony in the fact that the one part of the actual Catholic university that really succeeded was the school of medicine. Nevertheless in the four years during which Newman was head of it as a working institution it seems to have been a lively and attractive place.

One other unfavourable circumstance needs to be recalled, a more strictly personal one. The discourses were composed at the period of Newman's trial, and absurd condemnation, for libelling Achilli, a lecherous friar who had been unfrocked by the Inquisition. The fact is mentioned in *the Idea of a University* only in its dignified and moving dedication to the 'many friends and benefactors... who, by their resolute prayers and penance, and by their generous stubborn efforts, and by their munificent alms, have broken for him the stress of a great anxiety'.

## 3. The idea of an idea

Newman's final and best title for his book conveys an account of its nature and method. It is not any kind of comparative or historical study of the university as a widespread and developing institution. For that one must go to *The Rise and Progress of Universities*. It is not a detailed set of organisational recommendations. It is, rather, a philosophical inquiry into the essential nature of the university, an attempt at a deduction of its ideal form from first principles.

I would suggest that Newman got the word from Coleridge and in particular from Coleridge's *Constitution of Church and State*, whose title is completed with the phrase 'according to the Idea of each'. Coleridge is admirably explicit about what he means by the term. 'By an *idea*, I mean (in this instance) that conception of a thing, which is not abstracted from any particular state, form, or mode, in which the thing may happen to exist at this or at that time; nor yet generalised from any number or succession of such forms or modes; but which is given by the knowledge of *its ultimate aim*.'

This is one of the two main ways in which Plato presents his theory of idea or forms. In it they are taken to be ideals or paradigms, complete and perfect versions of the kind or class of things within which their actual instances fall. That account of ideas or forms does not combine at all comfortably with the conception of them as the nature common to all the instances of any class or kind, to everything to which a given general term or 'common name' can be correctly applied. Plato recognised the difficulty of conceiving an ideal paradigm of mud or dirt and also, if with less distress, of artefacts like beds.

The conception recurs in Aristotle's doctrine of essence, at least where that is taken to be a thing's final cause, its ideal end or goal, the form or set of characteristics of its perfect realisation. In Hegel's hands the idea is historicised, taken to be the ultimate fulfilment to which some thing or kind of thing is striving in a progressive way. The word occurs, in very much Newman's sense, in T.S. Eliot's *Idea of a Christian Society* and a word close to it in Ward's *Ideal of a Christian Church*.

There is nothing very metaphysical about Newman's conception of the idea he is elaborating. He proposes to rely on common sense and natural reason. 'The principles on which I would conduct the enquiry', he says, 'are attainable by the mere experience of life... and they are recognised by common sense.' He goes on, 'I am concerned with questions, not simply of immutable truth, but of practice and expedience.'

Nevertheless his approach is of high generality. 'I am investigating in the abstract, and am determining what is in itself right and true.' There is, after all, hardly any reference in his discourses to the special circumstances of mid-nineteenth-century Ireland. The historical knowledge revealed in *The Rise and Progress of Universities* may be at work in the background of his thinking, but it is not explicitly referred to or called upon. 'For the moment I know nothing, so to say, of history. I take things as I find them.' Nor are there references of a comparative kind to the current state of the universities of France and Germany. Nor does he engage in any sort of systematic consideration of possibilities that had not been realised in the essentially Oxonian model of an ideal university which he was delineating. He does not even consider the example of the early Italian universities of Salerno and Bologna, which were confined to a single discipline (law and medicine, respectively) and were run by their students, not their masters. Research is excluded in his preface on general grounds and without consideration of its pursuit in actual universities. In neglecting Hamiltion's criticism of Oxford in the 1830s, he fails to meet the claims of professors, as actively engaged in the advancement of knowledge, over those of tutors, who merely reproduce what they have learnt.

Certainly, writing in 1852, Newman had little to help him in the respects I have mentioned. Matthew Arnold's *Schools and Universities on the Continent* did not come out until 1868. Adequate histories were not available until 1885 with Denifle, the late 1880s with Paulsen and 1895 with Rashdall.

J.M. Cameron has convincingly argued that, as a philosopher, Newman is a fairly traditional British empiricist, deriving his ideas from Locke and Butler, and familiar with Hume. He was more or less innocent of knowledge of scholastic philosophy, although he had an extensive grasp of the Fathers. But that consideration is not needed to explain the absence of any suggestion of a return to some, perhaps idealised, version of the medieval university. To Newman it would be unattractive in three ways. In its preoccupation with logical disputatiousness it was too uncultured. In the unregulated, Chaucerian life of its poor scholars it was too undisciplined. In its fostering of mere argumentativeness and neglect of taste and a sense of the past it was too rationalistic. But Newman, like Oxford itself, kept on from the medieval university an insistence that training in arts – more broadly conceived, however, than the trivium, the quadrivium and the three philosophies – must precede professional training in theology, medicine or law.

Newman's basic loyalty was rather to the educational ideal of Renaissance humanism in its anglicised form, relying on Ciceronian Latin to produce the gentleman, a demure and respectable version of the virtuoso. But he was fully prepared to countenance an admixture of Renaissance naturalism. His view that natural science should be a university subject is congruous with his admiration for Bacon. Dwight Culler has perceptively remarked that unlike most nineteenth century religious thinkers, Newman was not really afraid of science. Since his faith was of an inward, essentially moral, nature he was indifferent to natural religion and so unaffected by the way in which progressing science undermined arguments from nature to God.

### 4. Copleston and Whewell

The spaciousness of Newman's achievement in *The Idea of a University*, for all the modesty of its specific occasion, is clearly brought out if it is compared with the defences of the traditional English university published some years earlier by Edward Copleston and William Whewell. In 1810 Copleston's *Replies to the Calumnies of the Edinburgh Reviewers* came out in response to their attacks on Oxford of 1808 and 1809. Whewell's *Principles of English University Education* of 1837 followed on from a slightly earlier dispute with Hamilton and it develops a root-and-branch demolition of Hamilton's professorial doctrine.

Copleston had been a fellow of Oriel since 1795 and had played an energetic part under Provost Eveleigh in carrying into effect two important reforms: the introduction of serious examinations for classified honours degrees and the opening of fellowships for competition exclusively on merit. Since Oxford had taken these two large steps, there is an understandable note of affront in his *Replies*. He was provost of Oriel during its greatest years, from 1814 to 1826, leaving three years after Newman's arrival for, briefly, a deanery and, a year later, the bishopric of Llandaff. Whewell spent his entire career at Trinity College, Cambridge and was master of it from 1841 until his death in 1866. He wrote copiously on the philosophy and history of science and on ethics and in the first of these three fields with great, and still perhaps not adequately recognised, distinction. Both men were remarkable for physical strength and vigour, appropriate equipment for controversialists.

The first two calumnies to which Copleston addresses himself, in a style of fairly tumultuous indignation which stands in the sharpest possible contrast to Newman's subtle and fluent persuasiveness, are of relatively minor importance. Oxford, he insists, does not teach Aristotle's physics; nor is mathematical instruction confined to elementary geometry. Although that was true as far as it went, it did not go very far. There was no serious teaching of physics, which was no more than a possible academic hobby for an interested handful, rather in the manner of archery in an institution addicted to team games. and after a good start early in the century, mathematical study dwindled.

Even less important, although all very well in its way, was his merciless demolition of some ignorant comments on an Oxford edition of Strabo by an insufficiently equipped Scotchman.

The nerve of Copleston's case for Oxford teaching lies in his defence of classical education against the charge that it lacks utility. The production of wealth is neither the only nor the supreme end of human action in general or university education in particular. The indispensable necessity of material provision for mankind does not endow it with prime value or, indeed, any value to speak of on its own. The community rightly expects more of an individual than his professional skill. And a generally cultivated education prepares a man for professional training and enhances the quality of his exercise of his skill when he has acquired it. These thoughts reappear in the fifth and seventh of Newman's discourses. In the latter Newman writes of Copleston and acknowledges his debt to him.

Whewell's defence of the English university, and pre-eminently Cambridge, is dry and almost military where Copleston's is luxuriant and judicial. With Copleston and Newman, but more emphatically, he holds that university study should be a business of the active appropriation of knowledge, not its mere absorption. From this principle he derives a distinction between the practical and speculative sides of a university education. In practical learning the student is made to do something, to prove a theorem in mathematics or to translate from an unfamiliar language in classics. In speculative learning, large and interesting vistas into the unknown are opened to him by professorial lectures. Hamilton's preference for professors to tutors is persuasively inverted. The temptation to quote is irresistible:

Professorial lectures appear to have very small attraction for the greater part of Englishmen... Even when the matter is interesting, and the manner striking, how rarely does the lecturer collect and keep together a voluntary audience in England! And if his topic be a subject of exact science or critical research, we are certain that his hearers will soon be reduced to a very few students, and perhaps a few personal friends. In the metropolis, most persons have known of many admirable lectures, delivered in various institutions, on subjects even of great popular interest, as geology or political economy, where general neglect was bestowed, so undeservedly, as to be a matter of grief and indignation to those who attended.

Practical learning, in Whewell's sense of the phrase, brings about clear ideas and a capacity for rigorous deduction. Civilisation and the progress of knowledge on which it depends do indeed require speculative thinking. But speculation must always be controlled by rigorous testing. Speculation alone, without the benefits of practical learning, leads to obscurity and vacant wrangling. Of the two practical fields, classics, by imparting a mastery of Greek and Latin, makes its students inheritors of a common European estate of culture. But classics by itself is not enough. Without mathematical stiffening it tends to give rise to mere elegance. Mathematics 'imparts the idea of fixed and immutable truth'.

A consequential advantage of practical learning is that it engenders the respect of students for the inevitably superior expertise of their tutors. Professorial lecturing, on the other hand, nourishes criticism. It is to this aspect of the professorial system, dominant in France and Germany, that the propensity of students in those countries to absurd rebelliousness can be traced. The direct instruction of a tutor inspires a love of knowledge for its own sake, as a result of which the knowledge is firmly and indestructibly acquired. That is much preferable to the examination system which accompanies professorial teaching, for that appeals to the student's love of distinction, and knowledge acquired for that reason, and merely got up for exams, is soon lost.

Whewell proceeds further to the question of discipline in a university or college, including compulsory chapel about which he felt strongly. The freedom allowed in German universities depraves the character of the students and corrupts their manners. It is impossible not to quote again:

Even tempers of great levity and stubbornness, if they are met at every turn of their extravagant and self-willed motions with

the calm but severe countenance of a system of rules like these
– imposing punishment for transgression, so long as it can be
ascribed to thoughtlessness, but pointing constantly to the
door, if transgression is persisted in – are awed and tamed; and
in a little while moulded to their position; while the great body
of young Englishmen, of the condition of those who come to
the Universities, conform, with a generous obedience of spirit,
to rules which are the very essence of the institution in which
they are placed, and of which all the better natures among them
see and feel the value.

This solemn austerity seems very remote from the high jinks and
billiard-room of the Catholic university of Dublin in Newman's time.
   There are evident anticipations of parts of Newman's doctrine
about universities in Copleston and Hawkins. He shares Copleston's
distaste for the idea that material utility is the touchstone of education and in his seventh discourse – 'knowledge in relation to
professional skill' – he repeats and endorses Copleston's arguments
on the topic. With Whewell he agrees that university education
should be a matter of active appropriation of knowledge, although
he expresses the position – in his sixth discourse: 'knowledge viewed
in relation to learning' – in a less breezy and hard-edged way.
   Despite these partial affinities Newman's *Idea* is of a completely
different order of magnitude from the others. It retains its large
perspective throughout and is nowhere encumbered with the refutation of mere silliness or ignorance of the most passing interest, as
is Copleston, nor grimly determined to find ironclad justifications
for almost every detail of the status quo in Trinity College,
Cambridge at the moment of writing, as is Whewell.

## 5. Newman's main theses

There are five main theses in *The Idea of a University*. The first of
them is that a university properly so called is a place of *teaching*, in
which *universal knowledge* is taught. In his preface Newman is at
pains to insist that teaching, the prime office of the university, is not
merely distinct from research or the advancement of knowledge but
should be carried on altogether separately from it. By 'universal
knowledge' Newman does not mean absolutely everything that
possible could be taught, but all theoretical subjects of a fair degree
of generality.

THE IDEA OF A UNIVERSITY

His second thesis is that theology is knowledge. It should, therefore, be taught in a university. It is certainly not a mere sentiment, not what Matthew Arnold was soon to call it: morality touched with emotion. As will appear, although Newman is very clear as to what theology is not, the exclusions are so lavish as to make it something of a problem to work out what it positively is.

Thirdly, he contends that knowledge is a unity. The intrinsic sense of this thesis is not altogether clear. But the purpose to which Newman puts it is definite enough. It is intimately related, almost as object to image, to his conception of intellectual culture, which is not high expertise in some particular branch of learning, the attribute of the scholarly specialist, but a just appreciation of the bearing of the different departments of universal knowledge on each other. A scholar who lacks intellectual culture will be the grotesque pedant of traditional comedy. One does not need to be a scholar to possess it, although one will have to understand what scholarship is. No student can hope to master more than a part of universal knowledge. A university can compensate for that human limitation in two ways. Collegiate residence, by bringing students of different subjects together, ensures that they will become acquainted with subjects other than their own. Secondly, it will impart, perhaps explicitly, perhaps in a more subliminal way by the manner in which it teaches its subjects, a 'philosophic habit', a 'science of sciences', an understanding of the strengths and limitations of the various constituents of universal knowledge.

The fourth, and really central, thesis is that knowledge, or, more strictly, the intellectual culture that acquisition of knowledge in a university should provide, is a good in itself.

But, fifthly and finally, it is not an *absolute good*. The ideal gentlemanly figure it produces is still a limited and imperfect being. It needs to be supplemented with morality and religious faith. It does not, indeed, promote sin, but it may divert energy from the eradication of sin. It is also calculated to turn the mind away from the grosser, more sensual sins. For these reasons it needs church control, especially since the scientific way of thinking can undermine religious faith, although it is not inevitable that it should do so.

It has been argued against Newman, by Dwight Culler for example, that there is a contradiction between his faith and his commitment to humanism and intellectual culture. There is certainly a tension and a number of weak points in the structure of Newman's doctrine which will be considered later. What is quite inescapable is that it is impossible to reconcile Newman's affirmation of the goodness in itself of intellectual culture with several of his best-known and most impassioned assertions. He once said, 'it would be a gain to the country were it vastly more superstitious.' Intellectual culture would seem to be in head-on collision with superstition as ordinarily understood: 'credulity regarding the supernatural, irrational fear of the unknown or mysterious'.

In an even more intoxicated vein is this famous effusion:

> She [the Church] holds that it were better for the sun and moon to drop from heaven, for the earth to fail and for all the many millions who are upon it to die of starvation in extremest agony, as far as temporal affliction goes, than that one soul, I will not say should be lost, but should commit one single venial sin, should tell one wilful untruth.

To ascribe such frenzied cruelty to the Church must itself be an untruth, even if hysterical rather than wilful.

## 6. Definition of the university

The first, since less controversial, element of Newman's definition of the university to consider is his assertion that it must teach universal knowledge. When first ascribing that task to the university, his use of the phrase 'as the name shows' suggests that he might be laying some argumentative weight on a mistaken piece of etymology. A *universitas*, in medieval usage, is simply a corporation and a *studium generale* derives its generality not from the range of subjects it embraces, but from its openness to students from anywhere and from the generality of its degrees as licences to teach.

Up to a point this defining characteristic of universities is simply a recognition of actual fact. Except in their earliest Italian stages and ever since the commanding model of Paris has been dominant, universities have everywhere taken the whole of knowledge as their province, at least in principle. Newman's real reason for insisting on it is his conception of the essential unity of knowledge and his connected idea of intellectual culture as a critical awareness of the scope of knowledge as a whole. That conception is presupposed by his thesis that if theology is knowledge, and, of course, he thinks it is, it is an indispensable part of a university's field of activities.

Newman's idea of knowledge, of the sort that should be conveyed in universities at any rate, is not unlimitedly hospitable. It does not include practical arts, the more concrete and earthy varieties of Ryle's knowing how; it does not include non-theoretical skills like cookery, car-driving or hotel management. Nor does it cover mere bodies of raw information, like the history of league cricket or air-mail stamps. To be studied in a university knowledge must be theoretically serious. Neither of these restrictions is an obstacle to the inclusion of theology in university studies.

His second defining characteristic, that universities should not engage in research, but should concentrate on teaching, is more debatable. In *The Idea of a University* he is altogether unequivocal about this. Research and teaching, he argues, call on different qualities in their exponents. Furthermore, the work of research and discovery needs special conditions of quiet and seclusion which a university full of lively students cannot provide.

At the time Newman was writing, absence of research was as conspicuous a feature of English universities as the attempt to teach 'universal knowledge', indeed much more so. That had been the case at any rate since the end of the seventeenth century. Hume, Bentham and Mill; Gibbon, Hallam and Macaulay; Johnson, Coleridge and Hazlitt were more or less metropolitan men of letters. Only in the more municipal universities of Scotland was there any substantial positive contribution to knowledge, as in the work of Thomas Reid, William Robertson, Adam Smith and Adam Ferguson.

In the middle of the nineteenth century that was beginning to change. Whewell and Mansel were followed by Sidgwick and T.H. Green; Freeman and Froude were at least Regius professors; Matthew Arnold and Pater had, in their different ways, a kind of loose university anchorage. For more than a century the universities of the English-speaking world and of western Europe have increasingly monopolised the advancement of learning. But although Newman's second defining characteristic was in fact as prevalent in universities as his first, it was not for that reason, but out of some kind of conformism that he espoused it. I am inclined to suspect that there was a circumstantial aspect to Newman's contention that universities should confine themselves to teaching. The pursuit of new knowledge is inevitably going to lead to more or less unsettling novelties which will tend to undermine the authority of knowledge as traditionally accumulated. Where Whewell had objected to the *rebelliousness* inspired by the professorial, knowledge-advancing university, Newman had set himself against *viewiness*, the excited enthusiasm for intellectual novelties fostered by periodicals, which we now see, perhaps, as one of the cultural glories of the nineteenth century. He wanted universities to act as a counterweight to that influence, as strongholds of established traditional learning. It was a notion calculated to reassure his immediate audience.

In *The Idea of a University* the alternative place for research which he proposes is academies. These had had a great past in Italy and France and had an important living example in Britain in the Royal Society. That division of intellectual labour has been generally adopted in eastern Europe and Russia and, in unpropitious circumstances, has much impressive work to its credit. It is, no doubt, congenial to despotic or authoritarian societies.

The depth of Newman's conviction in this matter is put in question by something he says in *The Rise and Progress of Universities*.

> Though the Roman schools have more direct bearing on the subsequent rise of the medieval Universities, they are not so exact an anticipation of its type, as the Alexandrian Museum. They differ from the Museum, as being for the most part, as it would appear, devoted to the education of the very young, without any reference to the advancement of science. No list of writers or discoveries, no local or historical authorities, can be adduced, from the date of Augustus to that of Justinian, to rival the fame of Alexandria; we hear on the contrary much of the elements of knowledge, the Trivium and Quadrivium. (*Historical Sketches*, 1873, vol. I, p. 100)

Nevertheless there is one kind of highly successful academic institution which conforms closely to Newman's prescription. That is the American liberal arts college, which is always called a college and not a university on the counter-Newmanian ground that it does not contain a graduate school. Colleges like Swarthmore and Oberlin are as highly regarded as any as places for undergraduates to study at. Indeed they are often preferred for that purpose to larger and better-known establishments because their professors actually teach undergraduates rather than concentrating on research, slightly mitigated by a bit of graduate instruction.

## 7. Theology is knowledge

After defining the university in his preface. Newman goes on in his first, introductory discourse to meet various possible objections to his project. He affirms, quite properly, that his views have not been specially got up for the occasion; that the matter at issue, a Catholic university for Ireland, is not a matter of immutable truth to be referred to church authority, but a question of practice and expediency, to be settled by the natural powers of reason; and that the project has been authorised by the bishops of Ireland and, above all, the Pope.

The main exposition is resumed in the second discourse, which is addressed to the question: should theology be excluded from university teaching? Given that the university teaches universal knowledge, he replies, it should teach theology if theology is a branch of knowledge.

In the present age that question has a slightly different inflection from the one it had when Newman was writing. He was not concerned with the now common conviction that the dogmas of religion are simply false, and theology therefore on the same footing as astrology and alchemy, but with the ideas that still prevail among more or less defeatist friends of religion that its beliefs are not really knowledge but rather a sentiment or attitude toward the world. Faith, he insists, cannot be detached from truth and knowledge; revelation is revelation of truth. Against the exponents of 'natural religion' who argue to God from the evidences of design in nature, he follows Hume. If to believe in God is just a way of looking at nature, then he is not a supreme being separate from nature and there can be no science of God. In an agreeable anticipation of the present, he asks if the then bishop of Durham believes in the same God as Catholics do. Their God is a supreme being beyond nature, not a constitutional monarch.

That is a characteristic expression of the essential inwardness of Newman's faith. It rests on conscience, not external evidences, on a sense of radical moral imperfection which he takes to imply an absolute moral authority.

What precisely Newman means by theology, or the science of God, seems to be something much more contracted than would ordinarily be understood by the term. In the third discourse he defines it as 'the truths we know about God put into a system'. That remark comes at the end of a long series of statements about what theology is not. It is not in itself Catholic; it is not 'physical theology'; it is not the polemical mobilisation of 'the evidences of religion'; it is not 'that vague thing called "Christianity" or "our common Christianity"'; it is not acquaintance with the scriptures.

After all these excisions not very much is left apart from an abstract monotheism, affirming an invisible being endowed with intellect and will, creator of the world, self-dependent, eternal, supremely good, governor and judge of all that he has created. That is not Christianity, although it is the crowning part of it. It is certainly only a very small part of what was then and is now the substance of theological instruction, which embraces the study of the Bible, the history of the Jews, the first Christians and the Church, moral and pastoral matters and much else.

It might be objected that the things I see him as discarding were thought by Newman only to be not the whole of theology. But the words in which he describes them are too dismissive to sustain the objection. It might also be said that, since God created the world and was incarnated in it as Christ, everything is really comprised in his 'science of God'. But neither the creation of the world nor the incarnation is *deducible* from the existence of a God like Newman's; both are free, unconstrained acts, operations of grace. For belief in the divinity of Christ the Bible is indispensable. In repudiating *acquaintance* with the Bible as part or all of theology may he not have meant to leave in a less casual attitude to scripture, perhaps its *reverent acceptance*. If that is to be at all intellectual it must presuppose acquaintance. If he had intended to keep the study of the Bible within theology he would have had to speak of mere acquaintance or something of the sort. The part of theology in which he was himself most expert, the study of the Fathers, is not among his exclusions, but it does not form an intelligible part of the science of God as he conceives it.

The question of the cognitive status of theology is still a live one, even in an age in which the multiplicity of quite distinct religions is at the forefront of consciousness because of improved communications and the failure of the missionary enterprise together with the imperialist assumptions which underlaid it. The general drift in universities is from theology to 'religious studies', from the authoritative exposition of a faith to comparative religion, the study of religion as a natural, earthly, human phenomenon.

In Newman's own university it is only in this century that the requirement has been dropped that examiners in theology should be Anglican clergymen. There is a conceivable middle path between a strictly external and a strictly internal attitude to religious teaching in a university. It has a measure of analogy to that which obtains in the teaching of law. Many from time to time disobey the law of the land or think it mistaken or even, in rare, passionate cases, deny its validity altogether. But the law of the land is what is taught as law, with comparative law as an optional attachment. In both fields of study the requirements of the profession to which it ordinarily leads exercise a formative influence. That is too pragmatic or worldly a solution of the problem to have appealed to Newman.

Newman's minimalism about theology is peculiar given the audience he was primarily addressing, who were not only Christians, but Irish Catholic Christians. They would have no doubt of the truth of the creeds and of what might be called the consistent residue of the Bible, as authoritatively interpreted (for they were not, of course, fundamentalists). He could expect agreement to the proposition that theology, conceived much more inclusively than it was by him, is a branch of knowledge. It may be that he was concerned to persuade a wider constituency than his immediate audience and also, in a philosophical spirit, to take as little for granted as possible.

## 8. The unity of knowledge

Newman's third thesis, that knowledge is a unity, is the main theme, whatever their ostensible topics, of the third, fourth and fifth discourses. For convenience, to secure the advantages of the division of labour and to take account of the limited powers of the human mind, the field of knowledge as a whole is parcelled out into separate sciences. But the essential unity of the object of knowledge must be accommodated in university teaching if it is to be genuinely educative, if the evils of what we now call specialism are to be avoided.

His basic argument for the thesis is brief and unconvincingly formal. Knowledge is one because its object is one, namely the universe. Behind this lies a more logically forceful, but more disputable, assumption: that everything there is is either God or God's creation. More specifically he argues that man is the topic of many different sciences. 'We treat of him,' he says, 'respectively as physiologists, or as moral philosophers, or as writers of economics, or of politics, or as theologians' (*IU*, p.55). Truth consists of facts and of their relations and those relations make the facts they relate into an integrated whole.

The relatedness of facts does not entail that they all integrate into a single all-inclusive group but the conclusion has much to be said for it. In the first place the recognised sciences stand in various relations of dependence on one another. Biology presupposes chemistry and chemistry physics; all natural and many social sciences presuppose mathematics. History draws on politics, economics and psychology; the study of literature on linguistics and history. Sciences melt into one another at the edges and, with the passage of time, the boundaries between them are redrawn, as witness the recent disintegration of geography, whose constituent parts are being redistributed.

Recognition of the precariousness of the boundaries between disciplines leads some people to say that the conventional divisions of learning are merely practical or administrative in nature. It is in that spirit that much is heard of the cross-fertilisation of disciplines. But there is also the possibility of cross-sterilisation. It would seem to be realised in the often quite successful attempts of pseudo-scientific ideologies like Marxism and psychoanalysis to take over the softer, more viewy subjects: history, social theory, the study of literature and art.

Nevertheless disciplines overlap, their exponents need to know what is going on elsewhere and, a point Newman insists on, how their speciality stands in relation to others. What he looks to to bring about a sense of the unity of knowledge is what he calls 'a science of sciences' or a 'philosophic habit'. He is quite explicit, in the paragraph immediately following his introduction of the idea of a science of sciences, that it is not theology, which, he affirms, is one of the sciences of which it is the science. So, although it is the central element in theology as he conceives it – namely God – that is the source of the unity of knowledge, theology is not the discipline with is to provide a sense of that unity to the university student.

Newman's science of the sciences does seem more like philosophy than anything else, even if it is philosophy in idealised form. More specifically it is, in its way, a theory of knowledge. As things actually are, the theory of knowledge is unfitted for the task he had in mind because of a certain silliness, abetted by a consequent introversion. The silliness is that, since Descartes, the philosophical theory of knowledge has been preoccupied with the refutation of doubts, which, however ingeniously reasoned for, no sane person would seriously entertain, about the existence of material things, minds other than one's own, the past and laws of nature. Introversion inevitably follows since most intelligent people do not see the point of refuting what no one – the refuters included – can seriously believe.

That is a somewhat philistine exaggeration. But it does serve to mark off the traditional core of epistemology from what might be called general methodology, an examination of the methods of various forms of inquiry and of the justification of the conclusions at which they arrive. That is pursued piecemeal in philosophy as it is by the philosophies of particular fields: scepticism-rebutting, epistemology does provide a crucial service for these special philosophies. It sets out in general terms the main sources of knowledge (perception, memory, inference, testimony and so forth) and offers fairly controversial distinctions between the kinds of propositions in which claims to knowledge are expressed (as, for example, empirical, analytic and evaluative). It makes explicit the principles of reasoning and the difference between proof and confirmation, knowledge and rational belief.

When a familiarity with this epistemological apparatus is combined with a fairly thorough understanding of one field of knowledge, or, preferably, more than one, a valuable result ensues. It is the acquisition of a kind of intellectual taste, an ethics of inquiry or belief, a sense of the relative strength of the claims to credibility of different bodies of alleged knowledge, a critical awareness of how these bodies of alleged knowledge stand in relation to each other. That, I believe, is what Newman meant by the phrase 'a science of sciences' and which he took to be the most important constituent of the intellectual culture which it is the office of a university to cultivate.

He did not take it to be a part of the formal curriculum but as something that would be absorbed by mixing with students on subjects other than one's own, by intellectually civilised teaching, by critical reflection on one's field of study, as opposed to loading its detail into one's memory. A useful addition to it, which he does not mention, makes large recollection of detail unnecessary: the knowledge of how to find things out, where to look them up.

The aim of Newman's prescription is the truly educated person, as contrasted with the pure scholar, the intellectual all-rounder, a C.B. Fry or Owen-Smith, not an over-muscled monster, an Arnold Schwarzenegger or Fatima Whitbread. That could have been a further reason, whether it was operative in Newman or not, for excluding research from the ideal university, since the researcher is likely to be a scholarly pedant. Whately, perhaps, was the sort of teacher he had in mind: Pusey he would have appointed to an academy.

## 9. Intellectual excellence a good in itself

The intrinsic value of intellectual excellence or intellectual culture, the thing that is imparted by a liberal education in which a 'philosophic habit' is inculcated along with knowledge of some particular subject, is asserted in the fifth discourse and the theme is developed in the two following discourses. A mind cultivated along the lines Newman has laid down may have various kinds of extraneous utility. Intellectual culture may enhance professional skill and, indeed, ordinarily will do so. It may be advantageous from a moral point of view, if only in a negative way, by leading those endowed with it away from the pursuit of grosser bodily pleasures towards that of 'higher things'. He takes it to be less dangerous to religion than specialised learning, which tends to reduce everything outside the specialist's own field to the terms of his speciality.

Newman does not appeal to much in the way of argument to support his principle of the intrinsic goodness of intellectual culture. He mentions the antiquity of the principle as embodied in Aristotle's account of human nature. For Aristotle, the essential differentiating feature of human beings is rationality and he concludes from that that the exercise of reason is the highest form of life. But for Newman, believing, perhaps, with Mill that 'questions of ultimate ends are not amenable to direct proof', it must have seemed enough to distinguish intellectual culture from other things with which it might be confused for its intrinsic excellence to be evident.

In saying that its extraneous utility is a secondary consideration he is emphatic that it is for *enjoyment* before it is for use. That calls to mind the boy who delighted Samuel Johnson by replying to the inquiry as to what he would give to know Greek, that he would give what he had. It is something that anyone, on thoughtful reflection, would like to have. Human beings are not just practically curious; they desire to know for its own sake, are more or less possessed by what Aristotle called wonder.

On the negative side of the argument, Newman follows Copleston closely. A person is more than his specialised professional role. As an end in itself intellectual culture is like health and virtue, but it differs from them in that there is no single English word for it. In fact, the word 'culture', central to the vocabulary of Matthew Arnold, came to be that single English word. For Arnold culture was a familiarity with the best that has been thought and said. But after him the sense of the word became aestheticised: culture turned into familiarity with the best that had been written, painted and composed. Arnold, devoted to Newman, may have derived the term from Newman's phrase 'intellectual culture', preserving the intellectuality in his definition, but adding to it familiarity with imaginative literature. Newman, as will be seen, would not have followed him there. Another possible source, both for Newman and Arnold is the idea of *cultivation*, defined in Coleridge's *Constitution of Church and State* as 'the harmonious development of those qualities and faculties that characterise our humanity'. That is clearly echoed in Arnold's remark: 'culture... leads us... to conceive of true human perfection as a harmonious perfection, developing all sides of our humanity'. And culture has an evident affinity with the German idea of *Kultur*, conveyed into the stream of English thought by Coleridge and Carlyle.

Culture, in Newman's view, like health, or, for that matter, wealth, although good in itself, is not an absolute good. There is a difficulty here in that, although he does not say in so many words that virtue is an, or more logically, *the*, absolute good, that is plainly what he believes. But, if that is the case, the goodness of culture would appear to be only presumptive, dependent on its contribution to virtue. And he is clear that it is not always contributory. It leads people away from the grosser forms of sin but the morality it inspires is of a social, polished kind, as set out in the ethics of Shaftesbury. It creates the gentleman, as described in the famous passage at the end of the eighth discourse; it does not create the saint. But it is saint-hood or, at any rate, holiness to which we are called, to which we must at all times endeavour to approximate.

There is a possible way out of the difficulty in the Catholic doctrine of supererogation and of two types of vocation, one for the religious in which the claims of duty determine every choice, the other for the laity in which the claims of duty extend only to specific acts and forbearances and which leaves room for extra-moral or morally neutral choices. Newman, possibly influenced by his evangelical upbringing in which such a distinction would have no foothold, does not avail himself of it.

An echo of Whewell is to be heard in Newman's insistence in the sixth discourse on liberal education as the active appropriation of knowledge, a process of 'comparing, ordering, digesting' and not mere storing of detailed information in the memory to be regurgitated in examinations. But that is something distinct from the philosophic habit, 'getting a connected view', 'seeing all in its place in the whole'. It is an inevitable acquisition of the pedantic scholar, however narrowly specialised. Education can be thoroughly expert without being liberal.

## 10. *The church and the university*

In the ninth and concluding discourse Newman draws out the consequences of his view that knowledge or intellectual culture is,
although a good in itself, not absolutely good. He has sought to
establish that a university does not exist to serve moral and religious
purposes any more than it exists to cultivate professional skills or
produce merely learned people or, even worse, merely informed
ones. It serves a purpose of its own.

The university, he says, 'concurs with Christianity a certain way,
and then diverges from it; and consequently in the event proves sometimes its serviceable ally, sometimes, from its very resemblance to it,
an insidious and dangerous foe.' He goes on a little later to conclude
that 'a direct and active jurisdiction of the Church over it and in it
is necessary' (*IU*, p. 183–4). Secular knowledge 'gives birth to a rebel-
lious stirring against miracle and mystery' (p. 136). Even in a
Catholic university there can be 'a recognition, indeed, of
Catholicism, but (as if in pretended mercy to it) an adulteration of
its spirit' (p. 187).

Turning specifically to the two main branches, beside the theological, of university study, he says that science excludes religion and
that literature corrupts it. Scientists are usually either indifferent or
positively hostile to religion. They reject the idea of final causes, their
discipline is inductive and progressive where theology is deductive
and based on a fixed and unalterable revelation. Imaginative literature has sinful man as its topic; it is 'the history and science of man
in rebellion'.

He sets out his specific proposals for church surveillance of literary
study in some detail. The church should not exclude but correct it.
It is morally desirable for the young to become acquainted with the
sinful world through study of literature at a university than much
more damagingly when they emerge into that sinful world itself.
Literature, on this view, is to be administered as a kind of inocula-
tion, in a supervised, antiseptic environment.

For his proposals for the church control of science we have to go
further back in the book, to the fourth discourse. There, to show the
tendency of specialists to usurp the field of other specialisms, he
instances the denial by physiologists of the immortality of the soul
and Milman's *History of the Jews*, in which 'a living dignitary of the
Established Church wrote a History of the Jews; in which, with what
I consider at least bad judgement, he took an external view of it, and
hence was led to assimilate it as nearly as possible to a secular history'

(p. 83). Earlier on he had said 'Revealed Religion furnishes facts to the other sciences, which those sciences, left to themselves, would never reach; and it invalidates apparent facts, which, left to themselves, they would imagine. Thus, in the science of history, the preservation of our race in Noah's ark is an historical fact, which history would never arrive at without Revelation' (p. 73).

These corrections of secular error, which at this date it is not easy to take very seriously, occur long before Newman's discussion of the role of the church in the university, at a point where he is concerned with the theoretical, rather than coercive, bearing of religion on other fields. The findings, or, more properly, doctrines of the theology department are, it appears, to be enforced, in Newman's scheme, by some executive arm of the church. From some points of view an education carried on under such conditions would hardly merit the description liberal.

This uncomfortable conclusion is another example of the tension between the claims of religion and intellectual culture in *The Idea of a University*, along with that of how the absolute goodness of virtue is to be reconciled with the intrinsic goodness of intellectual culture as end in itself. Behind it there is a tension in Newman's Oriel career: that between the protégé and collaborator of Whately and the tutor removed from his post by Provost Hawkins for importing too much moral and religious supervision into it.

Newman's instability on this point allows him to develop, despite the intensity of his religious commitment, an abidingly persuasive account of and argument for liberal education. Detached from that commitment by Arnold, particularly by his absorption, in effect, of religion by literature, it was also diluted and aestheticised. For all the complicating effect of its religious setting, there is still no more eloquent and finely judged defence of intellectual culture than Newman's.

*Delivered at a conference on Newman's centenary at St Andrews University, 1990.*

# The Idea of a National Library

## 1. Introduction

In choosing to talk to you about The Idea of a National Library I am relying on what I hope is a still extant readiness in Scotland for a moderately philosophical approach to the subject. Scotland, after all, is the home of the Gifford lectures and it is in the traditional idiom of the titles of many of these that my title is couched. Next year is the centenary of the inauguration of the Gifford lectures so my point of departure has a measure of ceremonial appropriateness.

When they spoke of the idea of something the more typical Gifford lectures had in mind a broadly Hegelian version of the theory of ideas propounded by Plato and amended, but by no means wholly discarded, by Aristotle. In one aspect Plato's ideas are the ideal or perfected forms of various kinds of things. For Aristotle, ideas conceived in this way are the implicit goals towards which things may be understood to strive, the ultimate fulfilment or realisation of their natures, which give sense and order to the process of their development. In the hands of Hegel, and applied to the contents of the human world, in particular to institutions, rather than to natural objects, the conception becomes more straightforwardly historical. It is taken to reveal the history of institutions, not as a more or less random and accidental sequence of changes, but as a rational progression, in which each stage is some kind of improvement on its predecessor and will serve, in its turn, as a taking-off point for further movement towards the ideal, pressing further onwards and upwards.

Adherents of this comforting doctrine supposed that by consideration of actual instances of an institution in its historical development a rational or philosophically enlightened intelligence could discern its inevitable and finally perfected stage. That often turned out to be something very much like the stage it had reached at the time and place at which it was being written about. Hegel is widely held to have seen his own philosophy as the culmination of thought and the Prussian monarchy of which he was a subject to be the final phase of history.

My intentions are less ambitious. although you may discern a certain tendency in what I have to say to draw attention to the glories of the British Library, as at present constituted, in comparison to other national libraries. But I do not claim to perceive in it. against the background of its predecessors and of its parallels in other countries, any such thing as the absolute or perfected national library. My use of the doctrine of the idea is merely expository. The aim is to consider what light the differences in the histories and present states of national libraries can throw on the principles which should be used to guide their future development, so far as we can see at present.

The point is. of course, that we can know perfectly well what a national library is without knowing what a perfect national library is, which is just as well since, perhaps, there is no such thing as a perfect national library. Also we can recognise that a number of very different institutions are national libraries without being at all clear as to how they should be ordered on a scale of comparative excellence. One does not really know what poetry is unless one knows it is different from doggerel, but the capacity to tell them apart does not automatically equip one to decide whether Yeats is or is not a better poet than Eliot.

In a Gifford-like manner, then, but without Gifford-like assumptions, I shall begin with a survey of the origins and present state of some major national libraries. I shall go on to examine the implications of their claim to be national and then to compare the varied conceptions they exemplify of the proper functions of a national library. While the right hand, so to speak, is occupied with this primary task, the left hand will also be working away. To vary the metaphor, there is another bird I hope to bring down with the stone of this lecture. When I was appointed to my present post with the British Library I received many kind messages from friends. Some of these wondered if there would be enough to do at the London Library to keep me out of mischief. Others were unaware of the fact that the British Library was anything different from the British Museum Library, although library and museum were institutionally separated in 1973 and, as the Library was then constituted, were to a very considerable extent physically separated as well. At present while the main reading rooms for the humanities and social sciences are still in the British Museum building in Bloomsbury, there are other departments and several storage buildings dotted about in London and a third of the library's employees work at the document supply centre in Yorkshire. So, while engaged in considering what national libraries are and ought to be in general, I shall hope also to supply some information about our own for which there may be room even here.

## 2. *National Library origins*

What we now think of as national libraries generally began as the personal libraries of monarchs, even if personal only to the limited extent that monarchs have private personalities. The greatness of royal book collections was not rigidly correlated with the enthusiasm of royal book collectors. As the chief persons in their communities, monarchs had to have the best of everything. From the Renaissance, at any rate, warfare and hunting were no longer seen as occupations fully sufficient for royal dignity. From then on monarchs themselves, or others working on their behalf, assembled libraries that soon surpassed those of the grandest ecclesiastical establishments.

National libraries can be dated either from the emergence of nation-states or from the public inauguration of the ideology of nationalism with the French Revolution. A weakness of the first criterion is that it is not very easy to date the emergence of the nation state. England had a single monarch from the time of Egbert and an effectively centralised monarchy from William the Conqueror. But it was hardly a nation until monarch and subjects spoke the same language or even until Henry VII controlled the nobility with the statutes of livery and maintenance. By the sixteenth century France, Spain and Russia, too, were single political entities with reasonably homogeneous cultures or, at any rate, a common language for each. But Vienna, centre of a dynastically assembled hotchpotch of cultures, had a great royal library with no corresponding nation to serve. And until the late nineteenth century, of course, the nations of Germany, and Italy, with distinctive national cultures, were divided into a number of separate states.

This untidiness is not a compelling reason for dating national libraries from a date later than the emergence of the nation state. However royal libraries were, on the whole, more for display than for use, museums of treasures rather than scholarly resources. The point can be illustrated from an episode in the history of our own national library. Four years after the British Museum was founded in 1753 to house the Cottonian, Sloane and Harleian collections, George II gave it the old royal library. This had started with Henry VII's collection but its most impressive constituent was the collection of James I's cultivated son, Prince Henry. Some seventy years later George IV handed over, for what is sometimes politely described as a 'monetary consideration', the substantial collection of – or perhaps one should say, put together for – George III. This acquisition doubled the size of the library's holdings. But George III can hardly have been a very serious reader. After all he observed to Fanny Burney 'Was there ever such stuff as great part of Shakespeare... Is there not sad stuff? what?-what?' That is pretty much in style of his brother, the Duke of Gloucester's, remark to Gibbon, on receiving the second volume of the *Decline and Fall:* 'Another damned thick square book! Always scribble, scribble, scribble! Eh! Mr Gibbon?'

There were exceptions. Henry VIII, a most energetic amateur theologian, was as assiduous marker of his own books in pursuit of support for his divorce from Anne Boleyn and for his assumption of supremacy of the Church of England. But his books, although used for study rather than display, were for his personal use and were not available to interested and qualified members of the general public.

Royal libraries, in those cases, where an emerging nation wholly or mainly composed the realm of their owners, are perhaps best seen as proto-national libraries. With the expression of national self-consciousness in political form, above all with the French Revolution, the national library proper may be said to begin.

The dramatic circumstances of its inauguration in the first year of the revolution give the French Bibliothèque Nationale a certain pride of place in the general history of national libraries. The British Museum had been set up over forty years earlier as an accessible public institution and, for all its once royally owned contents, it was outside royal dwellings and independent of royal control. But the French royal library, nationalised in 1789, was much larger. It originated, as a serious undertaking, with Henry VII's contemporary François I. Its comparative splendour must in part be traced to the greater wealth and populousness of France as compared to Britain until the end of the eighteenth century. Equally important for its head start is the nationalistic vigour of the revolutionaries and, even more, of Napoleon, who greatly enriched its collections with the spoils of war, not all of which were returned. In 1818, after the restoration of the Bourbons and the return of much stolen material, it still had some 800,000 volumes of printed books, many more than the British Museum. In 1929 the *Encyclopaedia Britannica* still saw it as without question the world's leading national library. With nearly four and a half million volumes it was well ahead of the Library of Congress with three and a half or the British Museum with three and a quarter million. The German State Library did not reach three million until ten years later and the outbreak of the war which was to dissolve it.

Thirty years ago, according to Arundell Esdaile's survey of the world's national libraries, the Bibliothèque Nationale was still ahead of the British Museum, with six million volumes to the Museum's five. Since then it has been overtaken. In the mid-1970s, with nine million, it was behind the British Library by a million. Today, with the British Library at fourteen million, it has fallen still further behind. But it was a glorious reign of a hundred and seventy years. To suppose that it is over is not to regard the raw number of volumes held as the crucial factor. Otherwise the Library of Congress, which has been for some time the world's largest national library, would have to be the best. But by comparison with the great European libraries, even those not of quite the first rank, its holdings of older material are not of the greatest distinction, apart from its naturally unrivalled collection of Americana.

The Library of Congress became, by a gradual process, the national library of a country that was historically new, and at the time of the library's foundation in 1802, an almost complete cultural dependency of Britain. Recurrent fires and various forms of political hostility and mismanagement led to its holdings being no more than 20,000 volumes at the middle of the nineteenth century. A decade later, at the beginning of better times, it was still only 80,000 books strong and was no more than a service facility for the legislature. From the Civil War onwards, and particularly since the forty year reign of Herbert Putnam as librarian began in 1899, things have been very different. Splendidly housed, supplied with funds in what is elsewhere seen as almost limitless profusion, it has become statistically the world's first library.

The legislative patronage of the national library of the United States is not peculiar to it. The National Diet Library of Japan is, however, not altogether an independent development. Formerly the Imperial Library it was turned into the library of the Japanese legislature by the American conquerors after 1945. In some relatively small countries the national library is the library of a university, in Finland and Israel, for example. In the surviving and thoroughly constitutional monarchies of north-western Europe and Scandinavia the national library is ordinarily called the royal library but this is no more than a verbal archaism.

Germany and Italy have both suffered from their common fate of having had a multiplicity of monarchs until their respective unifications in the late nineteenth century. Germany had the advantage of a dominant constituent part in Prussia, but the division of the country after the Second World War meant that its library became the national library of East Germany and today West Germany has no national library. Italy, on the other hand, has two, neither of the first rank; one in Florence, notable for older material and also the destination of all new Italian books, the other in Rome, the repository for books of foreign origin.

I cannot leave this survey of national library origins without a word about the unique case where the library of a particular profession became quite soon after its foundation in fact, but only after two and a half centuries in name, the national library of its country. Founded in 1682, the Advocates' Library in Edinburgh was given effective national status twenty-seven years later by the Copyright Act which endowed it with the right of legal deposit. From the earliest period, beginning before the end of the seventeenth century, it admirably refused to allow its scope and interest to be narrowed by its professional association, unlike the Library of Congress. The latter was burnt by the British in 1814, twelve years after its foundation, and was a pretty meagre affair, some three thousand volumes on law and foreign policy. Soon reanimated with the purchase of Jefferson's private library of six thousand books, it did not set itself to become a serious general collection until after the Civil War. Sixteen years after its foundation the Advocates' Library's acquisition of the Balfour MS showed a much broader view of its role than that of serving simply the professional requirements of Scottish barristers. It is appropriate that since the legal system was the part of the total Scottish political structure that survived the Act of Union with least change it should have proved the original patron for the country's national library.

## 3. The cultural background

If the great libraries of the early modern period from the Renaissance to the Enlightenment were assembled as the property of monarchs and for the purpose of display that was calculated to augment the glory of those monarchs in the eyes of the world, they gradually turned into something much more than that. A scholarly constituency existed which had an interest in gaining access to the royal collections and it was inconsistent with the liberality proverbially associated with princes to keep them out.

The idea that it was a natural and proper thing for a monarch to have a collection of hooks was part of a general change in the life of the mind in Europe whose main aspects can best be seen as supporting and reinforcing one another. These are the extension of literacy to laymen after about a thousand years of clerical monopoly;

a vast increase in the scope and quality of secular literature; the rapid domination of literary production by writing in vernacular languages; and, as a technological magnifier of these factors, the invention of printing.

Most medieval literature was produced for ecclesiastics and was directed towards their religious concerns. It was made up of theology, dogmatic and biblical, of writings on liturgy and church organisation and history, and of works of devotion. It was nearly all written in Latin, an international language. It was written by hand on vellum. It was, therefore, expensive, and copies of a particular book were few in number. It was stored in ecclesiastical buildings, particularly monasteries which were commonly out of the way. Physically it was comparatively fragile.

There were, of course, literate laymen, and women, in the middle ages, but they were a small minority of the literate, and a tiny minority of the population at large. There was some secular literature in circulation, most notably classical Roman works of poetry, history and oratory. (Some classical Greek writings existed, waiting in neglected corners of monasteries for the more enterprising scholars of the Renaissance to discover them. But little Greek was read until Manuel Chrysoloras arrived from Byzantium in Florence at the end of the fourteenth century.) There was not much new secular writing. What there was was generally in the vernacular languages that people actually spoke. From the twelfth century there were the epic *chansons de geste,* the romances, and the lyrics of troubadours and, later, the minnesinger.

Increasing comfort and security prepared men's minds for the acquisition of polite culture. Printing, towards the end of the fifteenth century, transformed the process into an explosion. In one of the less questionable of his audacious remarks, Marshall McLuhan observed that printing is the first example of mass production. It was certainly his view that it was also the most important one.

The printed book, the literate layman, the secular work in a vernacular tongue are not contemporary in their very first appearance. But they achieved what may be described as a critical mass at much the same time. The new secular and vernacular writing was met by a body of people with the capacity and desire to read them. The invention of printing ensured that they had the practical opportunity. What was further required for the royal collections of books that were brought together in these circumstances to become national libraries was the development of national self-consciousness, the diffused. implicit and comparatively non-combative form taken by nationalist ideology.

## 4. The national idea

People often deny, or at any rate try to minimise, the reality of national differences. A nation, in one version of this view, is the more or less illusory conviction imposed by a sovereign political authority on the collection of people who are subject to its rule. The conviction, they might admit, may acquire a measure of validity from various mind-conditioning influences exerted by a government on its subjects.

There are two reasons for attempting to eliminate, or, failing that, to play down, the concept of the nation. The first is ethical or emotional, the ugly emotions and ugly deeds to which conflicting senses of national identity give rise. There is in fact no irresistible connection between the recognition of national differences between people, in some sense that is more than merely formal or institutional, and their fearing, despising or hating each other and acting in accordance with those feelings. But there does seem to be a preponderating tendency for this kind of difference between people to express itself disagreeably, instead of being positively exploited and enjoyed.

But so far as that tendency does exist it is no use trying to control it by an unconvincing pretence that the state of affairs on which it depends does not exist. The tendency may be due to the fact that there is no automatic countervailing influence to the negative implications of national difference for feeling and conduct as there is in the case of difference of sex or even difference of age. Members of the opposite sex or at the opposite end of the age-range from one's own are not instinctively regarded as foreigners and enemies. Often, after all, their company is preferred to that of people of one's own kind.

There is also a more logical or intellectual reason for questioning the objective reality of national differences and of the nations these differences define. This is that there is no one clear criterion for determining whether a group of people constitutes a nation or not. But it is a cognitive superstition to suppose that a concept cannot apply to the real articulation of the world into different kinds of thing unless there is a single decisive characteristic that picks the members of that kind out from everything else that there is.

The case of nationality is an example of a quite common situation in which a concept is governed by a plurality of conditions, none of which is necessary or sufficient on its own for its application to a thing, but where the satisfaction of a majority or reasonable number of these conditions is sufficient and the presence of some of a crucial primary set of these conditions is necessary. Concepts of this relatively complex kind are typical of the apparatus we have for the discussion of human matters when they go beyond the most obviously physical. *Fat, white* and *bald* are not of this kind, although they are a little vague, with a frayed edge at the fringe of their field of application. *Mad, married, poet* are quite different; the ways in which these statuses are possessed are irreducibly various. The same is true of more explicitly social conceptions like *class* or, the topic in hand, *nation*.

There are two obvious conditions involved in the case of nationality: a common language and the occupancy of a continuous piece of territory, at least as the majority group in it. Neither of these is necessary: polyglot Switzerland is undoubtedly a nation, so were the scattered Greeks of the Ottoman empire and, up to more recent times, the Jews. Nor is either sufficient: there are two nations on Cyprus, and, perhaps, in Ireland and there are many nations of English-speakers, three, perhaps, on the island of Britain, not to speak of the Americans, Canadians and Australasians as well. Naturally the factors mentioned help to support each other: scattered members of a speech-community gravitate towards the main mass in times of public or private change and uncertainty, language habits are preserved when the language in question is spoken by nearly everyone one comes in contact with. Where both factors are present common nationality is almost assured. Where both are absent common nationality is pretty well ruled out.

As well as these primary conditions of nationality there are some others that deserve attention. A common religion can fortify a nation that is first identified on other grounds. A shared government, which will naturally work, deliberately or not, to strengthen cultural, non-political affinities, is inevitably secondary. Unless it were there could be no such thing as nationalism. More important possibly, but less palpable, is what may be called a common history, a set of emotionally compelling incidents and heroes, which again is clearly a by-product of other connecting links.

The Renaissance, I said earlier, saw the replacement of the religious literature of the middle ages as the dominant form by the emerging secular literatures written in vernacular languages, in other words by national literatures. For large, culturally advanced nations, widely spread in space and having broken out of the limits of a rigidly customary style of behaviour, a national literature is the most powerful expression of national identity. It serves in much the same way as memory does in the case of individual human beings by endowing nations with a sense of their continuity with their own pasts. Philosophers have often doubted the complete adequacy of the view that memory is the thing that makes a persisting individual out of a sequence of momentary states of mind. But a person whose memory of his past has gone irretrievably has to be considered as reborn, in effect, from the point at which it takes up again. The same is true of nations. And in all but the simplest national groups in which identity is sustained through time by oral literature, literally stored in human memory, the literature of a nation is the totality of a nation's books, all that is written in its language, or, sometimes, languages.

Now it is possible for this totality to be preserved in a scattered fashion, spread out, in some application of the principle of the division of labour, between a number of different holdings. But it is plainly more sensible, because more manageable and reliable, to ensure that there is at least one carefully and responsibly run collection of the whole of a nation's non-trivial literary production. That defines what is generally recognised to be the first and, I should argue, overriding function of a national library, the maintenance of the national literary archive.

Before I go on to consider this and other functions of a national library, the essentially national character of post-medieval literature should be examined a bit more fully. The two features characteristic of a national literature, its being in a vernacular language and secular in content, are both important. The vernacular characteristic confines its readers in the great majority of cases to the members of a particular nation. Imaginative literature, particularly poetry, is tied to a particular language. This is nearly always a vernacular one. There was some fine medieval Latin poetry and, as late as Milton, it was still reasonable to divide his works into 'English poems' and 'others'. But since his time the writing of poetry in any but the poet's first language is a statistical, and usually literary, oddity, like the French poems of T.S. Eliot.

Poems are essentially constituted by the language in which they are expressed. Two familiar considerations bear this out. The translators of poetry from one language into another are always apologetic and emphasise the very narrow limits of their ambitions.

Secondly, poets, like all other writers, are participants in a tradition, which influences them powerfully, even if not always in the oppressive fashion described by Harold Bloom as the anxiety of influence. This tradition is nearly always that of the poets of their own language. Where that is not the case, as it was noisily with Ezra Pound, more discreetly with T.S. Eliot, it is interesting that the poet in question is often *déraciné*, and, in the cases mentioned, a permanent exile from his homeland.

The tie to a language is also present in the next large section of a nation's literary output, the expository writing whose upper levels consist of scholarly work in the humanities and the social sciences. Criticism, in the service of a nation's imaginative literature, shares the national limitation of that literature. Only an occasional work of pure literary scholarship written by an author of one nationality about some element of the literature of another is taken seriously by the native experts in that literature. History when it ceased to be religious, on the whole became patriotic and was thus largely confined to a national audience. Even the advent of various forms of scientific history has not really eliminated this. The historians of different languages do read each other but they have significant differences of style and method which obstruct their reliance on the work of those they read for anything but the history of the latter's own countries.

Philosophy is not exactly national but it is carried on in almost entirely different ways in the English-speaking countries and Scandinavia, on the one hand, and continental Europe, on the other. The social sciences, in spite of the implied claim to universality in their name, also do not travel all that well. Economics is perhaps the least nationally confined of them and for a good reason. In this century it has been a highly mathematical undertaking and the language of number is the Esperanto of learning.

Its mathematical character associates economics with the natural sciences rather than the humanities, where numbers are, of course, to be found, but only in the crude, arithmetical form of the least theoretical kind of statistics. It is significant that some national libraries confine themselves to the collection of material in the humanities and social sciences. Where they do not there is commonly a clear separation between the two types of collection, one which corresponds to two very different styles of use.

I have been arguing that acceptance as the prime function of a national library of the maintenance of the nation's complete literary archive is founded on solider grounds than the vague idea that somebody ought to do it. Before going on to consider what other functions are and should be associated with it I want to digress briefly to consider the situation of nations which do not have a large national literature or a linguistically single one or any national literature to speak of at all. In the first of these conditions are polyglot nations like Switzerland and Belgium. Each of them has more than one literature which is a small part of the national literature of another, larger country. In such cases language is a less crucial part of national identity than in the usual case, but both are clearly nations: Switzerland with a long history, Belgium reaching back into the Spanish Netherlands. At any rate, in such cases it may be that the archival task will be discharged by the nation with the controlling share in the language in question.

A second kind of case is that of the fairly small country with a fairly small literature: Sweden. for example, or Hungary. In such cases, where the country is an advanced one, educated people tend to know other languages than their own reasonably well. They cannot bask in the monoglot complacency of the British, the French and the Americans. On that account a national library in such a country will serve general readers, and not just scholarly specialists, with its foreign collections. And that is just as well since a small national literature is not really up to the job of supplying adequate culture to the members of the nation in question.

Finally, there are countries in effect without a literature. Sometimes, as with African countries of low literacy, although there is no written literature there may be an oral one and. mindful of Homer and the heroic poems of the Scandinavian peoples before they became literate. we should not dismiss it on that account. It is plainly the task of the national library wherever there is an oral literature to record it. now that the spread of literacy and the general homogenisation of the world is undermining the traditional means of its transmission.

## 5. The first step beyond the archive

Anyone familiar with national libraries will realise that the kind of archive which I have described is seldom, if ever, found on its own: it is always embedded in a collection of books from other countries for purposes of general scholarly research. The principal administrative division between these two aspects of a collection lies in their mode of acquisition. The institution of legal deposit, clearly installed here in the reign of Queen Anne. and proclaimed much earlier, but none too effectively, in France certainly removes some of the pain of acquisition. It might seem odd that the two functions are seldom discharged by the different institutions, except in Italy.

I have said that the humanities and the social sciences have a national flavour and have implied that scholars on the whole write for their compatriots in the first instance, at least in non-linguistic subjects. Nevertheless that is not to say that humanistic and social-science disciplines are rigidly divided by national boundaries. Some of them are concerned with the history and literature of other countries, or its impact on the history and literature of their own. All are to some extent responsive to the work of foreign scholars in their own fields, even if the response is often remote.

On the other, practical, side the difference in mode of acquisition between legal deposit free of charge and purchase with foreign currency is not as far-reaching as it seems. It may take some of the sting out of acquisition to receive a new book for nothing. But national libraries also have to fill gaps in their collections of older books of native origin. Furthermore the cost of acquisition is only a part, and by no means an overwhelmingly large part, of the cost making a book an effective part of a national collection. Its arrival has to be registered. It has to be catalogued and the information about its presence in the library must be made available to readers. It has to be shelved in an environment which it is expensive to maintain in a desirable state of temperature and humidity. It has to be rendered secure from theft and natural hazards. Arrangements have to be made for its delivery and inspection. It has to be preserved from the effects of use and simple decay.

The entry of a book into a fully professional library is not unlike an old-fashioned marriage. The initial commitment is easy enough to set up. But then the heavy burdens begin to make themselves felt; orgies of expense not readily envisaged at the outset. No wonder librarians at quiet moments rotate in their minds the possibilities of weeding-out, their equivalent to divorce. Last year only about 7.5 per cent of the British Library's expenditure went on the purchase of books and periodicals. Most of the rest was, in effect, after-care.

It remains true that the maintenance of the national literary archive could be separated from the provision of the most extensive national collection of foreign books. But since books of the two kinds are typically studied together by scholarly users there would be no point in separating them. I spoke a moment ago of 'the most extensive collection of foreign books' and the phrase raises the question: should there be one'? If there is then pointless duplication of comparatively little-used material is controlled much more efficiently and conveniently than if the job were done by libraries telling each other what they were getting or had got.

In taking on the task of collecting, preserving and making available the national literary archive, a national library implicitly takes on another job, that of producing the authoritative bibliography of the national literature. This is not just a catalogue for its direct user. It is a necessary service for those concerned with books generally, above all libraries at home and abroad and the book trade. In fact the job was not done by the national library in this country until the British Library incorporated in itself in 1973 the British National Bibliography, which had previously been a separate, commercial organisation. In its service to the book trade this bibliographic function may reasonably be seen as the return to publishers for having to deposit their productions free of charge.

A good many other functions naturally follow on from the joint task of maintaining the national archive and holding the largest collection of the better books from other countries, whether imaginative or expository. A library with these responsibilities will be comparatively large and so a suitable place for research into matters of interest to libraries generally: techniques of conservation, automation, especially of bibliography. It can also help in training.

Another activity which is best, because most effectively and conveniently, carried out from the centre is that of exchange, whether international or between libraries within the country. International exchanges make purchase in both directions unnecessary. Since government publications are a major element in international exchanges between libraries and there is normally just one government per country, it is obvious that such exchanges are best done by national libraries. As for internal exchange I cannot imagine that there is a better arrangement than the Gift and Exchange Service of the British Library which achieves a great deal at a very modest cost. Libraries send books they no longer wish to house to the British Library's Document Supply Centre in Yorkshire. There a large proportion of them is added to the stock of the National Lending Library to be lent to users through their local libraries when those libraries, or those they are in direct touch with, cannot fill the need. The residue is listed and the lists are sent to public libraries for them to choose from. Decent fates are found for the ultimate left-overs. This seems to me to be very good housekeeping. I am afraid I have no idea if anything like it exists anywhere else in the world.

It is an implication of the responsibility for the national archive that its contents are not lent. And that principle is extended by a natural enough contagion to the national library's collection of foreign books, although not in its full rigour and with occasional exceptions. But readers cannot all readily come to the national library and a central lending library is needed to supply the inevitable deficiencies of local libraries. That implies, it is said, that legal deposit should be of two copies at any rate. For complex historical reasons in the British Isles six copies must be deposited. Three go to the national libraries. One each to the Bodleian and Cambridge and one, by an agreeable historical anomaly, to Trinity College, Dublin. Perhaps we should understand it as a retrospective apology for England's long denial of Ireland's nationhood.

Many national libraries have collections of newspapers. In Britain they were moved from Bloomsbury to the outskirts of London in 1902 to relieve congestion. In the same spirit national libraries collect non-printed material: tapes, discs, slides, film, particularly microfilm. In Britain we have developed an impressive national sound archive. There are other accumulations of matter on which it is possible to cast an imperialist eye from time to time.

## 6. The second culture

But there is one important variety of written material which I have mentioned so far only to distinguish it from the main, nationally-flavoured part of the nation's literary output. This is the books and periodicals on science and technology and the literature of patents which, because of community of use, it is natural to associate with them. It may be that the two cultures should not be as isolated from one another as they are, in the sense that few people display a competence in both. But nowhere more than in libraries is the fact that there are two cultures more irresistibly evident.

The fundamental difference between the two domains is that the scientific material required is all of the last few years while humanities material is required from all periods represented in the collection. A national library, being a library of last resort, will be very notably equipped with rarities and these, in the nature of the case, are as much of the remote as of the recent past. The curve of demand for scientific writing falls steeply away from the present and soon levels off at a small distance above zero where it is sustained by the relatively minute requirements of historians of science.

A second, connected difference is that scientific writing is almost all in periodical form. Since most of what people want to read is recent it is still in its pristine mode of expression. If it ever comes to be embalmed in a monograph it is likely to be used only for occasional reference. Some, of course, will filter into textbooks, but these will be widely disseminated, especially among university libraries. In the case of technology the material will solidify into handbooks with comparably wide dissemination.

These differences are the result of the different kinds of use to which the material is put. Humanistic study is ordinarily carried on by attention to a substantial body of texts and commentaries even if its particular target is a text or part of one. The scholar has to build up in his mind a mastery of the total linguistic and cultural circumstances of the work he is studying, or to enlarge what he has already. The scientist wants something that will throw light on a particular investigation he is pursuing; the technologist seeks light on a particular technical problem. The humanist is like someone trying to work out the precise shade of feeling that lies behind the words of a letter. The scientist is like someone who wants to know the time of the next train to Birmingham.

An implication of this comparative practicality of the uses to which scientific and technological material is put is that it often commands a straightforward market price. It can, therefore, help to finance its own provision. The user does not want to undertake elaborate searches for broadly interesting things; he wants rapid access to available material from any part of the world about a precisely defined topic. It is principally to be found in the last few years' issues of a very large array of scientific and technical journals and conference proceedings. Although the satisfaction of this need involves the acquisition, storage and delivery of printed matter (and, increasingly of surrogates for print) it is sufficiently different in its style to deserve another name than library, that, usually, of information service. Since the units of material required are comparatively small it is convenient to send copies to the user, by post or fax, rather than to draw the user to the stacks or to send him the original on loan.

At the Document Supply Centre at Boston Spa in Yorkshire the inflow from more than 50,000 different periodical subscriptions is stored, their regular arrival being carefully monitored every morning as they come in with the post. Last year 3 million requests for material were received, a quarter of them from overseas, naturally the more profitable end of the operation. Attached to it, as part of the Science, Technology and Industry division of the library as a whole, are the Science Reference and Information Service and the Patent Office Library in London. For some years the staff in this division as a whole at a little over a thousand, has slightly exceeded the numbers in Humanities and Social Sciences, at a little less than a thousand. A further development has been the creation of specialised information services for business and dealing in information about Japan.

The supply of information of this kind must occur in any advanced economy. Should it be taken on by the national library? It is no part of the work of the Library of Congress in the United States. In part that is due to the continuing primacy of that library's commitment to the service of Congress. More fundamentally, perhaps, it is traceable to a general American reluctance to have anything done by the state that can be done by private enterprise.

In France the state does take responsibility for the national information service, and, indeed, has recently taken to endowing it most handsomely. But it is an entirely separate institution from the Bibliothèque Nationale. In West Germany where one might expect such a thing to be done very well there is no national library to take it on.

Of the great libraries of the western world, then, the British Library is unique in the commanding position it gives to its information service. One argument in favour of it is that the traditional scholarly library uses just the same technology as an information service, in acquisition, storage, environmental control, cataloguing and conservation, even if the two diverge in the style of their delivery of material to readers. Many of the most traditionally scholarly of the British Library's curators have become enthusiastically expert in the new information technology. We have an automated catalogue of manuscripts as well as of biotechnology.

Another supporting consideration is that the scholarly, humanistic part of the library can benefit financially from being part of a total system containing a profitable information service. In France. where the two are separated, the Bibliothèque Nationale has tended to recede into a Cinderella-like status, huddled over the diminishing embers of its former glories, while the ugly sisters of science and technology go to the ball of publicity and ample public support.

But there are arguments on the other side. Objections from the staff and from experienced users of the scholarly research library to this expansion into services to the market-place are not just instinctive reactions to change or expressions of an élitist disdain for the practical. There is a fear that the traditional work of the library will be absorbed into, and smothered or marginalised by, its more politically glamorous associate. But the same obliteration could just as easily occur if the two were separate. If both are united in one institution the one that appears to be endangered can in fact be assisted by a common loyalty among staff, particularly if there is some movement between divisions or, at any rate, regular contact between them.

Scholars and the audience for scientific information are the two main groups of direct users of the national library in this country. My own hope is that, far from cutting the two domains adrift, we shall be able to do more for a larger constituency, that of general readers. At the moment, unless they visit it as a museum, to look at Magna Carta, Shakespeare's signature and the Lindisfarne Gospels, it cannot be much more for them than an object of distant pride like Concorde or the navy.

In the British Library's new building at St Pancras it is planned to set up a Centre for the Book in which the scholarly work of the library – lectures, conferences, learned publications – will have a focus. I hope it will also be used for the provision of guidance to readers of a less professional sort. What they need – as we all know, since we are all unprofessional about some areas of our reading unless we are narrow specialists of the most deplorable kind – is access to bibliographical knowledge in small chunks, in other words about some rather closely defined range of subject matter, not just raw information, but with some account and evaluation of the material listed. New techniques for the electronic storage of bibliographical data can satisfy the first need; the curatorial skills of the Library's staff could be drawn on most productively to satisfy the second. No institution is better qualified than the national library we have to perform a service which, added to those it already carries out, would complete its title to its description as national.

*Delivered as the Robbins Lecture at the University of Stirling, 3 December 1987.*

III

# The British Empire and the Theory of Imperialism

*1. The British Empire and theory*

The most famous remark about the British Empire was published just over a century ago, in 1883, in J.R. Seeley's *Expansion of England*. 'We seem', he said, 'to have conquered and peopled half the world in a fit of absence of mind.' Looking back on a process which he took to have been going on for nearly three centuries, he did not mean only that the great Victorian imperial contraption of his own time was the outcome of a series of accidents and improvisations, rather than the fulfilment of a grand plan consciously thought out in advance, true though that was. He was more concerned to point out that it had not attracted anything very much in the way of general reflection.

As a historian rather than a political theorist, he approached the fact from a historical point of view. In the first half of his extremely readable book he argues that since the seventeenth century the central issue in the political history of Britain, and above all its diplomatic history, had been the struggle for mastery of the New World with a succession of other western European states: first Spain, then Holland and finally France. Despite the setback of the American Revolution we had emerged victorious in 1815. Even if France, in revenge for its losses in the Seven Years War, had helped the United States to secure independence from Britain, that had not restored French power in the New World. The object of this attempt to redirect interest from the domestic constitutional struggles on which it was ordinarily focused to the development of a world-wide system of nations of British blood and culture was to encourage the further and more effective unification of that group of countries by some kind of imperial federation.

That idea attracted a good deal of support until at least the Boer War. By the time the 1914 war was over it lived on only in the circle of Lord Milner's adherents, gathered together at the Round Table, and in the form of occasional ebullitions from Lord Beaverbrook.

The aspect of Seeley's celebrated formula with which I shall be concerned is the remarkable absence of theoretical discussion of a general, or broadly philosophical, kind of the principles which should govern the relations between a country and its offshoots or conquests. Bertrand Russell wrote in 1938 in his *Freedom and Organisation* that the British Empire grew up, not only 'without the help of deliberate government policy', but also without 'the assistance of imperialistic doctrine' (p. 460). More recently A.P. Thornton has said that 'the adjective that best qualifies the British empire is not imperial, but empirical' (*From the File on Empire*, p. 295). He has also said that 'the British Empire was fortunate to have been served by pragmatists' (ibid, p. 28). Those pragmatists, it could be added, may have counted themselves fortunate not to have been encumbered by theorists.

Throughout Britain's imperial period there was effective parliamentary discussion of the activities of government and, spreading out from this to an even wider circle, public debate about political issues. But this was little influenced by anything much in the way of explicit political theory. There was plenty of polemical advocacy on the theme of empire, for and against. But its foundations were immediate sentiments of a patriotic kind on the one hand, occupied with power and glory, or on the other side, either of a simply moralistic character or reflecting economic self-interest.

At its Victorian apogee imperialism began to attract theoretical *explanations*, most notably J.A. Hobson's conception of it as a means for disposing of surplus capital on the part of a society suffering from the 'underconsumption' caused by the propensity of the unnecessarily rich to save too much. But the topic of the *justification* of empire was not addressed by political philosophers in a general and rationally detached manner.

Two great political philosophers did give some attention to the subject: Burke and John Stuart Mill. But the involved, detailed, essentially practical nature of their dealings with imperial matters only serves to enforce the point I am making. Burke was involved with the American colonies, with Ireland and, in his protracted efforts to secure the impeachment of Warren Hastings, with India, as a practising politician, in particular as the main source of ideas for the Rockingham Whigs. His general convictions are evident in determining the positions he took, to the extent that party loyalty allowed. He opposed inexpedient insistence on abstract right in the matter of taxing the American colonists for the expenses of their defence. He argued that the restrictions on Irish trade imposed in the time of William III should be removed, opposed the penal laws on Catholics and supported Catholic representation in the Irish parliament and Catholic access to the professions. In India he was concerned to bring the powers exercised by the East India Company under parliamentary control, both as a requirement of justice and to preserve the traditional social fabric of India. As Frank O'Gorman says, 'it is a large and dangerous assumption that Burke must have had a systematic imperial "theory"... his method was characterised by a fund of common-sense practicality and a distaste for abstract theorising' (*Edmund Burke*, p. 67). The fact of empire he was content to take for granted.

Mill devotes the eighteenth and last chapter of his *Considerations on Representative Government* to the topic of the government of dependencies by a free state. He too takes the existence of dependent possessions as a fact not in need of discussion. He praises the Durham Report for encouraging colonies with populations of European descent to take full responsibility for their internal affairs. He thinks they are too far apart for there to be an imperial parliament in Britain, dealing with foreign affairs and defence, and with the existing British parliament confined to the internal affairs of Britain. The present degree of union is beneficial: it favours peace, keeps markets open and lends force, as he puts it, to the one nation that fully supports liberty. But such colonies should be free to leave the union whenever they choose.

India is another thing altogether. Mill was an employee of the East India company for thirty-five years, from becoming a clerk at the age of seventeen, until he retired in 1858, after the Mutiny and the dissolution of the company. He maintains that vigorous despotism is required for non-European colonies and the despots should not be remote but must get to know those they rule. Good despots will preserve the generality of the native population from their two kinds of oppressor: white settlers and powerful compatriots. He puts 'improvement' forward as a general aim, but does not envisage it as a process with a completion. The chapter ends with some detailed practical wisdom about the need for a permanent delegated body to rule, not a remote minister, and the desirability of training young, competitively selected administrators on the spot.

The only book known to me to address the topic of empire in English in the rational tradition of general political theory came out in 1960, just as the last disembarrassments of decolonisation were taking place. This is John Plamenatz's *Alien Rule and Self-Government* and I shall be giving it some of the attention deserved by its solitary distinction later.

## 2. Two models of empire

The British Empire, at least from the time of the Seven Years War, was composed of two very different sorts of colony. On the one hand there were the colonies of settlement, communities of British, or at any rate European, descent, occupying parts of the world at once habitable by Europeans and with a small, thinly spread native population: Canada, Australia and New Zealand. On the other were the colonies of conquest; populous, tropical nations, some with advanced civilisations, particularly India, others, particularly those in sub-Saharan Africa, backward. There were, too, some mixed instances where a fairly numerous settler population was superimposed on a substantial number of indigenous people: South Africa, Rhodesia, Kenya.

In their difference of kind the two extreme cases correspond to the two kinds of colony to be found in the classical world. The colonies of Greece were formed by emigration from the mother country; the colonies of Rome by the imposition of Roman power on established non-Roman populations. But the correspondence is significantly imperfect in both cases. The colonies produced by the cities of Greece were politically independent from the outset, whatever links of sentiment and tradition there may have been to the cities from which they originated. Something more like an empire was contrived by Pericles out of the Delian League, the naval confederacy that was finally disbanded by Sparta after the Peloponnesian war. Here tribute was firmly exacted by Athens from the other members; there was some political interference; moneys raised were questionably diverted to work on Athenian temples. But Athenian control fell far short of that exercised by most imperial powers on their subject colonies.

The altogether more lasting and serious Roman empire also began from a single city. Between the fifth and third centuries BC the Romans established their rule over the whole Italian peninsula and then spread on outwards over the whole Mediterranean world and beyond. They established colonies in the areas they conquered and soon began the process of according Roman citizenship to everyone under Roman rule, a process more or less complete by the beginning of the third century AD. The armies they sent along the newly constructed roads did not outrage the religious loyalties of the conquered and often sustained the local form of government. With the replacement of the republic by the Augustan empire the grosser forms of exploitation were brought back within bounds.

In Britain's Greek-style colonies of settlement, the white dominions of more recent times, the purposes of trade were not the clearly predominant cause of colonisation. If Virginia was invested in as a source of tobacco and Canada penetrated for the sake of fur, many of the colonists were drawn to the New World as religious refugees or in the search for a standard of living they could not hope for at home. The climate was at least supportable; the native inhabitants few in number and thinly spread. Epidemics and alcohol ensured that the question of extermination or expulsion did not have to be raised, although wars against the Indians helped to reduce the indigenous population.

The Roman-style colonies of conquest were, to start with, wholly brought into being by trade. The East India Company was founded in 1600 and ran its affairs as a private business without government control until the Regulating Act of 1773. Clive, who won India for Britain, in effect, at Plassey in 1756, was an employee of the Company, not of the Crown. India had an advanced civilisation of its own and was economically active and politically sophisticated enough for secure and profitable trade to be carried on without large interference, to start with at any rate. Once India had been secured the necessities of its defence led to the conquest and domination of other countries, notably Egypt. In the second main phase of colonisation by conquest, in the late nineteenth century, in sub-Saharan Africa populations were taken over which were as unignorably numerous as the inhabitants of India but as primitive as the original occupants of the white dominions.

These demographic and cultural differences between colonies posed different problems of justification to advocates of empire. Seeley, and before him Charles Dilke, were mainly interested in the colonies of settlement and nourished hopes for a fraternal federation, of just the kind Mill thought impractical. As Thornton tartly observes, their calculations did not include an estimate of the attractions of the proposal to the colonists themselves. In the late nineteenth century, with Britain industrially overtaken by the United States and Germany, the colonies of settlement seemed an ideal receptacle for the surplus poor of Britain. On top of that those colonies, strengthened by immigrants from Britain – for it was clear they could absorb many more people successfully, as they have since done – and bound more closely to the home country, would restore Britain's strength in the competition with other nations.

Concern for the colonies of conquest, in particular for the new ones in Africa, was aroused by two distinct and largely opposed interests: the commercial and the missionary. For those not directly involved with profit-making or proselytising, expansion in Africa was attractive as enhancing national prestige, and possible power, and was inevitable if other competing colonial nations were to be pre-empted.

But there were many who either believed or suspected that the colonial empire did not pay and that provided a material support to the idea that the acquisition of colonies was morally disreputable.

## 3. The early history of empire

Conquest has historically been the normal method of empire-building. New nations formed by settlement are either never subject to the countries from which they began, as with the Greeks or the Normans, or soon break away into independence, as with the British Empire. But modern empires of conquest, the British very much among them, differ from those of the past in the oppressively external nature of their rule. It has often been noticed that Alexander the Great did not apply to his imperial conquests the principle of his teacher Aristotle that Greeks and barbarians were utterly different kinds of human being. There is no more obvious indication of the same non-discriminating attitude among the Romans than the fact that so few of their emperors were even Italian, let alone Roman.

Going further back than Greece and Rome, it appears that nations seem to have established empires wherever they were powerful enough to do so. Stone Age tribesmen fought each other, and no doubt exterminated other tribes from time to time. But they did not have the organisation to bring other tribes into a state of permanent subjection. It is only with the emergence of cities, made possible by the surplus food yielded by the agricultural revolution, that empire-building begins; It started with the Sumerian empire of Sargon, to be followed in the Mesopotamian region by the Babylonian, Hittite, Assyrian and Persian empires. Like the Romans afterwards they were drawn into expansion by the possession of disciplined military power and used it to spread social order by means of uniform laws effectively enforced, to improve communications and so, through both of these, to enhance trade.

The Greeks had a marked, and justified, sense of their intellectual and cultural superiority to the surrounding peoples with whom they came into contact. But, divided into warring cities, they could unite only for common defence against the barbarians of Persia. Not until

Greece had been unified by his father was it possible for Alexander to entertain the thought of a civilising mission, the first unquestionable example of an idea that has to support any imperial expansion that is to be more than appropriation or banditry. The Hellenisation which was an integral part of his great career of conquest lasted long after the political disintegration of his empire. It proved, indeed, to be more enduring than the elimination of Greek racial exclusiveness, which was symbolised by his marriage to the Bactrian Roxana and later to a daughter of Darius.

### 4. Empire and national interest

The simplest justification for empire is the claim that it is in the national interest to acquire colonies. The particular interests served, as has already emerged, are economic, in the first instance: those of trade and then of privileged access to needed resources and, ultimately, of investment. Secondly, there is the demographic interest of improving the lot of surplus population through emigration, turning them from dissatisfied citizens of the home country into possibly grateful and anyway prosperous citizens of a colony. Thirdly, there is the interest of defence. For an island nation this is a less pressing matter than for one with comparably powerful neighbours attached to it by land frontiers. The attempt to secure the original area by taking over regions around it is likely to export the original defensive anxiety to those conquered regions themselves, a Hobbesian process of restless desire for power after power, ending only in death, or rather, in this case, defeat. The defence interest in the British Empire was not of this sort. It was derivative from the need to secure colonies acquired from economic motives.

I shall not attempt to evaluate the extent to which these varied appeals to national interest have in fact been well-founded in the British case. But a few passing comments may be made. It was often argued that, although there was a sense in which the empire was a paying proposition, it was advantageous to some people – the traders and the accompanying retinue of administrators and officers – at the larger expense of the tax-paying population in general. Even more calculated to give pain is the argument that by sending people out to lord it over subject nations in places not permanently inhabitable by Europeans it was made certain that there would be a continuous inflow of returning persons with undesirably imperial attitudes.

That last consideration is the counterpart to a question about the desirability from the point of view of national interest of emigration, at least if it is voluntary emigration and not emigration of what may be called the early Australian kind, the enforced dumping of social rejects. Are not those who will choose to emigrate going to be the liveliest and most enterprising part of the population? No doubt the government was pleased to see the Pilgrim Fathers go. But was it in the national interest in the long run that people of above average ability and determination should be lost for good? There are good reasons for thinking that this country got much benefit from the Huguenot refugees who were driven here by the revocation of the edict of Nantes.

It may be worth dwelling for a moment on the idea of surplus population and on the correlative notion of overcrowding. Overcrowding, like expensiveness, is a relative term. And there are many different points of view from which it may be assessed. It may be conceived aesthetically, or in relation to transport (where increased mobility may lead to overcrowding without any increase in population), or as an economic matter as measured by unemployment or even starvation. But the fact of starvation is not a conclusive proof of overcrowdedness. It may be due to inefficient use of resources and could be got rid of by more fertiliser or better irrigation. To talk of surplus population, then, is always a highly contestable matter; there is no objective norm of the kind that there is for the blood temperature of the human body. Nevertheless no English person, living where there are eight hundred people per square mile, can be altogether immune to the appeal of the idea that if some fraction of the population were to emigrate, then they and we should both be better off.

Returning to my main theme of the silence of British political theorists on the subject of the empire at a time when they were citizens of the largest – if not exactly the most important, nor, as it has turned out, most long-lasting – empire in the history of the world: that silence is part of a more inclusive, even if not quite so unbroken, one about the principles that should govern the relations between sovereign states. Grotius, of course, is the magnificent exception. The rights of nations struggling to avoid the domination of others were inevitably present to the mind of a seventeenth-century Dutchman. Sixty-five years after Grotius's *De Jure Belli ac Pacis*, Locke adverted to the subject only in a very abstract chapter of his second *Treatise on Government* devoted to the topic of conquest. Denying any rights over the persons or property of their defeated opponents to unjust conquerors, he sought to limit the rightful claims of just ones. In particular he maintained that legitimate compensation for war damage could never extend to appropriating the land of the vanquished. That combines a little uncomfortably with his acceptance a few years later of a post as commissioner on the Board of Trade and Plantations.

It is obvious that governments have a duty to pursue the national interest of the nations they govern. It is ordinarily in the interest of a country that those who want to trade abroad should be allowed to do so and be protected where they do. The provision of such protection may, however, wind up with responsibility for Victoria's Indian Empire.

Do governments have a duty not to harm the interests of other nations if to do so is beneficial to their own? An extreme case of such harm would be the destruction of another country's independence, particularly where, as in the British colonies of settlement, the appropriation has disastrous consequences for the original inhabitants. In fact the problem never presented itself in quite that form. A small number of settlers arrive. They seek a peaceful accommodation with the natives. They go through the motions of buying land from the natives. The process continues and the natives begin to react violently. Death in battle is added to infection with unfamiliar diseases to reduce the indigenous population to a size at which it is easily contained in a few sequestered enclaves.

More generally it would seem that there is an inevitable convergence in the relations between different sovereign states to the Hobbesian position that no one is obliged to adhere to rules of generally beneficial conduct unless they have some guarantee that others will do so as well. So long as there are a few powerful nations who make it clear that they will be not bound by restraints it becomes foolish not to be prepared to follow suit. On the other hand, the better element may choose to band together to suppress the outlaw. I hope it is not nationalistic prejudice that leads most people in this country to see the last two major European wars in this light. That, of course, is to rest morality on long-term prudence. But, in a situation where there is no direct inclination to morality, that is the best that can be got.

The national interest is something that rulers or politicians need to be believed to be serving whether dependent on the electoral choice of the populace or not. But they often claim to be serving larger purposes as well. There can be no doubt that the British Empire was initiated by a combination of private commercial interest and government interest that was directly competitive with the military interest of other nations. That does not mean that the empire was entirely sustained or extended for these reasons. Government frequently intervened to protect non-Europeans in British possessions from the exploitative rapacity of traders and employers. Many justified their work or support for the empire on the ground that it was a force for civilisation and the true well-being of those it ruled.

## 5. The idea of a civilising mission

That claim that empire is justified as a force for civilisation is the basis on which imperialism must appeal to those who are not members of the nation whose interest is held to be served by colonial possessions, to those from whom self-government is withheld or removed by imperial appropriation and to those of the dominant nation who are not satisfied with the argument from national interest, either because they do not regard it as morally adequate or because they do not think that the colonies do contribute more to the national interest than they detract from it.

The principle should be formulated explicitly. *It is right to acquire or retain colonies because of the civilising effect that it has on their inhabitants*. That principle applies to colonies of conquest, with non-European populations in a markedly different cultural state from that of the colonial power. In the case of colonies of settlement, broadly speaking, the level of civilisation attained in the home country is directly implanted in a region where there was nothing at all. Then the principle is relevant only to the small indigenous population intruded on by settlement. Plainly it does not show up very well: moderately with the Maoris of New Zealand, badly with the Indians of Canada, very badly with the Aborigines of Australia. The cultural difference was so very large in the two latter instances that the massive infusion of the new culture was altogether destructive of the original one. I shall confine myself to the case of colonies of conquest.

The fact that this principle has often been sincerely and enthusiastically invoked does not mean that it is at all clear and definite. Before it can be critically examined it must be given a much more concrete interpretation than it ordinarily receives from its exponents.

The first element in need of examination is the idea of a civilising effect. That plainly has a number of aspects, each of them being some respect in which the advanced industrial societies of the jest differ from their non-European colonies. The most obvious difference is technological and economic. Colonies are agricultural and poor; their possessors are industrial and rich. There are all sorts of ways of measuring the difference: in terms of calories of food consumed per head, in terms of national product per head, in terms of the amount of available energy per head.

Other things being equal, which of course they are not, the colonial subjects will want more calories, disposable income and energy and that is as good a prima facie reason for supplying these things as could be hoped for. But the costs to the subjects are numerous and heavy. There is, first, the objectionable social transformation that will be involved. Change is upsetting anyway. In compelling movement from familiar villages to congested and insanitary towns it is so much the worse. Many non-European peoples – the Canadians of the Pacific North-West and some African tribes – were not undernourished or conspicuously subject to illness, at least until the colonists came. Furthermore they did not have to work as hard or at such disagreeable tasks as they were required to by the imposition of western methods of production. That revealed itself clearly whenever forced labour was introduced, either directly or by such devices as a head tax.

It is widely assumed that in the end everybody will have to be technically and economically modernised. Darwinism encouraged the acceptance of a doctrine of universal linear progress, which held that all human societies must pass through the same sequence of stages of development in the same order, even if not necessarily at the same speed. The Marxist theory of history is a melodramatic version of the doctrine. Even if it were correct, it would not follow that the change should be imposed rapidly and destructively from outside, rather than being managed by those it is going to affect in their own good time and in such a way as to allow mutual adjustment between the new procedures and the traditional culture.

It is nevertheless true that the attractions of greater wealth are so vivid as to obscure the accompanying costs. Starvation, sickness and infant mortality were much reduced in many countries that were colonially appropriated. The educated, westernised élites that developed in non-European colonies were strongly in favour of technical and economic modernisation. And, finally, what at first sight seems to be respect for the customs of primitive or undeveloped societies can also be viewed as condescension, a kind of indulgence of childishness.

To the administrator a different aspect of civilisation than that which interests traders and industrialists is important, the legal and political. Asian and African governments were, on the whole, seen as absolute, arbitrary and capricious. Their frequent tiresomeness to foreigners drew attention to their maltreatment of their own subjects. In India, even where as in the princely states, a community was not directly taken over, the native ruler was kept within bounds by an agent of the imperial power.

The forceful replacement of bad government by good is to be applauded. But rulers need, as well as virtue and a general knowledge of the business of government, an understanding of the ruled which will hardly ever be as penetrating as that of a compatriot. So good government is of no lasting value without a concomitant programme of creating a native political culture from which something better than the displaced absolutism can develop. History since colonial emancipation shows that such a programme was successfully carried out in India, but not in Africa, a fact attributable, no doubt, to India's long civilised past.

A third aspect of defective civilisation in colonial countries seizes much of the attention of missionaries, the agents of colonisation most explicitly committed to advancing the well-being of the native population. This is the prevalence of morally unacceptable customs. The laughable determination of missionaries to get naked women into print dresses should not be allowed to veil the force of this consideration. Headhunting, cannibalism, slavery, infanticide, female circumcision and the burning of widows on their husbands' funeral pyres are practices which surely fall outside the range of tolerance of moral disagreement. One might not feel justified in invading a country in order to put them down, but once installed in power there it would be morally unacceptable to endorse them, by allowing them to continue.

A final broad aspect of civilisation is that of intellect and culture, in a narrow but familiar sense of the word, of educatedness as that is understood in the advanced empire-holding nations. Of intellectual culture – science and learning – there was none to speak of in sub-Saharan Africa while in India, after auspicious beginnings, particularly in mathematics, it had succumbed to an oppressive religiosity. Artistic and literary culture was highly developed in India, but effectively available only to a few. African art has come to be admired in the West only in this century.

This and its more modest extensions in dress, furniture and style of personal, domestic life is the most central and intimate aspect of culture in the broadest sense and the one which all but the grossest and most parochial of modernisers would wish not to intrude on, except by the addition of knowledge, particularly by the dilution of superstitious error into innocuous legend.

The benefits of these various aspects of civilisation – prosperity, security, intellectual and personal liberty, moral improvement, education – are real enough and to some extent they go hand in hand. A degree of prosperity would seem to be necessary condition of the rest, although not sufficient for them on its own. It was this that utilitarian administrators and evangelical missionaries took as their goal in the nineteenth-century British Empire. No doubt there was some insincerity in this, less hypocrisy than self-deception. But it does provide an answer to the objection that it is wrong to keep people in political subjection, against their will and in your own interest: namely, it is really in their interest too. But it has a serious logical limitation if it is taken to justify permanent imperial rule.

This is that it is inevitably self-undermining. The justifying purpose is to bring the colonial possession up to the civilised level of the colonial power. To do that is, among other things, to equip it with that degree of political capacity on which the colonial power rests its own claim to self-government. If it is not so equipped then, unless some mystic racial theory of the intrinsic and unalterable political ineducability of the subject people is held to account for this very special unfitness, the civilising project must be judged a failure. And, if the other aspects of the civilising mission are to be transferable, why should not this one be too?

A version of the same argument can be used to counter the claim that since only the educated, westernised minority of the subject people calls for independence there is no sufficient reason to grant it. That minority is the part of the subject people that has so far most absorbed the politically educative lesson. Their wishes thus constitute good evidence for what the wishes of all are likely to be as the process develops.

Plamenatz points out the difficult position that an imperial power that is itself committed to liberal democracy is in by denying a say in government to its colonial subjects and persisting in despotic rule over them, however benevolent. The position becomes all the less defensible when the subject people themselves, or the politically articulate among them, become converted to liberal-democratic principles.

It is an interesting fact that progressive British political thinkers, from the Utilitarians to the Fabians, have held efficient government of non-Europeans to be incompatible with, and far more important than, self-government. One large part of the story is told in Eric

Stokes's illuminating book *The English Utilitarians and India*. Most utilitarians, from Bentham onward, were not very enthusiastic about democracy, a trait they shared with Milner. Only James Mill could be described as a convinced democrat, believing as he did that the only human group that has a direct interest in the general welfare is the populace at large, who should therefore rule. His extraordinary dislike of India is the explanation of his indifference to the idea that it could be developed there.

British policy towards its non-European colonies was always very external compared to that of France. In the early years of the nineteenth century, that reflected a conservative, Burkean respect for the traditional culture of India. The French in north Africa, later in the century, ruled people of comparable cultural development, formerly subjects of a great Muslim empire. They sought to make Frenchmen out of the inhabitants of their colonies. But even at its most interfering the British empire was never assimilative by design.

There was, of course a conceivable way of preserving the imperial union without denying political participation to the colonial population, the Roman procedure of extending full citizenship to them. That had, after all been the manner in which the conquered Welsh and Irish and the inherited, more or less peaceably absorbed Scotch had been accommodated within a unified Britain. Clearly the vast disparity of populations, added to distance and persistent cultural difference, ruled that out. The fact of common citizenship excludes the claim that nationalist movements of the Celtic peoples are standard cases of the pursuit of colonial liberation. It equally undermines the notion, polemically attractive to British sufferers from American criticism of empire, that Lincoln, in bringing the whole force of the North against the culturally different South, was himself an imperialist. The North, furthermore, had a very conspicuous civilising mission, the abolition of slavery, with which to consecrate the more lowly political object of preserving the union.

In the last half-century the most notable piece of imperial expansion has been the Soviet Russian colonisation of the previously independent nations of Eastern Europe. This was cloaked in an unconvincing veil of federation and of the pursuit of a system transcending nationalism. In fact these newly colonised nations have been ruled by local puppets set up by Russia and controlled by marginally visible Russian soldiers and police. In most cases there is at least some measure of Slavonic cultural affinity between the subject peoples and the ruling power. There is also a bleak and minimal applicability of the redeeming principle of common citizenship shared by the two parties to the relationship. The subjects have much the same political rights as the citizens of Russia proper. They may vote for a list of official candidates at election rituals and are free to express opinions licensed by the state. From a liberal-democratic point of view, that is to say, they both have no political rights at all.

## 6. Empire and evolution

There is a coarser, more down-to-earth version of the doctrine of the civilising mission of empire which had some currency during the revival of imperial expansion in the late-nineteenth-century scramble for Africa. That was the period in which implications for politics and society were being enthusiastically derived from the Darwinian theory of evolution. One of them was that the conflict between nations for imperial mastery was the competitive process which would help to produce and from which would emerge the nation or nations most fitted to survive. The pursuit of empire, on that view, is a sign of competitive fitness, and, by implication, of excellence.

In its most ruthless form that picture no doubt envisaged the complete elimination of the less successful populations, taking their cultures with them into oblivion. Less fiercely the competition was seen as one between the cultures themselves rather than between their educable human bearers.

The struggle and its ultimate end, the universal domination of the competitively strongest culture, were seen as inevitable. But, as with the equally deterministic Marxist theory of history, a place was left for those who perceived the way things were inevitably going to help in moving the process forward.

This activist version of the principle of lying back and enjoying it is not an irresistible implication of the discovery of some humanly interesting inevitability. To become convinced that they are eventually going to die does not lead people to commit suicide. It encourages them to eat a lot of fibre and to give up smoking. But that is not to the point unless the qualities of a culture in which fitness in the competitive struggle consists are bad. It was the belief of the social Darwinians that fitness, demonstrated by the fact of survival, was the criterion of superiority.

The military effectiveness on which this kind of success depends is a consequence of numbers, economic power and, up to a point, capacity for organisation. Impalpable psychological factors of resolution, ferocity and warlikeness have to be invoked when the outcome goes against form. If we can sum these things up loosely as *strength* we may say that it is a tautology that the battle is to the strong, in defiance of Ecclesiastes.

The question is still open as to whether the strong are more civilised or even more prosperous than those they overcome. Two large apparent examples to the contrary are the Mongols and the barbarians who at least contributed to, even if we should not say caused, the destruction of Rome. There is at least no Eurocentric absurdity in saying that in these cases culturally inferior conquerors prevailed over their cultural superiors. The point is enforced by the consideration that in both cases military conquest was not succeeded by cultural domination. The Mongols left nothing behind but a memory of horror. The barbarians were digested slowly, painfully and, as this century shows, imperfectly by the classical culture they over-ran.

## 7. The rights of nations

The evolutionary version of the civilising mission is too indifferent to the values that constitute civilisation to be very persuasive. But the principle that empire is justified by the civilising effect it has on the dominated may also seem too crudely utilitarian. Do nations, it may be objected, have no rights?

It could be said that they have legal rights under international law. That law requires that their territorial integrity be respected, provided that they respect the territorial integrity of others and perhaps satisfy other conditions which add up to being a member in good standing of the comity of nations, such as providing security for diplomats, extraditing criminals, putting down or helping to put down pirates and so forth.

There are two difficulties with this as regards the British Empire, the first of which still obtains. First of all, international law is law only in a sense somewhere between the literal and the metaphorical. There are lawyers and bills and courts but where, in ordinary legal systems, there is a sovereign source of law in the international case there are only treaties and occasional international conferences, and the only formal coercive power is a few soldiers here and there in blue berets carrying binoculars.

Secondly, Britain's Indian and African possessions at the time they were acquired were not part of the comity of nations in the sense I have described. Neither were really even nations. India had had a precarious imperial unity under the Moguls. But it disintegrated after the death of Aurungzebe in 1707 into a chaos of warring kingdoms. The parts of Africa brought under British control in the late nineteenth century were doubly non-national. They had not reached the level of political organisation to be recognised as members of the general, diplomatically interacting, comity of nations and, though they are even less to blame for that, the colonial units established by the British were not truly nations in the cultural sense. This has had grim consequences in Nigeria and elsewhere.

How are we to conceive the moral rights of nations, as contrasted with those of their individual citizens? The usual analogy of ruler and ruled to parent and child is a possible point of entry here. In the relevant case, that of the non-European colonies in Asia and Africa, the imperial parent has to be understood in the sense of Locke's notion of parental power, which implies no biological relationship, only the assumption of responsibility. India, to explore this comparison, might be seen, at the time in the eighteenth century when British rule was established there, as a highly gifted but wayward and disorganised child, in need of care and attention. The African colonies, seen in the same light, were, at the time of their acquisition, very young children found wandering about in a very rough neighbourhood. Taking them into care looks like a work of mercy when one remembers what the Germans did to the Hereros in south-west Africa or Leopold of Belgium in the Congo.

If this analogy is to be taken seriously at all it should be extended to accommodate the fact that children ordinarily grow up. Only the constitutionally retarded can rightly be kept in a state of permanent dependence and subordination. The normal presumption, in the cases of both children and colonies, is that they will grow up, that they will acquire the capacity to manage their own affairs. The criteria of this capacity for self-government and, more generally, the arguments for and against it are the topic of Plamenatz's admirable book *Alien Rule and Self-Government* which I mentioned earlier.

## 8. Plamenatz on self-government

Since my subject is the relation of the British Empire to the theory of imperialism and since the British Empire no longer exists, I have not been concerned with principles that have a direct practical application for Britain. So I have allowed myself to consider the problem of the justification of empire with the utmost generality. Plamenatz, writing in 1960, in the middle of the process of decolonisation, concentrated on the immediately practical problem of whether European rule of colonies with non-European populations should continue.

The largest empires of this kind still in existence when he wrote were the British and the French, the two geographically European major nations most committed to liberal democracy. Their continuing denial of self-government to their colonies had an element of inconsistency which required it to be justified.

He considered two ways in which capacity for self-government may be conceived. In the first, which does not require democracy in the self-governing nation, it consists in being a good neighbour to other nations, in being efficient and not too corrupt, in affording security and public order and in accepting the canons of acceptable behaviour as between nations which have emerged over time. The second requires that, in addition, or perhaps primarily, the social preconditions of effective democracy should be assured.

He considers various arguments for continued European rule; the social character of African communities means that they do not, perhaps cannot foreseeably, satisfy the second condition; that the populations of these communities would be at risk, if decolonised, from self-interested élites pretending to share liberal-democratic ideals, from oppression by a tribe other than their own, from some less genial alien ruler; that European settlers must be protected. On the other side he considers the arguments that the art of making democratic government work can be learnt only by practice, that the imperial powers only pretend to be interested in preparing their colonies for independence, that only compatriots of a subject people can be sufficiently ruthless to modernise them and that colonial peoples do not want western liberty and democracy, but prosperity and self-respect.

The central question in all this is how can a liberal-democratic imperial power reconcile being constrained by its principles to grant self-government to its colonies with the likelihood that the liberated colony will turn out to be neither liberal or democratic? Must not all imperial power, before it abandons its responsibilities, however questionably these may have been acquired, embrace Rousseau's paradox and force its colonial subjects to be free?

The paradoxical nature of Rousseau's notion can, at least in some cases, be circumvented. A child, unwilling to leave home, may, once ejected, find autonomy much better than he feared. There are two major examples of desirably forced freedom in recent history. Liberal democracy was forced on Germany and Japan in 1945 by force of American arms, in flagrant contradiction to the political traditions of both countries, and, it seems reasonable to suppose, to the wishes of most of their inhabitants. But in both cases it has flourished.

How has it worked out in practice with the British colonies of conquest? As far as India is concerned with impressive success. One does not have to endorse the completeness of Fitzjames Stephen's somewhat blunt description of India in his day as 'a land of cruel wars, ghastly superstitions, wasting plague and famine' to suppose that it was safer, healthier, more prosperous and more peaceable when the British left than it would have been if they had left after the Mutiny. A bonus has been the full satisfaction of Plamenatz's more demanding criterion of the capacity for self-government: India remains the world's largest democracy. The African story has been less consoling. The form of government is everywhere charismatic or military dictatorship. Violence abounds. Opportunities or economic progress are widely obstructed by what has been called kleptocracy, the rule of thieves. Whether we were justified in taking on a civilising mission in Africa or not, our presence there was hardly a success. Either we should not have gone in the first place or not have left so soon, or, perhaps, have acted differently while we were there. The present condition of uncolonised Ethiopia and independent Liberia suggests that the torments of post-colonial Africa are, at any rate, not entirely of our making.

*Auguste Comte Lecture at the London School of Economics, 1988.*

# Property

## 1. Persons and their property

People are ordinarily taken to be distinct from their property. The idea of a person who has no property at all is, to our normal way of thinking and speaking, a perfectly digestible one. He may have lost all he had through misfortune or folly; he may never have had anything. The requirements of public decency may seem to entail that everyone should at least own the clothes he stands up in. But that is not inevitable. The garment he wears may be on temporary loan from a welfare authority. Yet even in these understandable circumstances, the person himself exists and is no less a person than a millionaire landowner.

The distinction is most obvious when person and property are conceived in the simplest physical or bodily way. If a person is taken to be the same as a particular human body, clearly bounded in space by a characteristically shaped surface of skin, he can be marked off readily from other physical things with definite positions in space that may be items of his property: a building, a bicycle, a set of underpants. Even if the institution of slavery exists, and people can be things owned as well as owners, the owner and the thing owned can still be easily told apart.

Even at this level, however, some marginal obscurities are to be found. Is a set of false teeth which, although ordinarily contained within the body's surface, is readily and undestructively removable from the body, a bit of the person or a bit of his property? It is only mechanically connected to the rest of the body, in the way that a hat is, and not, like an eye or a kidney, organically involved with it. If false teeth seem to be property rather than person, along with wigs and spectacles, what about prosthetic devices of a more intimate kind: artificial limbs, pacemakers for those with defective hearts, the silver or steel pins with which diseased bone is replaced, plastic tubes introduced to supply deficiencies in the digestive system? What, finally in this sequence, about those undeniable parts of the body that automatically renew themselves and generally fall or are conventionally removed from the body: hair on the scalp or face, teeth, fingernails? Perhaps we should say that those are part of the person until actually detached from the rest of the body, at which point they become his property, if he cares to enter a claim for them. Most of us are content to leave them on the barbershop floor or in the dentist's basin.

But the identifications of a person with a particular known body and an item of property with a particular physical object are both over-simple and questionable. As to persons and bodies, there are human bodies that are not persons, namely dead ones. Usually, of course, corpses do not long remain describable as human bodies but they can be embalmed. In the other direction, non-identity of persons and bodies is less obvious. We do not know of any persons who are not, or do not have, bodies. The possibility is envisaged, of course, by everyone who believes in the disembodied existence of persons after the death and dissolution of their bodies. It is also envisaged, in a somewhat more pedestrian but still speculative way, by those who conceive of the possibility of brain-transplants, from say, the body of an elderly person to that of some otherwise youthful and healthy person who has died of brain damage incurred in an accident, in which case the person does not have a particular body.

Equally, not all property takes the form of physical objects, even if it has some exiguous physical realisation in the form of a piece of paper. My shares in a steel company, my bank deposit, the rights to shoot grouse I possess as member of a syndicate are not be identified with a particular chunk of machinery, bundle of banknotes or flock of birds.

Even when conceived as straightforward material things, then, persons and items of property reveal a certain penumbra of indistinguishability. When this conception of things is rejected as over-simple, as I think in both cases it must be, the difficulty of distinguishing between person and property seems to be augmented. Take the case of my reputation. The law of defamation lays down that I am to be compensated for its malicious destruction. Should this be assimilated to compensation for bodily assault, which would make my reputation part of me, or to compensation for malicious damage to my house, which would make it part of my property? To the latter, I suppose, since my reputation consists of the opinion of my character held by others, not of my character itself, which might be damaged by introducing drugs into my food, and is pretty obviously part of me.

## 2. *Labour, the body and life*

The object of this modest conceptual terror-campaign has not been to pursue answers to the specific questions raised in the course of it. It is rather to prepare the way for a much more comprehensive question: that of whether I cannot be said to own myself. More specifically, I want to suggest that there are good reasons for saying that if one owns anything one owns one's labour, one's body, as the primary instrument of labour, and one's life, as the condition of the body in which alone it can be an instrument of labour by the person whose body it is. (One man can use another's dead body as an instrument of labour but only in rather bizarre circumstances, for example, by using it to reach a third drowning man who would otherwise be out of range.)

The idea that one's self is one's property, as much as the things external to or no part of one's body, whether physical objects or not, which are usually alone so described, could well have implications for moral problems connected with the disposal of the aspects of the self or person I have picked out for consideration. If one's labour is one's own to dispose of, why should one not sell oneself into slavery? If one's body is one's own, has one not a right to sell one's organs for purposes of transplantation? If one's life is one's own, can there be any legitimate objection to suicide?

Of the three aspects of the self or person I have listed, labour is clearly the fundamental one. If my labour can be shown to be my property it will not be hard to show that my body and my life are. There is, of course, a familiar theory that labour is the primary source or origin of property, best known in the explicit form given to it by Locke but, I shall argue, adopted, by implication, by Marx. This holds that something becomes a man's property, in Locke's phrase, if he has mixed his labour with it, that is to say, if he has appropriated it in a case where it is ready to use or worked it into a usable form in a case where it is not, it being assumed in both cases that it does not already belong to somebody else.

This labour theory of property does not ordinarily maintain that property in a thing can be acquired only by the labour of appropriating or making it. But it does imply that this is the only way in which property can come into existence *de novo*. The recognised alternative ways of acquiring property, by gift or exchange, both entail that the person who makes the transfer already owns the thing transferred. I cannot logically give or sell you what I do not own, although I may go through the motions of doing so. From this it follows that all property must *ultimately* result from somebody's labour, however easy it may have been (for example, finding a huge diamond in a deserted area) and however many hands it may have passed through since by various terms of transfer. It is not the same thing as Marx's labour theory of *value*. Nor does it imply the stronger position that I want to defend: that labour is one's property, provided, of course that one has not already sold it or given it away.

To prepare the way for the establishment of this position I shall turn, first, to an attempt at a broadly adequate definition of property and then to arguing that property is a moral right before, and more fundamentally, than it is a legal one.

### 3. *The definition of property*

I propose as a definition of property that it is anything which someone has an exclusive right to the use and disposal of. Several items in this definition need further explanation. A man's right to the use and disposal of his property is *exclusive* in the sense that he has it and nobody else has. I have a right to make at least certain uses of a public park, I may walk, sit, picnic and exercise my dog in it, but then so may anybody else who chooses to do so. The possession of exclusive rights may indeed be invested in a group of people rather than a single person. But these rights, for the joint owners, exclude corresponding rights in everyone but members of the group. This element of exclusiveness, of being mine or yours and *not anybody else's*, seems to me the crucial element of the concept of property.

It is important, however, that the essential exclusiveness of property rights should not be interpreted as *absoluteness*. One's right, as its owner, to use a thing is circumscribed by the requirement that the use should not be, in the moral case, harmful and in the legal case, forbidden by law. If I own a gun I am not thereby morally or legally entitled to use it on anyone or anything. I am entitled to use it in safe or legally designated places, perhaps at suitable or specified times, on inanimate targets or on animals that I need to eat or live by selling or are designated as game. My property-rights in my house are not necessarily infringed, let alone cancelled or undermined, if I am forbidden by morality or law to run a brothel in it, or to paint it pale green to the aesthetic distress of my more sensitive neighbours. As a utilitarian I am inclined to believe that no moral rights whatsoever are absolute, except perhaps that of having one's interests taken into account in moral or legal decisions whose results may affect them.

The other problematic element in the definition is disposal. By that word I mean either the transfer of ownership of the thing in question to another, whether for a consideration and by sale or simply as a gift, or the destruction of the thing. In some cases, where the item of property is short-lived or edible or combustible, for example, the use which makes the thing worth owning at all may involve its destruction. The characteristic use of a dish of scrambled eggs or a cigarette necessarily involves its disposal.

Here too the right is not, or need not be, absolute to be a perfectly genuine property-right. I should not, morally or legally, give a large brandy to a child of five or, to dig out Plato's old favourite, sell my submachine gun to a lunatic. The limitations correspond to the restrictions on harmful or legally forbidden use that I have already mentioned. A further question arises with regard to disposal. If I have purposely acquired or made something which is or would be of very great value to people other than myself, without any appreciable loss of value to me, such as a great picture by Rembrandt, the fact that it is my property surely confers no moral right on me to use it to get the fire started? Similarly, if I own something whose value survives the lifetime in which alone I can use it, does my right to dispose of it stretch out in perpetuity? But even if these restrictions on the right of disposal are admitted, an exclusive right to non-harmful use remains and also exclusive rights to some kinds of disposal, quite sufficient for the thing in question to be described as property.

## 4. Property is moral before it is legal

Property is primarily, even if not most obviously, a moral rather than a legal concept. No doubt in a legally organised society most assumptions about property are made in an implicitly legal sense. Practically, the most important questions about the allocation of property are ones in which a legal decision is taken as both relevant and authoritative. But questions about property arise in domestic circumstances to which the provisions of the law either do not apply or would not be taken as relevant. Who owns the bicycle that was given ten years ago to John but which he outgrew two years ago and has since been exclusively used by James?

That the concept of property is moral before it is legal is maintained by both Locke and Hume. In Locke's case it is an immediate implication of his claim that property is a natural right. A minimal conception of a natural right is that it is a moral right that everyone has, prior to and independently of any positive legal arrangements and by reference to which the moral adequacy of a legal system is to be judged.

Hume maintains that respect for property (which he rather quaintly calls justice) is on a level with fidelity or recognition of the duty of promise-keeping and with allegiance or recognition of the duty to obey the law of the state, all three being what he calls artificial virtues, which are not instinctive like benevolence but have to be rationally worked-out as collective conventions that are advantageous for men in general. The best-known application of this classification together of duties is in Hume's criticism of the social contract theory. My duty to obey the law cannot derive from my duty to keep promises, without what he calls an 'unnecessary circuit', since both have the same basis. By exactly parallel reasoning he could have argued that my duty to respect the property of others cannot be derived from my duty to obey the law.

Insofar as Hume defines these artificial virtues as non-instinctive, as the product of reflection on the collective conventions of behaviour most propitious for the general welfare, it could even be argued that property should be detached from the palpably artificial institutions of law and promising and associated with instinctive benevolence. Young children and animals display indignant possessiveness without having any grasp of the notion of an advantageous collective convention, just as they are instinctively prompted, by something like Hume's sympathy, to acts of direct benevolence.

Hume's case suggests that it is not necessary to believe in natural rights to believe that property is primarily a moral concept. The matter is hard to settle in view of the indeterminacy of the contention that there are natural rights. If that is taken to mean, full-bloodedly with Locke, that there are universally possessed moral rights, independent of law, which hold quite absolutely and of which any legal curtailment is *ipso facto* invalid, that they can be apprehended as self-evidently true by the moral intuition of any rational being in that they can somehow be deduced from a grasp of the essential nature of man, then the primarily moral character of property does not presuppose belief in natural rights. But if, minimally, to believe in natural rights is only to hold that there are things which men in general ought to be allowed to do or be provided with, unless this would seriously detract from the general interest, then it does.

## 5. The priority of morals to law

To say that there are moral as well as legal rights is not to say that there is a system of categorical moral rules, authoritatively promulgated by a moral sovereign, by reference to which all moral conflicts and disagreements are to be settled. It is not, in other words, to hold that there is the articulate system of natural law corresponding in form to an explicitness to positive law. That doctrine is, however, an exaggerated expression of something true: that morality is prior to law, not in the historical sense that it preceded it in time, but in the sense that it is the touchstone by reference to which the adequacy or acceptability of law is to be assessed and that it is the principal source from which the *content* of a system of laws must be derived.

In holding that morality is the touchstone of law, I do not mean that one is absolved from the moral obligation to obey a particular law if its enforcement infringes the moral rights of any of the parties involved. The general utility of a legal system can compensate for a measure of morally unsatisfactory legislation. But if a legal system seriously and consistently ignores or overrides the moral rights of those to whom it applies, it should be disobeyed, a course which, if it is morally followed, will eliminate the 'habitual obedience' without which it is not a legal system at all.

Morality is not the source of all of the content of law. But the elements of law that do not have a moral foundation are comparatively trivial matters of convention or procedure. Morality does not determine whether people should drive on the left- or right-hand side of the road. It is only tenuously related to the decision to have a convention about which side of the road to drive on at all, although such a convention is so obviously advantageous that a state that failed to institute or enforce one could be regarded as having failed in its duty.

But morality does provide the content for laws forbidding killing people or assaulting them, taking their possessions without their consent, deceiving them in matters which seriously touch their interests, making defamatory statements about them, breaking agreements that have been formally and explicitly entered into with them about matters of importance. The morality in question might well seem problematic, given the emphasis by philosophers on the individuality of morals, the fact, so far as it is a fact, that each man has to come to his own moral conclusions, even if they have the economical form of 'the Pope is infallible'. Against this a measure of realism requires the recognition that there is no large disagreement, either in numbers of dissentients or breadth of dissension from the norm, about the moral principles supplying the basic, non-procedural content of law.

Not all the principles about which there is a broad consensus in a society will be embodied in its laws. Some may be legally unenforceable or not worth enforcing. Only those should be, and generally will be, embodied in law whose effective enforcement is required for preservation of social order and peace. The fate of prohibition in the USA shows what happens when a law is enacted that rests on insufficient consensus.

Property, then, is a moral notion before it is a legal one, and it is on the moral principles of property that the laws of property should, and no doubt largely do, rest. But these principles are not timeless intuitive certitudes. They may change with changing circumstances and forms of property.

## 6. The labour theory of property

Locke's theory that labour is the ultimate source or ground of property is one of those reasonable philosophical ideas that has been brought into a discredit it does not in itself deserve by the questionable company it was associated with on its first appearance in the world. The weaknesses of the further detail of Locke's doctrine are well-known and they have tended to infect its fundamental and much more defensible propositions with their own ill-repute. In the first place, labour cannot be the sole, but at best the ultimate, ground of property rights. Most of what we own we acquired not by making or appropriating it but by sale or gift. Secondly, most of what is produced is the work of many co-operating hands or, to the extent that it is the result of one man's labour, is the result of the application of that labour to utensils and instruments belonging to others. Thirdly, and most questionably of all, there is Locke's argument that since money owes its value to convention and can be accumulated without spoiling to any extent whatever, men can be assumed to have endorsed the large inequalities that result from its accumulation.

Yet Locke's fundamental idea seems a very sensible one. There are obvious utilitarian reasons for the existence of property-rights, for the exclusive allocation of things to particular persons. People need reliable and substantial access to all sorts of things to live effectively. If the world's goods are not parcelled out in this exclusive way, men's satisfaction of their needs will lead to incessant, destructive conflict.

Given the necessity of some such system of exclusive allocation, the most intuitively appealing answer to the question of how the allocation should be made is that each person should be accorded an exclusive right to what he has himself made or found. This consequence seems to have the backing of a natural property instinct, as I suggested earlier when I mentioned the natural possessiveness of young children and animals. Considerations of utility of a more indirect kind than the satisfaction or frustration of this immediate possessive instinct reinforce the conclusion. The expectation of an exclusive right to the use of what they find or make will greatly enhance the readiness of people to find or make useful things.

The productiveness of the division of labour makes it natural for people to produce goods they do not need in order to exchange them for things that they do. The unrequited transfer of property by gift is an inevitable consequence of the institution of the family in which productive individuals have responsibilities for providing for the needs of unproductive ones. From that it is a short step to the transfer of property by free gift from the owner to anyone he chooses to benefit. Where this becomes questionable is where the object in question is something that continues to be of value either in perpetuity, such as land, or at any rate for a period that is much longer than the life of the original owner during which he can make use of it. The law of entail, by which land is vested in a potentially immortal family rather than a passing individual, is one way of dealing with this problem, suited to a simple agricultural society. Graduated inheritance taxes are a more flexible device appropriate to more complicated economic circumstances.

The simplest argument for the labour theory of property is regressive in form. Property-rights are not part of the natural order of things, they are an originated social contrivance. Although most of my property may have been bought or given to me, not all property can be the result of transfers. There must be a point at which it originates, where something that is not property at all becomes someone's property for the first time. In the simplest, limiting case, this will be a matter of appropriating a free good that one finds. But, in all but the most extreme cases, things become items of usable value only by the investment of labour in them: fruit has to be picked, game killed and prepared, land cleared, articles of manufacture fashioned more or less laboriously from laboriously acquired raw materials. Labour stands to property, in other words, such as sense-experience does to knowledge, ostensive concepts to defined ones or the directly apprehended to the inferred.

I mentioned earlier that Marx, apparently the great opponent of property, is, as much as Locke, an adherent of the labour theory of property. The defect of capitalism is not that it is a property system but that it assigns property in valuable things to the wrong people, to those who have not produced them. Exploitation consists in depriving those who labour of what their labour produces. Men are cheated under capitalism by the fact that labour is not undertaken by men's own choice to produce things that they will own and control themselves. Marx's account of post-capitalist society is not of an idealistic communism in which men, animated by self-forgetting collective enthusiasm, wish to augment the common stock, as in a kibbutz or utopian settlement. His model for the unalienated producer is the artist who expresses himself in his work, even if he chooses, when it is made, to make it freely available to others rather than use it as the raw material of a commercial bargain. Only by a certain sleight of hand, by which labour is identified with manual work, is the entrepreneur who creates a great industrial monopoly denied the status of creative producer that Marx would wish to see accorded to his alienated and exploited workers.

### 7. Do I own my labour?

What I want to propose is that if labour is the ultimate *ground* of property it is also the primary or most elementary *form* of property. There are two arguments for this conclusion. The first is that it follows that it is property if property is defined in the way I defined it as that to whose use and disposal a man has an exclusive right. Unless I have contracted to put my labour at the disposal of someone else, I surely have an exclusive right to use it as I choose and no one else has a right to make this decision for me. Among the uses I may so choose is that of selling it to another, of taking employment under his direction, for a consideration, and also that of giving it to anyone I choose, as where I help a neighbour to pick his apples or repair his roof.

This conclusion, of course, could easily be avoided by adding another clause to my definition of property so as to make it read – that, external to the person himself, to whose use or disposal he has an exclusive right. Now I should agree that the definition so amended covers pretty well what we ordinarily mean by property provided that we do not make too much fuss about the precise interpretation of 'external to the person himself'. But it seems a somewhat arbitrary proceeding. Consider the request: list the people in this room who were born in the same year as Fred. Colloquially we should not include Fred himself in the list. But that is surely not because Fred was not born in the same year as himself; it is because it is so irresistibly obvious that he was, it goes without saying.

Another argument for rejecting the additional clause so as to preserve the vernacular, conversational sense of the word 'property' is that it makes it hard to explain the sense of the word 'slavery'. No doubt there morally ought not to be such a *thing* as slavery, but there undoubtedly is such a word and there has been such a legal status, even if the current applications of the word are, in most parts of the world, figurative. A man is a slave if he, or more narrowly, his labour belongs to somebody else. Here again, indeed, the conclusion that I own my labour would be avoided by defining a slave simply as one over whose labour another person has an exclusive right of use or disposal, but in this application the artificiality of the manoeuvre is more obtrusive.

Incidentally, in ascribing to a man an exclusive right to the use or disposal of his labour, unless he has transferred it by sale or gift, here again one is not necessarily ascribing an *absolute* right over it to him. Legal systems typically allow for conscription, military or even industrial, and this is commonly regarded as morally acceptable, at least in time of war and provided that conscientious objection is allowed for. Less formally, it would ordinarily be regarded as a man's moral duty to put his labour at the service of the injured and endangered in a situation of natural catastrophe, such as an earthquake or hurricane, which had happened to leave him in good working order.

The second argument is that labour is undoubtedly treated in the same way as property in all but the most individualistically primitive types of economy. It is bought and sold, the subject matter of contractual exchange, priced and advertised. As Marx said, it is a commodity. for most of us, of course, it is the most valuable thing we possess and without it, unless we are very lucky, we shall not possess anything else.

This second argument is, indeed, no more than a factual parallel to the normative state of affairs referred to in the first. Where the first said that it is generally required that people ought to be allowed to use and dispose of their labour, exclusively but not absolutely, in whatever way they choose, the second says that men act, both in law and in economic practice, as if they have exactly the same rights over their labour, provided they have not in some way transferred them to another, as they are taken to have over what would more straightforwardly be described as their property. What differentiates it from property in the conventional sense is that it is not *acquired*, but, as it were, innately or intrinsically *possessed*.

It might even be argued that if labour is recognised as the most elementary or fundamental form of property, the labour theory of property, the view that those things which are turned into useful or valuable goods by labour are the property of the labourer (or, one should add perhaps, whoever owns his labour), is rendered more intelligible. Certainly the intuitive appeal of the idea that labour creates property does not extend to a case where the labourer has in some way transferred his rights over his labour, or the relevant portion of it, to another.

Marx seems to have regarded any work that one does for another, except as a free gift, as morally objectionable, for this is at least part of what is meant by his view that it is alienating. Man, for Marx, is an essentially productive being. He realises his ideal nature to the extent that he is engaged in free and creative production. The model of the unalienated man is the creative artist, not in bondage to dealers and patrons.

## 8. Slavery

A possible reason for resistance to the idea that a man's labour is his property is the moral objectionableness of the institution of slavery. For if a man has an exclusive right to the use and disposal of his own labour, why should he not sell it outright instead of renting it out for a comparatively short period of time, determined by the length of the period of notice agreed to by the parties to the undertaking? In civilised societies some fairly protracted commitments of future labour are to be found, such as twelve-year enlistments in the armed forces, but they are comparatively exceptional and are usually reversible, if with some trouble and expense. A man's labour may in fact be monopolised throughout his working life by a single employer but that does not make him a slave. At any moment his labour is committed to that employer only as far into the future as the length of the agreed period of notice.

Why, then, should the outright and irreversible sale of a man's labour as a whole, parallel to his outright and irreversible sale of a house or a thing he has made, be morally and legally forbidden in the civilised world? For slavery does not necessarily imply that the labour sold will be harmfully used, to invoke the condition which restricts the absoluteness of the right of disposal of property of the ordinary kind. The tasks to which slaves have been put, domestic or industrial, have generally been at least harmless, and to a large extent beneficial. Detached historians, indeed, have justified the institution of slavery as a necessary education for the indolent majority of mankind in habits of useful and persistent industry, imposed by a minority consistently successful in the more immediately attractive arts of war.

Plainly one does not need to look very far for the harm involved in slavery. It does not lie in the uses to which the slave are put but in the way that the slaves are used. Roman slaves were in the complete power of their masters, including the power to put them to death; they could not own property or money; their children inherited their status as slaves. This degree of subjection is, no doubt, congruous with the way in which men have historically become enslaved, as the result of capture in war and as an alternative to instant death. But this, I suggest, is not a choice that it can ever be usually acceptable to offer. If it is ever morally right to kill anyone, it must then be morally wrong not to do so. The moral extremity of the case means that it can only be right to do it when it would be wrong to do anything else.

The nearest approach there is to voluntary enslavement is the situation in which men forfeit their freedom through debt. But attaching a portion of man's freely earned income, if adequately administered, can be as effective in getting a debt paid off as enslavement. Even the most humane and businesslike form of slavery that can be conceived, a commitment of labour for the whole of a man's working life, closes too may options for anyone to accept it except under some form of duress. Although very far from the kind of total and degrading subjection involved in slavery as it has historically prevailed, such an arrangement would correspond fairly closely to feudal serfdom, in which the lord had a claim only to a clearly defined portion of the serf's labour. The nearest thing there is to it is the kind of bondage many women, but also some men, enter into on marriage in a society in which there is no divorce. But even in such societies the status of fugitive spouse is much safer and more comfortable than that of a fugitive slave.

The idea that labour not only makes property but is a form of property itself does, then, leave the question of slavery open. It does not rule it out *a priori*. The only theory of property to do that is, I think, Hegel's, according to which property is essential to man, as necessary for the exercise of the will without which man's humanity cannot be actualised. For the slave, having no title to his own labour and its products, can acquire no property of his own by his own efforts. If the system allows him to hold property at all, it could only be property that he has received by way of gifts. However, even if the labour-is-property thesis leaves the question open, it can be readily closed by the kind of consequential considerations I have suggested. Plenty of people are comfortable enough in their work, or sufficiently unenterprising, to be virtual slaves, in the very mild sense that they serve only one employer throughout their working lives. In principle, it should be noted, certain special duties are incumbent on the slave-owner. He has to support the slave, he cannot dismiss him and should not be allowed to 'free' him against his will when he is no longer useful. He can dispose of the slave only to a buyer who will take over these responsibilities. The prevailing morality of employment contains a corresponding old-retainer principle with regard to those whom I have called virtual slaves. In general, there is no reason that supports absolute, unconditional and irrevocable contracts that is strong enough to outweigh the considerations that favour conditional undertakings which allow for the unpredictability of changes in the desires and the circumstances of the contracting parties.

## 9. Labour and the body

The main grounds that exist for regarding a man's labour as a part, indeed a constant and universal part, of his property apply also in the case of his body. If the colloquial restriction of the term 'property' to things external to the self or person is abandoned in the one case it can be no obstacle in the other. The body is not only another aspect of the self which, like labour, is something to whose use and disposal its possessor can reasonably be held to have an exclusive right. It would seem to follow that a man's body is his property if his labour is. For the body is the essential instrument of labour. Even the most spiritual forms of work require some bodily activity. The poet has to recite or write. The entrepreneur, although he does not get his hands, literally, dirty, has to read and write, talk and listen.

One could define labour as activity not undertaken for its own sake but for some further purpose. Activity undertaken for its own sake is simply play. This definition does not imply that one cannot enjoy one's work or that sport, which is a conventionalised development of play, cannot be a profession. It does not imply that all work is for somebody else. Dusting one's house and washing up one's plates are still work, even if not paid for. It does run into a bit of difficulty with cross-country running, undertaken with gritted teeth for the sake of health. Such activities are inevitably ambiguous, concerned as they are with the healthy maintenance of the body which is both a source of enjoyment and the primary instrument of labour. So I think the definition can withstand the difficulty posed by such marginal cases.

If one owns one's labour, then, it would seem that one must own one's body. One cannot own the products of some instrument unless one has a right to the use of the instrument in question. It can hardly be supposed that one has bought or hired one's body from some other owner and, although in a sense it is given to one by one's parents, that is really a way of saying that it comes into existence as a result of various activities of theirs which do not confer a right of property in it on them.

In selling one's labour one is, indeed, selling one's body or, at any rate, hiring out the use of it. The phrase immediately calls to mind improving tracts of the last century about fallen women – but in that specialised application it carries the implicit rider 'for immoral purposes'. There are other, more fundamental, ways of selling one's body that raise interesting questions. The idea that a man's body is his property is implicitly recognised in the practice of bequeathing it, when dead, for purposes of medical research. I believe it is sometimes possible to sell one's body now for such a use when it is dead. People give or sell their blood for purposes of transfusion. People give, and sometimes sell, organs for purposes of transplantation. In such cases, of course, it is not the use of the body that is transferred but part or all of the body itself.

Plainly people ought to be prevented from selling parts of their bodies if this is calculated to be highly disadvantageous to them. Here, as in the case of slavery, it is not the harmfulness of the use for which what is sold is put that constitutes the ground of objection but the harmful effect on the seller, which in this case is even more obvious than in that of slavery. Mill's theory of liberty would, no doubt, endorse a brisk market in transplantable organs from the living, but a more consistent utilitarian would move to protect people against their own follies.

On the other hand, the parent who gives a kidney to save the life of his dying child seems highly praiseworthy. His conduct approximates to that of the hero who gives his life to save that of another. Why should we make this distinction? Presumably because we feel that there cannot be the same kind of element of duress in the case where an organ is given as there could be in the case where it is sold. It does not, at any rate, conflict with the theory that one's body is one's property, provided the exclusiveness of one's rights in it is not confused with absoluteness.

Who, morally speaking, has the right to non-harmful use and disposal of a dead body (provided that explicit arrangements for its ownership have not been made by the living person whose body it was)? There was a case in England recently where the kidneys were taken from the body of a young man killed in a road accident at a time when his parents, who objected to transplants on religious grounds, were abroad and inaccessible. His possible wishes for the disposal of his remains might seem more relevant than theirs. Legally, no doubt, as his next of kin they had to be regarded as his dead body's owners if he died intestate.

If anything, the idea that his body is a man's property is more easily acceptable than the idea that his labour is. It, and its parts and contents, are, after, physical things of the straightforward kind within which the simplest instances of property fall. So far as this is so, the fact that one's body is one's property can lend support to the theory that one's labour, the most conspicuous activity of one's body, is one's property too.

A final point on this subject is suggested by Locke's theory that a limit is set to the amount of property a man may hold by his ability to use it. This is an application of the more general view that the possession of property carries with it certain obligations, as well as rights to make use of the thing owned. We are accustomed to the idea that objects of value should not be wasted, as well as to the idea that they should not be used harmfully. Laws against leaving land undeveloped are widely acknowledged as reasonable, as are laws against letting land deteriorate in such a way as to damage the land of others. If one's body and its labour are one's property, is one not at least morally obliged to actualise the potentialities of the former by using it to produce the latter? Were E.M. Forster and the historian F.A. Simpson blameworthy for, in effect, simply abandoning the work they were uniquely qualified to do at the height of their powers? Are their decisions something we can legitimately censure or should we merely regret them?

## 10. *Life and property*

The final aspect of the person I want to argue is as much one's property as labour and the body that executes it is life. In a way, the right of a person to decide whether he shall continue to live or not follows from his ownership of his body. His right of property in his body involves his having a right to its disposal as well as its use, and disposal includes destruction as well as transfer. To commit suicide is to eliminate the life from one's body, to convert it from a living body into a dead one.

Some traditional arguments against the moral acceptability of suicide traded on the notion that a person's life or body was an item of property. One's life, it was held, was not one's own but something conferred on one by God and, if one is to have no right to commit suicide, not as an outright gift, but rather as something put into one's custodianship. God as the maker of a man's life could be held to have a property-right in it by virtue of the labour he expended in creating it.

The more immediate and uncontroversial creators of a man's life are his parents. It is ordinarily morally incumbent on them to do everything they can to maintain and protect the lives of their children until their children are in a position to manage their lives for themselves. Locke, it will be remembered, tied parental power over children to the provision of life-maintaining services to them and dissociated it from the bare fact of physical parenthood. That seems reasonable enough. Suppose a man makes some fragile and interesting object, which requires, if it is to continue in existence, to be constantly and laboriously maintained. If he abandons it as soon as it is made and someone else takes on the task of keeping it in being, the longer the interval between its coming into existence and the present, the greater the proportion of the labour that is responsible for the thing's present existence that is attributable to the maintainer rather than to the original creator. Biological parenthood is, one may suppose, often achieved by accident. Its very first element is only in exceptional and usually very unfortunate cases a matter of labour, but the mother's concern for the unborn child within her could well be said to have the character of work.

If one feels, nevertheless, reluctance to consider children, at a time when they are wholly dependent on them, to be the property of their parents, it is perhaps because of the very personal circumscriptions of the rights of use and disposal in this case that follow from the requirement that harm to the children must be prevented. All the same, such as they are, the rights of use and disposal of children, the latter being limited to arranging for and deciding upon their adoption, are exclusively vested in the parents, unless they have proved themselves to be incapable of looking after them.

To return to the adult's right over his own life, the best-founded moral objections to suicide arise from the harms practical and emotional, that it may do to those who are in either of these ways dependent on the person who is thinking of committing it. The argument that things may get better, that the individual contemplating it may miss much enjoyment of life by deciding upon it, is only a prudential one. The legal punishment of attempted suicide has a somewhat comical quality, considered in the abstract. It is an offence to which is hardly appropriate to affix a capital penalty. The practice could, I suppose, be defended on the ground that suicide attempts, successful or not, are a public nuisance. It is not persuasive to say that the community has a right to the potential services from an individual of which it will be deprived if he makes away with himself. It is a bit more reasonable to argue that a man ought not to commit suicide if he is heavily in debt, provided there is a prospect of his being able in the future to work off a significant proportion of it. The argument from potential services to the community might be presented as a version of the argument for undischarged debt. It could be alleged that everyone is in debt to the community where labour has provided necessities which he has not been able to provide for himself. But that would be countered by a man who was in a position to say that he had paid his way.

Locke sometimes uses the word 'property' to refer not to a man's actual possessions to which he has an exclusive right, which he sometimes calls 'estate', but to the whole of that to which a man has a right, to everything that is, as it were, proper to him. My argument here has, in effect, taken this mode of expression literally and not discussed it as a verbal anachronism. In a somewhat insidious way, I suppose, I have been defending a kind of moral individualism, in supporting the idea that there are some things, at any rate, to which men have *exclusive* rights. I have suggested that Marx, too, although the greatest critic of the detailed property-arrangements of our civilisation, is in this respect ultimately a moral individualist. His implicit commitment to the idea that men have an exclusive moral right to their own labour and his image of the ideal human condition as analogous to that of the creative artist seem to me to put him at a considerable distance from the moral collectivism of totalitarian societies. In such societies, the welfare of the individual is entirely subjected to the welfare, as a unitary whole, of the society of which he is a member, a doctrine nowhere more thoroughly put into practice than in the societies which claim to be realising the doctrines of Marx. The point is that his criticism of the actual property-managements of capitalism objects not to the idea of property in itself, but to their exaltation of the property-rights of a ruthless or fortunate few at the expense of the property rights of the many.

*Not previously published.*

# Madness

## 1. Introduction

Madness is a subject that ought to interest philosophers; but they have had surprisingly little to say about it. What they have said, although often interesting and important, has failed to penetrate to the properly philosophical centre of the topic. They have concerned themselves with its causes and effects, with its social and ethical implications, but they have said little that is useful or definitive about what it is in itself. Preoccupied with its accidents, they have failed to engage with its essence.

They ought to have concerned themselves with madness just to the extent that they have taken themselves to be the custodians of the cognitive, of rational belief and valid reasoning. For madness is a cognitive defect, both as ordinarily conceived and, as I shall argue, in fact. Familiar idioms reveal the general prevalence of the assumption that madness is a cognitive disorder. We talk of mad people as having *lost their reasons,* as *being out of their minds* (using 'mind' here in the everyday sense of the intellect, the thinking capacity), of *having taken leave of their senses* (where it is common sense or judgement that is involved, not the perceptual functions).

Nevertheless, the proposition that madness is a cognitive disorder, however natural or instinctive it may seem, needs defence, for it is ruled out by such explicitly thought out accounts of the nature of madness as are available. The more professional of these tend to be statistical, to take what is, in matters of this kind, the coward's way out of defining the mad as those who are in some way abnormal, in the sense of forming a statistical minority. More thoughtful accounts of the nature of madness are to be found. One is the suggestion of Jonathan Glover (in Chapter 7 of his *Responsibility)* that, since the practical point at issue is whether to shut people up or not, or, at any rate, to take the management of their lives out of their own hands, the relevant consideration is simply whether people are likely to do themselves harm if not under supervision.

Others see madness as a personality disorder of a particularly intense kind in which disapproved-of emotions or desires lead to disapproved-of conduct. A sense of the arbitrariness of these disapprovals, heightened by the use of asylums as devices for the stamping out of dissidence in police states, encourages scepticism about the existence of a real distinction between the mad and the sane. The word 'mad' becomes, in Thomas Szasz's phrase, a 'derogatory label' attached by the powerful many to the defenceless few.

My thesis is, to put it more precisely, that madness is a systematic breakdown in the belief-forming mechanism or capacity of the mind, particularly in relation to those practical beliefs about oneself and one's immediate circumstances which most directly issue in non-verbal conduct. What reveals the breakdown is systematic unreasonable belief.

## 2. Philosophers on madness

What have philosophers made of madness hitherto? Plato, in the *Timaeus,* draws a distinction between madness and ignorance as two different kinds of defect of intelligence. This at least takes an intel-lectualist or cognitive attitude to madness, but since madness and ignorance are not likely to be confused it is not otherwise of much significance. Locke draws a more important distinction between what he calls madmen and idiots, describing them in terms of his own fundamental conception of the mind as having, respectively, too many ideas and too few. What he is reaching towards is the current distinction between madness (and other forms of mental illness) on the one hand and retardation or mental deficiency on the other. Madness is a disease, something that happens to a mind; retardation is a constitutional handicap.

Hobbes and Voltaire are to be celebrated for their humanity and good sense in arguing for a naturalistic account of madness, in oppo-sition to the prevailing theory of diabolic possession, endorsed by the Bible and, indeed, by the explicit words of Christ. But their accounts of madness itself are unenlighteningly statistical. Hobbes says that 'to have stronger and more vehement passions for anything than is ordinarily seen in others is that which men call madness' *(Leviathan,* part 1, c.8) and that 'all passions that cause strange and unusual behaviour are called by the general name of madness' (ibid.). This is an emotional theory of madness. The passions or emotions which Hobbes cites as constituting madness by reason of their exces-siveness or statistically unusual nature are fury and melancholy, anticipations, perhaps, of paranoid mania and of depression.

Voltaire's theory is cognitive, but still statistical. It is also physiological. He says 'we call madness that disease of the organs of the brain which inevitably prevents a man from thinking and acting like others' *(Dictionnaire Philosophique,* article Folie). He infers from the assumption that a madman has the same perceptions as everyone else that the faculty of thinking is as much subject to derangement as the senses. In fact the mad have hallucinations as well as delusions, auditory ones being of great diagnostic importance in schizophrenia.

Kant gives the subject thorough consideration in his *Anthropology.* After distinguishing the madman from the idiot he indulges in a characteristic orgy of classification. Some interesting points can be briefly discerned amid the interstices of this machinery. He argues that therapy cannot help the mad since, locked in their own worlds of fantasy, they do not realise that there is anything wrong with them. In current terminology they 'lack insight'. The madman lives in a world of his own, like a dreamer; there is no public confirmation of his beliefs. Kant mentions in passing the fact that there is a hereditary element in madness, but does not make use of it.

Schopenhauer's account of madness interestingly anticipates Freud. There is nothing wrong, he contends, either with the senses or the intellect of the madman. What is adrift is his memory. Finding his ordinarily remembered and actual past unbearable he creates for himself an imaginary and emotionally tolerable new one. In support of this bold theory of repression and compensating fantasy he claims that actors, who are compelled by their profession to perform outrages on their memories, are the human group in which madness is most often found. This imaginary piece of evidence would itself appear to be a piece of wish fulfilment. It should be noticed that although Schopenhauer says that madness is emotionally *caused,* he sees the condition as itself cognitive, as a matter of systematic false belief about one's past.

Descartes, taking a cognitive view of madness for granted, begins to go deeper into the subject, philosophically speaking, than anyone mentioned so far. As well as asking himself how he knows that all his beliefs have not been excited in him by a malignant demon, he raises, with almost parenthetical brevity, the question: how do I know that I am not mad? He then sidesteps it by saying that he would have to be mad to raise such a question. That implies, however, since he has raised it, that he must indeed be mad. For his purposes, at any rate, he does not need to pursue the question; its sceptical work can be done just as well by dreams and demonic deceit.

So far, then, as philosophers have reflected on the nature of madness they have not done so very thoroughly. But, for the most part, they have gone along with the assumption embedded in our common idioms for talking about it, in taking it to be a sickness of the intellect or reason, in adopting what I have called a cognitive theory of the matter. I shall now set out a theory of that kind in more detail and go on to consider actual and possible alternatives to it. Descriptions of the various forms of madness refer to a wide variety of manifestations, in thought, emotion and behaviour. As opposed to my view that the essential element in the whole complex is to be found in the domain of thought, the idea that peculiarities of emotion are what matters has its defenders, among them, as we have seen, Hobbes. In an epoch of principled hostility to the idea of an inner life, a behavioural conception of the nature of madness has an obvious appeal.

A suspicion that the picking out of certain emotions as definitive of madness is ultimately an arbitrary business underlies various kinds of scepticism about there being any objective difference between the mad and the sane. Sometimes this response to the problem has a right-wing flavour, as with Thomas Szasz; more usually it comes from the left, as with R. D. Laing and Michel Foucault. A cognitive theory can resist such scepticism more readily than an emotional one. The difference between the true and the false, and between the justified and unjustified in the way of belief are less subjective and arbitrary than that between emotions that are socially acceptable and emotions that are not.

### 3. A cognitive theory of madness

The first thing to do is to mark out as clearly as possible the field to which the theory under construction is meant to apply. I am not, to start with, concerned with retardation or mental deficiency, a constitutional weakness of the mind, but with mental illness or disease. Next by the word 'madness' I mean to refer to what psychiatrists, their textbooks and thus, following them respectfully, encyclopaedias, call *psychosis*. This is comprehensive, large-scale mental disorder, as contrasted with more localised troubles like neuroses, 'personality disorders' (criminality, alcoholism, sexual deviance, for example) and comparable 'abnormalities'. A crucial distinction between madness and these lesser evils is that the mad generally, in other words for most of the time, lack 'insight'. They are not aware that anything is wrong with them or that they are in need of care and treatment. That is not to say that sufferers cannot be aware, in periods of remission, that they have been mad in the past or, as in the case of Charles Lamb's sister Mary, that they are about to go mad again in the near future.

The natural place to start looking for guidance is the clinical descriptions that are given of the various forms of psychosis. Three main varieties are currently recognised. The first of them is schizophrenia, taking several forms, from catatonic at one extreme to hebephrenic at the other. In all of them the sufferer is out of touch with or cut off from the common world and has retreated into a world of his own imaginative construction. One symptom of schizophrenia is held to be of particular diagnostic importance. That is the phenomenon of *insertion,* the delusion of being controlled by, indeed of receiving spoken orders from, some external intelligence, what is vulgarly called 'voices in the head'.

Schizophrenia is the most obviously cognitive of the psychoses. It is associated with a wide range of moods and emotional states and with a comparably wide range of styles of behaviour, from the wildly frenzied to the wholly passive and inert. The common element is the schizophrenic's detachment from the real common world by a private system of false beliefs about himself and his circumstances.

The other main group of psychoses are the manic-depressive and the simply depressive. Wild behaviour and extravagant emotions whether of elation or despair, are characteristic of these forms of madness. The manic individual has delusions of his own power and importance, of his quite superb intellectual brilliance. These are often political, as when he rings up presidents and prime ministers at grotesque expense and impossible hours of the day so as to remove the scales from their eyes with his unique set of infallible solutions to the problems of the world. The depressive individual, who may, of course, be the manic one a few days later, has delusions about the particular awfulness of himself, his circumstances and his prospects. In this case, unlike that of schizophrenia, the delusory belief is connected with a specific kind of emotional state and a specific kind of conduct, whether absurdly self- inflated and overweening or desperately miserable and defeated. The primacy of the cognitive or belief aspect of the whole condition will need to be argued for.

Much the same is true of the third variety of psychosis, paranoia, which is ordinarily found in conjunction with one of the other psychoses. The essential belief here is that the sufferer is the victim of a large conspiracy, which may include everyone with whom he comes into contact and others beyond and behind them. The object of the conspiracy is to persecute him, to cause him pain, physical or mental, to humiliate, to disadvantage, even to destroy him. The associated emotional state is one of fear, suspicion and angry resentment which expresses itself in an appropriate style of behaviour: scowling, shrinking, hiding away.

In the general view of those who have most to do with the mad, then, there is to be found in each type of madness a comprehensive system of false beliefs. Where these beliefs are specifically about the sufferer's importance or desperate forlornness or organised victimisation, there is a specific emotional state and a specific style of behaviour associated with the false belief-system. My central thesis is that the primary and crucial element in these groupings of belief, emotion and behaviour is the belief or, more precisely, system of beliefs.

The primacy of behaviour can easily be disproved. Behaviour is mad only if it expresses the standardly correlated emotions. In some cases, however, it arises from a quite different emotional background. It may be carried out by an actor or for a bet or to distract attention or to get released from military service. If so it can be entirely sane and reasonable, whether or not it succeeds in serving the purpose for which it was intended. The madness of behaviour, in other words, is derivative from that of the emotion it expresses. A particular form of behaviour, running away, for example, may be a reliable indication of fear. It may be, according to recent accounts of the nature of mental states, partly constitutive of it. But there is no fixed and regular connection between running away and fear. The ascription of fear to one who runs away can always in principle be defeated by some other explanation, perhaps the desire to answer a telephone no one else has heard or a twinge of boredom or an irresistible call of nature.

A first argument against the primacy of emotion in the total characteristic condition of a psychotic has already been alluded to in the description of schizophrenia. There simply is no specific emotion associated with it. The schizophrenic may be happy or sad, excited or impassive. It follows that schizophrenia cannot consist in the emotions that accompany it since these are to be found generally among the population at large.

The main argument against the idea that emotion is primary in madness is a further development of the same point and parallels the objection to the idea that behaviour is the primary factor. This is that the emotions of the psychotic are not in *themselves* indications of madness. There are readily conceivable situations in which any of them may be felt by an entirely sane person, even the extreme emotions that are specifically associated with manic-depression and paranoia. Consider a mother who finds out or comes to believe that a much loved child has just been horribly killed. If she did not experience the emotions typical in depressive psychosis we should conclude that there was something mentally wrong with her, a temporary, perhaps protective, state of shock. Similarly if she finds out or comes to believe that the child has just narrowly and surprisingly escaped a horrible death she ought to have the wild euphoria of the manic. Much the same is true in the case of paranoia. The point is made obliquely in the saying that paranoids often have some real enemies. The emotions of the paranoid are appropriate and reasonable in a Jew in Warsaw under German occupation or a present-day Russian dissident.

The emotions characteristic of a psychosis, manic-depressive or paranoid, are signs of such a condition only if they are *unreasonable,* if they are utterly inappropriate to the circumstances in which the person who has them is. Just as apparently, because typically, mad behaviour is really mad only if it is the expression of the emotion that usually accompanies it, so apparently, because typically, mad emotion is really mad only if it is experienced in circumstances in which it is entirely inappropriate.

Emotions are not simply caused by beliefs, although beliefs do indeed cause them; they also embody beliefs. To be angry with someone is to believe that he has harmed one; to be pleased with oneself involves the belief that one has brought off something good (or could do so); to be hopeful involves the belief that something good is going to happen. As a first approximation it could be said that the inappropriateness to the circumstances in which the unreasonableness of an emotion consists is its embodying a false belief about those circumstances. My anger at someone is unreasonable if the belief it embodies about his having harmed me is false. Following on from this we might conclude that what makes the emotions of the madman psychotic is that his beliefs are false. The schizophrenic falsely believes his imagined private world is real. The depressive falsely believes that his prospects are dreadful. The paranoid falsely believes that every man's hand is against him.

But that needs qualification. In one way, indeed, if I falsely believe that someone has harmed me when he has done nothing of the sort, my anger at him – and any behaviour that results from it – is unreasonable. But that sort of unreasonableness is, as it might be put, objective. I am not shown to be an unreasonable person, even if I get angry with someone who has done me no harm (nothing that I would recognise as harm), so long as my false belief was itself reasonable or justified in the circumstances. Perhaps I misread or misheard as his a name in a letter or conversation which was that of someone who really had harmed me. I may have relied too much on a usually reliable informant. All the evidence I had might have supported the false belief that he had harmed me. If so my anger is subjectively reasonable even if not objectively so. It is appropriate to what I reasonably believe to be the circumstances, even if not to the circumstances as they actually are.

What is wrong with the beliefs of psychotics is not primarily that they are false, although they usually are. It is that they are unjustified. Emotions and, *a fortiori*, behaviour, are indications of madness only if they are expressions of defective beliefs, essentially of unjustified beliefs and so usually, but only consequentially, of false beliefs. We should consider the case of a man whose beliefs were subjectively unreasonable but nevertheless true. I might believe that someone had harmed me, without any reason for my belief, although he had in fact done so. In that case I am unreasonable, but, in a way, my emotion is not. People often say, truly or falsely, after winning some wild bet in a lottery or on an outsider 'I *knew* I was going to win'. If they believed they were going to win for certain they would be full of happy expectation. After the event we might say 'well, your confidence was justified', and so it was, in itself, as a belief; but they were not justified in being confident. In being concerned with madness, a condition of persons, not of propositions, the kind of reasonableness which is relevant to us is the subjective reasonableness of persons.

## 4. *Emotion and belief*

Before going any further it may be right to stop to consider an objection to the assumption I have made that emotions embody beliefs. I am inclined to think this is correct since it is a natural development of the reasonable view that emotions have objects or are intentional, in Brentano's sense. One cannot just hate or fear or hope but must hate or fear someone or something, hope that something will come to pass. Fear entails belief in some approaching evil. Hatred and hope do not directly entail beliefs, but, nevertheless, more loosely imply them. Hatred is intense dislike and primarily a desire for evil to befall its object where that object is a person, perhaps for its non-existence where the object is a thing or event, in either case for the minimisation, ideally the reduction to nothing, of its coming into contact with or affecting one. It seems at any rate conceivable that one should have a quite baseless hatred of someone, in the sense of being unable to identify anything about him in virtue of which one hates him.

Another line of objection to the view that emotions embody beliefs is that there seem to be objectless emotions, free-floating anxiety or Heideggerian *Angst,* for example. But it does not seem too artificial to say that in such a case the embodied belief is of a somewhat indefinite kind to the effect that *something,* one cannot say more definitely just what, is horrible and going to happen. (If Popper is right about the metaphysical nature of uncircumscribed existential propositions it would follow that Heidegger's *Angst* is indeed a metaphysical anxiety.)

It is not, however, necessary to hold that all emotions embody beliefs, only that those that are characteristic of madness, in the forms of madness with which specific emotions are associated, do so. I think it is clear that the elation of the manic, the despair of the depressive and the suspicious fear and resentment of the paranoiac are of the same uncontroversially belief-embodying sort as fear or, for that matter, of embarrassment (embodying the belief that one has made a fool of oneself) or regret (embodying the belief that one has done something in some way bad, whether morally or prudentially).

The manic's wild elation embodies a belief in his own supreme qualities of intelligence and, perhaps, virtue and in his power to bring off remarkable achievements with, so to speak, a flick of the wrist. It is not an objectless glee, as is shown by its leading its possessor into characteristically over-ambitious lines of conduct. The intense despair of the depressive involves a belief in his own worthlessness and perhaps his wickedness and in the incurable bleakness of his prospects. The fear, suspicion and resentment of the paranoid plainly presuppose a belief in the existence of a conspiracy directed towards his undoing.

The cognitive conception of madness I am proposing should be formulated, then, as the acceptance of unreasonable beliefs. We all accept unreasonable beliefs from time to time, indeed it may well be that we always have some unreasonable beliefs, with some of them persisting for a long time uncriticised and undisturbed. But that does not make us all mad. Two further qualifications need to be introduced. The first of these has been mentioned more than once in passing. This is that the unreasonable belief of the madman is systematic. The second is that the beliefs in question should be practical and directly relevant to the active life of the believer.

## 5. System and practicality

The idea of system I have in mind is not a very precise one. What is meant is that the unreasonable belief that constitutes madness is neither short-lived nor localised, in the sense of being confined to some fairly narrow section of the whole range of someone's beliefs. Under the influence of drink or drugs one can have a broad array of unreasonable beliefs about oneself and one's circumstances (usually of a kind that is embarrassing to look back on later) which would not amount to madness unless it were to persist for a long time or indefinitely. One can also have unreasonable beliefs about some fairly narrow domain of fact that does not amount to madness, but at most to neurosis. Phobias, neurotic fears of some particular kind of thing or circumstance – crowds, spiders, flying, heights and so forth – clearly involve beliefs about the dangerousness of the things feared that are at least pitched unreasonably high. There are, after all, mobs, black widows, air crashes and crumbling cliff edges or church towers. Compulsions are beliefs of an unreasonable sort, for example about the dirtiness of the hands that someone with a washing compulsion cleans dozens of times a day. They too are neuroses whose unreasonableness is recognised by the otherwise reasonable person who suffers from them. But in the case of the psychotic the systematic extent of his unreasonable beliefs leaves no room for a main mass of reasonable belief to contrast with them and to provide a standpoint from which they can be criticised. It is to the systematic nature of his delusions that the lack of insight character-istic of the psychotic must be attributed.

Another, equally imprecise but equally indispensable, qualifica-tion is that the unreasonable belief-system of the psychotic should be practical, concern his everyday active life, his primordial business of looking after himself: waking and sleeping, steering clear of obvious dangers, eating and drinking so as to prolong life not bring it to an end, conducting relations with other people so as to avoid trouble and so on. The psychotic is a danger to himself and a danger, or at least a nuisance, to others in the same way as a retarded person, but for different reasons. The retardate does not know what to do or how to do it; the psychotic does not realise, because of his delusions, that things he knows perfectly well how to do ought to be done.

A lot of people believe a great deal of what may be called theo-retical rubbish without being on that account in the least mad. Communication in seances with the spirits of the dead, miraculous spoon-bending, flying saucers are relatively inoffensive examples of the sort of thing I have in mind. Their main effect, one may hope, is to brighten the lives of those who believe in them, in the manner of fairy stories and tales of the uncanny or of astonishing voyages. A measure of suspension of disbelief, rather than outright acceptance, could have an intellectually therapeutic value, keeping the mind open, like other fictions, to possibilities one had not considered. They are unpractical in so far as they have little bearing on action, at least of a non-verbal kind.

Theoretical beliefs in a more respectable, academic sense of the adjective, about the distance from the earth of Alpha Centauri or the atomic weight of mercury or the causes of the collapse of the Roman empire can also be unreasonable without doing much damage. The only practical upshot they have for most people is verbal: in talk or in doing examinations. In themselves they do not give rise to emotion. I may hold on doggedly and angrily to an unreasonable belief of an academically theoretical kind. But that will not be because of the belief itself, but because of the historical circumstances of its adoption. I may have thought it up and committed my repu-tation to it. It is my true and reasonable belief that I am generally identified with it that endows it with an emotional force for me. Despite this not uncommon kind of obstinacy, it is often the case that theoretical beliefs are entertained hypothetically, in a specula-tive spirit. This methodological attitude is appropriate to the limited confirmability of theories. They should be held in a tentative spirit that is always ready to acknowledge a need to revise or abandon them in face of unfavourable evidence. That is the correlate in the academic or scholarly scientific domain of the playfulness or suspen-sion of disbelief appropriate to the kind of humble theoretical folklore discussed a little earlier.

There is one large and important variety of belief-system that must be considered at this point, in which theoretical notions about the world, man and society are intimately connected with practical beliefs or at any rate prescriptions for conduct. These are religions and full-blooded political ideologies. Very often here too there is an analogue to the tentativeness proper to academic speculation and the playfulness proper to tales of the marvellous. Hume observed how surprisingly slight the effect of a proclaimed belief in hell is on the actual conduct of those who profess it, which is often little different from that of those who do not. Lord Melbourne memorably approved of that. 'Things have come to a pretty pass', he said, 'when religion starts to invade private life.'

But much religious belief is, of course, serious and sincere and it typically protects itself from rational investigation by the principle that faith, which is, after all, something close to a euphemism for unreasonable belief, is a moral duty. Among the great religions Christianity occupies a kind of middle position between the Chinese form, in which there is no speculative, supernatural element to speak of, and the Indian form in which, both in Hinduism and in the less sophisticated types of Buddhism, the common world of practical everyday belief and action is held to be an illusion. Christianity asserts the existence of an elaborate supernatural order of things, but the reality of the created world is not denied. The Christian God, after all, incarnated himself in it. But apart from that and some lesser miraculous happenings, the common natural world is taken to be real on its own account in very much the terms in which it is conceived by everyday reasonable belief. Christianity adds a great deal of additional matter of belief to everyday convictions, but it does not conflict with or undermine them on the whole.

A significant residue of fanatical religion remains in which witches are identified and burnt, in which Moslems enthusiastically go to their deaths expecting an immediate move to paradise, in which Christian Scientists refuse medical aid for themselves and their children. At this level of intensity religion begins to look like collective psychosis. There is much more to be said on this subject and on the related topic of total political ideologies and, at a more modest level, about superstition. But ideologies and superstition resemble non-fanatical religious belief in adding to, rather than supplanting or suppressing, the reasonable beliefs about the world, about the believer himself and about the immediate circumstances of his life and field of his conduct which define his sanity. They do not, therefore, need to be further considered here.


## 6. Practical beliefs and evaluation

What I have called practical beliefs are, it might be objected, of a hybrid character, containing an unproblematically factual but also an evaluative element. Words like 'wonderful' and 'dreadful', 'good' and 'bad', 'harm' and 'advantage' occur in their verbal expression. But judgements involving these terms are intrinsically controversial,

are not or are not simply cognitive in nature, express the preferences
of their users rather than state what is objectively true or false. The
unreasonable practical belief-system of the psychotic is not, then, as
cognitive a matter as I have made it appear.

But the unreasonable aspect of the psychotic's characteristic
beliefs is not the evaluative but the factual one. Behind the manic's
elation lies the belief that he has a proposal which will bring peace
to the world and is also wonderful, a proper object of elation. But
there is nothing very questionable about the second, evaluative part
of his belief. If he really had a proposal that would guarantee world
peace who would question his right to be elated? The depressive
believes that nothing he could do would succeed and that that is a
bad thing, a proper thing to be depressed by. And so it is. What is
unreasonable about his belief is its factual part, its judgement of his
own potentialities. The paranoiac believes that everyone around him
is in a conspiracy to frustrate him or destroy his reputation and also
that if they succeed it will be very bad for him. Here again the evaluation is too obvious to question. What is wrong is his factual
account of what is actually going on.

But although this objection fails to show that an account of
madness in terms of systematic unreasonable practical belief is only
superficially cognitive it does raise a question that should be considered. In what has been said so far no mention has been made of the
desires or preferences of the psychotic. Might it not be here that the
essential core of madness is to be found?

It is quite true that the desires of the psychotic for the most part
display his condition, although it may take time for someone else to
recognise the fact. The mad are often 'rational', in so far as their
beliefs, emotions, desires and actions hang coherently together. It is
when we discover the systematic unreasonableness of his practical
beliefs that we catch him out. Many desires are not ultimate, are not
directed towards things we want as ends in themselves. They are for
things we want because we believe that they will promote our
achieving what we do want for its own sake. I want the waiter to
come to the table, not because I enjoy the pleasure of his company,
but so that I can order the meal. At the end of the chain of desires is
a plate of food that I want for its own sake. Likewise, the paranoiac
wants to get away from the other people in the bus shelter because
he believes they are conspiring to kill him and he does not want to
die. My summoning the waiter is based on the reasonable belief that
it is a means to the end of getting fed. His flight from the bus shelter
is an unreasonable means to self-preservation, because his belief that

his fellow-shelterers are conspiring to kill him is an unreasonable one. Non-ultimate, or mediate, desires are in the same boat as emotions. Their unreasonableness, which makes them candidates for consideration as mad, is derivative from that of the beliefs that they embody.

That leaves ultimate desires, which, if they embody beliefs at all, embody only the belief that the attainment of their objects will be satisfying. Could it not be said of them that they can be and sometimes are for things which although satisfying to the desirer are nevertheless things it is mad to desire? Possible examples are the psychopath, and his brother, the coldly calculating criminal, the sexual deviant and the eccentric. The psychopath is 'without conscience', the suffering of others plays no part in the determination of his actions. In notorious cases he combines a persistent taste for cruelty and murder with a measure of blithe imprudence that leads to his getting caught. There is no question that his motivation is abnormal, exceptional and repulsive. But is he mad? Apart from the absence of any sort of altruistic concern for others he has the usual Butlerian apparatus of self-love and particular passions. He pursues his ends with a reasonable system of practical beliefs. I should conclude that he is nasty, but sane, as does common legal practice and common opinion. The calculating criminal is also sane, as distinct from the mentally deficient criminal, the passionate criminal (provoked beyond endurance), the criminal who commits his crimes under the influence of drink or drugs (which, I suggested earlier, produce temporary states of belief derangement comparable to madness).

In this connection the case of the major political criminal, like Hitler or Stalin, should be considered. It has been objected to the cognitive account of madness I am proposing that it would imply the sanity, probably, of Hitler and, almost certainly, of Stalin. (The second consequence is generally found less offensive.) Now there are aspects of Hitler's personality that seem psychotic. I am not thinking so much of the alleged episodes of rug-chewing as of the central position in his whole system of ends of his hatred of Jews. But, given its ultimacy and primacy among his purposes, he handled it rationally. For example, when, after his seizure of power, he expelled all Jewish professors, he was told that this would cripple German theoretical physics, which, it was correctly pointed out, would be of great military importance. He answered that he would rather Germany failed than succeeded with the help of 'Jewish physics'. All the same his hatred of Jews was not all that ultimate, it was permeated with ridiculous beliefs. But on the whole he was far too shrewd and crafty an operator to be described as mad. Those who, often passionately, think otherwise, tend to subscribe to three inconsistent propositions: Hitler was mad, only the sane should be punished, Hitler should have been punished.

Hitler was certainly a psychopath, and thus far mentally deficient, and a neurotic, in the light of his unreasonable, not simply contemptible, hatred of Jews. Sexual deviants and eccentrics, by which I mean people indifferent to worldly success that is within their power, and who choose to pursue some unusual or exceptional end of a harmless sort, living in isolation on nuts and berries, are neither. The sexual deviant may be quite right in his belief that he will get erotic satisfaction only from members of his own sex. The more generally agreeable forms of sexual activity involve the participation of others and that creates a need for protection, from violent coercion in the case of adult partners, from any sort of interference in the case of children, who can be coerced very easily and, where there is no coercion, may not know what is happening and so cannot be said to choose to take part.

The psychopath, who is without conscience, has a counterpart in the realm of prudence, the rash or reckless person, who, for the joys of skiing or motor racing, is ready to pursue them at great risk of injury or death. In English English it is that sort of extreme imprudence to which the word 'mad' is colloquially used to refer, while 'crazy' does the same job in American English. In the latter dialect 'mad' is the colloquial equivalent of 'angry'. It may be hard to decide, here as in the case of the criminal, just how far it is a matter of unusually balanced ultimate desires that is at work and how far a matter of unreasonable estimates of the likelihood of death or serious injury. I should maintain that a risk-taker who, as the phrase is, 'knows what he is doing', is perfectly mentally healthy, while one who, with ordinary desires, nevertheless acts more rashly than most people is to that extent neurotic, for I believe this accords with our reflective intuitions on the subject. Deviation in patterns of desire is not a sign of mental illness, deviation in practical belief is.

Madness, then, and, by implication, neurosis, is a specific kind of mental weakness or defect. It is to be distinguished from retardation or mental deficiency, which is a constitutional inability to learn, to acquire and retain beliefs and skills; it is not ignorance or stupidity of any kind, which is a shortage of beliefs and not a collection of bad ones; it is not illogicality or muddleheadedness, which is a failure to see the implications and incompatibilities of beliefs. It is a matter of having a set or system of unreasonable beliefs, comprehensive in the case of madness, localised in neurosis.

## 7. Scepticism about madness

In defending a cognitive account of madness against an emotional or affective one I have had two ulterior motives. In the first place a cognitive theory makes the attribution of madness less disputable, more objective than the emotional alternative does. Unreasonableness of belief is a matter on which general agreement can be expected, while the characterisation of certain unusual emotions and supposedly perverse desires as unacceptable is hard to defend from the charge of being arbitrary. Secondly, a cognitive theory sets up a distinction between the mentally ill and the socially deviant. To treat the latter as more or less mad is doubly undesirable. On the one hand it puts calculating criminals from Hitler downwards outside the reach of punishment; on the other it exposes homosexuals and eccentrics to the comparatively benign but still disparaging and potentially compulsion-inviting category of the mentally ill.

The objectivity of the distinction between the mad and the sane, which I am anxious to secure, has been challenged from both ends of the ideological spectrum. Thomas Szasz has been mentioned earlier for his view that to call people mad is to tie a derogatory label to them. Those we describe as mad, he says, differ only in degree from the rest of us. We all have problems of life; theirs happen to be particularly severe. The ideological point of his position is that people should not be encouraged to give in, to be rendered passive by institutionalisation and subjection to treatment. They should be stimulated, rather, to pull themselves together and to take responsibility for themselves.

At the opposite extreme is Michel Foucault, who, in his *Madness and Civilisation,* plays rhapsodic variations on a theme he states at the beginning – the mad conspiracy of men to call some of their number mad and to confine them. Between tracts of pretentious verbal posturing the idea is insinuated that for their own convenience and profit the holders of power carried out this imposture. Some rational fragments can be picked out here and there in the flux. Confined madmen were for long thought of as monsters and wild beasts. But that was due to the religiously endorsed idea that the mad were diabolically possessed and also to the idea that only rational beings are proper objects of moral concern. In repudiating the

Cartesian tradition of intellectual hygiene for some dirty habits picked up from Nietzsche, he retains the French resistance to the idea that animals have rights, or even feelings. Of course the mad should be treated humanely, but neither distinguishing them from the sane, nor confining them for their own and other people's protection implies that it does not matter what is done to them in confinement.

A general merit of these scepticisms is that they raise the question as to whether the distinction between the mad and the sane is not some kind of put-up job. In the first place, it may be questioned whether the various forms of madness are diseases at all. Secondly, the usual ways in which sanity and madness are distinguished are unsatisfactory, although for quite different reasons. On the one hand there is the tight-lipped evasiveness of psychiatric professionalism, as revealed in textbooks. In imitation of the equally bogus rigour of ordinary pathology, disease is defined in purely statistical terms. On the other hand there are more or less affective accounts of madness, which define it in terms of radical failure of social adjustment or socially unacceptable behaviour caused by socially unacceptable emotions. The affective conception of madness I have already criticised. I shall now consider the claim that madness is a disease and then the idea that disease, mental or physical, is simply a matter of statistical abnormality.

Before leaving the sceptics I must explain why I have not included R.D. Laing among them. He, at least in his early work, gave an account of how people are driven into schizophrenia by disabling emotional pressures within the family. He held that the apparently senseless discourse of the schizophrenic can in fact be interpreted as a rational communicative response to the circumstances in which he finds himself. I am neglecting him because his main point is an account of what *causes* schizophrenia, not of what it is. It, like other forms of madness, may be emotionally caused, but that does not determine what it is. Even less does it imply that there is really no such thing. He does indeed go on to say that it is not what it is supposed to be. What casts doubt on any literary-humanistic theory of schizophrenia of this kind is the fact that it is to a considerable extent inherited. Even more striking, in view of the fact that most people are brought up by those from whom they get their genes, is the small variation in the incidence of schizophrenia as between one culture and another.

## 8. Is madness a disease?

The main argument for taking the various forms of madness to be diseases is their analogy to what are conventionally acknowledged to be diseases of the body. That argument does not raise the question of what a disease actually is, but it will be considered later. The mental and behavioural manifestations of madness – the unreasonable belief-systems, the absurd or unusual emotions and behaviour – would, if madness is a disease, be its symptoms. There is a close relationship between the ordinary sorts of madness I have been dealing with so far and the organic psychoses. The first and most powerful aspect of the analogy between madness and straightforward physical disease is that some kinds of madness, the organic psychoses, *are* physical diseases, or, at any rate, result directly from them.

A well-known and dramatic form of organic psychosis is paresis, the tertiary stage of syphilis, sometimes known as general paralysis of the insane, a complaint much favoured by cultural figures in the nineteenth century. More widespread is what is often called senile dementia, the mental collapse that can come with great age. Both of these are organic conditions since they are rooted in disorders of the brain, in cerebral lesions arising in one case from prolonged syphilitic infection, in the other from decay through the passage of time. The symptoms of these two conditions are very closely similar to those of functional schizophrenia, that schizophrenia which has no *known* physiological or organic basis. Other organic conditions of a more or less psychotic kind are delirium tremens, caused by alcohol, which is not easy to distinguish by way of its symptoms alone from the delirium of fever, and the dementia that arises not from old age but from injury to the head.

The boundary between organic and functional conditions, defined as it is in terms of what is currently known, is neither sharp nor permanent. A functional condition is one that is waiting for a physiological explanation, not one for which no such explanation can in principle be found. Over and above the close analogy between the symptoms of organic and functional psychosis a further reason for supposing that the functional psychoses of the present are the organic psychoses of the future is the fact that some functional psychoses, most notably depressive psychosis, respond to treatment with drugs. That is a more powerful consideration than may at first appear. For in this sort of case it cannot be argued that the drug serves merely as a symptom-suppressor, in the way that treatments for the common cold clear the nose and soothe the throat without getting to the root of the matter. The drug cannot get to the root of the matter unless there is a root of the matter to get to. If there is not the symptoms, or some of them, must actually constitute the disease.

Our ordinary notion of a disease is that it is a bad or abnormal condition which lasts for some time, perhaps a very long time. At the opposite extreme to things like cancer and tuberculosis are sudden attacks of pneumonia which can kill people off very soon after their onset. But even these last a few hours. If someone chokes on a bone or is suffocated or killed in a crash or by a fall a medical explanation is readily available for the cause of death. But the deaths are said to be due to accident or injury, not disease. Such deaths cannot be marked off from those due to disease by reference to the external cause of the body's malfunction and death because the lethal germs or viruses are just as much external as the choking bone or the fatal car. A reason for picking out longer lasting painful or fatal conditions as diseases is that their duration allows time for treatment.

The point of this digression is that we do seem to countenance the idea of momentary madness. Someone hit on the head or insulted or obstructed may be brought by it into a delirious, raving state that quickly passes. If this is correct it amounts to a marginal lack of analogy. A line of defence against it would be to say that the brain is the most delicate, complicated and volatile of all the organs of the body. It may be, too, that there are physical analogues: sudden, quickly passing bouts of fever.

A final reason for taking the analogy to justify calling the psychoses mental diseases is that some conditions that are unhesitatingly regarded as diseases of the body have obscure or unknown physiological bases, epilepsy and migraine, for example. They stand to the bodily diseases that have a known physiological basis as do functional to organic psychoses. I believe that all diseases, of the body and the mind, have a physiological basis. But that assumption is not presupposed by the view that madness is a disease. However, without it a certain whiff of the metaphorical clings to the idea that it is.

## 9. The statistical criterion of disease

Pathology textbooks usually begin, before they plunge into the honest, scientific detail of the subject, with some gruff and embarrassed preliminaries of a definitional kind. The student is told that a disease is an abnormal condition of the body and is made clear that the word 'abnormal' is being used in a strictly statistical sense. The advantages of this are obvious. The field of study is demarcated in an irresistibly objective and uncontroversial way. Or, at any rate, it seems that that is so.

What it actually does is to pretend to have given a truly scientific account of the field, which turns out to let into it much that its exponents would never think of considering. For example, the possession of naturally blonde hair is common in Sweden but unheard of in Japan. It is the property of a small minority in the human species as a whole. Is it, then, a disease? Are having dense freckles, being over 80 inches tall, being left-handed? These last three conditions, unlike naturally blonde hair, are all a bit of a nuisance. Respectively, they make one look silly when middle aged, require one to crouch when going through doorways, necessitate special golf clubs. But at least introducing the idea of a *disliked* bodily condition is a move in the right direction. It recognises an ineliminably evaluative element in the concept of disease.

The crucial negatively evaluated features in straightforward physical disease are pain, death and, more elusively, what is called dysfunction. The most obvious instances of disease are those bodily conditions which are either painful and will lead, if not corrected, to pain or death. Pain and death are unfavourably evaluated in almost all circumstances. But pain can trump death. When intense, prolonged and unstoppable it may make death relatively attractive. Dysfunction is harder to define. I cannot climb to the top of a gymnasium by a rope, but that does not constitute an illness But I should be ill if I were unable to walk from where I am writing to the door (provided that I had previously been able to walk that distance); if I had never been able to do so I would not be ill but handicapped.

A statistical account of illness in terms of abnormality is, if anything, even less enticing in the mental case. The reason is that we are – to speak with somewhat vertiginous generality – much more alike physically than we are alike mentally. To bring that large contention down to earth a little: there is a real point to the idea of a normal body temperature. For most people most of the time it is 98.4°F. People whose temperature departs substantially from that figure become distressed, wish they felt as they more usually do in certain respects, find it hard to do things that they want to do and ordinarily can do without difficulty. Allowing for differences of sex and age, we are all anatomically much the same, within a moderate range of shapes and sizes.

Mentally, however, we differ much more widely. Different cultures, different personal histories, different tastes and interests and preferences cause us to follow very different styles of life, to approach the world with very different aims and to react to it with very different emotions. Because of our physiological uniformity statistical abnormality is not too bad a guide to physical ill-health. As the examples proved, it is not a sufficient condition. But in practice it is approximately a necessary condition. If someone is ill then his body is in a statistically abnormal condition. If that abnormality is connected to pain, death or dysfunction we have an adequate working criterion of physical ill-health.

Is illness always statistically abnormal? The idea that it is not could be named 'Auden's conjecture' in virtue of his line, 'this England of ours where nobody is well'. Operating under poetic licence he announces that no one is well in England. Since there are plenty of different illnesses what he says is compatible with no disease ever affecting more than a small minority. Since there are well over twenty of them, the statistician's ninety-five per cent rule of normality can be complied with.

But is it possible for a majority to suffer from a particular disease? It could happen for a time, epidemically. A nation or the whole world could be temporarily afflicted for a while like a prison or a boarding school. Could some disliked bodily condition be suffered from by most of the people most of the time? Only, I suspect, if the identification of the disease was logically parasitic on the statistically abnormal character of most diseases. Otherwise it would be counted part of the general human condition, like getting tired after a long hard day.

Even if it is a necessary condition of illness, statistical abnormality is certainly inadequate as a criterion or definition unless an evaluative element is added. And the evaluative element must be of a particular sort, one that involves pain, death or dysfunction. A persistent, acquired condition of the body that is simply disliked, either by its possessor or by anyone affected by it, is not on that account a disease. An attractive child turns into an ugly adult. Its ugliness, although perhaps medically modifiable, is not an illness. Nor is early baldness, unless it is total and sudden. Nor are evil-smelling breath and body, even if not due to lack of hygiene.

The inadequacy of a statistical criterion of disease is even more patent in the case of mental illness. People with abnormally high IQs, calculating prodigies and the owners of enormously capacious memories are not insane. Nor are those with a compelling interest in Turkish carpets or real tennis or the breeding of decorative poultry. What is needed is some negative aspect to the abnormality. The wide range of mental abnormalities that falls under the consideration of the psychiatrist has little to do with pain (except in the sense of emotional distress, to which I shall return) or with death. It may be some kind of dysfunction, but that is even less clear a notion in the mental case than it is in the physical. To consider this problem the scope of the inquiry must be widened to include all mental illness, actual or alleged, neuroses and 'personality disorders', as well as psychoses.

## 10. What is bad about mental illness

Neurosis differs from psychosis in two connected respects. A neurosis – phobia, obsession or compulsion – is a local or partial oddity of belief, emotion and conduct in relation to some particular kind of thing: high places, the possibility of being attacked from behind, washing the hands. This will co-exist with reasonable belief, emotion and behaviour with regard to other matters. Secondly, the neurotic recognises this and deplores it. Like the physically ill person he will ordinarily admit that there is something wrong with him, even if he is unwilling to submit to treatment for one reason or another. The psychotic, just because his beliefs are systematically unreasonable, usually does not admit that there is anything wrong with him and cannot co-operate with the attempts of others to cure him.

What are called personality disorders are all localised in the way that neurosis is, but the attitudes to them of their possessors are very various. A good many alcoholics and drug addicts and some sexual deviants would like to have their personalities changed, and not just for the sake of convenience and so as to fit more smoothly into society. But many sexual deviants, all eccentrics and, I imagine, all criminals are unwilling to admit that there is anything wrong with them. They have insight in that they know what it is about them that brings social disapproval down on them, but they do not think these peculiarities ought to be eliminated and do not want them eliminated.

Perhaps it does not matter very much whether we see neuroses as illnesses or, on the other hand, take them to parallel those bodily deficiencies which, while not diseases, are medically treatable and, where disliked by those who have them, may be brought to treatment. Agoraphobia and washing compulsion could be categorised in the same way as an ugly face or early baldness. A reason for not doing so is the superficial and cosmetic nature of these disliked bodily defects. Their dysfunctional aspect is fairly trivial, more like conversational boringness or a stammer on the mental side.

The dysfunctions attributable to neuroses are more disabling, even though a neurosis can be accommodated, at some cost, in a life that is otherwise normal. So, given that the problematic mental conditions have no connection with pain and death, it seems reasonable to call them diseases too. If that is correct for neuroses it must hold all the more solidly for psychoses, since with them the dysfunction is very much greater. The total inability of the psychotic to manage his life does, indeed, bring pain and death in indirectly. If left to his own devices he may starve or may suffer and die as a result of dangers he is not in a condition to avoid or ward off.

Glover's proposal of a better criterion of mental ill-health than statistical abnormality exploits this fact about the extremely dysfunctional character of psychosis. He argues that, since the practical point of categorising people as mentally ill is, in extreme cases at least, that of whether to institutionalise and to force treatment on them, the mentally ill should be defined as those whose consistent pattern of action is harmful to them. One objection is that this would make retardation a mental illness, but that could be circumvented by redrafting. He attempts to minimise the contestable and controversial potentialities of his central evaluative notion of harm by saying it is what is unpleasant, unwanted and deprives one of pleasure without any compensating benefit.

On Glover's criterion a religious zealot who refused medical treatment when physically ill would be not just disastrously mistaken but mad. The reckless people who drink and smoke too much or drive too fast are not just unwise but insane. Not only does his proposal imply that a lot of people are mad who are not, but the converse is at least a possibility. Could there not be a man who lived in a complete fantasy world, but who was so happy in it that it would be cruel to cure him? Admittedly his avoidance of harm would be a piece of good luck, perhaps that of living in some affectionate human setting in which he was cared for and looked after. He could not flourish in the real world unless so protected.

The disastrous consequences to the psychotic of the behaviour to which his madness leads are the bad feature which makes that condition madness and not its statistical abnormality. But the madness is not in the consequences; it is in the mental condition from which those consequences ensue. They could have arisen from sheer bad luck or undetected malice on the part of others and then there would be no suggestion that the victim was mad. In fact such disastrous consequences are most unlikely unless they are the results of madness. The state of mind that the disastrous consequences show, if persistent enough to rule out other explanations, to be madness is required to explain why the behaviour is so persistently disastrous.

Earlier I ascribed the charm of a statistical criterion to psychiatrists to its apparently objective and scientific character. But if it is inadequate how do psychiatrists manage in practice to pick out for treatment, in marked agreement with each other as to those who need it, patients who are not picked out for them by the criterion to which they ostensibly subscribe? The answer, clearly enough, is that their practice is better than their principles. In their training they learn how to diagnose madness and can give provisional accounts of that practice in the form of open-ended lists of symptoms, that is to say the 'clinical descriptions' from which I started and on which I have, of course, relied. They are not trained to take a step further back and to produce a justification for classing together as psychoses the assorted set of clinically described conditions they deal with. They do not really need to until challenged by sceptical critics of the whole idea of madness. I have assumed that, in virtue of the wealth and intimacy of their experience, they know what they are doing when they diagnose people as mad. That does not entail that their attempts to summarise the principles embodied in their diagnostic practice have to be accorded the same authority.

## 11. Beliefs, consensus and Descartes' problem

My chief claim has been that madness should not be defined either in terms of the characteristic emotions of those identified as mad, nor in terms of their characteristic behaviour. Nor should it be defined in textbook fashion in terms of statistical abnormality or, again, functionally, as by Glover in terms of need for protection against a consistent behaviour pattern that is harmful to the agent. Madness consists in the systematic unreasonableness of a person's practical beliefs.

The effectiveness of the social practice of diagnosing some people as mad must, then, depend on some sort of consensus about the unreasonableness of the relevant, practical beliefs, to which, of course, the person under consideration can not himself be a party.

He is bound to agree with the consensus if he is sane and disagree with it if he is mad, since, in both cases, he will have to say that his own system of practical beliefs is reasonable. To say that it is not is as good as self-refuting. What he says about the system is not exactly part of the system of his practical beliefs. But each of them informally implies its own reasonableness and so the whole lot of them, taken together, informally imply the reasonableness of the whole system.

Does this requirement of consensus reinstate the statistical criterion? In a way it does, but it applies to a different and more narrowly circumscribed range of material. As things are, and given that the relevant beliefs are practical in the sense I have described, the consensus is very broad. In the case of psychotics, at any rate, there is no serious doubt about the characterisation of their beliefs as unreasonable. In the case of more localised peculiarities of belief, those of the fearful flyer, for example, there may be some opening for disagreement. But the possibility should be considered that the present state of affairs, in which the vast majority agree that the practical belief-systems of a comparatively small number of people are unreasonable, might not obtain.

Suppose that only a fifth of the population managed to precipitate the kind of consensus about the reasonableness of practical beliefs that is now much more widely shared. They could still regard themselves as the sane minority provided that no group as large as their own in the remaining four-fifths achieved a comparable consensus. As things are the sane inhabit a common world, while the mad live in worlds of their own, unable to communicate or cooperate effectively with each other or with the sane. In our epistemic democracy the mad are all fringe candidates of the most extreme variety. But if there were two belief-parties of much the same size we should be in a mess. Were such a state of affairs to seem to obtain it might inspire doubt in each party as to whether they really understood the remarks, and so had really identified the beliefs, of the other. We can understand what other people say only if we assume that most of what they say is true, at any rate (cf. my *Thoughts and Thinkers*, Ch. 8).

Another extreme possibility is intimated but not explored in the first of Descartes' *Meditations*. I have been considering the question how I, or anyone else, can reasonably conclude that anyone other than the inquirer is mad. Descartes touches on the question: do I know that I am not myself mad? It seems to me that others share my beliefs and regard them as broadly reasonable, at least on practical matters, and find my emotions and conduct not to be particularly surprising or absurd. But may they not all be humouring me? Or, to go a stage further, might my belief in their apparent endorsement of the reasonableness of my practical belief-system be only a large piece of my system of unreasonable practical beliefs.

It would seem that if one is mad one cannot know that one is or even seriously believe that one is. For to do so is to believe that one's capacity for forming reasonable beliefs has broken down, that one's system of practical beliefs is composed of unreasonable beliefs and also that, on that account, one's beliefs are different from those of most people, the epistemic consensus. But to do that is, in effect, to repudiate one's system of practical beliefs.

The belief that I am mad is, therefore, a more disturbing one than the belief that I am asleep and dreaming. Any evidence one could cite to show that one was not dreaming could simply be something that one only dreams to be at one's disposal. Likewise any evidence one might invoke to show that one was not mad might be just a lunatic fancy. But while one usually wakes up from dreams, madness is a more long-lasting condition. Sometimes there is remission in which people can look back and conclude, reasonably, that they were mad then but are so no longer. In that case the past mad self is, for most epistemological purposes, another person. On that basis they can reasonably predict the return of madness. On a smaller scale there can be moments of sanity when the psychotic makes a brief escape from his prison of delusion. But often madness is a dream from which the dreamer never awakes.

The thought that I am mad is also more logically disturbing than the belief that I am dreaming. For the belief that I am mad really does have the property ascribed by Malcolm to the belief (or assertion) that I am dreaming: it cannot be coherently framed. I can remember that I was mad. I can expect, or fear, that I will go mad. But I cannot believe that I am without undermining the grounds for supposing that my capacity to form reasonable practical beliefs has broken down on which the belief must rest.

*Published in* Philosophy and Practice, *edited by A. Philips Griffiths* *(Cambridge University Press, 1985).*

# Homosexuality

I am going to consider some common and, for the most part, fairly unreflective reasons for thinking that homosexuality is a bad thing and, therefore, something that should be extirpated, if that is possible, or suppressed, by, most obviously, legal prohibition or, falling short of that, by moral or social pressure. These reasons are five in number: homosexuality is held to be unnatural, abnormal, a perversion, morally wrong or sinful and aesthetically repellent or disgusting. The first three of these unfavourable characterisations of homosexuality apply to it primarily as an orientation, a disposition to engage in homosexual activity, whether the disposition is manifested or not. The other two, the moral and aesthetic ones, so far as most of their proponents are concerned, apply only to homosexuality, as manifested in actual conduct. The desire to sin, after all, is a necessary condition of virtue. There is no merit in not doing things one has no desire to do. Similarly the desire to do something disgusting is hardly, in itself, disgusting.

My subject spreads beyond the general formula of the series: philosophy and psychiatry. But it has a psychiatric component. Up until recent times, at any rate, text-books of psychiatry have classified homosexuality as an abnormality or 'personality disorder' and, within that general area, as one of the sexual perversions. This way of classifying homosexuality may be seen as reflecting the more primitive, commonsensical conception of homosexuality as unnatural.

*Unnatural*, like its counterpart *natural*, is a desperately flexible term. Natural law is one thing for the legal theorist, quite another thing for the theorist of science. John Stuart Mill engaged with this problem in a lucid and dignified way in his essay 'Nature' in his *Three Essays on Religion*. What he comes up with is a twofold account of the natural, neither part of which is of any use in the present investigation. The natural, he concludes, is either that which is in accordance with the laws of nature, which for him means everything that actually happens, or everything that exists or happens independently of human interference. On neither of these accounts is there anything wrong with being unnatural, unless non-existence is a fault. Greek tragedy, representative government, flower gardens and other objects of general admiration are none of them natural in Mill's second sense and none the worse for that. It might seem strange to call any of them unnatural, but such a description is not indefensible. Greek tragedy is formalised and unrealistic; representative government is at odds with men's unruly passions; flower gardens can seem objectionably artificial by comparison with wild, uncultivated scenery. What seems quite clear is that homosexuality is neither supernatural nor non-natural: it is not outside the spatio-temporal order of nature.

One interpretation of the distinction between the natural and the unnatural which is significantly relevant to the matter in hand is to take it to be that between the innate and the acquired. The two main theories about the cause of homosexuality adopt the contrary positions. On one view homosexual orientation is constitutional, an outcome of the individual's inherited bodily equipment. On the other it is acquired by way of profoundly influential emotional experiences from earliest childhood onwards. First of all there is a phase of narcissistic fixation, in which the idea is implanted that the self is the primary object of love and, by extension in due course, that love-objects of one's own sex are to be preferred to those of the other sex. Secondly, there comes to be aroused in the infant, once conscious of the great importance and comparative fragility of his genitals, a fear of the castrating woman (woman, not man, presumably because women, as mothers, nurses, bathers and so on, have more to do with his genitals and his disapproved behaviour with them than men do). Finally, and most emphatically, there is the tracing of homosexuality to the kind of family situation in which there is the combination of an absent or hostile father with an emotionally overwhelming mother.

In both these causal accounts of homosexuality it is represented as a kind of immaturity or arrested development, particularly in the case of the Freudian view of it as acquired. It is, fortunately, not necessary to adjudicate between the two for the purposes of this inquiry. The fact that a human propensity is acquired no more shows it to be bad (or good, for that matter) than the fact that it is innate. Cooking, shaving, the wearing of clothes, agriculture, industry, flying ('if God had meant us to fly he would have given us wings'), are all acquired, the products of learning, not the outcome of instinct. Aggression, whatever culturally influenced forms it may take, is innate, but then, so it would appear, is a measure of sympathetic response to the sufferings of others.

To describe something as immature or an instance of arrested development implies a mildly negative evaluation; whatever is so classified is being held to be somehow imperfect or incomplete. That is not a consideration that can be pressed very far. An eighty-year-old man with his own teeth and a good head of hair and with the bodily strength and energy of a fifty-year-old is an instance of arrested development. In practice we should probably call it delayed development or something of the sort to avoid the unfavourable nuance of 'arrested'. The condition is unusual or exceptional, but to be welcomed and even admired, not regretted.

There is possibly an implicit comparison between the conception of homosexuality as arrested development and the condition of someone whose sexual development in narrowly physiological terms is incomplete, where, for example, there has been a failure to attain positive sexual capacity. Unlike persistent youthfulness, that condition is one to which those subject to it are strongly averse and which they would wish to correct if they could. If they did not desire to be rid of it, it might be held that they would wish to if they knew what they were missing. This kind of sexual immaturity is analogous, to some extent, to such disabilities as congenital deafness or blindness. Some homosexuals wish they were not, but only a minority of them, and then largely for extraneous, contingent reasons such as social disapproval and fear of the blackmail which that disapproval makes possible.

The question as to whether homosexuality is innate or acquired is often thought to have a bearing on its alterability, which is practically important if it is, indeed, a bad or unwanted condition. Homosexual activity can be suppressed by sanctions (at great human cost, if the suppression is to be effective). Homosexual orientation is another matter. Whatever its cause or causes, it seems highly resistant to any way of altering it that has occurred to anyone. But this really has nothing to do with its innate or acquired nature. Innate deficiencies can be dealt with by medicine, as with insulin treatment for diabetes (which, being inheritable, is presumably innate). Acquired deficiencies, such as blindness or paralysis resulting from serious accidents, are often unalterable. If anything, homosexuality might be more alterable if it is innate than if it is acquired. If it is the result of some kind of hormonal imbalance that would seem to be the sort of thing that could be dealt with pharmacologically. In the other type of theory, the special kind of family situation held to produce homosexuals cannot be retrospectively corrected. The deed is done, as with a broken back; there is no simple deficiency, like that of insulin, to be made good.

In so far, then, as the natural is identified with the innate and the unnatural with the acquired, neither is good or bad on that account alone, nor would the innateness of homosexuality, if it turns out to be innate, show it to be unalterable, always supposing it ought to be altered.

The innate–acquired distinction is backward-looking, drawn in terms of past causes. Another biological distinction, this time forward-looking, could be used to provide an interpretation of the supposed unnaturalness of homosexuality. That is the distinction between what is biologically adapted, or, more specifically, what is reproductively efficient, and what is not. Homosexuals are obviously less likely to bring about their own replacement in the human species than heterosexuals. Most of them, after all, have no children, never act in such a way as to beget them. Some do: Oscar Wilde had two sons, André Gide a daughter, various royal homosexuals have submitted themselves to the call of dynastic duty – James I, for example. But such homosexual fathers must be a very small proportion of the male homosexual population as a whole.

The obvious reproductive inefficiency of homosexuals has been used as an argument against the idea that homosexuality is an innate, inheritable characteristic. If it were, it is argued, the relevant gene would not be passed on to subsequent generations and would be bred out. Against this some sociobiologists have claimed that a genetic package that ensured that *some* male offspring were homosexual would provide a supply of homosexual uncles to whom husbands could confidently entrust the protection of their wives and children when they were away from home, on hunting trips. Perhaps that consideration could be extended to apply to female homosexuals, who, unencumbered with children of their own, could help the over-burdened mothers who were their sisters. The style of male dominance conventionally ascribed to palaeolithic society might have excluded the possibility of homosexually inclined women in these circumstances following their inclinations and abstaining from heterosexual intercourse.

It would seem probable that, although the protective homosexual uncle may have been a reproductively useful part of the family circle in palaeolithic times, he can hardly have been so in the last ten thousand years. Therefore, if homosexuality is inheritable, it ought by now to have shown signs of fading away. On the other hand, ten millennia is a very small part of the history of the human species as a whole. We do inherit vestigial items, like the appendix, which seem to do no discernible good for the organism's chances of survival and only a modest and tolerable amount of harm. The neolithic increase in food supply made possible an enlargement in the number of children a family could bring to maturity more than sufficient to compensate for the failure of the persisting body of homosexuals to make a direct contribution to the number of children born.

A continuing problem for the human species has been, not its failure to reproduce enough, but, generally, the overabundance of its reproductive energy. Famine, disease and war must have killed many more people before they could reproduce themselves than have failed to be born by the abstention of homosexuals from the reproductive task. It is hard not to feel that nature has been more lavish than necessary in making human beings sensitive to pain as a warning against the injurious. In the same way the human sexual urge seems extravagantly strong. Males have the desire to do what would, if the necessary females were available, lead them to father thousands, not handfuls or Victorian dozens. Their reproductively essential female partners could manage at least twenty offspring. Just as anaesthetics enable us to receive the warning of pain without continuing to endure it once it has made its point, so birth control enables us to satisfy our sexual desires without leading to altogether insupportable overpopulation.

The population could be maintained if there were many more male homosexuals than there are. Fatherhood could become a specialised craft, as the growing of food has. That is not, of course, true of motherhood. If few women want to have more than two children and if the population is to be kept up then most women must become mothers. But must the population be kept up? There are few places in the world where the general level of contentment would not be greater if the population were smaller.

A somewhat more metaphysical conception of the natural derives it from the idea that each kind of thing has a nature, that is to say, an essence or ideal or perfect, completed form. It is presumably in this sense that it is said that it is unnatural to dress dogs up and train them to perform in circuses. That is, indeed, unnatural in Mill's second sense, as arising from human interference. But then so does inoculating dogs against distemper, which one might suppose enables them to realise their essence or ideal form. So also does training dogs to herd sheep, which exploits their sharpness of perception and speed, while interferingly inhibiting their 'natural' tendency to kill the animals they chase.

The idea of a thing's nature being its essence or ideal form is one that now has little philosophical currency. But its respectable Aristotelian ancestry makes it odd that Mill did not even mention it.

Its inescapably evaluative character – a thing's nature is what it *ought* to realise or accord with – makes it contestable and weakens its claim to objectivity. There is also a possible problem about kinds. To what kind does an individual primarily belong? It may be argued that it is part of the nature of a man, simply so characterised, to be heterosexual: most people are, he will in the end be happier if he is, and so on. But what if he is a male ballet-dancer?

The idea of something's nature as its ideal essence is rendered more solid by the religious conception that the kinds of thing that there are are the creations of a supreme intelligence. That is the point of view of the strictest sort of Christian morality. God made man to be fruitful and multiply, amongst other things, like fearing God and labouring in the sweat of his brow. It follows that our sexual capacities are to be exercised solely for the purpose of reproduction. And that is the official morality of the Roman Catholic church and, in a more vestigial way, of the other Christian churches.

That leaves homosexuality outside the pale as unnatural. But it also implies that nearly all heterosexual activity is unnatural too. Various methods of birth control are, and some always have been, very widely practised: coitus interruptus, condoms, diaphragms, spermicides – all, of course, condemned by the more rigorous Christian bodies. There is vasectomy, on a smaller scale. There is the widespread practice of oral-genital sex and the perhaps less widespread one of heterosexual sodomy. This array of stratagems and devices makes a vastly greater contribution to the avoidance of reproduction than homosexuality does. It follows that it is certainly no more unnatural in this sense than most heterosexual activity.

Until recently the prevailing style of psychiatric classification has located homosexuality under the general heading of abnormalities, as one among what are described as personality disorders. It was thus associated with neuroses, such as phobias and obsessive-compulsive disorders, with hysteria, hypochondria and psychopathic criminality. In 1974 the American Psychiatrical Association removed it from this classification, under pressure from homosexual activists, but that change has not yet been followed internationally. The idea that homosexuality is abnormal still widely persists.

Medical writers, most relevantly of text-books of pathology, tend to define abnormality or disease in barely statistical terms. Those who fall within some defined extremity of a distribution are on that account abnormal. But that, as many of them perceive, with varying degrees of embarrassment and response, is not enough. Being in a small minority with respect to some bodily feature or characteristic is not a sufficient condition of abnormality, if that is taken to imply that treatment aimed at its removal is appropriate. Having naturally red hair, being over six and a half feet in height, having perfect pitch or a taste for tapioca or tripe are all statistically abnormal, but they are not conditions calling for treatment; they are not diseases or disorders but idiosyncrasies or peculiarities.

It is not clear that statistical abnormality is even a necessary condition of disease. Auden's remark 'This England of ours where nobody is well' may be dismissed as an exercise of poetic licence, but the majority of a population, particularly an isolated and uncivilised one, may properly be held to have a disease, one arising for instance from parasitic infestation.

A sense of the inadequacy of the equation of disease with bare statistical abnormality is reflected in the tendency of pathologists to make some reference to function, such as 'the ability to function in harmony with one's environment'. Inability to function requires a distinction between disease and illness. One may have an undiagnosed and symptomless disease for years before becoming ill, that is to say feeling bad through pain or discomfort and being unable to do things most people do and one ordinarily can and which one regrets being unable to do. It is important to include pain since some loss of function attends the ageing process and it is statistically abnormal for it not to do so.

A disease, it is plain, is a *bad* abnormality, one which its possessor does not want to have. But the aversion to it must arise from a limited range of reasons. In the straightforwardly physical case this range is clear enough: it must involve pain or the likelihood of pain and the fairly vague factor of loss of function. Mental disorders do not typically involve any physical pain, even when, as with the organic psychoses, they have a physiological basis. In such cases all the unfavourable weight that must be added to abnormality to constitute disease or disorder has to be carried by impairment of function or the related feature of 'inability to meet the usual demands of everyday life'. That requirement could perhaps be more concretely expressed as the inability to do things that it is reasonable to want to do, in the light of what one has usually been able to do and/or what most people are ordinarily able to do. That qualification about what it is reasonable to want is designed to exclude unrealistic desires, such as, for most us, to run a mile in four minutes or lift a 200-pound weight.

Curiously, homosexuals have a lower expectation of life than heterosexuals. But that hardly makes homosexuality a physical disease. It is not attributable to any identifiable organic condition, and is probably to be explained by persistent anxiety and loneliness. A contribution to this lower life-expectancy is made by fact that homosexuals are three times as likely to attempt or achieve suicide as heterosexuals. That is not an intrinsic feature of the homosexual condition but a result of the pressure of social disapproval.

By and large those who suffer from recognised physical diseases acknowledge that they do, and are keen to get rid of them if they can. That is also true of most sufferers from the conventionally recognised mental disorders, with the exception of the psychoses, where 'insight', an awareness by the sufferer of his disordered condition, is lacking. The psychotic is subjected to sequestration, care and treatment on the authority of others – family and psychiatrists in particular – to prevent him from doing harm to himself and to other people. They can possibly justify their dictatorial conduct by the consideration that he would want to be shut up and treated if he were not mad. There are, after all, psychotics like Charles Lamb's sister Mary, who, in periods of sane remission, but feeling a psychotic episode was about to begin, got her brother to take her to the asylum.

With this last, intelligible, exception it is evident that a statistically abnormal condition is not a disorder or disease, calling for treatment and eradication, unless those with it do not want to be. There is evidence that a fair number of homosexuals, about one in three of a large surveyed sample, wish they were not. Presumably nearly everyone with a straightforward physical disorder, like cancer or tuberculosis, would like to be rid of it, indeed would be passionately concerned to get any possible cure. One might not want to be cured of a comparatively mild disorder, neither life-threatening nor seriously disabling, if it could save one from military service or even render one attractive to a ravishing, otherwise inaccessible Lady Bountiful. Here the disorder is acknowledged as such and disliked for itself, but favoured as means to a more desired end than a cure, in the unusual circumstances described. It seems reasonable to suppose that a much larger proportion than a third would wish to be cured of phobias, obsessions and so forth. The sufferer from such a condition is not likely to regard it as 'constitutive of their identity' in the way that many homosexuals regard their homosexuality.

The contrast is heightened if the reasons given by homosexuals for wanting to change their sexual orientation are considered. About half of them cite social disapproval and such unpleasant corollaries as liability to blackmail, dismissal or exclusion from many kinds of employment, and the consequent need to deceive people about one's sexual nature. Another quarter of those who would prefer to change mention having no children.

That leaves only a twelfth of the homosexuals surveyed as possibly hostile to their homosexuality in itself and not as a contingent obstacle in one case and a fairly contingent obstacle in the other. Social disapproval does not make homosexuality bad; it can be justifiable only if homosexuality is bad for some other reason. As for the desire for children: if homosexuals marry but remain actively homosexual the marriages involved are not likely to prosper; if they do not marry, they will be hard put to find women ready to bear their children without prospect of a lasting relationship. The least damaging tactic is for the child-loving homosexual to adopt children. That only partly satisfies the need. Against it must be set the characteristic instability of homosexual households. Even where there is a long-lasting partnership it is often combined in such households with an amount of cruising which is not paralleled in any but most promiscuous of heterosexual families.

The small proportion, then, of homosexuals who regret their homosexuality, and would be rid of it if they could, for non-extraneous reasons, is not sufficient to show that their statistical abnormality implies that there is anything wrong with them. Their situation may be compared with that of married heterosexuals who do not have children. These may be of three kinds: those who cannot have them but wish they could; those who cannot have them and do not mind; those who can have them but choose not to. All of these classes are statistically abnormal. Only the members of the first regret their infertility. Those of the second are content with it; those of the third act positively to bring it about. If, as seems likely, the second class is smaller than the first (which seems likely since most physically fertile married heterosexuals do choose to have children), it is reasonable to regard physiologically caused infertility as a disorder, as a bad abnormality. But can it reasonably be held that physically fertile married heterosexuals who choose not to have children suffer from a personality disorder and should be encouraged to receive treatment for it? Others may look down on them and deplore what they would regard as their selfishness. But the careful abstainers from reproduction are more properly to be compared to people who refuse to have anything in their gardens but mown grass, thus steering clear of the nuisance and worry of flower beds.

To characterise homosexuality as a perversion is to associate it with other non-standard forms of sexual behaviour such as fetishism, bestiality, incest, paedophilia, gerontophilia, necrophilia, voyeurism

and exhibitionism. Some of these alternatives to ordinary heterosexual activity are the product of unfavourable circumstances.
Bestiality is the legendary resource of shepherds stuck on remote
islands for long periods.

Homosexuality is often, in much the same way, the outcome of
sequestration from the opposite sex: in prison or a monastery or a
military barracks or, of course, a boarding school. In Kinsey's investigation 37 per cent of men said they had had homosexual experience
of some sort or other, but only 5 per cent really preferred homosexual relations. Incest, likewise, can be partly explained as taking
as sexual objects those who are most readily available and, perhaps,
those who are easiest to dominate.

Most of these perversions share with homosexuality the property
of being reproductively inefficient (in the case of incest the inefficiency is indirect, a matter of the likelihood of the offspring of
incestuous unions being in some uncontroversial way defective). But
are they bad, should they be dispositions we should aim to root out?
Incest and paedophilia normally involve fear, pain and an unacceptable level of coercion (and incest, as just mentioned, leads to
defective offspring). Voyeurism and exhibitionism may have the
effect, indeed exhibitionism is intended to have the effect, of
disturbing the people who are watched or exhibited to. The injury
to the voyeur's objects is very small; one can always pull the curtain,
or move to another part of the wood, unless the voyeur is very persistent. The purpose of the exhibitionist is to shock or upset. His effect
is more likely to arouse fear of rape or other sexual assault, although
I understand that this fear is usually without foundation.
Homosexuality need not, and ordinarily does not, involve any of
these objectionable consequences. Like heterosexuality it may take
frightening, painful or unacceptably coercive forms but to a serious
extent only in exceptional cases.

Bestiality might involve a measure of cruelty to animals, but seems
not far removed from weird eating tastes, as for grubs among native
Australians and for sheeps' eyeballs among desert Arabs. Fetishism
is pathetic, even comic, but harmless. As Philip Toynbee memorably
observed when reviewing G. Lowes Dickinson's autobiography:
there could be no more innocuous object of love than a pair of well-
worn boots. Gerontophilia seems positively philanthropic, providing
an opportunity for sexual pleasure for those for whom it has ordinarily run out. Necrophilia puts enlightened attitudes under some
strain. It does not, in itself, have to be associated with murder as a
way of acquiring the requisite objects, though most people have no

other reliable way of getting hold of dead bodies.

The crucial difference between homosexuality and all of these perversions evil, sinister or comic – is that in its ordinary form it is expressed in a reciprocal relationship with a consenting human partner. The perversions considered have all involved either a non-human object – animal, corpse or fetish – or some failure of consent, even of capacity to consent. As much as heterosexuality, it is a relationship between relevantly mature persons, capable of making responsible decisions. As much and as little, since there is plenty of heterosexual coercion of a degree less than assault or rape, plenty of taking advantage of the young and inexperienced that falls short of paedophilia.

Another crucial and fundamental likeness between homosexuality and heterosexuality is that both involve long-term partnerships; not just brief contacts for the sake of sexual pleasure but the sharing of lives, mutual concern over a long period. It is clear that a great deal of homosexual activity is casual and that energetic promiscuity is commonly combined with long-term homosexual partnerships. That is, after all, not unknown in heterosexual unions and even where a union is largely or wholly monogamous most husbands and many wives wish that it were not. But there is a real contrast here. What is common among homosexuals is more or less exceptional among heterosexuals. Married men take what they can get: a steady mistress kept of sight or quick frolics at conferences or on business trips. They do not, by and large, go out in an unconcealed way in pursuit of sexual pleasure in places set up for just this purpose and where it does not have to be paid for.

It cannot, I believe, be pretended that the general promiscuity of homosexuals is simply an effect of their oppressed or socially marginalised status. There is a biological explanation for it. Males aim to beget as many children as possible; females to conceive by mates who will look after them and their children. Males are genetically programmed to spread their genes as widely as possible; females to select mates who will give their children the best chance to survive. The relevance of this is shown by the fact that female homosexuals are not generally promiscuous and ordinarily establish life-long unions.

There is one social factor which may have helped to emphasise this difference between the sexes. There is no institution of homosexual marriage, although in recent years there have been calls for it and pretences of it (pretences, since, even if recognised by some sort of church, they have no official acknowledgement from the state). That fact partly reflects the more or less outlawed status of homosexual relationships. The state is not going to endorse relationships which it proscribes as illegal, or has until very recently. It could also be argued that there is no need for the institution of marriage for homosexuals, since there are no children of homosexual unions in need of legal protection, and in such unions there is not the asymmetry of power and wealth that is usual in heterosexual marriages.

So, although the sort of life-long and largely exclusive partnership that is reasonably, if decreasingly, common in heterosexual marriages, is a good deal less often to be met with in homosexual unions, it is not a large enough difference between the two styles of sexuality to outweigh the vastly greater difference between them together, on the one hand, as reciprocal personal relationships and sexual perversions, properly so called, on the other. There is an essentially masturbatory character to the perversions. Their object is not on a level with the subject; a reciprocal personal relationship is either impossible or, with voyeurs and exhibitionists, not intended by the subject.

The fourth common type of adverse characterisation of homosexuality is moral. It is, it is held, simply sinful, morally wrong. There is no profitable way of arguing with someone who bases such a judgement on revelation, incarnated in a sacred text or the traditions of a church. Indirectly one may question the way in which the revelation has been interpreted. Even more indirectly one may question the sincerity of the position of the person who regards homosexuality as a sin if he fails to condemn it in some instances. But arguments about the interpretation of texts, particularly very ancient ones, are notoriously indecisive and the censurer of homosexuality may be entirely sincere. Much the same is true of the position of someone who claims intuitive knowledge of the principle that homosexuality is wrong. Homosexuality is a suspiciously specific matter to be a topic of moral intuition as compared with such very general matters as the wrongness of promise-breaking or lying. The question can be approached most manageably by asking whether homosexuality does harm. It does not seem to offend against any of the moral principles that are ordinarily, and with some measure of plausibility, held to be known intuitively and not to be in need, or susceptible, of further justification. It is not unfair or unjust, it is not dishonest, it does not involve the breaking of a promise.

What harm, then, does someone do who persuades someone else to take part in homosexual activity with him? Much amorous persuasion is more or less coercive, much of it involves a measure of deceit. But these deficiencies are surely not greater in homosexual relations than in heterosexual ones. If anything they are probably less. The reproductively inconsequential nature of homosexual activity means that there is less at stake. The initiating partner does not have to promise that he intends the relationship to be persistent or permanent. Nor is there ordinarily the same sort of difference in physical strength between homosexual partners as there is between heterosexual ones.

It is argued that active homosexuals who persuade adolescent males, who have not yet arrived at a settled attitude towards sex, to have intercourse with them may instil an undesirable, harmful habit in them. If there is a choice heterosexuality is to be preferred to homosexuality simply on grounds of prudence, in view of the social disadvantages that still accrue to the latter. The older male who casually makes a young girl pregnant does comparable harm. What is more it is quite certain that older men do make impressionable girls pregnant with unwanted children. But it is far from obvious that some homosexual experience near the beginning of adult life largely determines the developed sexual orientation of those who engage in it. Kinsey's figures are the most objective foundation for this doubt; everyday observation of ex-public schoolboys, Guardsmen and so on is the most persuasive.

Are there any physical aspects of homosexual relationships which can be condemned as harmful? Sodomy is physically damaging to those who take a passive part in it. But it is by no means a universal element in homosexual relations, although commoner there, probably, than in heterosexual ones. The AIDS epidemic puts this in a somewhat different light. Homosexual sodomy has been much the largest contributor to the spread of this frightful disease (in the Western world, at any rate; the pervasiveness of the disease in Africa arises from the fact that women there suffer from lesions through which the virus can penetrate). AIDS has replaced venereal disease as the most serious pathological menace resulting from sexual activity, since the latter went into retreat in the face of antibiotics. The relevant moral considerations as regards the sexual conduct of the infected are the same in both cases. It is profoundly evil to engage in sexual activity when infected unless the partner knows about it. That last qualification is really redundant. No rational person will have intercourse with an infected one. But the fact that most of those who have, or are destined to get, AIDS are homosexuals does not imply that most homosexuals have AIDS. Many heterosexuals have it too: notably needle-sharers. So it is neither a peculiarly nor universally homosexual problem.

There is a fairly compelling moral consideration that can be adduced to support an adverse view of homosexuality, which is of a more or less Kantian nature. It is that in most homosexual relationships the participants do not treat each other as 'ends in themselves', but simply use each other as means to sexual pleasure. It is certainly true that long-term, morally and personally profound relationships are less common among homosexuals. How much does that matter? If I regularly play tennis with someone but do not see him except on the tennis court and at the health juice bar afterwards, if, in other words, I am interested in him only as a tennis partner, am I ignoring his status as an end in himself? More to the point, if I pick up different opponents every time I go to the courts, on a purely casual basis, am I acting immorally? I could embark on a deeper relationship: listen to their worries, exchange dinners and weekend visits, lend them books and so forth. I do not because I am interested in them only as tennis partners. Is that morally wrong? It is wrong, surely, only if I have led them to expect something more: a serious friendship. There would be nothing wrong if, in making use of him, I do not harm him and if, in particular, I am quite content for him to make use of me. We are reciprocally related by the coincidence of our interests; neither is profiting at the expense of the other.

Yet there is, I think, something wrong about the comparative lack of serious commitment among homosexual partners. But it is not a moral fault. It is a deficiency, due to the fact that both partners are male, which emotionally impoverishes homosexual relationships. Except for a minute number of people sex is a more important part of life than tennis. A life in which it is merely a source of short-term gratification and not an inseparable part of a whole shared life is to that extent trivialised. But triviality is not a moral offence; it is, rather, a missed opportunity and one which, in fact, many homosexuals do not miss.

The final objection to homosexuality, brought forward, perhaps, by the least reflective of those who condemn it, is that it is aesthetically disgusting. This is very much a last resort. In the first place I should not imagine that more than a minority of heterosexuals view it with more than moderate distaste, although they might find the thought of engaging in it themselves unpleasant. But then that is just what many homosexuals feel about heterosexual intercourse. There is something fairly frivolous about the objection anyway. In general heterosexuals are not compelled to witness homosexual activity, except by quickly correctable accident on wandering into a gay bar or visiting a public lavatory.

In general full-blooded sexual activity of any kind is not aesthetically suitable for close inspection. Heterosexuals and homosexuals alike adopt ridiculous positions, emit hoarse, inarticulate cries, twist up their faces absurdly in the culminating phase of their relations. It is interesting that in Chinese and Indian representations of sexual intercourse, a favourite subject, people's faces are generally serene, however bizarre the positions in which they find themselves. There are no twisted faces, no sweat, no secretions.

Those who find homosexuality disgusting do not need to see it taking place to be disgusted; it is enough for them to know that it is going on. That is a pretty tenuous basis from which to move to the prohibition and suppression of activity that is a great part of a large number of people's happiness. The aesthetics of the disgusting are worthy of investigation. Is disgust the result of some kind of conditioning or are some things, like putrefying flesh or slime, intrinsically disgusting? It is not necessary to go into the question here, for a simple reason. Most people find cannibalism disgusting, although some, cannibals, presumably do not. But its disgustingness is not the basis for the condemnation of cannibalism, which is that it leads, very directly, to the intentional killing of human beings. Generally the disgusting is condemned, not because it evokes a reaction of disgust, but because of some evil of which that reaction is a sign. Disgustingly violent videos are objected to because it is thought that they encourage unpleasantly violent behaviour. Disgustingness is not a reason on its own for suppression, there has to be something objectionable in the thing to be suppressed which justifies the reaction of disgust to it.

I conclude that none of the five familiar grounds on which homosexuality is condemned is sufficient. It is not in any relevant sense more unnatural than heterosexuality and it would not matter if it were. It may be statistically, but that does not show it to be objectionably, abnormal. As a reciprocal relationship between people old or sensible enough to be responsible for their own actions it should be classified with heterosexuality, not with the sexual perversions. It is not morally objectionable in itself, although, just like heterosexuality, it may be carried on in an immoral, in a coercive or deceitful, way. To the extent that it is aesthetically repellent it is no more so than heterosexuality. The special frisson that attends its contemplation in the minds of many people is simply superstitious.

*Published in* Philosophy, Psychology and Psychiatry, *edited by A. Philips Griffiths (Cambridge University Press, 1994).*

IV

# The Inner Life

Let me begin with the ancient philosophical injunction 'know thyself'. In the sense intended it means: find out what sort of person you really are, find out what you are good at and good for, find out what you really want from life. Such an enquiry is to a considerable extent one into what other people think you are really like. That is because the assessment of a person's character is an essentially comparative affair. To be mean is to be meaner than most; to be brave is to be rather braver than the average. Now it is hard to compare oneself with other people. It is not just that one may love oneself more than others, or at least be anxious to arrive at a kindly view of oneself, however clear-sighted one is prepared to be about others, though that may play a part in one's limitations as a self-assessor. More important is the fact that one has to compare oneself and others asymmetrically, from different points of view. One contemplates oneself inwardly; others one considers from outside. Thus, one is intimately aware of one's own good intentions, but one sees only what others actually manage to bring off.

The outside observer can compare people other than himself on a level. As a result his bestowals of comparative judgements about character are made on a single scale of measurement. It would seem to follow that other people must be better judges of a person's character than he is himself. To a very large extent they surely are. There is, however, one important thing that goes a little way toward counteracting the force of the outside observer's advantages of a single standpoint from which to make comparisons, and, in most cases, of a lack of emotional bias toward the subjects of comparison. This is that the subject has much more to go on than all but the most pertinacious and Siamese-twin like observers could possibly have. So his wealth of evidence may do something to compensate for his disadvantages in regard to standpoint and emotional neutrality.

Over the past half-century philosophers have been preoccupied with theories about the nature of the mind which connect our notions of the elements of mental life with the publicly observable circumstances in which thoughts and feelings occur, and with the publicly observable activity or behaviour in which they are manifested. What I have been saying about judgements of character, of the character which we are told to get to know in the old injunction, is in conformity with that more or less behaviouristic tendency in the philosophy of mind. And indeed it is the traits of character here in question to which such accounts of mental concepts apply most convincingly.

A conception of someone's character as an organised system of traits is very much in the nature of a theory, a fairly generalised, fairly abstract representation of the persistent ways in which someone's mind works. A theory of this kind is what we have most practical need of in our dealings with people. We look to it for answers to practically pressing questions about what another person is likely to do in such and such circumstances, how he will react to such and such a proposal, whether he can be trusted to stick to some undertaking he has made. But there is more to one than this practically interesting public self. There is also oneself as a continuing history (interrupted of course by bouts of sleep, at least to the extent that they are dreamless), a history of thoughts and feelings, wants, hopes, imaginings, likes, efforts, movements of attention and so forth. It is this inner life of private experiences which philosophers of a more traditional dualist kind have seen as the life of the mind proper. When they talk about self-knowledge it is to knowledge of this inner stream of conscious experience that they are referring. The standard account of this knowledge that we have of the historic detail of our own mental lives is provided by what Locke says, and, one should add, assumes, in his doctrine about reflection. We are equipped, he holds, with a faculty of reflection, over and above the coordinate faculty of sensation which supplies us, in an indirect and somewhat precarious way, with knowledge of the physical world outside us (including our own bodies). Reflection, he says, 'is the perception of the operations of our own minds within us, as it is employed about the ideas it has got', these prior ideas it is 'employed about' being ideas of sensation.[1] Specifically, the objects of reflection turn out to be the various kinds of perceiving, thinking and willing. Pleasure and pain and, by implication, the whole comparatively passive, emotional aspect of our mental life, is bundled, for an unconvincing reason, into a hybrid category of ideas of both sensation and reflection.

A crucial and philosophically problematic feature of this account of our knowledge of our historical, non-theoretical selves is that the subject's awareness of the experiences that make up the detail of his mental life is held to be infallible. Locke distinguishes between the

1. *An Essay Concerning Human Understanding*, ed. J.W. Yolton, (Everyman edn, 1965), 2 : 78.

ideas that we have and the objects to whose existence they testify, but only in the case of sense-perception is this distinction exploited. There the ideas present to the mind are clearly distinguished from the qualities of physical things, which he takes to be their causes and, in some cases, to resemble them. That admits a problem of how the ideas supply us with any knowledge about physical things and their qualities and offers a none-too-convincing solution to it. In the case of our mental states, although Locke goes through the forms of distinguishing them from the ideas we have of them, there is no suggestion that the two could conceivably be somehow out of alignment. Having the idea of a mental operation and being directly aware of the operation seem to be the same thing. Ideas of reflection are not intermediaries between the mind and its own operations.

Why did Locke adopt, or fall into, this questionable doctrine of the infallibility of our beliefs about our own mental states? Perhaps he confusedly thought that since ideas are experiences, all experiences must be ideas; in other words that for an experience to occur is for the mind it occurs in to have an idea. Perhaps it was a generalisation from the fact that it does seem in the case of some mental states – having pains or visual images are the most persuasive examples – that it is a necessary condition of the occurrence of the experience that the subject is conscious of it. Perhaps it was reverence for Descartes, whom he sometimes mentioned to disagree with, but more often followed without mentioning.

This curious view, with its implication that no one, not even ourselves at a later time, can correct us about anything we sincerely believe about our current mental state, has been extraordinarily tenacious. The unconscious was not, of course, discovered by Freud. His new contribution was the idea of unconscious mental states that are prevented by repression from entering consciousness. Simple dexterities of navigation around cluttered places by people fully engrossed in conversation that has nothing to do with the stuff they nimbly avoid stepping on proves the existence of unconscious perception, to carry the battle to the heart of Locke's fortress. People often dislike others they are generally expected to love, such as their brothers, and can manage to conceal the fact from themselves, though not from observant people around them, who may be able to enlarge the self-knowledge of the self-deceiver. There are mental states, that is to say, of which it is *not* the case that we *believe* we have them, although we do in fact *have* them. To say that is not to say we do not believe we have them since that is our idiom for believing that we do not have them. No doubt the unconsciously hostile sibling believes that he does not hate his brother. But the talkative person picking his way through the clutter probably has no belief either way about whether he saw the basket of light-bulbs he neatly stepped over.

Old-fashioned or dualist philosophers of mind implicitly reject the thesis of the infallibility of self-awareness in distinguishing, as they do when they are being moderately careful, between self-consciousness and introspection. Self-consciousness does not imply anything about the beliefs in which it results as being the outcome of any kind of deliberate scrutiny or investigation or purposive direction of attention. But introspection, on the other hand, is an active, exploratory survey of the contents of one's mind. If there is such a thing, and it succeeds in finding, say, a new view of the precise shade of enthusiasm one feels for a person of one's acquaintance, then what it finds must have been in one's mind already without one's having known that it was. The alternative is to hold that introspection, the attentive scrutiny of one's own mind, *creates* its objects. It is only proper to admit that there is an element of decision, of making up one's mind, in some of these attitude-considering situations, as there also is in belief. To come to a conclusion about how much one likes someone or wants something is often a decision on future policy towards them – how much time shall one spend with him, how much effort shall one put into getting it. But one can approach such an inner enquiry just as well in a cognitive, truth-seeking spirit as in a practical, policy-making one. We often take a fair amount of trouble about formulating satisfactory descriptions of our own states of mind. An honest autobiographer, aiming to avoid both self-deception and a mere superficial register of public events, would be constantly engaged in such perfecting of his self-description. To some extent, no doubt, his care and hesitation could be put down to distrust of memory. yet the same tentativeness is entirely conceivable in producing an account that is contemporaneous with its topic. It might be objected that in such a case we would be fully conscious or aware of the state in question, but would be having difficulty in finding the right words in which to clothe our awareness. Until the words are found, however, that awareness is only potential.

Finally, and most concretely, we find it natural to describe some of the contents of the mind as at the centre or focus of our attention and others as being at the margin of consciousness. To be so located is not ordinarily an immutable fact; it is something that can be altered by a shift of attention. But the shifting light here is something that illuminates what was there already; it is not like the beam from the projectionist's booth near the rafters that conveys the film we are watching on to a screen that in itself is blank.

I have been arguing that knowing oneself can be both a knowledge of one's publicly observable and comparatively assessable character – knowledge here taking the form of a practically useful, more or less systematic theory – and a knowledge of the historical detail of one's inner mental life, which is not something unproblematically self-luminous but a field of investigation that may call for attentive scrutiny and, no doubt, the exercise of skill.

The bottomless capacity for error that Descartes chillingly observed in philosophers may account for the curious imperviousness to fairly obvious fact displayed by the theory of the infallibility of self-knowledge adopted by him and by Locke and, indeed, by most philosophers until recent times who have considered the matter at all. One thing they might have been brought up short by is the work of novelists, particularly in the last hundred years. The greatest novelists of that period have been masters of subjective knowledge – James, Proust, Conrad, Joyce. What they have done, in comparison with such earlier novelists as Scott, Thackeray and Trollope, is to move the centre of gravity of the novel away from the systematic, practically useful kind of externalised representation of human beings. The difference between the two groups parallels that between two kinds of autobiographer. The first, who is perhaps more properly called the memoir writer, records events he has observed that he believes to be of interest, while remaining himself in a more or less Isherwoodian seclusion. The second, the autobiographer proper, is principally occupied with himself. It is the difference between Saint-Simon and Rousseau.

There are autobiographies earlier than the Renaissance. The one obviously great one, St Augustine's *Confessions*, is not quite a straightforward case. The detail of life is at once sketchily recorded and wholly subordinate to the main religious intention of the book, as in Newman's *Apologia*. The recording of experience for its own sake comes later. And it first appears in such extroverted narratives as those of Cellini, Lord Herbert of Cherbury and Casanova, as a form of boasting or self-inflation, formally comparable to the picaresque novel. The inner life, except in its religious aspect, does not arrive until the romantic epoch. Gibbon's account of the end of his early romance is characteristic.[2] 'I sighed as a lover, I obeyed as a son' stands to the circumstances it reports as the formally elegant balance sheet of a stormy and troubled theatrical production does

2. *Autobiography* (Oxford: World's Classics edition, 1907), pp. 83–4.

to the shouting and tears, the collapses of pieces of scenery, refusals to go on for Act III and so forth that lie behind it. Perhaps there was less inner life in the less leisured past or in a world where there was less privacy, to make self-contemplation possible. The introspective opportunities of shepherds and anchorites would have to be argued away on the grounds of their respective simplicity of mind and emotional obsession. There was clearly less recording of the inner life, and the imaginative literature of the age did not incite or develop a practice of attending to it.

Let us consider the first great European novel. *Don Quixote* undoubtedly contains characters. The two main figures are memorably distinctive and have a considerable attraction: Sancho, although down to earth, is not gross or squalid, as his equivalent in a contemporaneous drama would have been; and Don Quixote himself, although he has to be equipped with a kind of rubbery indestructibility, like a maths master in a farce, to survive the misfortunes into which his dignified illusions lead him, retains a gentle, exasperating nobility throughout. But while being memorably particularised, they are not creations it is possible to imagine oneself into. They are to be contemplated with patient delight. They can be sympathised with only in the primitive way we feel for the victims of drubbings, upended buckets and other such harassments in a pantomime. In the text the smaller part of the whole which does not consist of somewhat oratorical quoted speech is made up of running commentary of a purely external nature, essential explanations of who people are and what they are up to. The life of the mind is reduced to a very rudimentary keyboard of emotional notes: 'our knight was amazed at the goatherd's tale and more anxious than ever to know who the unfortunate madman was', 'Sancho had entered in the middle of this conversation and was much astonished and depressed to hear that knights errant were now out of fashion', 'goodness what a fury Don Quixote flew into when he heard his squire speak with such disrespect', 'Don Quixote was amazed to hear the Knight of the Wood, and was a thousand times on the point of telling him that he lied', 'the Duchess was astonished at Altisidora's effrontery'. Amazement, astonishment, fury – the emotions are intense and vivid, but they are very thin and, as it were, impersonal, states anyone might be in under the circumstances, the common condition of a crowd, not the distinguishing possession of an individual.

Scott, two hundred years later, and despite his justified categorisation as a romantic novelist, has not got much further under the skins of the people in his novels. In the following passage the young hero of *Old Mortality*, Henry Morton, is in difficult circumstances, for he is hiding a leading Covenanter from the royal troops who are pursuing him, and is in painful doubt as to which side loyalty calls him to:

'Young man,' returned Balfour, 'you are already weary of me, and would be yet more so, perchance, did you know the task upon which I have been lately put. And I wonder not that it should be so, for there are times when I am weary of myself. Think you not it is a sore trial for flesh and blood, to be called upon to execute the righteous judgments of Heaven while we are yet in the body, and retain that blinded sense and sympathy for carnal suffering which makes our own flesh thrill when we strike a gash upon the body of another? And think you, that when some prime tyrant has been removed from his place, that the instruments of his punishment can at all times look back on their share in his downfall with firm and unshaken nerves? Must they not sometimes even question the truth of that inspiration which they have felt and acted under? Must they not sometimes doubt the origin of that strong impulse with which their prayers for heavenly direction under difficulties have been inwardly answered and confirmed and confuse, in their disturbed apprehensions, the responses of Truth itself with some strong delusion of the enemy?'

'These are subjects, Mr Balfour, on which I am ill qualified to converse with you,' answered Morton; 'but I own I should strongly doubt the origin of any inspiration which seemed to dictate a line of conduct contrary to those feelings of natural humanity, which Heaven has assigned to us as the general law of our conduct.'

Balfour seemed somewhat disturbed, and drew himself hastily up, but immediately composed himself, and answered coolly, 'it is natural you should think so; you are yet in the dungeon-house of the law, a pit darker than that into which Jeremiah was plunged, even the dungeon of Malcaiah the son of Hamelmelech, where there was no water but mire. Yet it is the seal of the convenant upon your forehead, and the son of the righteous, who resisted to blood where the banner was spread on the mountains, shall not be utterly lost as one of the children of darkness'.[3]

3. *Old Mortality*. ed. Angus Calder (Harmondsworth, 1975), Ch. 6, pp. 104–5.

Balfour of Burley with his revolting flow of Protestant cant comes across as the cruel and repulsive creature he is, but within, he is just a hot amalgam of hatred and fanaticism, different only in temperature from others of his kind. There is less than that to the stilted Morton. And matters are not much improved when he has recourse, a few pages further on, to interior monologue:

> 'Farewell, stern enthusiast,' said Morton, looking after him; 'in some moods of my mind, how dangerous would be the society of such a companion!' If I am unmoved by his zeal for abstract doctrines of faith, or rather for a peculiar mode of worship, (such was the purport of his reflections,) can I be a man, and a Scotchman, and look with indifference on that persecution which has made wise men mad? Was not the cause of freedom, civil and religious, that for which my father fought; and shall I do well to remain inactive, or to take the part of an oppressive government, if there should appear any rational prospect of redressing the insufferable wrongs to which my miserable countrymen are subject? – And yet who shall warrant me that these people, rendered wild by persecution, would not, in the hour of victory, be as cruel and intolerant as those by whom they are now hunted down? What degree of moderation, or of mercy, can be expected from this Burley, so distinguished as one of their principal champions, and who seems even now to be reeking from some recent deed of violence, and to feel stings of remorse, which even his enthusiasm cannot altogether stifle? I weary of seeing nothing but violence and fury around me – now assuming the mask of lawful authority, now taking that of religious zeal. I am sick of my country – of myself – of my dependent situation – of my repressed feelings – of these woods – of that river – of that house – of all but Edith, and she can never be mine.[4]

To draw attention to the resolute externality of Scott's handling of a highly emotional confrontation and leave-taking between two emotionally excited characters is not meant as unfavourable criticism, even if a certain effort is required to accept the irresistible Old Testament articulateness of Balfour and the stuffy elaboration of Morton. The public world in which Scott's fictional creations move and act is an object of serious and satisfying imaginative interest,

4. *Old Mortality*, Ch. 6, pp. 109–10.

equipped with the traditional appurtenances of narrative excitement and picturesqueness. My purpose is simply to mark how far most of the novels that are comparably admired have moved since Scott's time into the inner life.

There is a remark in Chapter 9 of William James's *Principles of Psychology*, the famous chapter called 'The Stream of Thought' and in which the phrase 'stream of consciousness' appears, that it is appropriate to consider at this point. 'The important thing', he says, 'about a train of thought' – and by that he means any tract of mental life whatever – 'is its conclusion.'[5] His point here is that what is *practically* important about a train of thought is what it publicly eventuates in: an asserted belief, a resolved-upon action. Ryle subscribed more comprehensively to this assessment:

> If we ask a soldier to tell us about a battle, we do not expect to be told all or many of the myriad details of which the battle and the battlefield happened to consist. We do not care which of his boots he wore, when he had a cigarette, over what tussocks of grass he walked or what he said to the sergeant during a lull in the fighting. We want to know how the battle went, and why it went that way. We want the tactical and strategic plot of the story of the battle, and the telling of this requires careful neglect of its negligible detail. Detail is negligible when it could have been widely different from what it was without making any difference to the story of the course of the battle.[6]

It may be that a philosophical commitment to the demystification of the inner life is the force behind this judgement of its uninterestingness and unimportance. There is a quite general prejudice among philosophers against attention to it. F.P. Ramsey, who does not seem to have held a Rylean theory of the mind, in an agreeable paper read to a select Cambridge society about what there is left to discuss in the modern age, is dismissive about the comparison of introspective notes in non-scientific or gossippy psychology or in talking about literature and art. 'Although a pleasant way of passing the time,' he says, 'it is not discussing anything whatever.'[7]

Ramsey was, of course, talking about discussions to a society dedi-

5. (1890; reprinted New York, 1950), 1 : 260.
6. Gilbert Ryle, *Collected Papers* (1971), 2 : 266.
7. *The Foundations of Mathematics and Other Logical Essays*, ed. R.B. Braithwaite (1931), p. 289.

cated to the activity of discussion and was not quite saying that the inner life is unworthy of attention altogether. Admittedly, what we most need for purposes of practical dealings with other people is that kind of theoretical or systematic knowledge of character which we are told to acquire in the Socratic injunction with which I began. And that systematic knowledge of the characters of other people is not in fact dependent on any knowledge we may have of their inner lives in the sense in which I have been using it, that in which it is represented in the novels of the great masters of subjective description. Practical knowledge of others can be acquired from their overt words and deeds without any speculative circuit through their inner worlds of feeling and emotion. Such a behaviourally based knowledge of character is reliable and adequate for everyday purposes. I call it behavioural since it need involve no introspectively sympathetic construction of a picture of its objects' inner lives. There is no reason to suppose that Proust or Henry James would have turned out to be what are called 'good judges of men' in recruiting centres or probation offices or personnel departments. The kind of practical knowledge of character I am speaking of will be enriched and deepened if a conception of the inner life of the possessors of the characters is added to it, but is not necessarily made more effective. Cooks do not need to study chemistry.

Ramsey admitted that the comparison of introspective notes was a pleasant way of passing the time. That is too provocatively practical. Beyond the mild sort of pleasure he allows, there is also a kind of reassurance to be gained, a greater sense of affinity with others, a diminution of the estranging sense of their remoteness. That could almost be called the Kinsey effect, in memory of another breach in the isolating walls of human privacy. But, more than that, not all human relationships are practical and ideally all but the most fleeting and functional of such relationships – those with bus-conductors and telephone operators and attendants in shops, for which the formulas of politeness and geniality are enough – are improved if they are not wholly functional. An individual's capacity for the specifically personal relationships of love and friendship is enlarged by his sensitivity to the inner life of the people around him, although so too, no doubt, is his capacity for hatred and contempt.

The most obvious way in which the novelist can concern himself with the inner life is by the technique of interior monologue or stream of consciousness. This is a device of some antiquity. Sterne was inspired by the theory of Locke that the inner life of the mind consisted in a tidal flow of associated ideas to the striking technical idiosyncrasies of *Tristram Shandy*. In a way his representation of the inner life is more like Hume's than Locke's. Locke makes no reference to any kind of turbulence or disorder. As he depicts it, the life of the mind is more like a fairly sedate magic-lantern show. Hume is more tempestuous. 'I may venture to affirm of the rest of mankind' he says, ironically 'setting aside some metaphysicians', 'that they are nothing but a bundle or collection of different perceptions, which succeed each other with an inconceivable rapidity, and are in a perpetual flux and movement'.[8]

In fact the special style of *Tristram Shandy* has very little to do with the exploration of the inner life. A discursively jerky conversational mode of narration, with constant irrelevant side-trips, recurrent mentions of the narrator in the act of writing and ornamental devices of marble paper, blank pages, asterisks and large chunks of Latin, are used as a sauce to present thoroughly straightforward, charmingly petty material about Uncle Toby, Corporal Trim, the widow Wadman and, a little to the side, the narrator's parents. But the technique can be argued to be specially apt for what Ryle calls 'disclosure by unstudied talk'. Those who have attempted to fix on some particular distinguishing mark of the inner life of the mind usually characterise it in some metaphor of liquidity. It is said to be a stream, a flow, a flux a torrent. The theoretical support for this is given in Chapter 9 of James's *Principles* where he insists on the 'sensible continuity of thought'. 'Consciousness', he says, 'does not appear to itself chopped up in bits. Such words as "chain" or "train" do not describe it fitly as it presents itself in the first instance. It is nothing jointed; it flows. A "river" or a "stream" are the metaphors by which it is most naturally described. In talking of it hereafter, let us call it the stream of thought, of consciousness, or of subjective life.'[9]

The implied contrast, of course, is with the world of common objects with which we are concerned in the practical activities of everyday life. The obstacles we need to avoid, most of the food we eat, the items we buy and sell, the people with whom we co-operate and compete in work or in recreation, all those are solid, numerable objects, clearly marked off in colour and texture from their surroundings, sharply defined in their individuality. Admittedly along with these admirably docile solids we have dealings with labile material: soup and wine, milk and rain, the gas that hisses in the fire-

8. *A Treatise of Human Nature*, ed. L.A. Selby-Bigge; 2nd edn ed. P.H. Nidditch (Oxford, 1982), p. 252.
9. *Principles of Psychology*, I : 239.

place or the cooker. But here, as far as we can, we use cups and glasses and pipes to impose the semblance, the temporary discipline of solidity on what is not in itself solid.

It is to some extent a local peculiarity of our circumstances on the surface of the earth that most of what we are directly concerned with in practice is either reasonably solid or containable by things that are. This state of affairs prevails on that part of the surface of the earth on which our species is able to survive. But further down under the surface liquidity prevails. Furthermore, physical theory, resolving matter into energy, tells us that the solid objects of common life are ultimately composed of something that, however difficult it may be to grasp positively, is at any rate not solid. That idea is elaborated in various ways by process philosophers such as Bergson and Whitehead and was poetically anticipated in the metaphysics of Bradley who saw our raw, unanalysed and unorganised flow of conscious experience as a model of the true nature of reality.

Language is itself in a way atomic and discontinuous. Discourse breaks up into sentences (larger units like the paragraph are matters of style or rhetoric, not of essential grammar); sentences break up into words. We put words together to make sentences in a way that seems to demand metaphorical description in terms of building with bricks. To the extent that this is so, language seems to correspond in its principles of organisation to the world of solid common objects to which it is most crucially applied. It seems reasonable to say that language, in the discontinuous character in which alone we can conceive it, could have arisen only in an environment of solid and persisting objects, or what was thought to be such an environment. On the other hand, language as used seldom consists of solid objects of the most respectable kind, except in the very exceptional case of the name-plate or sign with separate metal letters. Written language perhaps just qualifies, as consisting of small, but not really detachable, mounds of ink. But the primary spoken language is rather weakly individuated within its continuum of sound. Nevertheless, we have to identify the individual ingredients of a piece of speech in order to understand it.

Speech, however, retains its intelligibility to a considerable extent when it moves away from syntactic propriety. A great deal of communication is carried on quite effectively in fragments of sentences or sequences of words in which what appear to be such sentence-fragments follow one another in a wholly irregular way. Anyone who has had the painful experience of seeing a transcript of his contribution to an unscripted discussion on television or radio will be familiar with this fact.

The political journalist Peregrine Worsthorne took part some years ago in a highly excited argument on television with Bryan Magee and the novelist James Baldwin about the position of the blacks in the United States. He then bravely published what were described as 'unedited excerpts' from the debate to show, in Worsthorne's words, that 'television has such a lowering effect on the human mind that only those with an exceptional gift of words, with more than ordinary fluency in ideas, can even utter a coherent cliché or produce a plain platitiude'.[10] Certainly some of the material he produced is remarkably chaotic, to an extent because of the excessively stimulating nature of the topic:

MAGEE: What is your answer to [Worsthorne's] charge that the Negroes have uniquely failed in the United States to work their way up from poverty in the way that all other immigrant groups have?

BALDWIN: Well the first thing I would say, we'll get to this later though, is up to...(inaudible)... but we'll get to that as I say later...
    All of the civil rights legislation is absolutely meaningless, and it was meant to be meaningless, and furthermore, the situation of a black man or woman, or boy, in any Northern ghetto is this: the school, which is not responsible because it belongs to the city, to the board of education, is a shambles, and in which no one is educated and in which no one is meant to be educated – the house in which he lives belongs to a landlord who is not responsible for anything whenever it's to collect his rent. Try to get through one winter ah in a Harlem ghetto. This is not either the black man's fault. Where do you go to complain if you want to complain? And we might even discuss the situation in the Labour Unions, which are geared to keep black people in effect in their place. And if you were right if you were right about the generosity of the American people then Governor Wallace... (inaudible) ... his conference in Florida the other day and Nixon will not be President, I am talking about a system which is not only historical but actual, I am saying in effect that the white people without going into any further...

10. 'Arguing on the Box', *Encounter* (September 1972), p. 22.

And furthermore the high income niggers such as you're really talking about, are listen... I can name many high come... high... income niggers whose name you would recognise, who can buy a house anywhere... and do, and also... (inaudible)... of them, by the population, by their neighbours, try to be Sammy Davis and raise your children. What we are trying to get at, what I am trying to get at because I'm not talking about high incomes, I'm you see, what I'm what I'm trying to suggest is that I reject that particular standard. I don't think a man's life is meant for that. I don't think. I'd rather die than be Richard Nixon.[11]

I suspect that Worsthorne is being over modest in thinking that such syntactically free-wheeling utterance is something in need of special explanation by reference to the disturbing presence of television cameras. Most people talk something like this most of the time. What is significant about this kind of loose or chaotic utterance is that it comes to us in a pristine and untouched-up form and so presents itself as a more faithful expression of the thoughts of the speaker, like an ageing face caught early in the morning and not made-up.

In its syntactical deficiencies it is not unlike the discourse of Mr Jingle in *Pickwick Papers*. but without the constraint of the specific subject to talk about he is much more irrelevant and diffused. There is also his special signature of talking in staccato bursts, a denatured correlate of a sentence division of more correct speech.

'Any luggage, sir?' inquired the coachman.

'Who – I? Brown paper parcel here, that's all, – other luggage gone by water, – packing cases, nailed up – big as houses – heavy, heavy, damned heavy,' replied the stranger, as he forced into his pocket as much as he could of the brown paper parcel, which presented most suspicious indications of containing one shirt and a handkerchief.

'Heads, heads – take care of your heads!' cried the loquacious stranger, as they came out under the low archway, which in those days formed the entrance to the coach-yard. 'Terrible place – dangerous work – other day – five children – mother – tall lady, eating sandwiches – forgot the arch – crash – knock – children look round – mother's head off – sandwich in her hand – no mouth to put it in – head of a family off – shocking

shocking! Looking at Whitehall, sir? – fine place – little window
– somebody else's head off there, eh, sir? – he didn't keep a
sharp look out enough either – eh, sir, eh?

'I am ruminating,' said Mr. Pickwick, 'on the strange muta-
bility of human affairs.'

'Ah! I see – in at the palace door one day, out at the window
the next. Philosopher, sir?'

'An observer of human nature, sir?' said Mr. Pickwick.

'Ah, so am I. Most people are when they've little to do and
less to get. Poet, sir?'

'My friend Mr. Snodgrass has a strong poetic turn,' said Mr.
Pickwick.

'So have I,' said the stranger. 'Epic poem, – ten thousand
lines – revolution of July – composed it on the spot – Mars by
day, Apollo by night, – bang the field-piece, twang the lyre.'

'You were present at that glorious scene, sir?' said Mr.
Snodgrass.

'Present! think I was; fired a musket, – fired with an idea, –
rushed into wine shop – wrote it down – back again – whiz,
bang – another idea – wine shop again – pen and ink – back
again – cut and slash – noble time, sir.'[12]

Jingle's mode of speech is undisciplined but really it is more of a
mannerism than a free flow of his unmodified thought. For that we
need to go to another loquacious creation of Dickens, Mrs Lirriper.

Whoever would begin to be worried with letting Lodgings that
wasn't a lone woman with a living to get is a thing inconceivable to me, my dear; excuse the familiarity, but it comes natural
to me in my own little room, when wishing to open my mind
to those that I can trust, and I should be truly thankful if they
were all mankind, but such is not so, for have but a Furnished
bill in the window and your watch on the mantel-piece, and
farewell to it if you turn your back but a second, however
gentlemanly the manners; nor is being of your own sex any safe-
guard, as I have reason, in the form of sugar-tongs to know,
for that lady (and a fine woman she was) got me to run for a
glass of water, on the plea of going to be confined, which
certainly turned out to be true, but it was in the Station-house.[13]

12. *Pickwick Papers*, ed. Robert L. Patten (Harmondsworth, 1972), Ch. 3, pp. 78–9.
13. 'Mrs Lirrper's Lodgings' in *Christmas Stories* (Everyman ed., 1982), Ch. 1,
    p. 343.

It is not just the respectability of her musings that distinguishes Mrs Lirriper from Molly Bloom. The most important fact is that she is directing her tumultuous narrative to someone else, its rolling contours are given some measure of defining restraint by a communicative intention. Molly Bloom is engaged in soliloquy, in a relaxed, unpurposive contemplation which drifts from the events of the day back over her vaguely remembered past.

I have been considering styles of linguistic expression which go some way in their self-liberation from ordinary syntactical bonds to conform the language in which states of mind are described more closely to the continuous, liquid nature that is held by William James and many others to be characteristic of those states of mind themselves. The early examples of Sterne and Dickens do not in fact use this mode of expression for the purpose of representing the inner life of the mind. But in more recent times, possibly since Dujardin's *Les lauriers sont coupés* of 1888, and very definitely since Dorothy Richardson's *Pilgrimage* began to come out in 1915, since Joyce's *Ulysses* in 1922 and Virginia Woolf's *Jacob's Room*, also in 1922, that has been its purpose.

Neither James Joyce nor Virginia Woolf committed themselves to interior monologue as the complete method of a novel until late in their careers: Joyce with *Finnegans Wake*, Virginia Woolf with *The Waves*. In *Ulysses* a wide range of other techniques is employed: parody, the expressionist phantasmagoria of the Nighttown section, dialogue of varying degrees of wildness and playfulness. Something of the same is true of Virginia Woolf's earlier but still formally experimental novels. In *Mrs Dalloway*, for example, there is a firm representation of the upper middle-class London scene, solidly there, around which the heroine's sensibility is rapidly deflected this way and that. In her more single-minded *The Waves* the revelatory potential claimed for the method of interior monologue does not materialise. The book remains an elegant abstraction, transcending personality. Its six characters are neither effectively individualised in anything like the way that the very different leading characters of *Ulysses* are, nor are they very perceptibly human but tend towards the condition of pure consciousnesses. Here, for example, are two different characters expressing themselves at opposite ends of the book and thus at different ages; first Neville in childhood, then Bernard in old age:

'After all this hubbub,' said Neville, 'all this scuffling and hubbub, we have arrived. This is indeed a solemn moment. I

come, like a lord to his halls appointed. That is our founder;
our illustrious founder, standing in the courtyard with one foot
raised. I salute our founder. A noble Roman air hangs over
these austere quadrangles. Already the lights are lit in the form
rooms. Those are laboratories perhaps; and that a library,
where I shall explore the exactitude of the Latin language, and
step firmly upon the well-laid sentences, and pronounce the
explicit, the sonorous hexameters of Virgil, of Lucretius; and
chant with a passion that is never obscure or formless the loves
of Catullus, reading from a big book, a quarto with margins, I
shall lie, too, in the fields among the tickling grasses. I shall lie
with my friends under the towering elm trees.
    'Behold, the Headmaster. Alas, that he should excite my
ridicule. He is too sleek, he is altogether too shiny and black,
like some statue in a public garden. And on the left side of his
waistcoat, his taut, his drum-like waistcoat, hangs a crucifix.'

    'Lord, how unutterably disgusting life is! What dirty tricks
it plays us, one moment free; the next this. Here we are among
the breadcrumbs and the stained napkins again. That knife is
already congealing with grease. Disorder, sordidity and corrup-
tion surround us. We have been taking into our mouths the
bodies of dead birds. It is with these greasy crumbs, slobbered
over napkins, and little corpses that we have to build. always
it begins again; always there is the enemy; eyes meeting ours'
fingers twitching ours' the effort waiting. Call the waiter. Pay
the bill. We must pull ourselves up out of our chairs. We must
find our coats. We must go. Must, must, must – detestable
word. Once more, I who had thought myself immune, who had
said, "Now I am rid of all that," find that the wave has tumbled
me over, head over heels, scattering my possessions, leaving me
to collect, to assemble, to heap together, summon my forces,
rise and confront the enemy.'[14]

There is nothing much to distinguish the individuality of the speakers
or to show that they are of very different ages. Both speak in an
incantatory, consciously memorable way, like the chorus in a
modern poetic drama attempting to sound Greek. Or again they
recall the sententious toddlers of Ivy Compton-Burnett, also making
a bid for accommodation in the house of Atreus. Only the mildly

14. *The Waves* (Harmondsworth, 1964), pp. 25–6, 252.

contemptuous note of surprise distinguishes the child from the
unteachably embittered elderly man.

In *Ulysses* there is indeed a great deal of recourse to internal monologue. but it is relieved with briskly peremptory but still entirely
objective description of the physical setting:

Mr Leopold Bloom ate with relish the inner organs of beasts
and fowls. He liked thick giblet soup, nutty gizzards, a stuffed
roast heart, liver slices fried with crustcrumbs, fried hencod's
roes. Most of all he like grilled mutton kidneys which gave to
his palate a fine tang of faintly scented urine.

Kidneys were in his mind as he moved about the kitchen
softly, righting her breakfast things on the humpy tray. Gelid
light and air were in the kitchen but out of doors gentle summer
morning everywhere. Made him feel a bit peckish.

The coals were reddening.

Another slice of bread and butter: three, four: right. She
didn't like her plate full. Right. He turned from the tray, lifted
the kettle off the hob and set it sideways on the fire. It sat there,
dull and squat, its spout stuck out. Cup of tea soon. Good.
Mouth dry. The cat walked stiffly round a leg of the table with
tail on high.

– Mkgnao!

– O, there you are, Mr Bloom said, turning from the fire.

The cat mewed in answer and stalked again stiffly round a
leg of the table, mewing. Just how she stalks over my writ-
ingtable. Prr. Scratch my head. Prr.

Mr Bloom watched curiously, kindly, the lithe black form.
Clean to see: the gloss of her sleek hide, the white button under
the butt of her tail, the green flashing eyes. He bent down to
her, his hands on his knees.

– Milk for the pussens, he said.[15]

Interior monologue begins, then, as an arresting presentational
device with Sterne. With Dickens it is a comical idiosyncrasy of utterance. It is used for the whole representation of Mrs Lirriper but again
with comical intent, more as a reflection, in her case, of mental indis-
cipline, of self-indulgent fatuity than, as in the case of Mr Jingle, of
a none too effective control on violent emotional centrifugality.
More recent and more earnest uses of the technique reveal the limits

15. *Ulysses* (Harmondsworth, 1971), p. 57.

to its more ambitious employment. In Virginia Woolf it is destructive of individuality; the liberated self encompasses the whole world and makes it its own. Even when there are six such selves, as in *The Waves*, all that we find are six such universes, prevented from collapsing into one only by the rags and tatters of objective individuality that are still left bobbing about on the surface of the stream of consciousness: being male rather than female, handsome rather than ugly, having an Australian accent. In Joyce either, as in *Ulysses*, the technique is kept within bounds by being embedded in a number of others, most effectively that of ordinary description of the physical setting in reasonably impersonal terms; or, as in *Finnegans Wake*, the collapse into undifferentiated subjectivity is at least mitigated by endowing H.C. Earwicker with mythic status as man in general, as Haveth Childers Everywhere, although hardly to the point of justifying it, over forty years after, to more than a handful of reflective readers of the novel.

Another point, perhaps a connected one, is that the fictional human beings presented in interior monologue tend to be human beings of a rudimentary sort. In being put forward as the stages, on which a host of impressions tumble past, some externally induced, others dredged up associatively from memory, they are inevitably more or less passive. This is connected with lack of individuality because we are most alike as mere wax tablets on which impressions are imposed, most distinct and individual when we react positively, with judgement, with persuasion, with policies of action, on the inflowing tide of material that is registered on our sensibilities.

Interior monologue, for all its formal congruity with the life of the mind as expounded in views like William James's, confines itself in describing the stream of consciousness to the readily visible surface of that stream, even if it allows a certain width to it and admits the existence of odd, disorderly, often disreputable eddies at the edge of it. It represents consciousness by a dramatised expression, the unedited verbal exhalations it gives off as it rushes by. It is, therefore, admirably suited to the representation of trivial or at any rate inconsiderable people, like Mr Jingle and Mrs Lirriper, or the more solid but still somehow manifestly incomplete and looked-down-on figures of Leopold and Molly Bloom.

The novels of the last century have moved away from the practically useful theory of a person embodied in a conception of character. The most obvious way of moving inwards from this, rather as moral assessments move from achieved actions to intentions, is to the episodic detail immediately available in Ryle's unstudied talk, the

unedited verbal by-product of the momentary contents of consciousness. It is not surprising that such a move came as an enormous relief
from the overdressed pretence of the kind of novel which has
passionate lovers addressing their loved ones as if they were the
Lords of Appeal. but these passing details can have beneath them a
compelling and illuminating order which the technique cannot really
reveal. The emotional life of civilised human beings has an intellectual complexity which no colourful sequence, however artfully
organised, can properly convey. For that we have to go to the great
bourgeois analysts of the inner life, Proust and Henry James. In them
we find people it would be worth getting to know and through
whom, by getting to know them vicariously in imagination, we are
enlightened about ourselves. Swann's musings about the gross
Odette are significantly unilateral. While awaiting her lovers she is
unlikely to read Proust.

The unique human individual is a remarkable invention, first
clearly in evidence in Athens in the fifth century BC, extinguished by
the totalitarian blight of religion and politics from time to time but
nevertheless from time to time revived. Today the species from which
it emerged is endangered and if the species survives it may be at the
expense of the individual. The great analytically introspective novels
of the last century testify both to the existence of the individualising
inner life and to its value. I should not like philosophy to jump on
the dungcart that seeks to destroy it.

*Delivered as a Chichele Lecture at All Souls College, Oxford in 1982.*

# The Divergence of the Twain:
## Poet's Philosophy and
## Philosopher's Philosophy

There are at least three distinguishable ways in which literature and philosophy are interestingly related. For convenience I shall identify these relationships with the phrases: philosophy *as* literature, philosophy *through* literature and philosophy *in* literature. By philosophy as literature I mean the fact that philosophy is a part of literature, at the very least an indispensable element in the classificatory system of any general or comprehensive library. The idea need not be quite so modest as that suggests and may distance itself even further from the sense of the word literature in which we speak of election literature or a salesman says that he will give us some literature about sofa-beds or washing-machines. It implies that philosophical writing is, or is sometimes, or, at any rate, can be worth reading for its own sake and not merely for the sake of the philosophical understanding or knowledge to which it conduces.

By philosophy through literature I mean the use of imaginative literary forms as devices of exposition, for the more effective communication of philosophical conceptions that have already been fully worked out. In this case philosophy is not being conceived as a species of literature, but is to some extent contrasted with it. More precisely it is conceived as a kind of content which is not primarily or usually expressed in the forms of imaginative literature and, on the other hand, which the forms of imaginative literature are not typically or commonly used to express.

By philosophy in literature I mean a more indirect kind of expression in imaginative literature of ideas or beliefs of a philosophical character. The philosophical content is not the primary, immediate sense of the literary work; it is latent, not manifest; it is to be discerned by a process of interpretation that goes beyond a straightforward reading. Secondly, the author is not required to be philosophically educated or competent and will not usually be so, although he may be. Thirdly, and arising from the second point, the philosophical content that is more or less buried in the work is not supplied with the kind of context that it would have if it were to be the substance of a work which we should unhesitatingly describe as a piece of philosophical writing. In particular, the depth at which the philosophic content is embedded in the work and the author's lack of standard philosophical qualification ensure that the philosophical beliefs involved will not be sustained and systematically organised in relation to one another by explicit argument.

Let me put some flesh on these bare and abstract bones. Historical conceptions of literature, in the simplest form, perhaps, of a catalogue of the leading writers in some language of a given epoch, will naturally include writers whom it is most natural to describe as philosophers. Bacon and Hobbes could not reasonably be omitted from such a catalogue of English writers of the seventeenth century; nor Descartes and Pascal from a comparable list of French writers of the same age. Books of general literary history will always include philosophers even if they may tend to find themselves segregated as such from writers of other kinds in the treatment of a given period. But it is not out of the question for them to break out of this measure of classificatory quarantine even when their literary production is exclusively philosophical in a narrow and professional sense of the word. A chapter on the French literature of the early seventeenth century could as well be titled 'the age of Descartes' as 'the age of Racine'.

Philosophers, furthermore, must figure in any history of prose or prose style. Bacon, Hobbes and Berkeley would have to be included in any serious enumeration of the greatest writers of English along with the less purely philosophical Burke and Newman, the only vestigially philosophical Dryden and Swift and the almost wholly unphilosophical Scott, Jane Austen and Henry James. In this connection the philosophers involved will be the objects of a rather strictly formal literary interest. Judgement about their excellences as writers of prose will stand in a very loose and distant relation to the matter of the cogency of their reasonings and the truth or justification of their conclusions. George Saintsbury and Herbert Read are qualified to discuss philosophical stylists as such even if they are not in a position to criticise them philosophically and do not have any real philosophical comprehension of what they are saying.

This is not a subject that has been very much considered. There is a characteristically assertive and idiosyncratic chapter on it at the end of Collingwood's *Essay on Philosophical Method* and a characteristically elegant long essay by Brand Blanshard *On Philosophical Style*. An interesting question that arises in principle is that of whether a really bad philosopher could nevertheless be a great or fine prose writer. No uncontroversial examples occur to me. Bolingbroke is probably the most obvious candidate. There is a temptation to put Bergson in this rather humiliating pigeon-hole. But despite his pervasive incoherences and his argumentative whimsicality he is unquestionably an interesting philosopher, with bold and original thoughts to express even if they are communicated in a philosophically disreputable idiom.

It is much easier to find examples of the contrary case, that of a major philosopher who is a bad writer. Kant and Hegel stand in a mixture of glory and disgrace, at the head of a great host of significant philosophers who are inept as writers, one that is to a considerable extent populated by their followers and disciples. It is not of course inevitable that a Kantian or a Hegelian should be a bad writer. Schopenhauer was pretty much a Kantian; Bradley and McTaggart in their very individual ways were pretty much Hegelians. Nor are only adherents of German idealists at fault. Some recent philosophical writing of high intellectual quality and of scientistic allegiance is very casual and slovenly and reads as if it had been dictated while the writer was having a bath. And some sort of wooden spoon must be awarded to Dr A.C. Ewing who, as well as being learned and productive, served the useful purpose of firmly adhering to just the positions that his livelier contemporaries were most anxious to controvert. His famous pronouncement 'the sole purpose of language is not to communicate thought' is a not unrepresentative piece of inadvertent Wildean paradox. Further back in time is the dismal Latin of the general run of medieval philosophers, perhaps best seen as a kind of stylistic hair-shirt.

Philosophy through literature is a less clear-cut category, at least at the further end where it merges indefinitely into that of philosophy in literature. But at the hither end there are some obvious examples, notably Lucretius's exposition of Epicureanism in *De Rerum Natura* and Pope's account of the philosophy of Bolingbroke in his *Essay on Man*. In Pope's case certainly and in Lucretius's probably we have a poet who is not a philosopher taking hold of a fully articulated system of ideas and supplying it with a formally attractive literary expression. The work is analogous to translation to some extent but it is not beset by the usual problem of translation, that of preserving as much as possible of the verbal form and character of the original without too much distortion of its sense. The imaginatively literary expositor of a pre-existing philosophical system need feel no obligation to the words or form of the original from which he is working. His object is simply to provide the paraphrasable content of his original – which is something it unproblematically has and which is all that is important about it – with a more agreeable verbal realisation. It is really more like gift-wrapping than like translation. Once we move on from Lucretius and Pope, the most docile and subservient of producers of philosophy through literature, the path soon divides. In one direction lies a series of imaginative writers who are all writing poetry or fiction in consciously close connection to a body of philosophical ideas which they accept with understanding and in many cases, have worked out for themselves. These are the true philosopher-poets and philosopher-novelists. That is to say, they are not just imaginative writers, the full significance of whose work cannot be grasped without an awareness of the philosophical ideas expressed in it. They are both imaginative writers and philosophers and not in a compartmentalised fashion, but writer-philosophers whose imaginative writing is seen by them as a way of communicating their philosophies.

Dante, the author in his *De Monarchia* of a work of technical political philosophy, is the exemplary prototype of this group. It also includes Milton, Diderot, Rousseau, Schiller, Coleridge, Tolstoy, Unamuno, Santayana and Sartre. These are all notable imaginative writers who are at the same time serious philosophical producers. They are not consumers either in the way that Pope and, presumably, Lucretius are, or in the way that Goethe and Shelley and Thomas Mann are. The latter group, who lie in the second direction taken by the path of which I have spoken, contains writers who are not substantive philosophers but who nevertheless see their poetry and fiction as embodying philosophical ideas which they accept. At the same time they are not, despite their comparatively dependent status as regards philosophy, literary couturiers, setting themselves to the professional task of expressing externally provided philosophical material in an attractive literary form. Where the members of the first group – Dante, Rousseau, Tolstoy, Sartre and their kindred – are philosopher-poets or philosopher-novelists, the members of the second – those of the party of Goethe and Shelley – are best described by the significantly different terms philosophical novelists and philosophical poets.

The application I have assigned to these contrasted pairs of terms is, of course, a piece of legislation, though not, I hope, a gratuitously eccentric or unintelligible one. But it does differ from other more or less familiar conventions of application. In Cyril Connolly's magazine *Horizon* there was published a series of fifteen articles under the general heading 'Philosopher-novelists'. (Eight of them, incidentally, were French; two were American; England, Scotland, Italy, Russia and Spain were allotted only one article each.) Of the fifteen only two would count as philosopher-novelists as I am using the phrase: Sartre and Camus. Three others – George Eliot, Gide and Malraux – at least qualify for consideration. The remainder may be seen as the beneficiaries (or victims) of editorial licence, which reaches an extreme of licentiousness in the cases of Robert Louis Stevenson and Ernest Hemingway.

Santayana's three philosophical poets are Lucretius, Dante and Goethe, whom I see, respectively, as couturier, philosopher-poet and philosophical poet. Joseph Brennan's list of three philosophical novelists – Gide, Joyce and Mann – interposes a novelist of philosophical interest, Joyce, between a marginal and a central instance of the philosophical novelist as I understand him.

A possibility that presents itself for consideration is that of a philosopher-poet or philosopher-novelist, a writer, in other words, who is serious and committed both as a philosopher and as an imaginative writer, uncontroversially to be included in encyclopaedic catalogues of both, who separates his two activities from one another, as might a philosopher who was also an entomologist or historian of furniture or expert on diseases of the liver. It would certainly be possible for a genuine philosopher to write detective stories, indeed, I have always understood that Willard Huntington Wright, author of the detective novels of S.S. Van Dine, had some measure of philosophical competence. A philosopher's detective stories would be preserved from the influence of his philosophy by the artificiality of the form, the rigid conventions that constrain characterisation, incident, the flow of reflection.

In a novel that set out to be more than the ingenious manipulation of stock characters in stock situations – and I realise that there are detective stories and many thrillers that are not limited in this way – and that was written by a philosopher it seems inconceivable that his philosophical convictions about the world, human nature and right conduct could fail to find expression in it. It may be that the kinds of poetry and fiction effectively separable from serious commitment to philosophy should be allowed to be rather more numerous than the rather lopsidedly commercial case of the detective story, whose poetic correlate might be the advertising jingle. Brief lyrical poems like those of Herrick or historical novels that strive for verisimilitude, rather than use the past as a cover for philosophical purposes, would seem reasonable instances of imaginative

productions which need show no trace of their author's philosophical convictions, on the supposition that he had some.

The idea that the separation we are considering could occur,
provided that the imaginatively literary side of the duality is in some
way limited, by conventions of artificiality, in the most obvious case,
or by modesty of scale, inspires the thought of a counterpart style of
separation in which a comparably limited philosophy is prevented
from interacting with serious poetry or fiction. There are, after all,
highly abstract and formal kinds of philosophical work which would
seem to have no very evident, perhaps even no conceivable, bearing
on any imaginative writing that might be done by someone involved
in them. Where philosophy approximates to the condition of mathematics, not just in style but in substance, in the manner, that is, of
Carnap rather than that of Spinoza, it simply fails to engage with the
fundamental concerns of imaginative literature with human nature,
conduct and destiny. The possible worlds of modal logic have
nothing to do with the possible worlds of fiction.

Nevertheless what might be called strictly formal philosophy, of
the sort that could not have any direct bearing on imaginative literature, need not always be produced under conditions of extreme
division of labour. An interest in it need not always be motivated by
a taste for the investigation of abstract structures, even if it often
comes to he sustained by such a taste once it is developed. Plato's
ideas about mathematical knowledge and the meaning of general
terms were firmly connected for him with his ideas about the right
conduct of life and the right ordering of society. The implication is
that formal philosophy can be preserved from all possibility of influence on imaginative writing only if it is first separated from the kind
of philosophy that is inescapably influential by a rigid confinement
of attention to it and a resolve not to pursue its possible larger consequences.

Those writers, at any rate, who actually merit recognition as
philosopher-poets or philosopher-novelists in the sense I have specified do not in general try to separate the two aspects of their activity
or suppose that the two are separated anyway without their trying.
But it is essential to recognise the fact that they do not use their imaginative works to expound their philosophies in the manner of the
practitioners of what I have called philosophy through literature.
Lucretius's poem is not misdescribed as a philosophical treatise that
happens to be written in verse. To call it that is not to deny its greatness as a poem, even if it does imply the distinctness of the epicurean
content and the poetic form.

Philosopher-poets and philosopher-novelists, as contrasted with the philosophical poets who do not embark on their poetry or fiction with the settled intention of conveying philosophical ideas they have already formulated and accepted at least begin with the purpose of communicating ideas that are, in a phrase of Leavis's 'previously definite'. It may well turn out that the imaginative project, in its development, takes on a life of its own that leads it away from the initial communicative purpose. It may even happen that the independent development of the imaginative project reacts influentially to bring about changes in the 'previously definite' set of ideas. But the fact that in these cases there is an independently accessible presentation of the writer's philosophical ideas in a conventionally philosophical form – for unless that were the case they would not be describable as philosopher-poets or philosopher-novelists in the sense I have given those terms – means that it is quite clear what the philosophy is that the philosopher-poet or philosopher-novelist is seeking to express in the different medium of his imaginative writing. Also it is quite clear that it is philosophy in a narrow and literal sense that is involved and not something that may loosely be given that name.

There is no such assurance in the case of those I have called philosophical poets and novelists, those less deliberate, less technically equipped, altogether less explicit conveyors of philosophical ideas to whom critics and students of literature, unless they are of a very up-to-date austerity are in the habit of ascribing a philosophy. Virgil, Shakespeare, Wordsworth, Baudelaire and Tennyson were not philosophers, so they cannot be philosopher-poets in my sense. For the same reason Cervantes, Richardson, Balzac, Dickens and Dostoevsky are not philosopher-novelists. But if one were to come upon an article claiming to be about the philosophy of any of them it would not be shocking or paradoxical or even stupid.

All the same I should claim that of those ten only two are unquestionably philosophical writers, namely Wordsworth and Dostoevsky, while the other poets have at most candidate status, as perhaps only Cervantes does of the novelists, the remaining novelists being either marginally philosophical or not philosophical at all. What is true of them all is that they have fairly coherent general opinions about matters of human interest about the right way to live, the nature of true happiness, the proper response to the great problems of life and so on. But to say that is to say no more than that they are intelligent and reflective people. What is needed is a conception of philosophy that is closer to the concerns of the organised intellectual activity that has historically borne that name and which is not promiscuously bestowed on the general beliefs about life of anyone serious-minded enough to have any.

I would agree that it would be possible to let it go at that, to endorse the very inclusive practice of calling the general beliefs of anyone who is sufficiently mentally organised to write poetry or fiction their philosophy, as in the usage of those who confide that their philosophy is look after number one or perhaps that it takes all sorts to make a world. But to do so would be to obliterate a difference that is of some importance both in life and literature. There are unreflective people who manage their lives by some combination of habit and impulse and feel no need to introduce any sort of explicit order into their preferences and valuations or to relate those practical attitudes to any general conception about the nature of human beings and the world they inhabit. There are imaginative writers of this kind as well, devoted to and adept at the description of nature, the narration of action, the representation of human variety, the precise delineation of feeling.

What differentiates them from those who have a philosophy, however unprofessionally and even inarticulately, is that the practical attitudes of the latter, their ideas of right conduct and of sensible conduct, of what is important to pursue or preserve, of what gives genuine enjoyment and so forth are not only internally ordered through being consistent and of a degree of stability, but are also associated with some reasonably articulate conception of the nature of human beings and of the world in which they find themselves; a theory of human nature, in other words, and a metaphysics.

A hundred years ago the idea that a philosophy, properly so called, consists of a metaphysics, a theory of human nature and a system of values, coherently arranged, would have been a commonplace. In this century it has had a hard time, even if it seems now to be recovering a measure of acceptability. Metaphysics was proscribed as without meaning. For knowledge about the reality there actually is, nature and ourselves, we were sent to natural science and psychology. Values were wholly detached from such matters of fact as we could get to know about and understood as matters of ultimately arbitrary choice. The residuary legatee of what had been philosophy came to be the analytic study of our ideas and beliefs, more precisely, of their linguistic expression. If that is all that philosophy is then there is no such thing as what I have called philosophy in literature, no such people as philosophical poets or philosophical novelists, only at most some people who, as well as writing poetry and fiction, have a quite independent interest in or capacity for the logical analysis of ideas and beliefs.

What I have just said may, from its somewhat Gifford lecture-like tone, have led you to suppose that I am announcing some massive, elderly repudiation of the kind of analytic philosophy with which I have always been associated. But I intend to do nothing so drastic. Like most of my fellow-members of the analytic tribe, I have long been persuaded that metaphysics, of a reasonably cautious kind, is a rationally acceptable undertaking, that there is no such thing as the naturalistic fallacy and that philosophy neither needs to be nor can be carried on in a position of neutral detachment from all matters of fact and value.

But even if that were not the case, I should still contend that the word *philosophy* should be allowed a sense in between the analytic minimum of the 1930s and the all-inclusive reading in which it applies to any old fragment or assemblage of proverbial wisdom. The primary reason is historical. There is a recognised tradition of philosophers and of philosophical problems and doctrines from the pre-Socratics to the present day to which, even at their most combative, the minimalists never denied that they had a measure of affiliation. In strict consistency with their professions they ought, perhaps, to have regarded the long pseudophilosophical past as a kind of junk-yard in which they, the true builders, were practising their skills in demolition. It may have been the institutional influence of having to expound the ideas of their predecessors in courses on the history of philosophy that kept them from going so far. Wittgenstein alone seems to have had the courage of his evictions and he was magnificently impervious to institutional influence.

There is not time, and there would not be much point, in trying to be more precise than I have been about the definition of this tradition-including but still not unlimitedly hospitable conception of philosophy. I must hope that it is clear enough not to come to pieces in my hands as I start to apply it to various propositions about philosophy in literature.

What I have called philosophy through literature, the direct exposition of philosophy in the medium of imaginative literature, is rare in its pure form. The examples I have given, those of Lucretius and Pope, stand alone so far as imaginative writing of any distinction is concerned. In discussions of the topic they are often associated with Dante, who is taken to stand to Aquinas as they do to Epicurus and Bolingbroke. But that is to ignore an important difference. Lucretius and Pope write in an expository way. Dante's *Divine Comedy* is not a versified presentation of Thomism; it is the narrative of a fabulous journey in which the poet is conducted, first by Virgil and then by Beatrice, through the imaginary worlds of hell, purgatory and paradise, in the course of which a large array of characters is encountered, all with stories attached. It is, of course, informed by the Christian philosophy of the Middle Ages, but it is not an exposition of Thomism in particular. As Eliot said, 'Dante's debt to Thomas Aquinas... can be easily exaggerated; for it must not be forgotten that Dante read and made use of other great mediaeval philosophers as well' *(Selected Essays,* p. 257). Even if he had not, the main point would still stand: the *Divine Comedy* is not a treatise in verse but a poetic narration in which a host of other narratives is contained. Its form is more that of the *Canterbury Tales* than that of the *Summa Theologica.* Much the same is true of Goethe. The first part of *Faust* is a love story, not a versified treatise, and there is no one philosopher or independently identifiable system of philosophic ideas on whom or on which it is dependent.

Altogether more important than philosophy through literature is philosophy in literature, whether produced by philosopher-poets like Coleridge or philosopher-novelists like Sartre or by philosophical poets and novelists like Wordsworth and Kafka. The business of determining what the implied philosophical content of poetry or fiction is is made easier if the author is a philosopher-poet or philosopher-novelist. The fact that he is also the author of explicitly and literally philosophical work is at least a powerful indication of the latent philosophical content of his work. It does not follow that the implicit philosophy of his poetry or fiction is exactly that of his explicitly philosophical writings, even if he claims that his intention was to give it expression in his imaginative work. A sincere statement of intention, it is generally recognised, can fail to correspond to the real character of the product with which it is connected. But there is at least a presumption in favour of the author's conception of the meaning, even the implicit meaning, of his own work, particularly when he identifies it with the main content of substantial philosophical writing of the standard variety. The ideas in question will have been in the forefront of his consciousness, have commanded his attention, for a considerable time.

This is not a rule to be relied on unreservedly. It would be wrong to infer from the fact that T.S. Eliot wrote a reasonably professional-looking book on the philosophy of F.H. Bradley that the underlying philosophy of *The Waste Land* and *Four Quartets* is Bradleyan. In this example we have Eliot's own authority for the fact that, rereading the book after many years, he found it unintelligible. Eliot's deviousness and general lack of candour about himself throw some doubt on his disavowal. More to the point is the considerable lapse of time, relative to Eliot's age, a time in which his life and interests were undergoing large and rapid changes, that elapsed between finishing the Harvard dissertation and the writing of *The Waste Land*. Bradley is not the philosopher of the shattered urban sensibility of the twentieth century. He combines a measure of mystical detachment from the plural, changing world with a traditionalistic scorn for well-meaning efforts to improve it. I think he would have regarded The *Waste Land* as the wounded cry of a rather unmanly character.

There are two diametrically opposed views about philosophy in literature, one negative, the other affirmative, both of which I believe to be mistaken. The negative view is more a cluster of opinions than a single definite proposition, a cluster united by shared hostility to any intrusion of philosophy into imaginative literature. It cannot reasonably be denied that philosophy is present in literature after a fashion, but the adopters of the negative attitude seek to minimise its significance.

One line of approach is to say that it does not matter from the point of view of one who is concerned with the literary value of a poem or novel whether the philosophical beliefs implicit in it are true or false or even whether they are believed in by the writer. It is a somewhat indirect answer to the thesis that the truth of the philosophy in an imaginative work does not matter to reply that nor, in any absolute or conclusive way, does the truth of the philosophy in a philosophical work. Spinoza and Leibniz are great philosophers and ought to be studied by everyone seriously interested in philosophy, but few would hold that much, let alone all, of what they assert is true. The object of philosophy is, indeed, truth, but the best way to set about its pursuit is to follow the efforts of great philosophers to achieve this, if only to acquire through the process the critical capacity to realise that they have not succeeded. In all spheres of thoughtful inquiry, but above all in the more speculative, the discovery of the actual is nourished by a lively antecedent conception of what is possible.

Although this reply is indirect it is relevant. If truth is not a necessary condition of the interestingness and importance of a belief in philosophy itself, as we now understand it, in what may be seen as the official residence of philosophical beliefs, although possibly not their birthplace, it must be all the less a necessary condition when they are found in another context.

Philosophy, in the intermediate sense I have given it, in between the analytic minimum and any large general beliefs whatever, is something which those who have a taste for it take very seriously; it is a significant fact about them that they have the philosophy they do. In particular if a poet or novelist is philosophical it is a significant fact about him and his work; it will order and to some extent explain the way he perceives his manifest subject-matter. The role of coincidence in Hardy's plots is at any rate accounted for, shown not to be a gratuitous trick, when it is understood as expressing his sense of the cruel indifference to human wishes of a natural world with no loving God behind it.

Two critical controversies of the comparatively recent past turn on the issue of the literary importance of philosophy in literature. The first began with René Wellek's friendly criticism of Leavis's frequently deplored failure to make his critical assumptions explicit. Wellek ingeniously frustrates a charge of misrepresentation in advance by giving his account of these assumptions in the very phrases Leavis himself uses in the appraisal of particular works and passages. His point is not that this muteness in respect of principles makes Leavis's criticism obscure or arbitrary but that it makes him unresponsive to the idealist and romantic tradition, in which philosophy, rather than the simple moral assertiveness that Leavis favours, plays an important role. Leavis, says Wellek, ignores Wordsworth's philosophy of nature, which he describes as 'important and defensible' and fails, in his hostility to Shelley, to acknowledge Shelley's 'unified and coherent' philosophy. Leavis had justified his distaste on the strength of Shelley's 'weak grasp of the actual', his 'wordy emotional generality', his reliance on 'feeling divorced from thought' and had reinforced it by a telling comparison of Shelley's 'Mont Blanc' with Wordsworth's 'Simplon Pass'.

Leavis answers the complaint of inarticulateness about principles by a familiar and not unpersuasive line of argument which maintains that criticism should be a total response, in the light of the whole range of the critic's reading, not by any judicial application of abstract rules. That seems a little squeamish. It does not follow from the critic's abridgement of his critical experience in some general principles that he will be led into total dependence on them, forgetting the particulars from which they were derived, or, again, that they will be impervious to the corrective influence of further reading.

More to the point on this occasion is Leavis's defence of his inattention to the philosophy of the Romantic poets. How, he asks, can

Romantic philosophy be of literary interest if it covers such different poets as Blake, Wordsworth and Shelley? That observation betrays very profound inattention to the philosophies of the three poets. Their three philosophies, although all Romantic or at any rate idealistic, are as different as their poetries. The label Romantic no more implies detailed identity in the one case than in the other.

He goes on, in discussing the philosophical interpretation of Blake's symbolism, to make the following weird remark: 'I do not believe that it will ever turn what was before an unsuccessful poem into a good one.' No doubt a change in the reader's understanding will not turn a bad poem into a good one, but it can obviously turn a poem that was unsuccessful, to the extent that the reader did not previously get anything much out of it, into one that he does find rewarding. And it does so by giving the reader a fuller understanding of the poem as a whole, by making him aware more fully of what actually constitutes the poem. Just as you will simply fail to apprehend much of a play of Shakespeare's if you come to it unaware that many of the words in it bore different senses four hundred years ago from the ones they have in colloquial speech today, so you will not have a full comprehension of a literary work unless you grasp its underlying theme, philosophical, merely moral or of another kind. I believe that that is true even where the underlying philosophy is, taken *au pied de la lettre*, merely silly, like the eerie contraption set out in Yeats's *A Vision*. In fact I do not think Yeats's official occult doctrine can be taken to be the real underlying content of his mature poetry, but, even if it were, the case would be too exceptional to invalidate the general rule.

A more sophisticated controversy about the significance of philosophy in literature is that between T.S. Eliot and Professor Erich Heller, occasioned by Eliot's views on the subject in his essay of 1927, 'Shakespeare and the Stoicism of Seneca' (in *Selected Essays*, pp. 127–40). Eliot maintains:

> When Dante says *la sua voluntade e nostra pace* it is great poetry and there is a great philosophy behind it. When Shakespeare says *As flies to wanton boys, are we to the gods;/They kill us for their sport* it is *equally* great poetry, though the philosophy behind it is not great. (pp. 136–7)

We can accept the relative estimation of the two underlying doctrines without leaping to Eliot's conclusion: 'I can see no reason for believing that either Dante or Shakespeare did any thinking on his own... that was not their job; and the relative value of the thought current at their time, the material forced upon each to use as the vehicle of his feeling, is of no importance' (p. 136). One short answer to that is that not all thinking is philosophical reasoning. A further point is that the view that the philosophical content of a literary work is a part of its constitution does not imply that the value of the whole work is determined by that of an integral part of it, considered on its own.

Heller fastens on another passage in Eliot's essay and memorably dismisses it. Eliot says, 'Champions of Shakespeare as a great philosopher have a great deal to say about Shakespeare's power of thought, but they fail to show that he thought to any purpose; that he had any coherent view of life, or that he recommended any procedure to follow' (p. 135). Of this Heller says:

> In other words 'thought' in this sense appears to be the preoccupation of a group of men among whom the professional bores are in the majority. The three criteria amount to a definition of a certain type of rationalism. It excludes, first, the thinker for whom thinking is not a means to an end, but a passion; secondly, the thinker who knows that no system of thought can ever be completely coherent without the knowledge of the indispensable measure of incoherence worked into the whole structure of the system; and thirdly, the thinker whose thought does not issue in recipes for action, but in invitations to think. In short, it excludes the thinker. (*The Disinherited Mind*, Pelican edn, p. 132).

Eliot in an essay of 1955, 'Goethe as a Sage' *(On Poetry and Poets,* pp. 203–27) replies courteously to Heller, saying 'Some of what I then said I would not now defend, and some I should now be inclined to qualify or put differently' (p. 222), without going into detail. He goes on that the problem of ideas in poetry or of the philosophy of poets is that of whether a poet holds an idea in the same way as a philosopher, of whether he should believe it and of whether a reader has to believe it as well to appreciate a poem. The last of these three elements of the problem as Eliot sees it is not worth bothering about. It is simply fanaticism to be unable to appreciate the writings of people whose beliefs you do not share. Only where the beliefs are disgusting is there proper occasion for that throwing the book into the waste paper basket which is more broadly appropriate to bad writing. It would be unsettling to discover that a work in which some philosophical ideas were powerfully expressed was totally insincere. A pious impulse leads one to imagine that the fact would reveal itself somehow in the work itself.

But these are not the problem as I have been considering it. I have been urging that where a work of imaginative literature has a latent content or underlying theme of a philosophical character it is essentially constitutive of the work itself and is a proper, indeed, indispensable concern of critical interpretation of the work. This is denied by Eliot's thesis that poets do not think, but deal rather in what he calls the 'emotional equivalents of thought'. I have also claimed that the truth or even reasonableness of a work's philosophical content has no bearing on the value of the work that contains it. Nor must the underlying philosophy of a novel or a poem be accepted by any reader who is able to appreciate the work. But it is necessary, if he is to respond to the work in its fullness, that he should be aware of the philosophy it contains. And, whether the more jealously proprietary students of literature like it or not, a lot of imaginative literature does have an underlying philosophical content.

The final question I want to consider is whether all imaginative literature has a philosophical component. The notion that it has is not without defenders. S.H. Olsen, in his contribution to a Royal Institute of Philosophy series of lectures *Philosophy and Literature,* says that what he calls *theme* is 'of the essence of literature' and that 'literary appreciation necessarily involves the recognition of theme'. Themes, he goes on, may be topical or perennial and the latter are philosophical or philosophico-theological, they deal with 'mortal questions' in the sense of Thomas Nagel. He illustrates the recognition of themes by a consideration of Blake's 'The Sick Rose' which takes the rose to be the individual erotic impulse and the worm to be love as socially defined by the institution of marriage. He allows that this theme is not itself philosophical but claims that it is an instance of a theme that is, namely that of individual impulse and the demands or requirements of others. If he allows himself that much liberty of interpretation it would seem that a philosophical theme could be found in anything. In fairness it should be said that he does not himself go so far, saying that Elizabeth Gaskell's *Mary Barton* has no perennial theme but only the topical and passing theme of the harshly oppressive treatment of industrial workers by their employers in the early nineteenth century, and contrasting it with *Bleak House,* which he sees as having a deeper theme than the law's delays. But *Mary Barton* might well yield something to the technique that elicited a philosophical theme from 'The Sick Rose'.

It seems best to approach the question through examples. It is surely clear, and I have no doubt that Olsen would not disagree, that the literature of pure entertainment has no underlying philosophical content. P.G. Wodehouse's kind of comedy, adventure novels like those of Jules Verne or, for that matter, *Treasure Island,* stories of horror by Poe and Lovecraft, most erotic novels could have a philosophical content ascribed to them only as some kind of playful trick. There are some works of modest pretensions that carry a large freight of moral guidance, the older-fashioned kind of boys' story, for instance. But simple moralising falls well short of philosophy even in the less than minimal sense I have attached to it.

Walter Scott's novels, the Scottish ones rather than the medieval romances, certainly have an underlying theme which is what makes them more than merely descriptive or narrative works. It is the conflict between the old tribal Scotland of the Highlands and the new urban Scotland of the Lowlands, between ancient honour and business-like good sense, between tattered glory and comfortable prudence. Scott, of course, is strongly attracted to both sides; by his primitive and domestic loyalties to prudence and by his historical imagination to glory. This is a social and political theme, but it is not a philosophical one. Its recognition is indispensable to a full apprehension of Scott's better novels and it does not take much burrowing to extract it. But it would be hopelessly strained to see it as an instance of the general problem of risk and security in choice. Scott has no articulate, personally achieved theory of the world, of human nature and right conduct; he takes the commonsense assumptions of his time, place and social situation for granted and as needing neither to be thought about nor expressed.

There is no theme at all in the better, intendedly realistic novels of Balzac, described by him as *Etudes de moeurs.* Even what he calls the *Etudes philosophiques* are hardly philosophical although they are mystically symbolic and describe more or less philosophical quests by their characters.

These examples, if they are acceptable, show that it is not necessary for works of imaginative literature to have an implicit philosophical content if they are to have a proper claim to be taken seriously and even to be of the highest excellence. I am inclined to agree with John Laird that although there are quite a number of references to philosophy in Dickens there is nothing much in the way of philosophical content proper. It is principally a topic for jocularity as with Mr Squeers or the lady who went to lectures on the philosophy of crime on Tuesdays and on the philosophy of vegetables on Wednesdays. Of course Dickens was a warm-hearted, sometimes sentimental, moralist and a critic of social abuses, but that does meet the point.

It is harder to find examples of poets whose work has no implicit philosophical content. There is the rather forced case of Mallarmé. But allowing for a certain rhetorical afflatus, perhaps the affirmative answer is correct to Santayana's question: 'does all poetry teach philosophy?', although the answer must be in the negative to the accompanying interrogation: 'is philosophy nothing but poetry?'

Fifty years ago the philosophy of philosophers and the philosophy of poets seemed to be completely out of touch with one another. I have urged the claims of a more inclusive conception of philosophy as one that would not be indignantly repudiated by those who practise the subject professionally and, at any rate, as one that their current practice would not justify them in repudiating. The two divergent things have come closer together.

It may still be argued that they remain irreducibly different. The philosophical theses which figure as the conclusions of philosophers and the underlying content of the works of poets and novelists could be held to be only superficially identical, because although expressed in the same words they derive a fundamental difference of sense from the radical difference between the contexts and styles in which they are affirmed. Philosopher's philosophy is explicit and expressed in a setting of dialectical argument; poet's philosophy is implicit and intimated through the primary, concrete meaning of the poetry. This fact leads R.S. Crane, for example, to say that the two kinds of philosophy have a common basis, namely the ideas that are studied by the historian of ideas, but the poet thinks *with* them, while the philosopher thinks *about* them. There is a common material but it is given different forms and the ideas themselves are 'affected, even determined' by the wholes in which they figure, poetic or argumentative. The same view is suggested by Leavis's question whether philosophy that is any good could be as loose as the second book of *The Prelude*.

One short answer to this is supplied by two distinguished philosophers who firmly separate what they see as a philosopher's central insight or vision from the argument by which it is sustained. Russell observes that the vision comes first and the argument is a subsequent process of defending it against objections. Waismann, in a late essay 'How I See Philosophy', is more emphatic, maintaining that it is the vision that is really important, not the argumentative scaffolding.

It would be possible to take the view that the true unit of philosophical discourse is not the proposition but the argument. But all that one can reasonably contend is that for philosophy philosophical propositions are primarily interesting in the light of the reasons given for them. If the literal sense of a proposition were determined by a given argument then no one could add another argument for that proposition to the first one, since he would be arguing for something else, and no one, presumably, could argue for the negation of a proposition, since in the process the proposition being negated would have been detached from the argument that determined its sense. What is true is that the argument a philosopher gives for some proposition helps to make clear what that proposition exactly is, but that does not take such propositions out of the reach of poetry.

There is an attractive counter-attack to the notion that the philosophy of philosophers is thoroughly divergent, exemplified by John Holloway's *The Victorian Sage*, which sees the imaginative form in which philosophical ideas are expressed in poetry and fiction as supplying them with a different kind of support from that provided by standard philosophical reasoning. It would be misleading to call the poet's grasp of philosophical ideas intuition, which suggests some direct, unitary apprehension. More appropriate is the notion embodied in Pascal's *esprit de finesse* or Newman's illative sense, the kind of unmethodical, accumulative procedure by which a mass of sensitive responses are precipitated into a philosophical belief. The imaginative literary work gives any philosophical content latent in it a concrete embodiment which renders it accessible to the reader's illative accumulations, his sense of how people and the world they inhabit really are. To unbending rationalists that will appear as something far too deeply interfused, but to me it is a promising conception.

*Delivered as the inaugural lecture to the Centre for Philosophy and Literature, University of Warwick, 1985.*

# Books and Culture

## I

There are two very different conceptions of culture in circulation to each of which books are relevant. The first of these is the more objective and inclusive of the two. It is that which defines the field of study of the anthropologist and it refers to the social inheritance of human communities, acquired by one generation from another through learning, and not by biological inheritance as part of the new generation's innate equipment. It consists of customs, techniques, attitudes and beliefs: ways of behaving, of pursuing chosen ends, of feeling and valuing, and of thinking. It is comparatively objective in that it is the common property of the community in question.

The second, the narrower and more subjective conception, is the concern of intellectuals and educationists. Although there is a common stock from which it is drawn, composed of bodies of knowledge and of works of art, literary and other, the emphasis is on its possession by individuals, between whom its extent, of course, varies very greatly.

The conception in its wider sense was established in Tylor's pioneering book *Primitive Culture* in 1881. The narrower conception is older, at least as old as Matthew Arnold's *Culture and Anarchy* of 1869. But it is present earlier in Coleridge and perhaps can trace its ancestry to the Renaissance humanist idea of the goal of liberal education.

Books are obviously not essential to social culture as conceived by the anthropologist. Anthropology proper, after all, is the study of the culture of pre-literate peoples. Social culture precedes literacy but is not brought to an end by it. Where literacy exists a whole new realm of evidence is available to the investigator, who has to rely on archaeology for the study of past pre-literate societies, or on participant observation where such societies still survive. What is necessary for human societies to count as cultures is language, the acquisition that makes us truly human and marks us off from all other animal species. The history of writing is a very small part of the history of language. If the populations of literate and non-literate societies are used as a basis of comparison rather than their historical duration, the balance between them is much redressed, possibly reversed. Hunter-gatherers need a great deal of space. Literacy and dense populations go together. Without written records and regulations only the most rudimentary economies can flourish. At any rate literate societies now cover the world, apart from a few small pockets here and there.

For some purposes it is important to distinguish between the restrictedly literate societies that run from the river valley civilisations of Mesopotamia and Egypt to that of eighteenth-century Europe from the comprehensively literate societies of the modern industrial world. But all, with the fascinating exception of the Inca civilisation of Peru, are marked off by writing as civilisations proper from the societies that preceded them. Writing and large cities appeared together between five and six thousand years ago, some time after agriculture had brought about surplus food. The unsurpassed excellence *so far* of the book as a way of packaging writing – a subject I shall come back to – makes written matter more comfortably and conveniently available, but it is not essential to civilisation in the way that the writing it contains is.

Karl Popper has advanced a striking argument, or, as he would say, thought-experiment, to show how profoundly modern industrial civilisation depends on books, or, to be scrupulously precise, written matter.

> Imagine that our economic system, including all machinery and all social organisations, was destroyed one day, but that technical and scientific knowledge was preserved. In such a case it might conceivably not take very long before it was reconstructed (on a smaller scale and after many had starved). but imagine *all knowledge* of these matters were to disappear, while the material things were preserved! This would be tantamount to what would happen if a savage tribe occupied a highly industrialised but deserted country. It would soon lead to the complete disappearance of all the material relics of civilisation. (*Open Society*, II.11.iii)

He writes here of knowledge rather than of written matter or books. But the knowledge on which civilisation depends most directly has to be stabilised in written form. The science that sustains technology is through and through mathematical and there is no such thing as truly oral mathematics (despite the existence of mental arithmetic). The short flights of calculation which are all that the great majority

of us who are not calculating prodigies can manage are parasitic on
written-down mathematics. Secondly, administration, although for
the most part not very sophisticatedly mathematical, is highly
numerical, and the numbers involved are too complex and on too
voluminous a scale to be carried in the head.

Furthermore, the knowledge that an individual uses is much
greater, in all but the most old-fashioned employments like that of
shepherd or ploughman, than he can keep in his head. So far as heads
are concerned it is very widely scattered. Some of it, like telephone
numbers, may be in very few heads. For quick information about a
lot of telephone numbers a directory is infinitely to be preferred to
personal consultation of members of the small informed groups
involved. At a less trivial and, so to speak, granular level, technical
and professional skills can be conveniently contained in manuals and
text-books, only a fraction of whose content will actually be in the
possession of their compilers at any one time. What is more, books
are much more amenable to repeated consultation than live infor-
mants, who move about for their own purposes and may prove
emotionally resistant.

Serious mathematics, then, which is such an integral part of the
industrial and economic aspect of our civilisation, is inconceivable
without writing, and so, therefore, are science and technology. The
other ingredients in social culture are not so radically dependent on
writing. Customs and attitudes are acquired through imitation of
parents or other guides. The more elementary beliefs are picked up
by observation or by word of mouth (those bits of lore often asserted
after an initial 'they say'). But beyond this preliminary outfit all
beliefs that do not have an anchor in one's immediate personal environment, those that concern history and geography, the temporally
and spatially distant, are got from written sources, which, for us,
means almost entirely from print. Beliefs react powerfully on
customs and attitudes. Where, as with us, the flow of print brings
about constant additions to and changes of belief, customs and attitudes will be stirred into a corresponding turmoil.

I have had to be careful in describing the role of written matter in
determining the character of social culture not to insist that books
are the indispensable things. But although in principle other forms
of writing could serve the purposes they do, it would be only at an
intolerable cost. This is the moment for a panegyric on the book as
the solution of a technical problem, like the safety pin or the Q-tip,
but on an enormously greater scale, surpassing even that great sparer
of the human back, the fork-lift truck. Once written matter was

mainly applied to paper (rather than stone or clay blocks or, getting warmer, flattened reed stems or the skins of sheep or calves), the next big step was to write on both sides and sew the sheets together. The process was consummated with the invention of printing, allowing for indefinite and reasonably reliable reproducibility. Once mechanical printing arrived, this became comparatively effortless, and, in consequence, cheap.

The practical virtues of the book, although obvious, are worth dwelling on. It is, so long as not a folio, easy to carry about and convenient to store. It stands up to use and movement much better than its predecessors. Light in the hand, it is easy to hold and, particularly since printing and other such improvements as punctuation and the breaking up of words, easy to read, both for long periods of time. The replacement of oral by written literature has both benefits and costs. The bards who were the main carriers of oral literature developed prodigious memories and it may be presumed that their audiences had much more impressive powers of memory than we do. An oral epic, passing through a sequence of bards or skalds, is likely to undergo a lot of change, where a printed work, with a bit of luck, will outlive marble and the gilded monuments of princes. That is surely a benefit. What is beyond question is that easy and copious access to literature is enormously enhanced, first, by writing, then by books and finally by printed books. Bards were probably a nuisance: not available when one wanted them, too obtrusive and demanding when they were present.

Our social culture, I have argued, is dependent on and penetrated by books, by far the most practically successful way discovered until now of holding written matter. New technology is superannuating many of the less graceful tasks that books have traditionally performed. The account book can no longer be a very widespread device for the recording of commercial transactions, as we all know from visiting our banks. Old expectations are met by print-outs, a subsidiary by-product of the main record. The printed or written library catalogue is presumably on its way out, although here again the needs of distant users may for a while be served by printed volumes rather than compact discs or online provision.

As things stand there is no clear indication of a way in which the literary components of individual culture, culture in the Matthew Arnold sense, are to be shifted from books into a new and distinct form. Scholars study microfilm, but usually without enthusiasm. The reading apparatus is cumbrous and pretty immobile; the illuminated object read is less pleasant to read than ordinary print. But these disadvantages may be put up with in the case of a rarity which one would otherwise have to go to Berlin or Naples or New York to read. From a librarian's point of view microfilm is attractive because it takes much less space than its original and is of a much more standard size. One of its great successes has been in making available items that are rare because not enough people are interested to make it worth while printing them, in particular doctoral dissertations. A sign of this is the very much grater frequency with which they appear nowadays in the bibliographies of works of humanistic scholarship. That is not due to the fact that there are many more such dissertations than there were fifty, or even thirty, years ago. Mere numbers need not affect the routine of a dissertation's readership being confined to its author, its typist (if different) and its examiners.

## II

It is time to turn to culture in its narrower individual sense, gestured at rather than defined by Matthew Arnold with the phrase 'the best that has been thought and said'. There are two points to be made about this formula. The first is that it assumes without argument that culture is something essentially literary or, at any rate, verbal. Since in our world we largely become acquainted with the best that has been thought and said in written, and, indeed, printed, form, the idea that culture is verbal and that it takes culture to be something impersonal and objective. It sees it as a common stock, or, as a currently favoured term has it, a *canon*, of literary material of the highest quality. Culture as a personal acquisition is an individual's experience of and familiarity with the items making up this common stock or canon. It is not, although it may be helped by, physical possession of the books, or, as people often prefer to say, texts, that compose it.

That is a pretty innocuous ambiguity. What matters about the books or texts is their meaning and as a property of the books themselves meaning is only a potentiality, which is realised to the extent that it is apprehended by a reader. In that operation the reader is ordinarily supposed to be reviving in his own mind the thoughts, and perhaps the feelings, of the author. But he may miss much, he may discern things the author was not consciously aware of and he may be prevented from getting hold of the author's meaning by historic shifts in the senses of words or, where the text is a translation, by the familiar hazards of that undertaking.

These qualifications rub the edges off the unreflective assumption that a text is a unitary, definite thing, a timeless and immutable abstraction, a structure of meanings fixed once and for all by the author's intentions. Recent theorists of criticism have become rather over-excited by these considerations, to the extent of taking a text to be a kind of discarded and highly elastic bathing-suit which can be pulled into any shape he likes by anyone who gets hold of it. That notion is clearly false as applied to abstract, cognitive texts like Euclid's *Elements*, Newton's *Principia* or the *Meditations* of Descartes, and above all the gloriously academic Aristotle, prime intellectual authority of the high Middle Ages and still dominant in the curriculum of Western higher education until well into the nineteenth century (in Oxford, of course, he is still alive and well). Circumstantial obstructions to understanding like shifts of meaning in, or total difference of, language can be overcome by appropriate effort, learning Shakespearian English or – rather harder – Russian.

There are interesting questions here about the accessibility of texts originating far away in time or space from their readers. It may be that some, like distant mountains, can be discerned only dimly. But the existence of a great deal of mutually intelligible communication about texts between present day readers who are not driven by a theoretical conviction that mutual intelligibility is impossible is an index of the semantic commonness of the physically common stock or canon.

Arnold's assumption that culture is essentially literary in character calls for further examination. A less minimal account of the constituents of culture, given by T.S. Eliot in his notes towards a definition of the idea, includes things it may well seem to have left out. Eliot lists four. First, a little surprisingly, *manners*, polite or civil conduct towards other people. Secondly, *learning*, the defining characteristic of the scholar. Thirdly, what he calls *philosophy*, which is something much less scholastically contracted than what currently goes by that name, in universities at any rate, and which he describes as the domain of abstract ideas and theories, of argument about topics of high generality. Fourthly and finally, there are *the arts*, comprising (over and above imaginative literature) painting, sculpture, architecture, music, the most insistent claimants left out by Arnold's formula.

The inclusion of the non-literary arts is reasonable and in accordance with our current understanding of the word. Of two people of equivalent literary knowledge and sensitivity, the one who was also familiar with visual art and music would be regarded as more, or more widely, cultured. But someone with no knowledge of or interest in imaginative literature who was responsive to visual art or music would, I think, be seen as rather trivially or marginally cultured. A reason for that is that the appreciation of art and music, if it is to be more than passive immersion, requires some knowledge of history and of the general cultural background. But the appreciation of imaginative literature involves no comparable familiarity with visual art or music.

There is a memorable scene near the beginning of E.M. Forster's *Howard's End* which may help to support my contention of an asymmetry of this kind. A brother and two sisters are at a performance of Beethoven's Fifth Symphony. The brother urges his sisters not to miss a particular transitional passage on the drum. One sister, Helen, is led by the music to imagine an invasion of the world by a race of horrible goblins. The other sister, Margaret, listens attentively to the music as music. She has a cultured approach where her brother's is merely technical and her sister's passive, wallowing and inattentive.

If interest in and familiarity with the non-visual arts can add to the culture of an individual, but cannot wholly compose it if it is to rise above a trivial or marginal level, the primacy of literature is still secure, even if it is no longer, as with Arnold, the whole content of culture.

Eliot's other addition, that of manners, is surely to be resisted. There are, and always have been, a great many people with no aspirations to culture but with excellent manners. A community can get on well enough if only a minority of its members are cultured (which is not to say it would not get on better, or be a better community, if more or all of its members were). It does not get on very well if most of its members are ill-mannered. I do not think we should deny culture to someone who was exceedingly bad-mannered provided that he had a profound knowledge of literature and ideas. Two men who knew more about literature and ideas than anyone else in their respective ages were Samuel Johnson and Edmund Wilson. Both were memorably bad-mannered. Johnson was particularly bad at the dinner table. Both were great shouters-down of people they were talking to. Both were unquestionably people of the highest culture, although deeply uncivil and, to that extent, uncivilised.

It may be that the underlying reason for Eliot's inclusion of manners among the constituents of culture is the fact that the approximate eighteenth-century synonym for *culture* was *polite learning*. *Polite* was the adjective that marked off culture and civilisation from savagery or barbarism, which was correspondingly *rude*.

These words have shifted in meaning as much as *nice* (from *exact* to *agreeable*) although they have not gone through a hundred and eighty degrees like *let* (from *obstruct* to *permit*).

There is a serious connection between courtesy and culture strictly so called. The feudal nobility of the high Middle Ages were neither polite nor cultured. Their behaviour was gross and they were not literate. (I realise that this is a wild exaggeration, but it oversteps the mark in the direction of the truth.) The new ideal of conduct of Renaissance humanism as set out in such courtesy books as Castiglione's *Cortegiano* includes the study of classical literature and the ability to write verse as well as etiquette proper. Good manners and culture became part of the educational diet of the European élite as a single package.

The final point about Eliot's inventory of the elements of culture that calls for consideration is the distinction he draws between learning and what he calls philosophy, the predilection and aptitude for the handling of general ideas. The two are certainly distinct. Wilamowitz is one sort of thing and Trotsky another. But Trotsky knew something and Wilamowitz had some general ideas. He was not quite the spinsterish pedant that his shocked reaction to Nietzsche's *Birth of Tragedy* suggests. Among lesser men the two capacities are often found in their pure form. There are scholars like the elderly Oxford Latinist who, when asked if the author whose text he had painstakingly amended was worth reading, replied 'to be quite frank, I don't go in much for the gush side of criticism'. And there are philosophers, in the strictly academic sense, who know nothing that they did not learn at their mothers' knees, G.E. Moore, perhaps, and a good many of the adherents of Wittgenstein. (He did know quite a lot in a haphazard sort of way. His followers sometimes use his anguished repudiation of nearly all previous thought, which he had at least some acquaintance with, to excuse not getting to know anything about it at all.)

Scholarship, or humanistic learning, is philosophical, historical or literary. Philosophy being what it is, it is hard to study it without having some traffic with general ideas, although I did know an expert on Arab philosophy who was almost perfectly innocent of intercourse with them. History and literature do not compel it in their students, but they give every inducement to it. Historians, embarrassed by Spengler and Toynbee, avoid comprehensive historical systems. Under the thumb of Marx or Namier they ritually deny the influence of general ides in history. But they admit it in practice, as in the case of Christopher Hill's Marx-rejecting title *Intellectual*

*Origins of the English Revolution.* Correspondingly a literary scholar who does not confine himself exclusively to textual criticism must give attention to general ideas. They are a substantial element in nay interpretation of a work of imaginative literature and in any placing of an imaginative work in the intellectual background of its age.

So although scholarly learning and a concern with general ideas are distinguishable, they have a marked tendency to combine in the minds of all but the purest of scholars and the most prophetic or vacuously ideological of men of ideas. Even when they are both present, are they enough to make their bearer cultured if he is without interest in or knowledge of imaginative literature? I am inclined to think that they are not, for two reasons. One is superficial: the fact that our current way of using the term requires those to whom it is applied to have such interest and knowledge. That does not matter much, since the word has varied in meaning and the Matthew Arnold sense which is under discussion at the moment is, for reasons that will emerge, engaged in something of a struggle for existence with the social conception of culture employed by anthropologists and sociologists. In many works of reference, such as the *Encyclopaedia Britannica*, the social conception is the only one that is given serious attention.

But a more solid reason is available. The general doctrines, with which the man of ideas, Eliot's philosopher, is preoccupied, are as closely involved with imaginative literature as they are with scholarly learning. Christians, Marxists, liberals and conservatives must rely on the findings of scholars to supply their doctrines with rational credentials, on history proper and on the record of past dealings with general ideas, that is to say, the history of thought. But, on the other side, they are as closely linked to imaginative literature, since it is as large and as influential a bearer of general ideas as philosophy in Eliot's wide sense. Only an exceptionally pure poet like Herrick or Mallarmé can be described in the phrase, misapplied to Henry James, as having 'a mind too fine to be ravished by an idea'. General ideas are also present in painting – ideas of human perfection or style in portraiture, for example, attitudes to war, conceptions of family life and so on. I would not press the argument to include music.

### III

I do not think it is just old age or personal idiosyncrasy that leads me to think that culture in the personal sense is in a comparatively bad way. The comparison yields its melancholy result most definitely when applied to the production of culture. There has been no writer in the years since 1945 of the stature of Proust, Mann, Yeats, Joyce or even Eliot and Auden. Some fine talents have emerged – in English – Burgess, Golding, Iris Murdoch in fiction, Hughes, Hill and Heaney in poetry. There have been no French novelists of the standing of Gide, Malraux and Montherlant, no French poet to put beside Valéry. The most interesting writers of the post-war period are all in a sense hold-overs from an earlier age: Borges, Lampedusa, Nabokov. I shall abstain from comment on the non-literary arts.

Much the same is true in the domain of learning and general ideas. In philosophy Russell and Wittgenstein eclipse those who have emerged since the war. (Ryle and Ayer, as Quine is, were men of the 1930s.) Richards, Leavis and Empson in criticism, Tawney, Namier, Bloch, Febvre and Meinecke in history equally have no one of the same distinction among their successors, with the possible exceptions of Northrop Frye and Braudel. The ablest British humanistic scholars of the present age – Strawson in philosophy, Kermode in criticism, Keith Thomas in history – all have a cautious, self-effacing quality, in which the most scrupulous professionalism is combined with a marked distaste for adventure. In France, if history is doing well – as my reference to Braudel suggests – the condition of philosophy and literature, dominated by Foucault and Derrida and by Barthes, is an occasion for concern. The German army was finally defeated in 1918 and 1945, but German ways of thought, in a particularly wanton and delirious form, have conquered French intellectual life. Its pantheon consists of Hegel, Husserl and Heidegger, with Nietzsche as a presiding deity. The outcome is a bacchanalian revel of paradox and oracular chatter, as far removed as can be conceived from *la clarté francaise* of Descartes and Pascal, or of Renan and Taine. But the previously accumulated capital of culture is still there to be enjoyed.

The consumption of culture is harder to appraise. Academics complain of the cultural malnutrition of their students: most of whom have read very little and few of whom can spell. Mechanical aids to leisure – television, video, CDs, swimming-pools and so on – are taken to reduce the time available for reading, or, at any rate, the time devoted to it. On the other hand there is, for most people, more leisure. It is possible that it comes at the wrong time, in adult life and, in particular, at the ever earlier age of retirement. The habits of culture are best acquired early in life. Tastes and mental appetites will become fixed narrowly and at a low level by middle life unless such habits have already been acquired.

For the three centuries preceding the twentieth the most widely effective cultural force in this country was the Bible. It was for the sake of access to it that a great proportion of the community made the often considerable effort to become literate. It did its cultural good inadvertently. Its readers were animated by a desire for eternal life. What they got was familiarity with a great and varied literature in a form superior to its original expression and to any other translation. It was an extraordinary bit of luck. Now the religious motive has drained away for all but a few. And they are likely to be exposed to the appalling stylistic barbarities of the *New English Bible*, whose composition appears to have been modelled on leaflets from the DHSS.

But there are some countervailing considerations. We know that the number of new titles that emerges from the publishes every year is constantly increasing. The fact that a lot of these are reissues is all to the good from a cultural point of view. Another edition of *Bleak House* is to be preferred to an illustrated biography of Kylie Minogue or a collection of Terry Wogan's favourite Irish jokes. Presumably the actual number of books bought is also increasing. It is not relevant that not all of them are read, for that has always been the case.

Even television is not an unqualified delinquent. Some culturally respectable mater gets on to the screen and the existence of special racks of paperbacks of books from which TV programmes have been derived is some sort of proof of TV's positive support for reading, even if it is only a modest compensation for the reading it prevents. Another faintly comforting thought is that television seems to be running out of steam. Can any even mildly cultured person watch much of it, now there has been about forty years for the novelty to wear off? It is an essentially parasitic affair which draws its content from other sources: literature, films, the music hall, even the parish hall. Its only real innovation has been the game show, for the soap opera came from radio. Might it not be that it is fading away, like the films before it and the music hall before them? Admittedly there is video to take its place, but, since video requires some action more positive than pressing a button, it is less McLuhanesque, less of a warm bath of collective mindlessness for the dazed peasants of the global village.

The superannuation of the Bible and the intrusion of TV and other mechanical leisure-fillers are not the only external factors which endanger culture. The rapid process of conglomeration in the publishing industry seems to mirror the replacement of the corner shop by the supermarket. But supermarkets have delicatessen counters as well as great cemeteries of detergent (the Harold Robbins of grocery) and, even if they obliterate the grocer on the corner, they co-exist with specialty shops. There is really no reason to impose on the publisher the duty of creating the appetite for the kind of books we should ideally prefer him to sell.

It may be that the most serious threat to culture at the present moment is not any sort of external pressure, but is the challenge that has been mounted against its claim to have special, uniquely superior status as compared with the rest of the products of the human mind. This is the assault against the idea that there is any canon at all, any objectively definable élite of books which should be attended to in preference to others. The assumption that there is such a thing is built into Arnold's notion of 'the *best* that has been thought and said', is embodied in the concept of *classics* or such productions as *The Great Books of the Western World.*

Some critics of the canon come forward as the champions of a neglected or undervalued group: women or blacks or homosexuals or proletarians. Their interest is in securing recognition for their clients; not total destruction of the canon, but the enlargement of its boundaries. In a way that enlargement is going on all the time, as new books come before the reading public and as older books are re-evaluated in relation to one another. Longfellow is shown the door; Hopkins and Octavio Paz are let in.

A more radical point of view is that which rejects the idea of canonical status altogether. It draws strength, none too logically, from hostility to social élitism. Against that, the first consideration to bear in mind is that, even if those capable of genuine enjoyment of the canon are a minority, as, at present, only a minority in practice is, the cultural élite is not coincident with any of the other élites, those of the powerful, the rich and the well-born. Each of these three overlaps its neighbour to a significant extent: many of the rich are powerful and many of the well-born are rich. The cultural élite is only very modestly represented among the membership of each of the three groups and most of its members are not contained within any of them.

More important is the fact that culture is not necessarily the possession of a small minority. The cultural élite is probably a larger portion of the community than it was in the eighteenth century, although not, I should imagine, than it was in the nineteenth. It is possible to suspect that it is smaller in Britain than it is in France, where there is not to be found the same brutish hostility to culture which is so firmly established here. All the same unlike wealth and power, culture is not a comparative term, so there is no logical limit to its width of application.

How is the sceptical objection to be met that the idea of a canon is a put-up job, a self-sustaining conspiracy kept going by people anxious to differentiate themselves at modest cost from the rest of the population? The only way to a response is through the appeal to experienced judgement, the convergence to agreement on the excellence of particular works of those who have studied them and other works in an informed and closely attentive way. That principle is uncontroversially admitted as justifying judgements of sporting excellence and physical beauty.

Librarians do not have to guide their acquisitions and recommendations by reference to the canon. But like a serious butcher, who will urge the claims of sirloin steak in preference to hamburger, it is surely natural for them to do so, and not to see themselves merely as passive satisfiers of independently generated demands made on them. A sensible butcher will not press sirloin steak on a totally toothless person and, in the same spirit, librarians must take account of the limits of their reader's appetites. But I hope they will not succumb to the policy of whatever turns you on, or, more specifically, whatever you want to turn the pages of.

*Not previously published.*

# The Tribulations of Authors

If these remarks were a sermon, which they are not intended to be, they would have to take as their text some passages from that holy writ of authorial misfortune: Johnson's *Life of Savage:*

> During a considerable part of the time, in which he was employed on this Performance (writing his tragedy *Sir Thomas Overbury)* he was without Lodging and often without Meat; nor had he any other Conveniences for Study than the Fields or the Streets allowed him... He generally lived by Chance, eating only when he was invited to the Tables of his Acquaintances, from which the Meanness of his Dress often excluded him, when the Politeness and Variety of his Conversation would have been thought a sufficient Recompence for his Entertainment. He lodged by Accident as much as he dined, and passed the Night sometimes in mean Houses, which are set open at Night for any casual Wanderers, sometimes in Cellars among the Riot and Filth of the meanest and most profligate of the Rabble; and sometimes, when he had no Money to support even the Expenses of these Receptacles, walked about the Streets till he was weary and lay down in the Summer on a Bulk, or, in the Winter, with his Associates in Poverty, among the Ashes of a Glass-House.

These parts, at any rate, of Johnson's biography of his unfortunate friend can be taken as authoritative. Johnson knew at first hand of what he wrote. As Boswell records:

> It is melancholy to reflect that Johnson and Savage were sometimes in such extreme indigence that they could not pay for a lodging; so that they wandered together whole nights in the streets. Yet in these almost incredible scenes of distress, we may suppose that Savage mentioned many of the anecdotes with which Johnson afterwards enriched the life of his unhappy companion and of other Poets. He told Sir Joshua Reynolds that one night in particular when Savage and he walked round St. James's Square for want of a lodging, they were not at all

depressed by their situation: but in high spirits and brimful of patriotism, traversed the square for several hours, inveighed against the Minister and resolved they would stand by their country.

Other aspects of Savage's story, the parts Johnson faithfully and perhaps too credulously reports on the authority of their subject, it is reasonable to doubt. In particular, there is Savage's claim to have been the child, by the Countess of Macclesfield, of Earl Rivers. The Countess, according to Savage, was anxious to get free from her husband and used the illicit romance of which he was the fruit to accomplish her purpose. From that moment on she treated him, he always insisted, with the utmost malignity: handing him over to the care of a nurse, repelling all his approaches and doing him out of a bequest that his natural father had designed for him.

Boswell argues against this melodramatic history of Savage's origins in a creditably lawyer-like way, pointing out enough discrepancies between it and pieces of evidence that could be independently discovered to sink it without trace. Or almost. Savage's best, or, at any rate, most frequently anthologised poem is *The Bastard,* and we may conclude that he was one, certainly in the legal, and possibly in the colloquial, senses of the word.

Even without suffering at the hands of his mother Savage's misfortunes were substantial enough. He was not successful as a writer so that he is known to us today only as the occasion of one of Johnson's first publications of note and continuing value. He was not only poor but kept poor by certain peculiarities of character; profuse extravagance when in funds, incessant sponging when out of them, violent alterations of attitude to benefactors, staying far too late in the houses of people good enough to entertain him. It is not surprising that he died while imprisoned for debt. But he must have had some attractive qualities. Johnson's charity, although very great, was not indiscriminate and he writes of Savage with tenderness and even a measure of admiration. And what can have induced a body of gentlemen to raise funds to set Savage up in a pensioned state in Wales but some good that they saw in him, although the remoteness of his intended retreat suggests another explanation?

Savage is probably the most extreme case of authorial distress and dereliction that can be found. But the condition has always been widespread as some poet has observed (intruding one musician among his host of authors, no doubt for reasons of euphony):

Cervantes, Dostoevsky, Poe
Drained the dregs and lees of woe;
Gogol, Beethoven and Keats
Got but meagre share of sweets.
Milton, Homer, Dante had
Reason to be more than sad.

Wyatt and Thomas More were executed, but not on account of what
they had written. Villon was sentenced to death several times.
Dostoevsky was reprieved from being hanged at the last moment,
before he had embarked on his career as a writer. However epilepsy
and a passionate addiction to gambling ensured that his life was
pretty much of a torment. A great many writers have, like Savage,
been to prison: Malory, Cervantes, Bunyan (for twelve years), Ben
Jonson, Defoe and Oscar Wilde. Genet does not really count, being
even more of a prisoner than an author by profession. W.E. Henley
and W.H. Davies each lost a foot and Cervantes had his left hand
maimed at the battle of Lepanto. The blind make up a particularly
distinguished group: Homer (on the traditional account of who he
or she was, or, for that matter, they were), Milton, and, on the whole,
Joyce. Baudelaire and Maupassant may be cited to represent the
throng of those who died of venereal disease. Pope was a hunchback
and Byron had a club foot. Barbellion, the 'disappointed man', died
after a long struggle with disseminated sclerosis. Tuberculosis laid
waste the Brontë sisters, Chekhov and D.H. Lawrence among many
others. Cowper, Ruskin and Ezra Pound went mad as, broadly
speaking, did Swift and Blake. Intense trouble with wives was undergone by Tolstoy, George Meredith (whose wife ran away) and
Thomas Hardy (whose wife did not). Pushkin and Lermontov died
in duels – an indication of the practical ham-fistedness of authors –
and Marlowe may have done so as well, unless that is too dignified
a way of referring to a pub brawl. Suicide brought to an end the lives
of Seneca, Chatterton, Stefan Zweig and Virginia Woolf. Coleridge,
De Quincey and Poe were drug addicts. The greatest American
writers of the interwar years – Faulkner, Fitzgerald, Hemingway and
O'Neill – were alcoholics, as were Hammett and Chandler. Kipling
and Saki endured miserable childhoods as the victims of cruel aunts.
Lucretius is said to have died from taking too large a dose of love
philtre. Cicero was killed by soldiers of the triumvirate. Rousseau
suffered in nearly every conceivable way but, most distinctively, from
an unusual complaint that cannot be specified in mixed company.
Robert Graves had Laura Riding.

These examples all have two features in common. Everyone in the list still survives as a writer, indeed more than survives, is still celebrated and enjoyed. That is why we all know about their misfortunes. Secondly, the troubles enumerated could, as the saying is, have happened to anyone. They are in no way peculiar to the race of authors, but are distributed with much the same broadcast generosity among any definable group one might select from the population at large.

There are pains and difficulties which are more or less peculiar to authors. The most poignantly intense of these is cruel reviewing, as with the handling of Keats by the *Edinburgh Review,* or, along the same lines, the kind of abusive public reception endured by Henry James when he tried his hand at play writing. The unkindness of other authors is a yet further version of the same thing: the portrait of Hugh Walpole as the greasily ingratiating Alroy Kear in Somerset Maugham's *Cakes and Ale* and the treatment of Henry James by H.G. Wells in *Boon.* Some bad reviews at least do no financial harm. James Gould Cozzens's *By Love Possessed* was already a best seller when Dwight Macdonald set about it.

Less wounding to *amour-propre,* but still a frightful nuisance, is the loss or destruction of manuscripts, as in the case of Carlyle's *French Revolution,* used to light a fire by John Stuart Mill's maid, and T.E. Lawrence's *Seven Pillars of Wisdom,* left, so he said, in the waiting room at Didcot station. Both these works were reconstructed by their authors, so the disaster was not total. William Empson's time in the East led him to write a large book, called, I think, *The Faces of Buddha.* He lent the manuscript to a drunken, and possibly envious, friend and it was never seen again.

When a book emerges into public view it usually needs to be noticed right away if it is to be noticed at all. One that has had the bad luck to come out just at the moment when general public attention is fixed on some such event of overwhelming concern as the outbreak of a war risks oblivion. There is an agreeable indirect recognition of this possibility in the preface to the second book of the philosopher C.D. Broad, which came out in the early 1920s. 'I hope', he wrote, 'that the publication of this book will not, like that of its predecessor, be the occasion of a general European War.' One might possibly add the difficulty of writing in an unusual language like Albanian or, indeed, a language of one's own construction, like the Lallans of Hugh MacDiarmid.

A further hazard is the villainy of publishers like Dr de Villiers of the enchantingly named Watford University Press, who first brought out Havelock Ellis's *Studies in the Psychology of Sex,* or merely incompetent ones like Ballantyne whose financial collapse brought ruin, and the drudgery needed to repair it, to the ageing Walter Scott. Then there are the oppressions of censorship undergone by Flaubert, Joyce and D.H. Lawrence, not to mention its grotesquely magnified versions in Stalin's empire.

But, in the end, authorship is a career; a career is undertaken, first of all, to earn a living, whatever may be the secondary allurements of fame. So the crucial tribulation of authorship is poverty, the consequence of most of the specifically authorial kinds of misfortune which have just been enumerated. From the seventeenth century onward the DNB entries of many well-remembered authors, who managed to survive into old age, report depressingly often that their subjects died in abject poverty.

For a long time after the invention of printing those who relied for survival mainly on their income from writing constituted a fairly disreputable fringe of the profession as a whole. The most dignified procedure was to emit an occasional piece of writing from a secure position in the upper ranks of society. Sir Thomas Wyatt, the earl of Surrey, Sir Philip Sidney, Anne, countess of Winchilsea, the first baron and the first earl Lytton reveal their status by their familiar designations. Although socially noble, these writers are, in the class system of literature, only petty bourgeois. For the most part the greatest authors in English were civil servants. Chaucer was employed in various foreign missions and then settled down in the customs service. Spenser worked for the government in Ireland. Milton, after a spell of teaching, served as Latin Secretary to Cromwell, a relationship approximately parallel to that of Sir Edward Marsh to Sir Winston Churchill. In more recent times this source seems to have run a bit dry. Serious government employment merges, at least in the disreputable past, with the enjoyment of sinecures bestowed as patronage. Wordsworth's post as distributor of stamps is a late but glorious instance of such an arrangement. But Trollope had a real job in the Post Office and held it until 1867 when he was fifty-two.

Once upon a time literacy was on the whole monopolised by the clergy. Most medieval writing that is not by clerics is anonymous and of oral origin. The lay author in the Christian west is a product and symptom of the Renaissance. Langland, Skelton, Hooker, Donne, George Herbert and Herrick were, in their choice of profession, more the rule than the exception in their epoch. Some of them, as one might put it, do not write like priests and do not confine themselves to devotional topics. That is conspicuously the case with the two great clergymen in eighteenth century literature; Swift and Sterne. Since 1800 there have been great writers who were priests, above all Newman and Hopkins. In recent times there have been some fine clerical poets: Andrew Young and, happily still living and writing, R.S. Thomas. But the clergy have not contributed much to the novel in the last two centuries. The largest achievement in that field I can think of is that of the Rev. S. Baring-Gould. Their contribution to general literature has been scholarly for the most part, as with Dean Milman, Bishop Mandell Creighton and more recently, David Knowles. The last important clerical philosopher was Dean Mansel who died in 1871. (Father Copleston is more a historian of philosophy than a philosopher proper.) Dean Inge and Monsignor Knox, somewhat incommensurable near-contemporaries, were the last distinguished controversialists to be in holy orders.

Authors who lived, or starved, on their writing, do not appear until the sixteenth century and the establishment of printing. The purest of them, in a superficially paradoxical way, were the pamphleteering hacks. The Martin Marprelate controversy of the 1580s was a godsend to many of them. The university wits were largely kept afloat, to the extent that they were kept afloat, by work of that nature. A more satisfactory procedure, or, at any rate, one more productive of memorable writing, was the composition of plays. In an illiterate age drama was the main method of conveying literary material to the public at large. It did what is done today, as we slide into another age of general illiteracy, by television. Udall, Peele and Nashe were the analogues of modern scriptwriters. The greatest dramatists, Shakespeare and Ben Jonson, not only wrote plays but acted in them. Play writing was the main support of Dryden a hundred years later and in the following century it was the chief resource of Fielding in his early life. Giving it up for the magistracy, he secured what he needed for his work as a novelist.

Actors have contributed little to literature since the Elizabethan age, apart from their ghosted reminiscences. An analogous combination, that of author and printer, has, so far as I can see, only one notable instance, that of Samuel Richardson. Since printers were publishers in his day it seems a shrewd manoeuvre, at least providing some guarantee of publication. Since publishing became a profession on its own there have been comparatively few publisher authors of importance. But some important authors have turned into publishers, most notably T.S. Eliot and Herbert Read.

It is from the pamphleteering hacks that the literary profession proper, relied on as the primary source of income, really derives. Defoe and Smollett turned their hands to all sorts of literary rough trade. Defoe, indeed, made ends meet, from time to time, by various forms of humble government service, spying amongst them. A more dignified approach to literature properly so called has been parliamentary reporting, an important mainstay for both Samuel Johnson and Dickens at certain stages in their careers.

The truly successful professional author first makes his appearance in the eighteenth century. In England there is Pope with his translation of Homer (he had some private means to keep him going until that success), in France Voltaire, who, of course, was initially admired for just that part of his gigantic output, his plays, that is least admired today. Johnson in England and Diderot in France had a much harder time until they went into the reference book business with dictionary and encyclopaedia. In the undergrowth were melancholy figures like Stephen Duck (1705-56), the 'thresher poet'. *The Concise Cambridge History of English Literature* says of him that he was a 'truly tragic figure. A Wiltshire farm labourer with a gift for verse he was taken up by the "best people", but, feeling unable to fulfil the absurd expectations of his backers, committed suicide.'

We meet with him an actual instance of the form of authorial disaster depicted in Max Beerbohm's *Enoch Soames*. Soames is a reminder that the examples, both of suffering, general or specifically authorial, and of ways of making a living that have so far been considered, apart from those of Savage and Duck, have all been those of writers who are still remembered as writers. But they are the survivors of an unrelenting and continuous process of competitive sifting. Their works have been more or less lovingly preserved in the original editions, have been kept in print in a succession of new editions or, at least, in pellet form in anthologies. Behind these compelling presences in the foreground can be dimly perceived a phantom horde of desperately gesticulating postulants, engulfed in an oblivion from which only some unlikely accident of research or casual browsing can rescue them. They did not live well then; they do not live at all now.

Enoch Soames is a vivid representation of the self-destructive pertinacity of authors, their determination in the face of every kind of ill-success – financial, critical, even social – to persevere with their work. If one were to start a career in the colonial service but found the heat unbearable and the mental processes of the natives impossible to understand, if one were to be recruited as a salesman of second-hand cars and found oneself incapable of keeping quiet about the defects of the vehicles one was selling to prospective buyers one would soon seek other work: in the accounts department of the town hall, perhaps, or as a carpet layer. One would regret the time wasted, but not feel desperately mortified.

Disraeli's father, Isaac, has a rather reductive explanation for this peculiarity of unsuccessful authors. Once embarked on authorship, he maintains, one is soon no good for anything else. But, on a second glance, that thesis is more a redescription of the phenomenon than an explanation of it. It is not that the committed author is incapable of doing anything else so much as that he is immovably unwilling to try a new line of work.

It is too simple, I think, to assimilate the persistent author to the sweatered lovelies who used to congregate in the drugstore at the intersection of Hollywood and Vine. Those appetising young women did not much want to act in films; they wanted to be stars, to enjoy the rewards and fame of Joan Crawford and Lana Turner. A similar gambler's conviction of the accessibility of the big prize, of becoming the glory of an age like Shakespeare or Goethe, may well be present to aspiring writers. But that kind of impulse eventually fades away under the sustained pressure of failure.

The writer, and above all the imaginative writer, is peculiarly close to the material in which he deals. It is not just a mass of external stuff, in itself more or less indifferent to him, which he handles in the normal course of business. It is himself, his inner being, his emotions, his memories, his beliefs, his ideas of good and evil. Once he is set upon formulating this intimate essence in words there is no going back on it. To do that would be a kind of suicide, a repudiation of what most truly constitutes one's existence as an individual. If you do not fancy my second hand cars you have not injured me as a person. But if you think my poems are awful you have wounded me in my most spiritual, personal, sensitive part. However art is long and life is short. Readers have only so much time and attention to bestow. Writers have bottomless supplies to offer them. The inevitable result is glut, an unwanted superfluity of production.

And, of course, critics and the contemporary public err. Writers ignored in their own age do sometimes achieve glory in the fullness of time, even if only, and not very rewardingly for them, after their deaths. Kafka, as an incorrigible non-publisher, has, one might say, only himself to blame. But a relevant contemporary is Italo Svevo. More recently there is the heartening story of Barbara Pym, rescued by Philip Larkin and David Cecil from premature burial by her publishers, in time to enjoy her resurrection.

It was the thought of some such rediscovery that induced Enoch Soames to sell his soul to the devil, that night in the inexpensive restaurant in Soho in the 1890s, for a glimpse of the relevant bit of the general catalogue of the British Museum a hundred years later. (The precise date is 3 June 1997. Beerbohm's prescience did not quite extend to envisaging the contemplation by Soames of a terminal of the online public access catalogue at the new St Pancras Building. It will probably be best to position discreet observers both there and at the Round Reading Room when the time arrives.)

Enoch Soames's anguish was caused not by lack of money but by lack of applause. The poem Beerbohm quotes from Soames's slim volume *Fungoids* certainly makes that state of affairs plausible. You will not blame me for quoting it.

> *Thou art, who hast not been!*
>     Pale tunes irresolute
>     And traceries of old sounds
>     Blown from a rotted flute
> Mingle with noise of cymbals rouged with rust,
> Nor not strange forms and epicene
>     Lie bleeding in the dust,
>     Being wounded with wounds.
> For this it is
> That is thy counterpart
>     Of age-long mockeries
> *Thou hast not been, nor art!*

In fact this poem of Soames's is more often read than any passage in the verse of Arthur Symons, or indeed all of it put together. But that is not for reasons that would relieve Soames's distress.

A more straightforward example of authorial suffering, in which poverty is more insistent than the lack of recognition from which it flows, is that of Edwin Reardon, the pathetic hero of George Gissing's *New Grub Street,* to some extent a self-portrait of the author. Reardon, like Gissing, is essentially a lover of the literature of classical Greece and Rome. For some time he beats fruitlessly against the ramparts of editorial indifference with dainty essays on topics in that field. Driven into fiction he does get published. But his fifth book, cruelly titled *The Optimist*, is a failure. Its four predecessors had earned, respectively, nothing, twenty-five, fifty and a hundred pounds.

Reardon has an attractive, hard, practical wife and a young child who serve to enhance the awfulness of his situation. Gissing's own matrimonial set-up was even bleaker. He got involved with a prostitute while a student at Manchester, stole some money, went to prison and, when he got out, married her. There is an oblique reference to all that in a short excursus in New Grub Street about the tendency of authors to marry badly, particularly below themselves. First there are the Hinkses. Mrs Hinks 'was the daughter of a laundress in whose house he had lodged thirty years ago when new to London but already long acquainted with hunger; they lived in complete harmony, but Mrs Hinks, who was four years the elder, still spoke the laundress tongue, unmitigated and immitigable'. Secondly there are the Gorbutts: 'this lady had an inclination to strong liquors'. Finally there are the Christophersons, who 'were as poor as church mice. Even in a friend's house they wrangled incessantly, and made tragi-comical revelations of their home life. The husband worked casually at irresponsible journalism, but his chosen study was metaphysics, for many years he had had a huge and profound book on hand, which he believed would bring him fame, though he was not so unsettled in mind to hope for anything else... Mrs Christopherson came from Camberwell, where her father, once upon a time, was the smallest of small butchers. Disagreeable stories were whispered concerning her earlier life, and probably the metaphysician did not care to look back in that direction. They had had three children; all were happily buried.' The characteristics of the first Mrs Gissing seem to have been distributed among these ladies.

Reardon's self-torturing commitment to a literary career is highlighted by its contrast with the altogether tradesmanlike point of view of his friend, Jasper Milvain. When the book opens Milvain is living on a substantial part of his widowed mother's small annuity, to the alarm and disgust of his spinster sisters. He sees his comparatively luxurious manner of life as necessary to establish the contacts required for success as a writer. Urging his sisters to a literary career on severely practical lines, he observes:

I tell you, writing is a business. Get together half a dozen fair specimens of the Sunday-school prize; study them; discover the essential points of such composition; hit upon new attractions; then go to work methodically, so many pages a day. There's no question of the divine afflatus; that belongs to another sphere of life ... If only I could get that into poor Reardon's head.

Reardon's view is altogether different:

How I envy those clerks who go by to their offices in the morning! There's the day's work cut out for them; no question of mood and feeling; they have just to work at something, and when the evening comes they have earned their wages, they are free to rest and enjoy themselves. What an insane thing it is to make literature one's only means of support! When the most trivial accident may at any time prove fatal to one's power of work for weeks or months. No, that is the unpardonable sin! To make a trade of an art! I am rightly served for attempting such a brutal folly.

In something like the spirit of Mrs Reardon one might wonder whether it would not be better to regard inveterate perseverance in an author despite repeated failure as a mental condition that needs to be treated rather than as something to be subsidised. Does it not call for therapists and sanatoriums rather than grants and retreats? The main argument against that reductive proposal is the large number of writers subsequently recognised as great or gifted who spent all or part of their lives in or near destitution. These are usually writers of an original, innovating kind, who present, to an initially resistant public, novelties of form or style or diction or subject-matter for which that public is unprepared and to which it takes some time to become accustomed.

Many fine writers succeed rapidly, but for every Scott there is a Wordsworth, for every Kipling a Conrad, for every Shaw a T. S. Eliot, for every H. G. Wells a James Joyce. When a writer's work does succeed financially, it is often for irrelevant reasons. The relation of the revenue to T. S. Eliot's estate from *Cats* to the return from the entire non-Possum body of his work hardly bears thinking about. Nabokov's *Lolita* became a best-seller in the teeth of its literary qualities. Support for poor authors now is a generalised variant of the institution of the publisher's advance. It is a prospective investment in a large number of projects only a few of which are going to succeed, but some of which will succeed gloriously Creative advance cannot be predicted specifically. The most we can be sure of is that it will take place.

The history of the Royal Literary Fund provides some detailed factual support for this general argument. Among its beneficiaries have been Coleridge, Conrad, Lawrence and Joyce, to mention only the most eminent. One writer, not quite of that class, who was helped was Thomas Love Peacock, seemingly the most blithe and genial of authors. In 1812 when he was twenty-seven years old and had written nothing to speak of, he received a grant of £30. At the time he was in a state of suicidal depression and the grant may well have saved his life.

A moment ago I raised the question whether obstinate persistence in authorship did not require treatment rather than financial support. Let me end with a story which brings them together. It was recalled by Nigel Dennis from a time when he was working as secretary to Alfred Adler, who had arrived in Britain not long before as a refugee. Nigel Dennis was at a sherry party Adler was giving and was in a depressed state. He was involved in a romance with a woman older and smarter than he was and he did not know where to turn to retain her affection by providing the kind of expensive pleasures to which she was accustomed. Adler's glance lighted on Dennis for a moment and he said, 'Oh look, Nigel is down in the mouth. I know what he needs. He needs a cheque.' He took out his cheque book and wrote one out.

Nigel Dennis recalled that incident to confirm his claim of Adler's brilliance as a diagnostician. That Adlerian gift has lain behind the two hundred years of the life of the Royal Literary Fund. I am honoured in having had this opportunity to congratulate and commend it.

*Address to celebrate the two-hundredth anniversary of the Royal Literary Fund, given at the Royal Society of Arts, 17 May 1990.*

# Wodehouse and the Tradition of Comedy

It is as dangerous to talk in public about Wodehouse as it must have been to go on at length about the prophetic books of the Old Testament in the more mountainous and agricultural parts of mid nineteenth-century Wales. It is quite certain that there will be several people in the audience who know vastly more about the subject than you do, whose depth of knowledge of the text is the product of life-long and uninterrupted study. I hope to skirt round this difficulty as far as possible by concentrating on breadth rather than depth. My aim is to reclaim Wodehouse from the segregation to which he is consigned both by devotees and belittlers and to indicate his place in literature proper, more specifically the tradition of comedy. In a very small way I am trying to do for Wodehouse what was done for the Bible in the mid-eighteenth century by Robert Lowth, a New College man who eventually became bishop of London. Lowth's *Interpretations of Hebrew Poetry* treated the Bible as part of the general corpus of the world's imaginative literature, not as a collection of intelligence reports on the supernatural to be mastered and memorised in detail.

For the most part critics do not know quite what to make of Wodehouse. In his *Enemies of Promise*, Cyril Connolly, after lumping him together with the *Oxford Book of English Verse*, Edgar Wallace and Mary Webb as 'politicians' reading', suggests that critics do not make anything of him at all. 'The entertainer', he says, 'suffers from no criticism whatever. No one has told P.G. Wodehouse which is his best book, or his worst, what are his faults and how he should improve them.'

Although this is simply false as it stands, it is true that most of the standard guides to or surveys of English Literature have nothing or next to nothing to say about Wodehouse. *The Literary History of England* by Albert C. Baugh, working in association with Brooke, Chew and a host of others, the compendium on which the teeming millions of American students of English literature are brought up, does not mention him, although, to move to a different margin of the subject, it treats Lewis Carroll at some length and has a solidly-built footnote about Edward Lear. The same silence prevails in David Daiches's *Critical History of English Literature*, in F.W. Bateson's handy *Guide to English Literature* and in Martin Seymour-Smith's copious *Guide to Modern World Literature*.

Sometimes he is let in, but only at a respectful distance, as in the *Concise Cambridge History of English Literature*, which refers to 'his gift for highly original aptness of phrase that almost suggests a poet struggling for release among the wild extravagances of farce'. G.S. Fraser, in *The Modern Writer and his World*, says of Wodehouse's novels 'if they are to be counted as literature, (they) are just to be counted so and no more'. The same point is made in more genial terms by Anthony Burgess when he says, 'the stories and novels of P.G. Wodehouse do exactly what they set out to do and their humour does not ask for close analysis: to it, as to *The Blue Danube*, we bring the tribute of unanalytical enjoyment.' Only with W.W. Robson's fairly recent *Modern English Literature*, in which Wodehouse is treated as a substantive Edwardian writer, along with, even if not of the size of, Conrad, Bennett and George Moore, is something like the attitude to Wodehouse I wish to promote reasonably discernible. Robson says, 'Wodehouse preferred to perfect an art of recreation. It depends so little on fashion and circumstances that it has survived into an entirely different world from his own. It may survive that world too.'

A few casual references may be mentioned from critics writing with no comprehensive intention. Edmund Wilson, betraying the dyspepsia that often accompanied his literary omnivorousness, says, apropos Max Beerbohm, 'I asked him what he thought of P.G. Wodehouse – the enthusiasm for whom of some people I have never been able to understand – he replied that he could never read more than fifty pages of any of Wodehouse's books. But now people – not I however – laugh their heads off over P.G. Wodehouse and pretend to take him seriously as a writer.' It is, of course, possible that Max Beerbohm found it hard to read more than fifty pages of *any* writer, before the powerful tug of his gift for parody led him off to the writing desk. The point is that is not necessary to share Wilson's unwavering solemnity, or his Anglophobia, to agree that there is a way of taking Wodehouse and other immediately entertaining writers which can obstruct their considered appreciation.

What I have in mind is pseudo-criticism in the style of Ronald Knox, applied by him most notably to Sherlock Holmes and to the Barsetshire novels and, in a slightly wilder form, to the cryptographic interpretation of *In Memoriam*. I have no wish at all to condemn these agreeable exercises. Indeed, if pressed, I should find myself reluctant to exchange them for the critical *oeuvre* or Roland Barthes. But they may distract attention from the primary source of our enjoyment of the works to which they re applied. In fact neither the more central and relevant criticism of the Barsetshire novels, nor any assistance that criticism may give to their enjoyment by readers, is interfered with by Knox's topographical frolics. It is only if such play is taken to be the mainly appropriate criticism for the writing at whose expense it is conducted that a sensible appreciation of that writing is prejudiced.

Wodehouse, in short, is too good a writer to be used exclusively as material for a kind of parlour game. People who preoccupy themselves with the problems of whatever became of Ukridge's wife and of whether Bertie Wooster really was at Magdalen are failing to attend to the real sources of the profound satisfactions to be derived from his work.

I think that something of the same irrelevance infects the extremely favourable judgements of Wodehouse made by Hilaire Belloc and Evelyn Waugh. Belloc described Wodehouse as 'the best writer of English now alive' and as 'the head of my profession'. As Bertie Wooster sagely reflected, in becoming the recipient of some deeply fatuous observation of Madeline Basset's to the effect that rabbits were gnomes in attendance on the Fairy Queen and that the stars were God's daisy chain: 'Perfect rot, of course. They are [and in this case, he is] nothing of the sort.' If Belloc had said rather that Wodehouse was perhaps the most brilliant and dexterous user of language among the writers of his epoch he would have been nearer the truth. There is an obvious sense, after all, in which Wodehouse is a secondary or derivative writer. His work is parodistic, the sustained, good-natured mockery of various familiar styles of variously defective utterance in life and literature: those of the fashionable simpleton, the pompous higher servant, the saloon bar tyrant and the obsessed golfer, in the one case, and of the romantic novelette and the manly tale of adventure on the other. As a result it is filled with clichés and stock phrases, brilliantly deployed, varied and superimposed, but clichés and stock phrases nevertheless.

Furthermore Wodehouse's work is to a great extent farcical or fantastic. Its engagement with the actual nature of human beings and the actual conditions of human life is at best remote and indirect. Wodehouse, it will be agreed, particularly by him, is not Tolstoy although their names are significantly linked by Vladimir Brusiloff. Only the most unrestrained and uncompromising aestheticism could take its very real merits to justify the kind of praise Belloc inundates it with. And since Belloc and Waugh are by no means pure aesthetes, but the devoted and combative adherents of a moralistic faith, their exaggerated praise of Wodehouse is really not concerned with him so much as with the condemnation and discomfiture of less verbally fluent but more morally earnest authors whose moral bias is opposed to their own.

Auden, with his characteristic literary generosity and inclusiveness, gives a good example of a more measured view of Wodehouse. Explaining the difference between being boring and being a bore, he contrasts Wodehouse who is neither with Shakespeare, who is sometimes boring but not a bore, and with Dostoevsky, who is a bore but seldom boring. In the light of the general critical status of Wodehouse it is bold to take him to be naturally comparable to the two giant figures, but Auden is not being insincere or frivolous.

So much for the critical consensus about Wodehouse. I shall pursue my aim of situating him in literature generally, and in the comic tradition in particular, in two ways. On the one hand there is the procedure of working from the top down, from prevailing or widely accepted conceptions of the comic and related literary or sub-literary types; on the other that of working from the bottom up, by considering him in comparison with writers firmly established in the literary canon. In fact I shall follow both procedures together, moving from one to the other: using the definitions to pick our particular instances for consideration and using likely instances to qualify the definitions.

Everyone knows what Aristotle had to say about tragedy, but his views on comedy have not survived. Perhaps that is significant, specifically of the common tendency to question the literary credentials of anything that makes people laugh. A work of the first century BC, the *Tractatus Coislinianus*, purports to fill the gap by describing his views on comedy, but it is really no more than an extrapolation, the result of reversing the sense of the crucial terms in his definition of tragedy. So where tragedy represents noble people succumbing to misfortunes that are only vestigially their fault, comedy represents ignoble people avoiding the worst consequences of their own follies.

Tragedy starts with certain advantages. Its dignified and edifying subject-matter implies that it does not merely occupy its reader's time interestingly or pleasingly; it is also calculated to improve him, to enhance or awaken morally creditable sentiments in him. Comedy, where it answers to the pseudo-Aristotelian definition, ministers to a less admirable appetite, at least to the extent that it does more than amuse: it affords us the unwholesome pleasure of looking down on the follies of others.

In fact the old comedy of Aristophanes fits the definition less well than does the new comedy of Menander and his Roman successors, Plautus and Terence. Aristophanes' comedies are vigorous political satires, attacking identifiable individual targets, and sauced with obscenity. With Menander wronged young women, young men of fashion and revelations of identity which make marriage possible are standard equipment and of a recognisably Wodehousian nature. Aristophanes was not simply out to entertain, nor was Ben Jonson, nor was Shaw. But Menander and the new comedians were not animated by any obvious moral or social purpose. Indeed the Roman new comedians were close to Wodehouse in a further respect. They followed Menander so devotedly that they situated their plays in Greece, even if a little Roman material crept in. Their comedies had a stylised, conventional quality on this account which parallels a measure of sociological unreality in the Drones Club and Blandings Castle.

What I am calling the comic tradition does not have to consist exclusively of works that would count as comedies proper in terms of some fairly exigent definition of the term. I intend to confine it to imaginative writing, and so to rule out funny, laughter-provoking expository works and, at the opposite extreme, books of jokes. In the imaginative domain there is, alongside comedy, overlapping it on some accounts, but never wholly identifiable with it, an array of cognate forms of which the farce and the burlesque are the most important. Farce is what Bergson's theory of laughter most directly applies to, the theory that we laugh when what is living, and meant to act in a plastic, intelligent way, comes to behave mechanically. In farce proper, from Feydeau to Ben Travers, more or less stereotyped and individually undistinctive characters, because they are locked up in themselves and are inadequately aware of the people around them whom they systematically misunderstand, find themselves in problematic situations for which they are unprepared and to which they react with extreme ineptness.

Burlesque, on the other hand (and I am not concerned here with burlesk in the American sense, often with a terminal *k*, and always with naked girls), is a matter of ridicule or mockery of an individual person or of a human type by exaggerated imitation, with particular reliance on the device of having trivial topics talked of in a high and grandiose manner.

There are, undoubtedly, large elements in Wodehouse both of

farce and of burlesque in the interpretations that I have outlined. There is quite a lot of hiding in cupboards and under beds in his narratives. The series of events in which Mr Mulliner's nephew is involved in the story 'The Truth About George', from the moment at which he addresses his fellow-passenger in song in the corridorless train to his taking command of himself in his loved one's cottage and delivering himself of his sublime proposal ('from the unspotted heart of an Englishman'), is paradigmatically farcical. So too are Gussie Fink-Nottle's frightful experiences in his rented Mephistopheles fancy dress.

Burlesque features are prominent in Wodehouse's exaggerated imitations of the conversational idioms of rustic noblemen, avantgarde artists, rich aunts, lady novelists, American millionaires and so forth, on the one hand, and in the grandiloquence with which Jeeves treats topics of the utmost insignificance at the same time as Wooster applies his basic vocabulary, in all its boyish impoverishment, to graver matters, on the other.

But it would be a mistake to infer from these facts that Wodehouse's writings are thus no part of literature proper and are merely material for entertainment purposes of a more or less disposable kind. Elements of farce are by no means absent from the works of those commonly regarded as the masters of comedy. Ubiquitous in the plays of Molière, farce is particularly evident in *Georges Dandin* and *Le Médecin Malgré Lui*. The business with the laundry basket in *The Merry Wives of Windsor* is by no means the only intrusion of farce in Shakespeare, although with him the farcical is neither central nor important. Burlesque, again, is to be found in Molière's *Les Précieuses Ridicules*.

What lies behind the habitual undervaluation of Wodehouse is a general prejudice against what it is no way tendentious to describe as pure comedy: drama or fiction, that is to say, whose dominant intention and effect is to entertain. Against such works the distinct censoriousnesses of moralists and aesthetes combine. Serious comedy, it is implied, comedy sufficiently dignified to be treated as literature rather than mere writing, must either have a morally improving or socially reforming purpose *or* it must be an originally creative exercise of the romantic imagination. The models of these two endorsed kinds are, respectively, Ben Jonson (and, at the historic beginnings of the genre, Aristophanes) and Shakespeare, in particular the Shakespeare of *Midsummer Night's Dream* and of the comedies of his last decade of production from *As You Like It*, *Much Ado* and *Twelfth Night* to *The Tempest* and *The Winter's Tale*.

In his remarkable investigation of literary genres, *Anatomy of Criticism*, the Canadian critic, Northrop Frye, distinguishes four main kinds of narrative structure: comedy, romance, tragedy and satire, associating them, in a somewhat fanciful way, by which we need not be detained, with the seasons of the year from spring to winter. The disparagement of pure comedy to which I have referred amounts, in Frye's terms, to an insistence that comedy, if it is to aspire to true literary status, must approximate either with Aristophanes and Ben Jonson to satire or with the later Shakespeare to romance. A further mode of conceivable literary promotion for comedy lies in its approximation to tragedy in Chekhov. It is not enough that it should delight, it must be morally instructive or imaginatively elevating or, perhaps, in the manner of tragedy, emotionally purgative as well.

I do not wish to dismiss this assumption as merely the expression of some kind of puritan asceticism or sanctimoniousness. We must, of course, always be on guard against the self-mutilating attitude expressed by Auden's celebrated don who announced that he was not quite happy about pleasure. But there is a substantial inductive basis for the comparative disregard for pure comedy. The greatest comic achievements of literature have all been in the impure forms. In claiming Wodehouse for literature I am not trying to rate him as equal to Aristophanes, Shakespeare, Chekhov and Shaw, let alone to rank him above them. My object is the more modest one of securing for him consideration on the same sort of terms that are customarily given to them.

There are two ways in which this object may be more concretely pursued. The first is by showing how close in many ways Wodehouse's work is to that of the acknowledged masters of comedy. Secondly, I shall examine the justice and relevance of the criticisms brought against him by those who would exclude him from literature properly so called, a body that includes many who would readily admit to greatly enjoying him.

The word *comedy* originates in the Greek word for a revel. Etymology is not a very reliable guide to essence, even if it may sometimes be a suggestive one. In this case we should be put on our guard by the fact that the Greek origin for tragedy is goat-song, an item of information that is of very limited critical use. More to the point is the association of tragedy and comedy in early ritual with, in the first case, the slaying of the god as a symbol of the harvest at the end of the vegetative cycle of the year and, in the second, with the riotous rejoicing that heralds the return of vitality.

This ritual origin corresponds to Frye's account of the fundamental structure of comedy. It begins with a young person who is frustrated by parental, or at any rate elderly, obstruction. The action consists in the outwitting or exposure of the obstructing character or characters. In this the hero is frequently assisted by some skilful trickster who makes up for the lack of combative resources entailed by the hero's essential innocence. In the end the society of the narrative reaches a more ideal condition, closer to the desires of ordinary, reasonable people than the artificially regulated state of affairs maintained earlier by the obstructive seniors.

It has often been pointed out, in support of the general line of my argument, that the relationship of Jeeves and Bertie Wooster echoes a long and glorious tradition of comparable partnerships: Sancho Panza and Don Quixote, Leporello and Don Giovanni, Figaro and Almaviva, Sam Weller and Mr Pickwick, Mark Tapley and Martin Chuzzlewit, Zahar and Oblomov, Passepartout and Phileas Fogg, the admirable Crichton and Lord Loamshire, even, pushing out a bit further, the ass and Balaam and Ariel and Prospero. The clever servant or *servus dolosus* was standard equipment in the new comedy of the ancient world.

This is really less important, being a single point of likeness between works of very different kinds, than the structural correspondence between a great part of Wodehouse's mature work and Frye's formula. Wooster is not obstructed by parents but they are amply compensated for by Aunt Agatha and such Freudian surrogate fathers as Sir Roderick Glossop. Others of the sympathetic youthful innocents of Wodehouse's fiction are heavily encumbered with parental authority, buttressed in the English cases by titles and status, in the American ones by large quantities of money and habits of asperity undiluted by considerations of good manners.

To a considerable extent, particularly in the Wooster and Jeeves stories, the liberating subversion of irrational authority is not carried on by the primary team in Wooster's direct interest but because of his unwavering commitment to the chivalric principle that one cannot let down a pal.

The tradition of the *Tractatus Coislinianus* picks out four main character types as proper to comedy. These are the impostors (both conscious and hypocritical and unconscious and self-deluded), the self-depreciators, the buffoons and the boors. Between them they form two pairs of opponents. The impostors seek to control and exploit the self-depreciators; more marginally and ornamentally, the buffoons raise the intensity of the action by wild and extravagant behaviour, while the boors constitute large, insensitive surfaces for the buffoons to throw themselves against and to rebound from.

In their different ways both Wooster and Jeeves are self-deprecators. We have no doubt of Bertie's candour when he observes, 'I mean to say I know perfectly well that I've got, roughly speaking, half the amount of brain a normal bloke ought to possess.' Jeeves's formulas of self-belittlement are, indeed, a professional mannerism. One would be shocked to find him saying, in reply to one of Bertie's admiring comments on the power of his brain and the instant need for its maintenance by a large meal of fish, 'Yes, I was pretty good in there,' like some oaf in Hemingway, instead of his more usual 'One endeavours to give satisfaction, Sir.' But though proud, he is modest, as his genuine regard and affection for his master make clear.

Bertie is by no means as much of a fool as he says and thinks. He is not well-educated and the idiom in which he expresses himself is threadbare. I cannot remember if it is he or a fellow drone who says somewhere 'do you know, I don't know, don't you know', but it is certainly in his style. He is not prudent or calculating. If he were his prodigies of knightly behaviour would never occur. R.D.B. French points out, on this score, that, far from constantly falling in love with girls on his own account, in the eight novels and thirty-four shot stories in which he appears, in twenty-five he is largely concerned with assisting others in their amorous affairs, in twelve he is trying to escape from girls who are pursuing him (usually with some ghastly aunt-like project of amendment in mind) and in only two is positively in love with someone. But he is quite perceptive and, as their association continues, plainly learns a lot from Jeeves. Furthermore, the two principal imitations of Wooster – John Buchan's Archie Roylance and Dorothy Sayers's Lord Peter Wimsey – are both represented by their authors as capable and heroic. Lord Emsworth, however, really is a fool, his mental deficiency being only compatible with the very limited measure of freedom allowed him by his fearful sister, Lady Constance, because of his unenterprising torpidity.

In Wodehouse as in life it is not always easy to draw the line between the hypocrite and the self-deceiver, the conscious and the unconscious impostor. By and large the more socially established or English heavy characters are the more self-deluding, the more self-made or American ones the more hypocritical. That is wholly intelligible. Those who have had deliberately to work for the position in which they can interfere with the desires of others are more likely to maintain the public display of that position with conscious artifice than those who have grown up with their status as part of their apparent natural endowment.

The most notable of Wodehouse's buffoons is Uncle Fred, the 5th Earl of Ickenham. Wodehouse himself describes him as a kind of 'elder Psmith'. He is an earl of misrule who comes from the country to quarter himself on his moderately vapid nephew Pongo and engage in various forms of misconduct which sometimes lead to trouble with the police and magistrate's courts and frequently involve sublime acts of impersonation, for example of Sir Roderick Glossop, nerve-specialist, and of several different people in a short space of time in 'Uncle Fred Flits By'.

Lord Emsworth is something of a boor or churl in the typology of the *Tractatus*, but Ukridge is harder to classify, being a boor who acts in the manner of a buffoon. There is something of him in Nicholas Jenkins's Uncle Giles in Anthony Powell's *The Music of Time*; they certainly share a mass of unreliable lore about how to get on in the world, an indeterminate social position often uneasily remote from the upper reaches of the middle class, and a psycho-pathic lack of awareness of the thoughts, and lack of interest in the feelings, of other people.

There is something mildly Ukridgian in the ancient-mariner-like resolve to dominate a captive audience displayed by those very similar narrators: Mr Mulliner of the Angler's Rest and the Oldest Member. Ukridge essays real sins: theft (lightly disguised as borrowing), lying, betrayal. Mulliner and the Oldest Member are entirely sedentary and act, and can therefore sin, only as narrators. It is a little odd to see how firmly Mulliner has to repress the budding narrative ambitions of his fellow-drinkers, or the Oldest Member shout down the pleas of those he has buttonholed, given the splen-dour of the stories that they both have to tell. Perhaps it is an oblique apology by the always self-depreciating Wodehouse for the volumi-nousness of his literary output.

The two narrators are instances of a well-established literary tradi-tion which is not primarily comic. Dickens tried the device of a narrator with Master Humphry, with his clock, in *The Old Curiosity Shop* and *Barnaby Rudge*, but soon tired of the contraption, which served no useful purpose, and abandoned it. Walter Scott's Jedediah Cleishbotham hangs rather vestigially about in the novels described as *Tales of my Landlord*. The closest parallel to Mulliner and the Oldest Member is really Conrad's Almayer; he, like them, has a char-acter, by no means a wholly admirable one, of his own.

Even more than in the characters, close adherence to the comic tradition is evident in Wodehouse's plots. In all the stories about young men, from Psmith and his attendant Mike through to Wooster and the members of the Drones and Mr Mulliner's superb array of nephews, the ancient struggle of the young against the old in search of love, a modicum of fortune and the power to run their own affairs constitutes the main structure of the action. Impersonation and concealed identities, chases, aberrant behaviour brought on by drink or falling objects, elaborate conspiracies fill the spaces between the chief structural members. Everything formal in Wodehouse's work is traditional, and everything material – by which I mean the date, social status, occupation and personal idiom of the characters – is familiar, either because it is an enhanced version of something in Wodehouse's own experience or because it is a burlesque of some prevailing literary form, usually not a very ambitious one.

In saying this I am led immediately to the first criticism made of Wodehouse, which deplores the unreality or artificiality of his characters and their circumstances. The answer to this is that it is partly false and to the extent that it is true it does not matter. Certainly the events narrated are of the sort which seldom occur and never in the kind of profusion with which he presents them. But there are now, as there were when Wodehouse was young, plenty of vacant young men about, some of them, like Bertie, not quite as vacant as they look. The aunts in Wodehouse are the product of observation not theory, and so are the great narrators: Mulliner and the Oldest Member. Jeeves is, indeed, an idealisation, as, one hopes, are Lord Emsworth and Ukridge. But they are exaggerated versions of something recognisable.

But what is so disastrous about this kind of artificiality, the reliance on a conventional repertoire of characters and incidents? It is not the melodramatic extravagance of Dickens's characters that deserves opprobrium but the frequent sentimentality of their delineation. In his early work there were elements of that in Wodehouse, first manly house prefects and, a bit later, brave young women with roguish smiles. In the mature Wodehouse all that has been smoked out. Bobbie Wickham is brave enough, but more in the style of an S.S. officer than that of a tubercular sempstress. Is its lack of Zolaesque naturalism seen as a weakness of *The Rape of the Lock*? Are pastoral poems taken to task for their inadequacies in the light of the oviculture of their time?

This criticism implicitly invokes a principle so plainly absurd – roughly, that the comic writer must be treated as if he is speaking on oath – that some more serious objection must lie behind it. Given the prominence of Wooster and Blandings in the minimal or everyday understanding of Wodehouse, it is probably the objection that he deals with morally and politically indefensible people, rich and well-born idlers, engaged in trivial activities involving cow-creamers, sexless flirtations, pig competitions, the enticement of French chefs and so forth. In this version the objection is that although Wodehouse's world may be actual to some small extent it is not truly or metaphysically real; it ought not to exist and is not worth thinking about.

Once again, when baldly stated, the principle involved shrivels in the light of critical inspection. Shakespeare's greater comedies are just those which are furthest from the obvious social realities of his own time and place. *The Merry Wives of Windsor* is much closer to *Bartholomew Fair* and to late Elizabethan England than are *The Tempest* and *A Midsummer Night's Dream*. But has it ever seriously occurred to anyone to conceive that that makes it a better play than they are? It must also be acknowledged that by no means all of Wodehouse's fiction is set in the world of the idle rich, which would, in so vast an *oeuvre*, bring on the danger of monotony. Mulliner's world, especially that part of it which falls under the eye of the inde-fatigable Miss Postlethwaite, embraces the entire middle class, even if only in its moments of leisure.

There is some repetition in Wodehouse, not surprisingly in such a large output. He took quite a long time to find his feet as a writer, in this respect being closer to John Cowper Powys than to Rimbaud. But the firm limits he set to the range of human types he would treat and the sorts of circumstances in which he would imagine them constrained him into ever more agile plotting, elegance of diction and economy of style. There are many things we find and enjoy in literature which he does not attempt. Since they include the things in literature that give us deepest satisfaction, any claim to serious literary consideration made on his behalf must be correspondingly limited and qualified. But that claim is not of a different kind from the claims that would confidently be made about many figures in the remoter literary past.

There is another, more specific comic tradition in which Wodehouse can be enlighteningly located. It is that of the amazing efflorescence of popular humorous writing of the late Victorian and Edwardian period. Among its more lasting constituents, in chrono-logical order, are: Anstey's *Vice Versa* (1882), Jerome's *Three Men In A Boat* (1889), Wilde's three-year career as a playwright, begin-ning in 1892, E.F. Benson's *Dodo* (1893), the Grossmith brothers'

*Diary of a Nobody*, Beerbohm's *A Christmas Garland* and Anthony Hope's *Dolly Dialogues* (all 1895, something of an *annus mirabilis*), Somerville's and Ross's *Experiences of an Irish R.M.* (1899), Ernest Bramah's *Kai Lung Unrolls His Mat* (1900), Saki's *Reginald* (1904) and George A. Birmingham's *Spanish Gold* (1908).

Much of this brilliant outpouring of material first appeared before the public in magazines. The first, and most tentative, part of Wodehouse's career coincided with the last, Edwardian, decade of the progression I have sketched. Between 1902 and 1909 he was an active magazine contributor, beginning very soon after he was removed from the Dulwich he found so delightful to the spiritually bleaker environment of the Hong Kong and Shanghai Bank. The school stories, which are the best part of his production during this early stage, were largely published by *The Captain* before their collection in book form. The more dispensable romantic items were only very selectively brought together in books and not until a good deal later. *Love Among The Chickens*, his first true comic novel, in which Ukridge is first revealed, came out in 1906, and was later much and wisely revised.

No very profound sociological penetration is needed to explain this copious effusion of comic literature in and beyond the last years of the nineteenth century. A large increase had taken place in the numbers of people literate and leisured enough to read for the sake of reading, and not for some extraneous practical or devotional purpose. The contrast between the new magazine audience, largely, but not exclusively lower middle class in composition, and the reading habits of all but a fairly contracted élite in the preceding period, is conveniently brought out by the list of Gabriel Oak's books in his shepherd's hut given by Hardy in *Far from the Madding Crowd*, which was published in 1874 and whose action is assigned by F.B. Pinion to some point in the previous four years. It consists of *The Young Man's Best Companion*, *The Farrier's Sure Guide*, *The Veterinary Surgeon*, *Paradise Lost*, *The Pilgrim's Progress*, *Robinson Crusoe*, Ash's *Dictionary*, and Walkingame's *Arithmetic*.

The new magazine-based popular literature of the late Victorian years was not only comic. Another successful development was that of the detective story, pioneered by Wilkie Collins and Dickens but reaching a Wodehousian apogee in the Conan Doyle's saga of Sherlock Holmes. Conan Doyle also contributed substantially to others popular forms: scientific adventure in the Challenger stories, historical romance, both humorous and straight. This was also the epoch of the best ghost story writing, despite its also being a period in which domestic lighting continuously improved. Le Fanu wrote in the 1860s and 1870s; Stevenson in the 1880s; Kipling and Arthur Machen in the 1890s; Algernon Blackwood, M.R. James and Henry James in the Edwardian decade.

On the whole ghost stories have been treated less standoffishly by critics than comic, detective, adventure and science fiction. The most probable reason for that is the extent to which writers who are admired for other, more conventionally respectable, work have contributed to that genre, while the others have to a great extent been in the preserve of specialists. And Wodehouse is, unquestionably, a comic specialist. But should this exclusiveness persist?

It is certainly true that a great deal of completely ephemeral, more or less mechanically imitative stuff has been produced in these marginal genres (most of them, with the exception of the comic, falling within Frye's broad category of romance). But that does not justify the refusal of serious consideration to the exceptional cases in which fine work is produced despite the influence of a particularly voracious and indiscriminating market. Should Wodehouse not be seen in relation to the great flood of comic writing on which he is borne in something like the way Shakespeare is in relation to the very varyingly meritorious theatrical production of the Elizabethan and Jacobean age, much of it churned out to satisfy a coarse and undiscrimating public appetite?

It may be that the reluctance of people of some degree of literary sophistication in general, and of critics in particular, to see Wodehouse, or, for that matter, Simenon and Raymond Chandler, as part of general literature, and thus to be examined and judged in the same way, can be partly explained by a literary habit. This is the practice of more or less affectionate regard for and attention to books that he reader knows are bad, but from which he has to admit he gets pleasure. The words *camp* and *Kitsch* come to mind as apt for describing the attitude and the objects to which it is directed. It is hard to suppose that a fondness for Rider Haggard, Dorothy Sayers or Dornford Yates could be reconciled with a claim to literary taste in any other way.

In these cases the self-indulgent reader knows perfectly well what is wrong with the books he is fond of, but he enjoys them none the less. One way of enjoying them is at one remove, by laughing at them, in the style of Theseus and his equally objectionable sycophants as they watch the groundlings' play in the fifth act of *A Midsummer Night's Dream*. But I suspect that this is more often an outward defence, used to conceal an attraction it would be embarrassing to admit, than a settled and stable point of view.

More usual, I believe, is a positive identification with the more innocent being, often one's younger self, for whom such books represent the highest conceivable level of literary art. In his discussion of 'Good Bad Books' George Orwell lists Sherlock Holmes, *Vice Versa*, *Dracula*, *Helen's Babies* and *King Solomon's Mines* and says: 'All of these are definitely absurd books, books which one is more inclined to laugh *at* than *with*, and which were hardly to be taken seriously even by their authors.' 'Yet', he goes on, 'they have survived and will probably continue to do so... there is such a thing as sheer skill, or native grace, which may have more survival value than erudition and intellectual power.'

This is a sympathetic but inadequate position. *Dracula* and *King Solomon's Mines* are, as he says, books to laugh at, but one would have to be in an extraordinarily confused state of mind to laugh at *Vice Versa*, though a sensible person could fail to laugh with it if he was sufficiently low-spirited, I suppose. Where Orwell has gone wrong here is in running together the psychologically somewhat complex business of enjoying something one knows to be bad, by dint of adopting a special, primitive attitude towards it, with the quite different business of recognising the literary excellence of works in a genre which is disvalued as a whole because so much of what it contains neither aims at nor achieves merit.

In one of the critical remarks about Wodehouse that I quoted at the beginning, Anthony Burgess observes that the humour of Wodehouse's books does not ask for close analysis. It is certainly true that a very great number of people have enjoyed Wodehouse's works without reliance on analytic criticism. It may, nevertheless, be of some interest to look into the manner of working of Wodehouse's humour. I believe that it will show that there is a distinctive and consistent moral outlook behind his writing and that it is not as is often said, even by those who are well disposed towards it, merely 'delightful nonsense'.

I shall concentrate exclusively on the minimum units of Wodehouse's writing, the individual jokes, described by Richard Usborne in his useful compilation as 'nuggets'. A starting point is the fact that a number of the best of these are metaphorical connections of men and animals. For instance, a girl says to Wooster: 'You're a pig, Bertie' and receives the reply 'A pig maybe – but a shrewd, level-headed pig.' At one level this is enjoyable because of the absurdity of ascribing level-headedness, which implies that his condition has been achieved despite the temptations of flightiness, to a creature as sedate, predictable and unenterprising as a pig. But there is a further aspect. The comparison invites us to feel rather more fellowship with the pig than is customary. Something that is ordinarily seen as compensating for its unpleasant appearance and manner of life by supplying us with ham, sausages and the better sort of suitcase is suddenly represented as having its own point of view.

The same latent moral content is also present in an example which might seem at first to be sheer flight of fancy. George Mulliner reports – and his uncle is admittedly inclined to discount it – that when he was running from a crowd of rustics led by a man with a pitchfork 'he distinctly saw a rabbit shoot an envious glance at him as he passed and shrug its shoulders hopelessly'. This serves as an implied reproof to the philosopher Descartes and his followers who suppose animals to be automata and their cries of pain to be no more than the squeaking of an unoiled door.

This duality of point is not universal. There are pure jokes, as remotely abstracted from the general human condition as anything in Mallarmé. For example, 'A certain liveliness was beginning to manifest itself up in the gallery. The raspberry was not actually present, but he seemed to hear the beating of its wings.' This fine image is of the same order as Orwell's Wodehousian fragment from an imaginary article of 1945; 'The Fascist hyena has sung its swan song; the jackboot is cast into the melting-pot.'

But some gentle moral point is conveyed by many of Wodehouse's comparisons within the human domain. This example I have not been able to track down in his works. It may not even be his, but is unquestionably in his manner. It concerns a stockbroker. 'His conduct in the city was calculated to cause raised eyebrows on the fo'c'sle of a pirate sloop.' As well as the pleasure we feel at the vertiginous breadth of the comparison, there is the thought that pirates, for all their faults, are members of the human race, not to be seen as mere blind fists of passion, whirling cutlasses.

Tolstoy maintained that the true value of art lay in its contribution to the enhancement of a sense of human brotherhood. By that somewhat extravagant criterion Wodehouse must stand very high, along with Tolstoy's particular favourite *Uncle Tom's Cabin*. In fact Wodehouse surpasses Harriet Beecher Stowe because he writes with the greatest delicacy and precision and, perhaps, because he is intentionally funny.

It could be argued that in practice Wodehouse was too trusting and uncritically forgiving. If he had been less genial and indulgent he would never have been involved in the broadcasts from Germany that caused him so much trouble. Nor would he have harboured the almost abject amiability which he showed afterwards to the repellent 'Cassandra'. But his general message is always apposite, even if, like other good things, it can be carried to excess.

In his 'Notes on the Comic' W.H. Auden says: 'Among those whom I like or admire, I can find no common denominator, but among those whom I love, I can: all of them make me laugh.' Much humour depends on making men look like fools. A special excellence of Wodehouse is that, over and above his purely literary excellence, he makes fools and knaves look like men.

*Delivered as the Tredegar Memorial Lecture to the Royal Society of Literature on 6 February 1986.*

# Wittgenstein

Wittgenstein, most English-speaking philosophers would agree, is both the most influential and the greatest of twentieth-century philosophers. There are good reasons for questioning both of these judgements, but he is plainly one of the most intriguing and distinctive philosophers of the century. Although the greater part of' what he wrote was composed in German, he still occupies only a very marginal position in the consciousness of continental Europe. However, Suhrkamp Verlag has been publishing his writings since 1960 and in France Pierre Klossowski has translated his two chief books, the *Tractatus Logico-Philosophicus* and the *Philosophical Investigations*.

In the English-speaking philosophical world, in which in many ways, as will be seen, he was very insecurely anchored, he remains the object of a fair-sized and energetically devotional cult, a continuation of the circle of profoundly self-abasing disciples with which he surrounded himself from his return from Austria to Cambridge in 1929 until the end of his life. For most of those outside this dedicated group he is the object of somewhat uneasy, even intimidated, reverence. In Germany his ideas have some circulation through the measure of attention given to them by Apel, but elsewhere in continental Europe he is not much more than a remote and enigmatic oddity. Erich Heller is quite right in classifying him together with Plato, Augustine, Pascal, Kierkegaardd, and Nietzsche as a passionately prophetic thinker, in contrast to such orderly bureaucrats of the intellect as Aristotle, Aquinas, Descartes, Locke, and Kant.[1] Yet it is Aristotle's party who are the paradigms of proper, serious philosophic activity for most philosophers in the English-speaking world and Plato's group who are looked up to and imitated on the far side of the English Channel.

Just how large is Wittgenstein's influence in the part of the world where it is supposed to predominate? For a long time, certainly,

---

1. Erich Heller, 'Ludwig Wittgenstein: Unphilosophical Notes', *Encounter* 13 (September 1959), p. 41.

Russell and Moore were more *conspicuous*. There were excellent reasons for that: they were on the scene earlier, they published more (Russell very much more), they were more accessible.

Moore woke Russell in the late 1890s from the dogmatic slumbers in the bosom of the British version of Hegelian idealism from which he too had only just emerged. The result of their mutual incitement to fresh thought was the remarkable set of writings they published in 1903, which soon installed a new system of ideas at the centre of philosophical attention – realistic about matter and the objects of thought, pluralistic about the contents of reality and so disposed toward an analytic method. It was the year of Russell's *Principles of Mathematics,* of Moore's *Refutation of Idealism* and also his *Principia Ethical* By the time Wittgenstein appeared in Cambridge in 1912, the new Russell–Moore philosophy was well on the way to becoming the prevailing orthodoxy it remained until the second half of the 1930s.

Russell kept up a continuous stream of philosophical publication from 1897 until 1948 and *Human Knowledge,* his last large contribution in the field. After his essay-collection *Philosophical Studies* in 1922, Moore did not publish a book until 1953, when he brought out, as *Some Main Problems of Philosophy,* some lectures he had given in the winter of 1910–11! But during the interwar years there was a steady flow of carefully written and carefully studied articles from him, for the most part contributions to the annual symposia of the Aristotelian Society, at which he was a dominating presence.

Russell was a notable public figure, energetically and very perceptibly involved in all sorts of reforming causes. Excluded physically and, to some extent, spiritually from the academic world, to which he never seriously returned after the First World War, his writings on philosophy still commanded the close attention of academic philosophers. Moore was unknown to the general newspaper-reading public, but by way of his role (unsought by him, it would appear) as spiritual guide to the Bloomsbury group he was at least familiar to the literary intelligentsia.

Wittgenstein remained in Cambridge for less than two years after his arrival there in 1912. Late in 1913 he departed for seclusion in Norway and stayed there until the war came. He did not return to academic life until 1930. The Second World War uprooted him from that and he retired from it altogether in 1947, four years before his death and only three years after coming back to it. Russell was still replying sharply to philosophical critics in the late 1950s. During his life Wittgenstein published only one book, the *Tractatus,* 75 pages of resonant aphorisms, and one article of ten pages, which corrects an error in the book, although it was later disowned by its author (and when it was to be delivered as a talk, Wittgenstein characteristically talked about something else altogether). Only since his death has the great cascade of his writings burst into publication through the obstacle of his ferocious reticence. Their bulk is perhaps magnified by his insistence on having the original German put opposite the English translation, but even if halved they are bulky and there is no apparent end to them.

Wittgenstein kept fiercely to himself and to the very small number of admirers prepared to pay the high cost of securing his tolerance of their company. He attended no conferences and was once seen ostentatiously leaving Cambridge as a train-load of conferring philosophers arrived there. He kept clear of the sociabilities of life in his Cambridge college.

In the face of these differences, it is remarkable that he should have succeeded in dislodging Moore and Russell from the centre of influence as he did in the late 1930s, soon after his return to philosophy and to Cambridge in 1929. However, the contrasts between him and them that have been mentioned are in need of some qualification. Wittgenstein came to Cambridge, at the suggestion of Frege, to study under Russell. As it turned out, it was not long before they were talking philosophically on equal terms and even with Wittgenstein in the ascendant. This process of reversal culminated some time in May 1913, when Wittgenstein had been in Cambridge for less than a year and a half. Russell had been writing a book on the theory of knowledge, modifying and developing some of the ideas in his *Problems of Philosophy*, published in the previous year. He gave Wittgenstein 200 or so pages of manuscript to read and had them returned with some devastating comments. He says in his *Autobiography*, quoting a letter to Ottoline Morrell, 'I saw he was right, and I saw that I could not hope ever again to do fundamental work in philosophy... I became filled with utter despair.'[2]

From then on Russell and Wittgenstein drifted ever further apart. Russell worked to get Wittgenstein released from his prisoner-of-war camp in 1918, arranged for the publication of the *Tractatus* a few years later, and helped to secure attention to it with an introduction that annoyed the author. From this time on, as Russell became more and more consciously hostile to Wittgenstein, it must be admitted

2. Bertrand Russell, *The Autobiography of Bertrand Russell* (3 vols, Boston, 1967–9), 2: 57.

that his philosophical power and originality waned and he published nothing of importance on the subject between 1926 and 1940. In short, when they were close Russell soon became more intellectually dependent on Wittgenstein than the other way round, and it may well be that Wittgenstein's confidence-destroying criticism of Russell helped to drive Russell from the subject at just the time Wittgenstein was coming back to it.

Moore, equally, was not really in a position to obstruct the influence of Wittgenstein. In the first place, although he kept active, with a thin but steady flow of small publications, from about 1910 he appears to have been largely content to repeat himself, a procedure simplified but in no way obscured by the extravagant repetitiveness of his style, a heavy-footed parody of plain statement. Most of what he had to say on his three subjects of sense-perception, the concept of goodness, and the nature of philosophical analysis had been said by 1912 and he did not manage to advance materially beyond the inconclusive positions he had reached by that time. He retained an influence, in many ways stronger than Russell's, but it was less for what he had to say than for his manner of saying it. It is worth noticing that a number of the most loyal and intimate Wittgensteinians wrote in Moore's plodding style, among them Norman Malcolm and Morris Lazerowitz.

In the ten years after 1929 Moore and Wittgenstein were colleagues in Cambridge, inevitably close colleagues since they were in the same minute philosophy department and also, much less significantly, in the same very large college. They got on well. Moore attended Wittgenstein's lectures and expressed his respect in suitably humble terms. He tugs his forelock in an autobiographical essay: 'I soon came to feel that he was much cleverer at philosophy than I was, and not only cleverer, but also much more profound, and with a much better insight into the sort of inquiry which was really important and best worth pursuing, and into the best method of pursuing such inquiries.'[3] Moore, then, had nothing new to say on his own account and was honestly content to join the small but gifted and determined band of Wittgenstein's votaries.

The received view about Wittgenstein's influence is that it lay behind the two most important philosophical movements in the English-

3. P.A. Schilpp, ed, *The Philosophy of G.E. Moore*, 3rd edn (LaSalle, Ill., 1968), p. 33.

speaking world in the fifty years since the early 1930s. His ideas are the ultimate substance of, first, logical positivism and then, after his return to the subject, of the linguistic philosophy so triumphant in the early postwar years and still far from extinct. Logical positivism is not exactly an English-speaking phenomenon, but then neither exactly was Wittgenstein. It began in Vienna in the 1920s, after Schlick's arrival there in 1922 to take up a chair in the philosophy of the inductive sciences. Soon a group around him had turned into an institution, issuing manifestos, publishing a series of important books, producing, in conjunction with some like-minded Berliners, the review *Erkenntnis*. It was anxious to internationalise itself still further, conscious of the diverse national origins of those it actually recognised as its intellectual ancestors, and did so by means of conferences at which allies outside Austria and Germany were fortified to spread the new gospel. Ayer in Britain, Quine and Nagel in the United States, Rougier (less successfully) in France brought back the exciting message. What they had to say was soon amplified by the members of the original circle, expelled by fascism for the liberal, cosmopolitan character of their thought and conduct and, in many cases, simply because they were Jewish.

Just how far was Wittgenstein the ultimate inspirer of the logical positivism of the Vienna Circle? One way of testing this claim is to consider the role he and his ideas play in the works of the acknowledged leaders of the movement. As regards Schlick, there is no mention of Wittgenstein in the text of his chief publication, *Allgemeine Erkenntnislehre,* in its second edition of 1925, and there is none in the first volume of his papers, those written between 1909 and 1922. It must have been about this time that Schlick encountered Wittgenstein's *Tractatus* and was bewitched by it. Schlick was about 43 at the time and, one might say, fully formed intellectually. In the excitement of his encounter first with Wittgenstein's work and then with the man himself, he may well have exaggerated the change it wrought in him. He certainly acquired some ideas from Wittgenstein, in particular the view, highly questionable in itself and undesirable in its practical consequences (for it serves handily as a way of evading criticism), that philosophy 'is not a theory but an activity.' Schlick's friend, Herbert Feigl, suggests also that the realism that Schlick abandoned, as being emptily metaphysical, after falling under Wittgenstein's spell was at least partly dropped because of Wittgenstein's influence.

The other main figure in logical positivism was Rudolf Carnap. With the rest of the circle he discussed Wittgenstein's *Tractatus* in

1924/25 and met him personally in 1927. In Carnap's first important book, *Der logische Aufbau der Welt,* there are a few references
to Wittgenstein, specifically to his views about the analysability of
such intentional contexts as 'I believe that it is raining' and about
the limits of knowledge and significant discourse. On the second,
anti-metaphysical point, Carnap's position is really very much
opposed to that of Wittgenstein. Carnap's 'There is no question
whose answer is in principle unattainable by science' is much like
Wittgenstein's 'If a question can be put at all, then it can also be
answered.' But Wittgenstein goes on, 'We feel that even if all possible
scientific questions are answered, the problems of life still have not
been touched at all.'

Reflecting on his relations with Wittgenstein a quarter of a century
later, Carnap admitted that he had not understood Wittgenstein's
position: 'I had erroneously believed that his attitude toward metaphysics was similar to ours. I had not paid sufficient attention to the
statements in his book, because his feelings and thoughts in this area
were too divergent from mine.' He says of himself and Schlick:

> Our attitude toward philosophical problems was not very
> different from that which scientists have towards their prob-
> lems... Wittgenstein, on the other hand, tolerated no critical
> examination by others, once the insight had been gained by an
> act of inspiration. I sometimes had the impression that the
> deliberately rational and unemotional attitude of the scientist
> and likewise any ideas which had the flavour of 'enlightenment'
> were repugnant to Wittgenstein.

And finally, 'All of us in the Circle had a lively interest in science and
mathematics. In contrast to this, Wittgenstein seemed to look upon
these fields with an attitude of indifference and sometimes even with
contempt.'[4]

Carnap, then, soon realised the gap between his ideas, and those
generally characteristic of the Vienna Circle, and, on the other side,
the ideas of Wittgenstein. Schlick spent the last ten years of his life
as a close adherent of Wittgenstein, but his main positivistic views
had been formed already. Other members and associates of the Circle
were, with one exception, even less involved. Reichenbach barely
mentions him apart from a very occasional reference to his theory

---

4. P. A. Schilpp, ed., *The Philosophy of Rudolf Carnap* (LaSalle, Ill., 1963), pp. 24–9.

of necessary truth and, unfavourably, to his inductive scepticism. Neurath, according to a pupil, 'made frequent interjections "Metaphysics!", during the Circle's reading and discussion of Wittgenstein's *Tractatus,* to the irritation of Moritz Schlick.'[5] Popper, not in the Circle but not far from it, was from the first an outspoken critic of what he saw as Wittgenstein's irrationalism and oracular posturing.

The exception mentioned was the unfortunate Friedrich Waismann, who, with Schlick, was personally closest to Wittgenstein and spent many years fruitlessly trying to keep up with Wittgenstein's demands for revision of a book he was trying to compose about Wittgenstein's philosophy. It came out finally in 1965, six years after Waismann's death.[6]

So far Wittgenstein's relation to the Vienna Circle has been considered from a comparatively superficial, biographical point of view. More crucial than what those involved thought or said about the matter is the extent to which the actual doctrines and arguments of logical positivism come from Wittgenstein.

The main theses of logical positivism are the 'elimination of metaphysics' that follows from limiting significance to utterances that report matters of fact or that exemplify formal relations between concepts; the theory that all factual propositions can be reduced to basic propositions that are somehow directly connected with experience; the theory that the necessary truths of logic and mathematics are factually empty and 'say nothing about the world', and the view that philosophy proper is concerned with the logical analysis of meaning. Most logical positivists agreed with Carnap that judgements of value are not propositions, capable of being true or false, but are noncognitive, commands, as Carnap himself thought, or expressions of feeling.

There is something corresponding to each of these five doctrines in the *Tractatus.* There is a page at the very end where metaphysical utterances are held to be meaningless. The principle of reducibility is affirmed strongly in the claim that all propositions are truth-functions of basic or elementary propositions. The basic propositions themselves are declared to be pictures of facts. The thesis that necessary truth is analytic or, as Wittgenstein puts it, 'tautological' is

5. Otto Neurath, *Empiricism and Sociology,* eds Marie Neurath and Robert S. Cohen (Dordrecht, 1973), p. 82.
6. The story is told in my introduction to Friedrich Waismann, *Philosophical Papers,* ed. Brian McGuinnes (Dordrecht, 1977).

neatly and graphically conveyed by a technique of showing that what is logically true is true whatever assumptions are made about the truth or falsity of its components (a formal realisation of the idea of being true in all possible worlds). As for philosophy, 'all philosophy is "critique of language"', the object of philosophy is the logical clarification of thoughts. 'Philosophy is not a theory but an activity... The result of philosophy is not a number of "philosophical propositions", but to make propositions clear.' Finally, 'there can be no ethical propositions', 'ethics cannot be expressed'.[7]

Nevertheless, in the form in which these views were held by the logical positivists there were sources for them closer than Wittgenstein. For them the most important antimetaphysician was Ernst Mach, the first holder in Vienna of the chair occupied by Schlick, who expounded an antimetaphysical reductivism in his *Analysis of Sensations* in 1886. And where Wittgenstein left the concrete character of the basic factual propositions open, Mach, in the tradition of Hume, firmly identified them with reports of the subjective experience of observers. Wittgenstein's account of logical necessity benefited from his invention of truth-tables, but the idea that such necessity is formal or verbal in nature is clearly stated by Hume, and in the work of Frege the analytic nature of arithmetic is powerfully argued for.

Hobbes and Locke had both subscribed to a nominalistic view of logic, conceiving its subject matter as essentially verbal. At times Locke treats philosophy as a natural science of the human mind, for example where he speaks of his 'historical plain method' of inquiry into the understanding in the introduction of his *Essay*. And the attack on innate ideas in Book I is carried on as an investigation of straightforward psychological fact. But in the *Essay's* final chapter he distinguishes inquiry into signs from the study of things (physical or mental) and the study of right action, and, since signs include both words and ideas, most of what has gone before falls under this head.

Even if philosophy as practised by the older British empiricists from Hobbes to Mill carried out its conceptual inquiries in too psychologistic a way, by reason of their view that concepts are psychic entities, of the nature of images, a very clear and explicit subscription to the method of extricating the logical from the psychological was to hand in the work of Frege, both as precept and as practice. Carnap had studied with Frege at Jena between 1910 and

---

7. Ludwig Wittgenstein, *Tractatus Logico-Philosophicus*, translated by D. F. Pears and B. F. McGuinness (New York, 1963), prop. 4.0031.

1914, when Wittgenstein was only making his first steps in philosophy.

There is no doubt that ideas corresponding to those of the Vienna Circle are to be found in Wittgenstein's *Tractatus* and that some members of the Circle had a measure of reverence for him, even if others did not. But the shared ideas could have been acquired from other sources and, it seems reasonable to suppose, largely were. The importance of the *Tractatus* was not as a source of new ideas for the Vienna Circle but as an encouragingly independent endorsement of the ideas it already had.

The encouragement was perhaps magnified by the exaggerated fashion in which the shared ideas are expressed in the *Tractatus*. To the extent that he was a positivist, Wittgenstein was a positivist at the top of his voice. Vanity and hysteria seem to have co-operated in making him repress the thought that he could possibly be wrong. Wittgenstein's exaggerations include the view that everything except the 'propositions of natural science' is literally senseless and that the propositions of traditional philosophy are senseless, not in the manner of logical truths as being void of factual content, but in the fullest possible fashion, as altogether without meaning, mere nonsense. At first this version of antimetaphysics was an agreeably iconoclastic way of securing attention for the Circle's ideas. Eventually it became an embarrassment, a nihilistic tin-can tied to the tail of a respectably liberal and enlightened bandwagon.

A less publicly tiresome Wittgensteinian extravagance was the theory that the truths of logic are tautologies. What the Circle defensibly believed is that the truths of logic are at bottom identical propositions. In its everyday meaning a tautology is a *blatantly obvious* identical proposition, something that is true of only a handful of the truths of logic. In the particular meaning that Wittgenstein seems mainly to have intended the word to be understood, a tautology is a proposition that can be shown to be true in all possible worlds by a mechanical decision-procedure. The claim that all truths of logic are tautologies in that sense has been proved to be false (by Alonzo Church in 1936).

A comment of Kolakowski's about Marx is appropriate here:

> Marx at times enunciated his theory in extreme, dogmatic and unacceptable forms. If his views had been hedged round with all the restrictions and reservations that are usual in rational thought, they would have had less influence and might have gone unnoticed altogether. As it was, and as often happens with

humanistic theories, the element of absurdity was effective in transmitting their rational content.[8]

So far attention has been fixed on the ideas shared by the Vienna Circle and the Wittgenstein of the *Tractatus*. But each party to this relationship had ideas and interests that it did not share with the other. At the concrete level of specific doctrines, as distinct from conceptions of method and of the purpose of philosophy, of its place in culture, the most important logical positivist view that is nowhere present in the *Tractatus is* what might be called experientialism. This is the view that the basic propositions of any system of knowledge or rational belief must be descriptions of the immediate subjective experience of the believer.

To be accurate, this was at most a majority opinion among the members of the Circle. Schlick held firmly to it. It was central to Carnap's early theory of knowledge, in particular to *Der logische Aufbau der Welt,* although he was converted to the view that basic propositions are descriptions of intersubjectively observable material objects in the mid-1930s by Popper and Neurath (who agreed on this if on little else). Ayer propagated the experientialist view in the English-speaking world, where it attached itself comfortably to the old empiricist tradition still very much alive in the theories of perception of Russell and H.H. Price.

However, the alternative, physicalist theory of basic propositions of the later Carnap and Popper was even further from the *Tractatus* than experientialism. Whatever Wittgenstein's ultimate propositions of fact were, they were like nothing in ordinary discourse. They appear to consist of names alone and to refer to points in space. In the late 1920s, when Wittgenstein was involved in regular discussions with select members of the Circle, he seems to have moved some way toward their theory of the basic propositions. But this 'positivist interlude', as Peter Hacker convincingly calls it in showing the dishonesty of Wittgenstein's later denials of any such thing, did not last very long.[9]

Another major concern of the logical positivists was with the inductive or probable reasoning they held to be the other pillar, alongside its empirical basis, sustaining the rationality of natural science. In the *Tractatus* there are some interesting pages in which

8. Leszek Kolakowski, *Main Currents of* Marxism (3 vols, Oxford, 1978), 3: 524.
9. P. M. S. Hacker, *Insight and Illusion: Wittgenstein on Philosophy and the Metaphysics of Experience* (Oxford, 1972), ch. 4, sec. 4.

the 'law of causality' is interpreted as a Kantian a priori intuition of the form of the propositions of natural science. At another place there is a brisk, objection-ignoring sketch of what has come to be called the range theory of probability.

The main tendency of the Vienna Circle was toward a very different account of probability, that which defines it in terms of observed frequencies and not in terms of alternatives discriminated a priori. Reichenbach and von Mises both elaborated carefully detailed systematisations of the frequency theory, as, at his usual distance, did Popper. For all the *Tractatus*'s occasional genuflections toward the 'propositions of natural science', there is remarkably little concern in it with two of their salient features, their generality and their incomplete justifiability.

Finally, on this score, the Vienna Circle concerned itself to quite a considerable extent with its updated version of the mind-body problem – the problem of the relations between physics and psychology. In the *Aufbau,* Carnap reduced the minds of others to the observable behaviour of their bodies and then reduced the latter to patterns in the private experience of the observing subject. Later, in the epoch of physicalism, the former reduction was endorsed. Although the problem of other minds was to be crucial in Wittgenstein's later philosophy, the only reference to the mind in the *Tractatus* is in a pregnantly obscure discussion of solipsism where he affirms both the truth and the unsayability of 'the world is my world'.

If the doctrines and concerns of the logical positivism to which nothing much corresponds in the *Tractatus* are substantial, the contents of the latter which were ignored by the Vienna Circle form an even larger portion of the whole. The most obtrusive of these neglected Wittgensteinian items is his picture theory of meaning. The logical positivists seem never to have wavered from the rather obviously correct view that the relation of language to the bits of the world it is applied to is conventional. They also, perhaps naively, took Wittgenstein to be denying this and so took themselves to be in disagreement with him.

There are crepuscular developments of the picture theory which are ignored even more thoroughly. One of these is the idea that the picture must share something called a form of representation with what it is a picture of in order to represent it. Another is the theory that, in the ultimate analysis, a sentence consists of object-naming words. There is much attention in the *Tractatus* to something called the 'general form of truth-function (or proposition)'. These matters are not only ignored by the Vienna Circle but by everyone else except the devoted band of commentators on the *Tractatus*. On that group alone have they exerted any influence. But to the extent that the commentators have done other philosophical work, the influence has not got through to it, remaining confined, in perfect doctrinal quarantine, to the commentaries.

Carnap was probably representative of most of the Circle in his lack of sympathy for the mystical side of the *Tractatus*. Apart from a somewhat formal or ceremonial endorsement by Schlick, Wittgenstein's view that 'philosophy is not a theory but an activity' was simply ignored. The idea on which that rule of procedure was based is that philosophy, even the good philosophy of the *Tractatus*, tries to say what can only be shown. There is an echo of that in the rather widespread conviction of leading members of the Circle in the mid-1930s that any attempt to talk about the relations between language and the world must be metaphysical and senseless. This led to Carnap's attempt to carry on philosophy or the 'logic of science' in a purely syntactical way, as a matter of a logical relations between expressions, and to the coherence theory of truth defended by Neurath and Hempel for a while. They took themselves to be released from this self-denying ordinance by the work of Tarski, with his arguments for the scientific legitimacy of semantics, studying the relation of words to the things denoted by them, and the correspondence theory of truth which was the first, nourishing fruit of the new discipline.

There is a vast difference of style between the *Tractatus* and the writings of the logical positivists. Where the latter are objective to the point of impersonality, with arguments fully set out, terms defined or explained, every effort made to achieve clarity, and the whole approximated as far as possible to a textbook of mathematics or physics on conventional lines, the *Tractatus* is a wilful sequence of gnomic sayings, often with no visible argumentative connection at all between them, only a certain community of unelucidated terms of which all that is reasonably clear is that they are not being used in their familiar senses. These sibylline properties make the *Tractatus* an ideal topic for the commentators and exegetes.

This difference of style can be expanded into a difference of a more or less ideological kind. Wittgenstein makes clear in his letters to Engelmann (although it may be that he is no more candid here than he is generally when talking about what he is or has been up to) that what really concerns him is *what cannot be said*. He is known to have been much affected by a devotional work of Tolstoy's, picked up in the ruins of a Galician village during the First World War. Broadly speaking, Wittgenstein was a religious pessimist, with no formal creed but a strong negative attitude to the world and the flesh, convinced of the deep-seated wickedness of men and the absurdity of expecting much of them.

The logical positivists, despite the bogus trappings of nihilistic destructiveness, of an almost Mongol antagonism to ancient decencies and pieties, were in fact liberal-minded people of the utmost seemliness, believers in the possibility of progress under the guidance of scientific knowledge. Positivists, Kolakowski has written, are

> convinced that their programme is eminently educational; it is a call to tolerance, moderation, restraint, and responsibility for one's own words... They represent a humanitarian protest against a world entangled in bloody conflicts and are convinced that spreading the so-called scientific attitude is an effective antidote to the madness of the ideologists.[10]

Nothing could be further from Wittgenstein's deepest feelings about man and life. He was in constant fear of going mad, talked frequently of committing suicide (two of his brothers killed themselves) and may have attempted it. He was liable to behave in a ludicrous fashion. Believing that riches were evil, he gave his own away, but only to his rich relations, on the ground that, being rich already, they could not be further corrupted. Presumably homosexual in disposition (the 'three words' of the dedication of the *Tractatus* to a male friend must have been 'Ich liebe dich'), he was not made for happiness. He extorted absolute subservience from his votaries and treated them cruelly. One, a young man of humble origin who had achieved a post of distinction at Cambridge by hard work, was told he was no good and should go and work in a factory. He did, and was heard of no more.

As far as his first philosophy is concerned, then, I do not believe that Wittgenstein had much influence. To the extent that his ideas are much the same as those of the positivists, the latter almost certainly got them from other sources and relied on his agreement with them simply for moral support after the event. His versions of these shared ideas are usually advanced in an exaggerated and fairly easily refutable form. Much of what he concerned himself with in

10.  Leszek Kolakowski, *The Alienation of Reason: A History of Positivist Thought* (Garden City, N.Y., 1968), p. 204.

the *Tractatus* had no discernible effect on the positivists or on anyone else apart from his scholarly commentators, and on them only when they were expounding his thought. More generally his method of expressing himself was objectionably oracular but, happily, little imitated. His general outlook had nothing to do with the mood of disillusioned secular hopefulness with which logical positivism was associated, the larger, non-treacherous part of the intellectuals' popular front of the interwar epoch. Beside Carnap with his interest in Esperanto and belief in international understanding, Wittgenstein displays the gloomy fanaticism and unintelligibility of a dervish.

After 1929 Wittgenstein devoted the two decades that remained to him to the development of a very different system of philosophy. It is still concerned with the same central topic: the relation of language (and therefore of the thought that is not possible without language) and the world. Also Wittgenstein did not waver from his old conviction that 'there are no philosophical propositions.' Now, in the *Philosophical Investigations,* he says, 'We may not advance any kind of theory... We must do away with all *explanation,* and description alone must take its place.'[11] In the *Tractatus* he had said, 'Philosophy is not one of the natural sciences,' and in the *Investigations,* 'Our considerations could not be scientific ones.'

The comparison of his later philosophy with psychotherapy, a long-drawn-out process of relieving puzzlement or mental cramp, not by direct statement, but by the assembling of reminders of how language actually works so as to dispel the bewitching hold of misleading analogies, is quite a long way from the *Tractatus*'s view of itself as a self-destructive device. But philosophy remains activity, not theory. However, the content of the two philosophies, as distinct from their main topic and their antitheoretical presupposition, is utterly opposed. The logical atomist principle of the exact reducibility of all significant discourse to absolutely simple propositions about absolutely simple objects is rejected and replaced by the conception of language as loose federation of particular language-games, established linguistic practices with distinctive purposes, pursued by distinctive rules or modes of working. Against the positivist dogma of verifiability Wittgenstein urged the obvious but still important truth that making statements of verifiable fact is only one

11. Ludwig Wittgenstein, *Philosophical Investigations,* translated by G. E. M. Anscombe (New York, 1959), par. 109.

of the uses to which language can be put. Other uses, not exactly unfamiliar to grammarians and students of language generally, of emotional expression, of incitement to action, of interrogation and so on, are just as meaningful as statement in that they are governed by rules that have to be learned and are subject in some measure to the constraints of logic.

A casualty here is the picture theory of the *Tractatus*. Despite the protestations of Anthony Kenny at the conclusion of his excellently lucid and well-informed book on Wittgenstein, the view that a meaningful sentence is a tool or instrument with a use or variety of uses, within the context of an established social arrangement, a 'form of life', is about as contrary as it could be to the view of a sentence as a picture, reflecting a concatenation of objects to a pure logical intellect.

In the *Tractatus* the formal logic of Frege and Russell is seen as revealing the essential structure of all language. Later Wittgenstein asserts that language has no essence; variety, not uniformity, is what is really to be found in it. Precipitate attempts to generalise about its workings lead to the typically philosophical kind of puzzlement, in which there seem to be reasons for asserting something, some paradoxical thesis, that we know in our hearts must be false.

The claim that language is a nonsystematic accumulation of instruments used for a great variety of distinct purposes is not very interesting, even if it has to be said to correct the errors of monolithic theorists. Wittgenstein admits this. 'If one tried to advance *theses* in philosophy, it would never be possible to question them, because everyone would agree to them.'[12] It is a kind of admonitory throat-clearing before the proper, concrete business of alleviating puzzlement.

There is, of course, plenty of such solid matter in the later Wittgenstein. It is here, indeed, that the later philosophy attends to subject matter barely considered in the *Tractatus,* above all in the philosophy of mind but also problems about knowledge and certainty. Other concrete issues are more intraphilosophical, as critical of Wittgenstein's own earlier beliefs: the distinction of meaning from naming, the rejection of absolute simples. A new idea, perhaps more calculated to relieve the puzzlement of academic philosophers than of ordinary thoughtful people, is the theory that general words apply to the things that they do, not because of a single common property of those things, but through a family resemblance between them.

12.  Ibid, par. 128

In the briefest possible terms the later philosophy of Wittgenstein comprises a purpose (the relief of puzzlement generated by linguistic misunderstanding), a method (the removal of the misunderstanding by assembling reminders of the way in which language actually works), and applications of the method, most notably to the questions of meaning (which is neither the relation of a name to its bearer nor that of a general term to a Platonic universal) and of mental life (which is not a matter of inner events, inscrutable to outside observers). In each case, the subject is opened up or publicised. The meaning of an expression is not a privately apprehended relation between it and some item in the world; it is its place in an established social practice of utterance. A mental state, like understanding something heard or feeling a pain, is not a secret episode, which others can at best guess at; it is inextricably implicated with the public activities and circumstances of the person who has it, with the verbal and other performances which reveal understanding; with the wounds, cries, and backings-away of the sufferer.

This publicised, more or less behaviouristic, account of meaning and mind is neither too obvious to state nor impossible to state (although it is hard to state clearly because here, as so often, Wittgenstein uses fairly ordinary terms such as *criterion* and *grammar* in unexplained senses of his own). It is fairly original in general and wholly original in detail. By that I mean that accounts of meaning and mind that do not rely on abstract semantic entities in the first case and on private inner states in the latter had been put forward before Wittgenstein's later period. Pragmatism in general and Dewey in particular had anticipated his publicisation of things usually treated as somehow esoteric, A possible source of influence here is F. P. Ramsey, one of the only philosophers Wittgenstein respected and from whom, indeed, he was even ready to accept reproof. (Ramsey said about Wittgenstein's theory of the unsayable, 'What we can't say we can't say, and we can't whistle it either.'[13]) Ramsey had been much impressed by the first writings of Peirce to become readily available to British readers (Morris Cohen's selection, *Change, Love and Logic,* published in the same year as the *Tractatus).*

The valuable side of the detailed originality of Wittgenstein's later thought about meaning and mind is that it respects the specific peculiarities of the objects of its investigation. But there is a cost to be paid. There are controlling principles to be found in the inconclu-

13. F. R. Ramsey, *The Foundations of Mathematics and Other Logical Essays* (New York, 1931), p. 238.

sive ramblings of Wittgenstein about the will, understanding, sensations, and a host of other mental phenomena, but he does not bring
them to the surface. There is seldom more than a thematic connection displayed by him between one of his typographically separated
paragraphs and its neighbours. This mode of presentation in printed
form as well as style is called on to avoid any sort of definiteness.
Where summary is inescapable, for example in introducing what he
is talking about, he resorts to devices of evasion. *In many cases,* he
says, or *in a large class of cases,* if he is feeling very bold; or perhaps
*often;* at his most defeated-seeming, *sometimes.* It is as if he were
nauseated by the idea of generalisation in philosophy and so put all
his great intellectual and literary skill to the task of concealing the
fact that generality is essential to the interest of rational discourse.
Even at its most poetic, in the aphoristic form he was most happy
in, philosophy is still general, saying something about the one world
all its readers inhabit or about the common aspects of the human
nature they share.

It is often said that the philosophy of the later Wittgenstein is the
chief influence on what is called 'linguistic philosophy'. A distinction needs to be drawn here. From 1945 until the 1960s, there was
a moderately self-conscious movement of ordinary language philosophers whose centre was the comparatively very large philosophical
community of Oxford. That 'Oxford philosophy', as I shall call it,
was administratively and, as it were ceremonially, headed by Ryle.
Its most exquisite practitioner was J. L. Austin. It was a much larger
and more impressive affair than the true Wittengensteinian church,
which is a quite different body altogether. But the Oxford philosophy of Ryle and Austin no longer exists as a movement, whereas
the Wittgensteinians proper are still in being as a self-conscious
party.

Both of these groups should be distinguished from a number of
very able philosophers who are great admirers and champions of
Wittgenstein but show little or no influence of his ideas in their work.
The most notable of them are Professor G. H. Von Wright of
Helsinki, Professor Michael Dummett of Oxford, and Professor
Peter Geach, until recently at Leeds in England. Von Wright is a
latter-day Carnapian, whose work shows no trace of Wittgenstein's
influence whatever. Dummett and Geach are, above all, Fregeans.
Frege was the philosopher Wittgenstein held in the greatest explicit
respect. But he deviated from Frege in a way that Dummett and
Geach have not. The admiration of these distinguished philosophers
is plainly sincere, but it seems to have no discernible effect on their

ways of going about the subject. All are committed to rigorous argument and express themselves within the intellectual constraints definitive of professionalism in the domain of formal logic.

On them, then, Wittgenstein has had no direct philosophical influence. But he did influence Oxford philosophy, although very much less than is usually supposed. The most obvious receptacle and further disseminator of Wittgenstein's later ideas is Ryle's much more intelligible *Concept of Mind*. In being made broadly accessible in Ryle's forceful, concrete, and entertaining prose, Wittgenstein's thought underwent a transforming simplification. Ryle's identification of mental states with the dispositions of their possessors to behave in certain ways in certain hypothetical circumstances is a much blunter resolution of the other-minds problem than Wittgenstein's elaboration of the much-interpreted motto, 'Inner processes stand in need of outward criteria.' Ryle's bold assertion that volitions or acts of will are mythical is unsophisticatedly categorical by comparison with Wittgenstein's account of the difference between one's raising one's arm and one's arm going up.

But for all the difference of tone, there can be no doubt that Ryle's philosophy of mind is a transcription of his understanding of the later Wittgenstein's views in the same field of interest. Ryle enthusiastically endorsed Wittgenstein's later theory of meaning, but he did not accept the idea that there are no philosophical propositions and he always remained a reductive sort of philosophical analyst in the manner of Russell or, for that matter, the Wittgenstein of the *Tractatus*.

There is a difference of fundamental outlook lying behind the difference between their prose styles: Ryle's bluff, breezy, unceremonious, and jocular; Wittgenstein's consciously elegant and melodious, conveying a strong belief in the depth and seriousness of the problems under discussion. Where Wittgenstein sees philosophical problems, for all their roots in linguistic misunderstanding, as profound and with consequences for life as a whole, Ryle persistently refers to them not as problems but as puzzles or even 'brain-teasers', 'posers', and 'riddles', assimilating them to devices for whiling away the idleness of energetic minds. Philosophy, Wittgenstein declared, 'leaves everything as it is'. He did not really mean that, but Ryle did.

Austin did not find it easy to take Wittgenstein altogether seriously. There was an overheated, absurdly foreign quality about Wittgenstein's intellectual manner which he thought ridiculous. Like Ryle, he was brought up in the atmosphere of an Edwardian reaction against Hegelian idealism in Oxford that was initiated by John

Cook Wilson and most ably and pertinaciously developed by H. A. Prichard. Ryle and Austin had had thorough training in Greek and Latin and their concern with what it is correct to say has a school-masterly character, a touch of the error-detecting red pencil, about it. Both Ryle and Austin conceived the kind of philosophical inquiry they were making into language as in principle systematic. Ryle called what he did a study of the 'logical geography' of concepts; Austin called what he did 'linguistic phenomenology or rational grammar'.

In sum, although Ryle owed a lot to Wittgenstein, he submitted what he took from him to a large digestive change. With a strong intellectual personality of his own and much repelled by the syco-phancy and cringing that prevailed in Wittgenstein's circle, he had means and reason for keeping his distance. Austin seems almost wholly independent of Wittgenstein. Their Oxford philosophy lost its specific identity after Austin's death, but the gap thus opened was not filled by the ideas of Wittgenstein. Wittgenstein's writings provide a seemingly inexhaustible educational and hermeneutic pabulum. But the doctrines that excite positive enthusiasm, rather than reverent study and exposition, are of American origin for the most part, those of Quine and Davidson, Putnam and Nozick.

There remains the sect of true or orthodox Wittgensteinians. This was a dangerous loyalty in Wittgenstein's lifetime. Excom-munication was easy to incur. As untimid a person as Professor Anscombe produced the following abject footnote: 'Everywhere in this paper I have imitated his ideas and his methods of discussion. The best that I have written is a weak copy of some features of the original, and its value depends only on my capacity to understand and use Dr. Wittgenstein's work.'[14] To the extent that Wittgenstein's work is of value, gratitude is due to those willing to endure an atmos-phere in which the quoted obeisance seemed natural.

The first of the devotees was John Wisdom, who from the late 1930s was a leading source of information about the direction of Wittgenstein's thinking. As it turned out, the information was a little flawed. Wisdom is a colourful and arresting writer, too imaginative to serve as a perfect medium. Nevertheless, his problems were Wittgenstein's, as was the apparently interminable method he had

14. C. E. M. Anscombe, 'The Reality of the Past', in Max Black, ed., *Philosophical Analysis: A Collection of Essays* (Englewood Cliffs, N.J., 1963), p. 53.

of dealing with them. He arrived at a conception of his own about the nature of philosophical problems as being intellectually irresolvable and to be settled only by a decision.

In the United States several of Wittgenstein's pupils have had distinguished philosophical careers, notably Professors Norman Malcolm, Alice Ambrose, and Morris Lazerowitz – at positions increasingly remote from that of their teacher. Professor O. K. Bouwsma carried the dialectical inconsequentiality of Wittgenstein's mode of writing to previously undreamed of lengths, sometimes very amusingly. Numerous able philosophers of a younger generation would not, I imagine, object to being labelled Wittgensteinians. The chief parallel group in Britain is largely composed of people who teach or have taught at the university of Swansea. They have exploited Wittgenstein's view that 'philosophy leaves everything as it is', and that a form of life can be understood only from the inside, to maintain that it is impossible to understand a society different in its institutions and customs from one's own (and, therefore, impossible to criticise its customs in the light of some objective standard of rationality) and also that religious belief is intelligible only to those who have it.

It cannot be said, then, of the later philosophy of Wittgenstein, as it can, I believe, of the earlier, that it had nothing like as much influence as is usually supposed. Logical positivism was not dependent on the *Tractatus;* it got only encouragement from it. Where the ideas of the two coincided, they were exaggerated into obvious unacceptability in the *Tractatus*. To a large extent the ideas of the two did not coincide. The positivists ignored a great deal of what was said in the *Tractatus* and had substantial interests which it did not share. The later Wittgenstein, however, left a band of disciples who had been directly exposed to his teaching, some of them still active, and they, in their turn, have inspired others. Through Ryle, at any rate, there was some, rather modified, influence of Wittgenstein on the Oxford philosophy of the first two postwar decades.

But Oxford philosophy as a whole was more powerfully affected by the wholly non-Wittgensteinian Austin than by the partially Wittgensteinian Ryle, and many of those who speak most respectfully of Wittgenstein show little evidence, if any, of having been influenced by him. Despite all the honour it is conventional to do him, the energy that is put into interpreting his dark utterances and the incessant sitting of examinations and composition of theses on his work, his actual influence is now confined to what I have called the true church, a decent but not particularly productive or distinguished group, at least in its second generation. The point to which I am building up is that the alleged colossus-like bestriding of recent philosophy by Wittgenstein is an illusion, a confusing miasma generated by his own desperate seriousness about himself and his work, his great and provoking obscurity, and the intense devotion of those who have felt the attraction of his personality and his ideas, directly or at one remove.

This illusion of his importance, as I see it, is assisted by the fact that, not only is he extolled by widely admired philosophers who do not in fact follow him at all in either their methods or their conclusions, but that, uniquely for a philosopher of his standing and reputation, he has been exempted from criticism. Russell, toward the end of his life, released a few disobliging asides. Popper, in various places, has objected in a rather generalised and casual fashion to the oracular and irrational nature of Wittgenstein's philosophy, making capital out of such obvious follies as the self-annihilating aspect of the *Tractatus*. But, apart from philosophers at a very different point of the compass like the courteously critical Professor Brand Blanshard, no one else of note cares to speak out.

Is this silence produced by fear of the counter-attack that would be inspired in the intensely loyal members of his cult? Is it, perhaps, caused by sympathy for Wittgenstein's sufferings, for he clearly found philosophy quite as painful as anything else in what was generally a painful life? Since he has now been dead for thirty years, is it not time to treat him in the same critical, selective manner that everyone else interesting enough to be studied at all at that lapse of time is treated?

In this essay I have been concentrating on the case against the widespread conviction that Wittgenstein has been of the highest importance in his influence on philosophy in the English-speaking world. A great philosopher need not be influential: Bolzano died in 1848 and is still largely unknown. But, where a philosopher's work is easily available to anyone interested, influence is at least the measure of the prevailing estimate of greatness. Wittgenstein was plainly a very remarkable and gifted man, although also a fairly dreadful one. He devoted a powerful mind to philosophy with a degree of intensity and seriousness possibly unprecedented in the history of the subject.

But that does not make him a great philosopher. The limits of his influence, in fact as distinct from conventional opinion, are due to things about him which also detract from his claim to greatness. The chief of these is his obscurity, whether that of the unexplained and undefended dogmas of the *Tractatus* or that of the directionless and inconclusive meanderings of his later work. Because of this his admirers can repel all criticism on the ground that it is based on misunderstanding. Because of this there is controversy about the sense in which most of what he wrote is to be taken.

Wittgenstein was a tormented and paradoxical figure. A central European of *nouveau riche* background and aristocratic outlook, of mixed religion, with a well-founded fear of madness, a leaning toward suicide, sexually uncomfortable, a high stylist with a taste and gift for aphorism, widely cultured but uninterested in and unimpressed by learning, almost a human embodiment of the fascinatingly disintegrating city and empire of his birth, he becomes a professor, an academic in the most complacent city in generally complacent England, the most philistine of major European nations. Hoping to change men's lives, he writes about the highest logical and semantic abstractions, and leaves behind not saved souls but decent academic functionaries who occupy a crucial position in the industry of explaining his works so that they are suitable for purposes of teaching and examination. It was an ironic situation, the attempt of an eagle to make a career in a cuckoo clock.

*First published in* Social Research 49:1 *(Spring 1982).*

# Index

108, 302
Descartes, René 9, 13, 18, 26, 29, 31, 24, 60,
  62, 66, 72, 93, 148, 215, 236, 237, 257, 276,
  302, 333, 335
d'Holbach, Mme 35
Dickens, Charles 48, 104, 269, 270, 272, 281,
  290–1, 312, 327, 328, 330
Dickinson, G. Lowes 248
Diderot, Denis 35, 278
Dilke, Charles 179
Disraeli, Isaac 313
Domitian 26
Donne, John 310
Dostoevsly, Fyodor 102, 281, 308, 321
Doyle, A. Conan 330
Dryden, John 276, 311
Duck, Stephen 312
Dujardin, Edouard 270
Dummett, Michael 351, 351–2
Duns Scotus 17, 25, 38

Eddy, Mary Baker 30
Egbert the Hairy 156
Einstein, Albert 30
Eliot, George 24, 279
Eliot, T.S. 135, 155, 163, 164, 283, 284–5,
  287–9, 298, 301, 302, 311, 316
Ellis, Havelock 310
Empson, William 302, 309
Epictetus 28
Epicurus 16, 283
Erigena, John Scotus 33
Esdaile, Arundel 157
Euclid 298
Evans, Christopher 107
Ewing, A.C. 277

Faulkner, William 308
Feigl, Herbert 339
Ferguson, Adam 35, 143
Feyerabend, Paul 86, 107, 108
Fichte, Johann Gottlieb 29
Ficino, Marsilio 34
Fielding, Henry 311
Fitzgerald, F. Scott 47, 308
Flaubert, Gustave 310
Flexner, Abraham 118, 133
Forster, E.M. 92, 209, 299
Foucault, Michel 37, 59, 62, 69, 71, 75–6, 216,
  228, 302
Franklin, Benjamin 45
Fraser, G.S. 319
Frege, Gottlob 61, 337, 342, 351
French, R.D.B. 326, 352
Freud, Sigmund 22, 47, 48, 53, 215, 257
Fry, C.B. 149
Frye, Northrop 312, 324, 331

Galileo, Galilei 5, 8, 20
Gardner, Martin 86, 107
Gaskell, Elizabeth 289
Gassendi, Pierre 31, 34, 60
Geach, Peter 351–2, 362
Genet, Jean 308
George II, King 156
George III, King 156
George IV, King 156

Gibbon, Edward 116, 143, 157, 259
Gide, André 242, 279, 302
Gifford, Adam 154, 155, 236
Gissing, George 314–15
Glover, Jonathan 213, 235, 236
Goethe, Johann Wolfgang von 278, 279, 284,
  313
Golding, William 302
Graves, Robert 308
Green, T.H. 74, 143
Grotius, Hugo 182

Habermas, Jurgen 62
Hacker, Peter 344
Haggard, H. Rider 331
Haldane, R.B. 28
Hamilton, William 36, 60, 132, 137, 138
Hardy, G.H. 21
Hardy, Thomas 286, 308, 330
Harvey, William 8
Hastings, Warren 176
Hazlitt, William 143
Heaney, Seamus 302
Hegel, Georg Wilhelm Friedrich 29, 63, 154,
  277, 302
Heidegger, Martin 61, 62, 63, 64, 67–8, 69,
  70, 221, 302
Heller, Erich 287–8, 335
Helvétius, Mme 35
Hemingway, Ernest 279
Henley, W.E. 308
Henry VII, King 156, 157
Henry VIII, King 157
Heraclitus 29
Herbert, George 310
Herbert, Lord, of Cherbury 259
Herodotus 128
Herrick, Robert 279, 301, 310
Herzberg, Alexander 24
Hill, Christopher 300
Hill, Geoffrey 302
Hipparchus 15
Hitler, Adolf 61, 226, 227
Hobbes, Thomas 29, 33, 34, 60, 62, 100–1,
  131, 214, 276
Hobson, J.A. 176
Hölderlin, Friedrich 69
Holloway, John 292
Homer 308
Hooke, Robert 19, 20
Hopkins, Gerard Manley 304, 311
Hughes, Ted 302
Hume, David 24, 26, 34, 44, 50–1, 52, 54, 62,
  66, 79, 136, 143, 198, 199, 265, 342
Huss, John 33
Husserl, Edmund 61, 62, 63, 302

James I, King 156, 242
James, Henry 61, 259, 264, 274, 276, 304, 331
James, M.R. 331
James, William 263, 265, 270, 273
Johnson, Samuel 66, 127, 143, 150, 299,
  306–7, 312
Jonson, Ben 308, 311, 322, 323
Jowett, Benjamin 116
Joyce, James 259, 270, 273, 279, 302, 308,
  310, 316